# The Politics of NGOs in Indonesia

Non-governmental organisations have proved crucial to political and social development in developing countries, and perhaps none more so than Indonesia, Southeast Asia's biggest country.

This book deals with two major issues: how Indonesian NGOs survived under Suharto's authoritarian rule; and how NGOs contributed to the promotion of democracy in the post-Suharto era. NGOs are often perceived as the cornerstones of a vibrant civil society, providing voices for the disenfranchised and creating centres of influence outside the state. Yet through an analysis of primary material, Bob S. Hadiwinata's fascinating study argues that NGOs must adjust their activities in accordance with local social and political conditions, and that NGOs are sometimes at odds with the local communities they purport to represent. If NGOs are to change from 'development' to 'movement' in democratic post-Suharto Indonesia they must adjust not only their management and working style, but also their very ideology.

This comprehensive study will be an important book for scholars interested in Asian studies, Indonesian politics and development studies.

**Bob S. Hadiwinata** is Head of the Department of International Relations at the University of Parahyangan, Bandung, Indonesia.

# Rethinking Southeast Asia
Edited by Duncan McCargo
*University of Leeds, UK*

Southeast Asia is a dynamic and rapidly-changing region which continues to defy predictions and challenges formulaic understandings. This series will publish cutting-edge work on the region, providing a venue for books that are readable, topical, interdisciplinary and critical of conventional views. It aims to communicate the energy, contestations and ambiguities that make Southeast Asia both consistently fascinating and sometimes potentially disturbing.

This series comprises two strands:

*Rethinking Southeast Asia* aims to address the needs of students and teachers, and the titles will be published in both hardback and paperback.

*RoutledgeCurzon Research on Southeast Asia* is a forum for innovative new research intended for a high-level specialist readership, and the titles will be available in hardback only. Titles include:

1 **Politics and the Press in Thailand**
   Media machinations
   *Duncan McCargo*

2 **Democracy and National Identity in Thailand**
   *Michael Kelly Connors*

3 **The Politics of NGOs in Indonesia**
   Developing democracy and managing a movement
   *Bob S. Hadiwinata*

4 **Military and Democracy in Indonesia**
   *Jun Honna*

# The Politics of NGOs in Indonesia

Developing democracy and managing a movement

Bob S. Hadiwinata

LONDON AND NEW YORK

First published 2003
by Routledge
2 Park Square, Milton Park, Abingdon, Oxfordshire OX14 4RN

Simultaneously published in the USA and Canada
by Routledge
711 Third Ave, New York, NY 10017

First issued in paperback 2015

*Routledge is an imprint of the Taylor and Francis Group,
an informa business*

© 2003 Bob S. Hadiwinata

Typeset in Times New Roman by
Newgen Imaging Systems (P) Ltd, Chennai, India

All rights reserved. No part of this book may be reprinted or reproduced
or utilised in any form or by any electronic, mechanical, or other means,
now known or hereafter invented, including photocopying and recording,
or in any information storage or retrieval system, without permission in
writing from the publishers.

*British Library Cataloguing in Publication Data*
A catalogue record for this book is available from the British Library

*Library of Congress Cataloging in Publication Data*
A catalog record for this book has been requested

ISBN13: 978-1-138-12210-9 (pbk)
ISBN13: 978-0-415-27229-2 (hbk)

# Contents

| | |
|---|---|
| *List of tables* | vi |
| *Preface* | vii |
| *Acknowledgements* | xi |
| *Abbreviations and acronyms* | xiii |
| 1 Introduction | 1 |
| 2 NGOs, community development and social movements | 23 |
| 3 The social and political settings | 48 |
| 4 NGOs in Indonesia: strategies and approaches | 90 |
| 5 Development, empowerment and professionalism: the case of development NGOs | 120 |
| 6 Building constituencies and institutionalising a movement: the case of women's NGOs | 168 |
| 7 Developing democracy through a local network: the case of the Yogyakarta NGO Forum | 206 |
| 8 Conclusion | 241 |
| *Glossary* | 256 |
| *Notes* | 258 |
| *Bibliography* | 268 |
| *Index* | 296 |

# Tables

| | | |
|---|---|---|
| 1.1 | Population distribution and density according to the districts in the Yogyakarta Special Province (1999) | 8 |
| 1.2 | Percentage of population below the poverty line in Yogyakarta Province | 9 |
| 1.3 | The number of industrial establishments in Yogyakarta, 1998–1999 | 10 |
| 1.4 | The number of work force and employment sector in Yogyakarta (1999) | 10 |
| 1.5 | The profile of NGOs used as case studies | 17 |
| 3.1 | Election results (1971–1997) | 56 |
| 3.2 | President Abdurrahman Wahid's controversial acts, November 1999–July 2001 | 86 |
| 4.1 | Trends in major components of central government expenditures, 1980–1990 | 93 |
| 4.2 | Different orientations of 'development' and 'movement' NGOs | 104 |
| 5.1 | The social safety-nets programme funding allocation, 1998–2000 | 125 |
| 5.2 | Village government in 1979 and 1999 | 133 |
| 5.3 | Backgrounds of KSM members in Wedi ($N=38$) | 142 |
| 5.4 | Methods of appointment of health workers in Donorojo ($N=26$) | 143 |
| 5.5 | Outline of ORA's problem identification and recommendations | 150 |
| 5.6 | BSY's revenue from internal and external financial sources (2000) | 157 |
| 5.7 | CD's revenue from internal and external financial sources (2000) | 159 |
| 6.1 | The rates of cleaning fee (regulated by Perda No. 9/1982) and the new tax systems of 1992 and 2000 | 179 |
| 6.2 | Rural factories and workforce in Gadingan (2000) | 181 |
| 6.3 | Background of specialisation of staff members of SBPY and Yasanti | 199 |
| 7.1 | Age distribution of members of Forum's governing body during 1996–1998 and 1998–2000 | 219 |
| 7.2 | Forum's political statements 1993–1996 | 222 |
| 7.3 | Forum's political statements and public hearings, 1998–2000 | 224 |
| 7.4 | Performance of Forum's *ad hoc* committees, 1993–1996 | 234 |
| 7.5 | Performance of Forum's *ad hoc* committees, 1998–2000 | 236 |
| 7.6 | Forum's annual budgets in 1995/1996 and in 1999/2000 | 239 |

# Preface

This book argues that a complete understanding of NGO operations as the 'third sector' organisations can be achieved if we perceive NGOs as both 'institutions' (since they have permanent office, organisational structure, leadership, management, staff members, statute and the like) and 'movements' (with commitment to political transformation, revolutionary change, informality, flexibility, spontaneity and so forth). It is this dual identity that makes an NGO an interesting agency.

Although the NGO movement is not a new phenomenon for Indonesia, an enlightened version of them thrived from the late 1960s and early 1970s when students and intellectuals formed organisations which were dedicated to community development activities. In the 1970s, amid the realisation that the government was unable to reach the poorest, NGOs received full support from the New Order government as they were expected to help the government in providing low cost health care, small credits and training on micro-enterprises.

From the mid-1980s, however, Indonesian NGOs entered a new era when the New Order government sought to co-opt or in some ways neutralise their activities as a manifestation of President Suharto's 'de-ideologisation' and 'de-politicisation' strategies. In this situation, no organisations – including NGOs – were allowed to pursue any ideology other than *Pancasila* (the five moral principles); and they were not allowed to carry out any activities without the government's consent. As a result, there was no room for Indonesian NGOs to nurture a strong ideological basis which would have been crucial in guiding their attempt to generate a movement. They were also compelled to adjust to the political situation by adopting a low-profile approach in which political controversies and strong words that may arouse suspicion were avoided.

The research for this book was carried out in the last years of the New Order government and again in the years following the fall of Suharto. During my first field research (October 1996–September 1997), I was able to record NGOs' attempt to help the underprivileged in the area of community development, grass-roots empowerment, and democratic education amid the government's constant attempt to control their activities. My second research in May–August 2001 had allowed me to learn about new hopes as well as challenges faced by Indonesian NGOs after the fall of Suharto. The post-Suharto government's decision to allow the formation of new political organisations and the removal of all regulations controlling organisational activities in 1998 seemed to have provided ample opportunity for society to become involved in political activities. The impact of this new development on NGOs' activities was obvious. If during the New Order government NGOs had to compromise their radical ideologies to avoid a possible ban or dissolution, in the post-Suharto era they can openly disclose their radical identity without the risk of being repressed.

In the post-Suharto era, the role of NGOs in both community development and empowerment becomes more crucial for at least two reasons. First, the economic disruption and widespread impoverishment after the collapse of the Indonesian currency, the *rupiah*, in 1997 and the political persecutions and civil disturbances in 1998 brought new demands from society to which NGOs cannot turn a blind eye. NGOs committed to both 'development' and 'human rights' would seem to play a greater role in mitigating the impact of the economic downturn. Poverty has opened up new opportunities for development NGOs to expand their charity, self-help and micro-enterprise activities to help the underprivileged. One major concern in the post-Suharto era is the decline of living standards in both urban and rural areas as a consequence of the implementation of the structural adjustment policies, which generates unemployment, the removal of government subsidies on basic items and the collapse of the social security system. Some new NGOs are formed to distribute loans and grants from various international development agencies – the World Bank, IMF, USAID, UNDP, and so on – to the urban and rural poor, especially those who are badly affected by the financial crisis (urban workers, farmers and the like). During 1998–2000, thousands of NGOs were involved in the disbursement of the government-sponsored *Jaringan Pengaman Sosial* (social safety-nets) programme. Moreover, the lessening of the military's political control of societal activities has increased NGOs' acceptability among the rural poor. Beneficiaries are no longer demanding approval from the local authorities prior to NGOs' operation in their neighbourhood.

Second, in a situation where the opportunity to engage in political activities arises, those NGOs committed to 'democratisation' have much to do to create a condition that will allow the democratisation to proceed. As a result, facilitating the transition to democracy becomes an agenda for Indonesian NGOs, including those which are previously considered to be conservative. Indonesian NGOs had undoubtedly contributed to the fall of the New Order government. Their endless pro-democracy campaigns and political education programmes since the early 1990s had generated a feeling of being oppressed among the people, especially those in the marginalised spectrum both in urban and rural areas. More importantly, notwithstanding the New Order government's systematic attempt to control all types of organisation in society (students, workers, peasants, professionals, women and so on), Indonesian NGOs were able to preserve the idea of people's sovereignty (*kedaulatan rakyat*) and conveyed it to the grassroots population. Thus, when the transition to a more democratic political system was initiated in 1998, it did not take much time to encourage grassroots population to support the *gerakan reformasi* (reform movement) since they were already familiarised with the idea of people's sovereignty and were prepared to defend it at all costs.

Although NGOs' ability to facilitate the transition to democracy is debatable, their access to grassroots organisations and their commitment to empower the marginalised groups have generated optimism that NGOs will contribute to the strengthening of Indonesian civil society much needed to generate demand for a more accountable, clean and transparent government. Some politically oriented NGOs have attempted to boost the democratisation by focusing on three crucial activities. First, an attempt to draw political and ideological boundaries within the existing groups in society. Second, an effort to develop a common political platform that should lead to the formation of a collective action involving different social and political groups. Third, a more serious attempt to form grassroots networks and coalitions in order to build a strong civil society.

These activities are crucial in Indonesian context, given that the democratisation is seriously challenged by the feeling of frustration towards the volatility of the political transition. Frustrated with ongoing conflicts and public disorder during the transition to democracy, some conservative elements of the society express their demand for a possible return of a Suharto-like authoritarian government. Having enjoyed a relatively stable political situation during Suharto's authoritarian rule, the conservatives are convinced that limitation on political activities of society will guarantee order and stability. This new development has alarmed NGO activists of a possible disruption to the democratisation which evolved from 1998. In order to prevent this conservatism from spreading across the country, NGO community feels it necessary to strengthen their attempt to establish networks and to replicate their workshop, training and campaign activities. This is exactly what has been done by many NGOs in the post-Suharto era.

Despite their success in making grassroots people determine their own development and in facilitating the transition to democracy, Indonesian NGOs remain unclear about their management system. Although they develop a more or less sustainable organisational structures, they remain ambiguous about the issues of career progression, staff development, leadership, managerial authority and accountability, financial management and other essential components of a modern management. Our cases seem to indicate that small NGOs tend to face less pressure of professionalisation, which affect their seriousness in developing the technical and managerial skills of their employees and in adopting an effective leadership. Meanwhile, large NGOs have more serious concern on staff development, career progression and leadership due to their awareness to act as a professional organisation. As a result, the activities of small NGOs often depend on the presence of a strong leader, while large NGOs depend on the rules and procedures, which guarantee more stability and sustainability. In terms of financial management, those NGOs capable of running commercial programmes tend to be more financially self-sufficient, which ensures stability and independence. Meanwhile, those NGOs focusing on mobilisation and empowerment activities are dependent on foreign donors. In judging NGOs' accountability, one should consider both external and internal dynamics of NGO operation. Our cases suggest that factors such as NGOs' status of being *yayasan* (which implies a non-democratic character), their role as 'virtual representatives' of the people whom they represent and the low level of demand for accountability both from target groups and public in general appear to have prevented Indonesian NGOs from developing an effective accountability system.

In this study, although a great deal information is drawn from participatory observation and in-depth interviews, it is not a pure ethnography. My analysis is also based on what other authors or scholars think, write or say about Indonesian NGOs in general as well as those NGOs used in the case studies. Since Indonesian NGOs rarely write about themselves, except what they write in their reports, the only information I can find from 'insiders' is through NGO activists whom I interviewed, their reports, bulletins, leaflets and meeting minutes made by NGO staff members. Data from state agencies and other external sources are also used insofar as they support the arguments developed throughout this study. In selecting NGOs in a place where organisations have been and continue to be numerous, varied and active, and often act in concert with each other, I hope to indicate the range of issues that arise in assessing NGOs in Indonesia or Yogyakarta (Java) in particular.

# Acknowledgements

The research for this book was carried out in Yogyakarta, Indonesia, from October 1996 to September 1997 and again from May to August 2001. The first research was supported by The British Chevening Awards administered by The British Council Jakarta. I am grateful to The British Council Jakarta's administrators, especially Dr Alan Rogerson and Yeyet Sriyanti for their support.

Additional support was provided by King's College, Cambridge University, for which I am grateful to Dr Basim Mussalam and Janet Luff who helped me to obtain support from King's College fellowships. Sylvana Dean generously provided institutional support during my study at the Faculty of Social and Political Sciences, Cambridge University.

The Parahyangan Reseach Institute at Parahyangan Catholic University, Bandung, has provided Indonesian institutional assistance in every conceivable way. I am deeply grateful to my colleagues at the Faculty of Social and Political Sciences, Parahyangan Catholic University, especially Pius Suratman, Aleks Jemadu, Mangadar, Pius Prasetya, Nyoman Sudira, Purwadi, Andre Pareira, Nur Indro and many others whose encouragement and friendship have kept my research going. I must thank Frank Landsman at the Language Centre of Parahyangan Catholic University who has patiently helped me in making the manuscript more readable. Jeff Lenz also helped me in improving my writing.

In producing the early draft of the manuscript, I have incurred a large number of debts to a number of people. I sincerely thank Geoffrey Hawthorn (my supervisor) for his stimulating comments and suggestions of my early drafts. I must thank David Lehmann for his support and encouragement during my study at Cambridge. I also thank Charles Elliott and John Sidel whose critical comments have substantially improved my early draft. Of course, I bear sole responsibility for the contents and analyses in this book. I am deeply grateful to Herbert Feith whose friendship and encouragement had helped me to turn my dissertation into a book. He made me think differently about Indonesian politics. I was so appalled by the tragic accident in Melbourne, Australia, that took his life. For this reason, this book is dedicated to him.

Several others deserve special mention. I thank Mike and Vi Webb, Keith and Susanne Heywood, Ryan and Wai-Li Rabbet and others at Link House for helping me make Cambridge feel like home. Craig Fowlie and Jennifer Lovell at

Routledge were patient and encouraging at all stages of the production of this book. I sincerely thank Duncan McCargo for his support and guidance – often given from far-distant places. My largest debt, however, is to my wife Dinari whose love, encouragement and endless support have kept my work going.

Bob S. Hadiwinata<br>
Bandung, Indonesia<br>
February 2002

# Abbreviations and acronyms

| | |
|---|---|
| ABRI | *Angkatan Bersenjata Republik Indonesia* or Armed Forces of the Republic of Indonesia |
| ADB | the Asian Development Bank |
| ANGOC | the Asian Non-Governmental Organisation Coalition |
| APBD | *Anggaran Pendapatan dan Belanja Daerah* or Regional Development Budget |
| Apsari | *Akseptor Keluarga Berencana Lestari* or Family Planning Group |
| BAKIN | *Badan Koordinasi Intelejen Negara* or State Intelligence Co-ordinating Board |
| Bandes | *Bantuan Pedesaan* or village development assistance |
| Bappeda | *Badan Perencanaan Pembangunan Daerah* or the Regional Development Planning Board |
| Bappenas | *Badan Perencanaan Pembangunan Nasional* or the National Development Planning Board |
| Bimas | *Bimbingan Masyarakat* or Agricultural Mass Guidance |
| BIPIK | *Bimbingan dan Pengembangan Industri Kecil* or Guidance and Development of Small Industries |
| BPD | *Badan Perwakilan Desa* or Village Representative Body |
| BPS | *Badan Pusat Statistik* or Centre of the Statistical Bureau |
| BRAC | Bangladesh Rural Advancement Committee |
| BRI Unit Desa | the village units of the Indonesian People's Bank |
| BSY | *Bina Swadaya* Yogyakarta |
| Bulog | *Badan Urusan Logistik* or the Food Logistics Agency |
| BUUD | *Badan Usaha Unit Desa* or Village Unit Enterprises |
| BTI | *Barisan Tani Indonesia* or Indonesian Peasants' Front |
| Camat | sub-district head |
| CD-Bethesda | Community Development Unit of the Bethesda Hospital |
| CGI | Consultative Group for Indonesia (replaced IGGI in 1992) |
| CODE-NGO | Caucus of Development Non-governmental Organisations Networks |
| COME'NGOs | Come-and-go NGOs (fly-by-night NGO entrepreneurs) |
| CPSM | Centre for Participatory Social Management |
| Danramil | *Komandan Koramil* or the Sub-district Military Commander |
| DIY | *Daerah Istimewa Yogyakarta* or Yogyakarta Special Province |
| DPR | *Dewan Perwakilan Rakyat* or People's Representative Body |
| DPRD | *Dewan Perwakilan Rakyat Daerah* or Local People's Representative Body |
| FKMY | *Forum Komunikasi Mahasiwa Yogyakarta* or Yogyakarta Student Communication Forum |
| FPIS | *Front Pembela Islam Surakarta* or the Islamic Defense Front of Surakarta |
| GAD | Gender and Development |

| | |
|---|---|
| Gerwani | *Gerakan Wanita Indonesia* or Indonesian Women's Movement (operating under PKI's influence) |
| Golkar | *Golongan Karya* or Working Groups (the ruling party in the New Order) |
| Golput | *Golongan Putih* (white groups) or the non-voters |
| GRINGOs | Govenment-run, -inspired or -initiated NGOs |
| GSOs | Grassroots Support Organisations |
| GTZ | *German Technische Suzammen Arbeit* or German Technical Cooperation Agency |
| HBK | *Hubungan Bank dengan Kelompok* or Groups and Banks Relationship Programme |
| HIP | *Hubungan Industrial Pancasila* or *Pancasila* Industrial Relations |
| HKTI | *Himpunan Kerukunan Tani Indonesia* or Indonesian Farmers' Association |
| HNSI | *Himpunan Nelayan Seluruh Indonesia* or Indonesian Fishermen's Association |
| HYVs | High Yielding Varieties |
| ICF | Indonesia-Canada Foundation |
| ICG | International Crisis Group |
| ICMI | *Ikatan Cendikiawan Muslim Indonesia* or Indonesian association of Muslim intellectuals |
| IDT | *Instruksi Presiden untuk Desa Tertinggal* or the presidential instruction of the less-developed village assistance |
| IGGI | Inter-Governmental Group for Indonesia (reformed as CGI in 1992) |
| IMF | International Monetary Fund |
| INFID | International NGO Forum for Indonesian Development |
| INGI | International NGO Forum on Indonesia |
| Inmas | *Intensifikasi massa* or mass intensification agricultural programme |
| INPI-Pact | Indonesian NGOs Partnership Initiatives |
| Inpres | *Instruksi Presiden* or Presidential Instruction |
| Insus | *Intensifikasi Khusus* or Special Intensification Programme |
| ISJ | *Institut Sosial Jakarta* or Jakarta Social Institute |
| ITP | *Ikatan Tani Pancasila* or Pancasila Farmers' Association |
| JBIC | the Japan Bank for International Corporation |
| KADIN | *Kamar Dagang dan Industri* or Indonesian Chamber of Commerce |
| Kapolda | *Kepala Kepolisian Daerah* or the Provincial Chief Police |
| Kapolsek | *Kepala Kepolisian Sektor* or the Sub-district Chief Police |
| Kecamatan | sub-district administration |
| Kelompencapir | *Kelompok Pendengar Pembaca dan Pirsawan* or Radio listeners and Newspaper Readers' Group |
| Keppres | *Keputusan Presiden* or Presidential Decree |
| KIK | *Koperasi Industri Kecil* or Small Industry Co-operatives |
| KIK/KMKP | *Kredit Investasi Kecil* or Small Investment Lending Scheme |
| KKD | *Kader Kesehatan Desa* or Village Health Cadres |
| KKN | *Korupsi, Kolusi dan Nepotisme* or Corruption, Collusion and Nepotism |
| KMKP | *Kredit Modal Kerja Permanen* or Permanent Working Capital |
| KNPI | *Komite Nasional Pemuda Indonesia* or the National Committee of Indonesian Youth |
| Kodim | *Komando Distrik Militer* or District Military Command |
| Komnas-HAM | *Komisi Nasional Hak Azasi Manusia* or the National Commission for Human Rights |

| | |
|---|---|
| Kopinkra | *Koperasi Industri Kerajinan Rakyat* or People's Handicrafts Co-operatives |
| Koramil | *Komando Rayon Militer* or Sub-district Military Command |
| Kowani | *Konggres Wanita Indonesia* or Indonesian women's congress |
| KSK | *Kas Solidaritas Kelompok* or central solidarity fund in *Bina Swadaya*'s joint effort groups |
| KSKPKO | *Kelompok Solidaritas Korban Pembangunan Kedung Ombo* or Solidarity Group for the Victims of Kedung Ombo Construction Project |
| KSM | *Kelompok Swadaya Mandiri* or People's Self-reliant Group |
| KUB | *Kelompok Usaha Bersama* or Joint Effort Group |
| KUD | *Koperasi Unit Desa* or Village Unit Co-operatives |
| KUK | *Kredit Usaha Kecil* or Small-enterprise Credit Scheme |
| Kupedes | *Kredit Usaha Pedesaan* or Village General Lending Programme |
| KUT | *Kredit Usaha Tani* or Farmers' Enterprise Credit |
| LKMD | *Lembaga Ketahanan Masyarakat Desa* or Village people's Defense Council |
| LMD | *Lembaga Musyawarah Desa* or Village People's Consultative Assembly |
| LP3ES | *Lembaga Pengembangan, Penelitian, dan Pendidikan Ekonomi-Sosial* or Institute for Social-economic Research, Education and Development |
| LPSM | *Lembaga Pengembang Swadaya Masyarakat* or Self-reliant Community Support Institutions |
| LSM | *Lembaga Swadaya Masyarakat* or Self-reliant Community Institutions |
| MPR | *Majelis Permusyawaratan Rakyat* or People's Consultative Assembly |
| MSOs | Membership Support Organisations |
| NKK/BKK | *Normalisasi Kehidupan Kampus/Badan Koordinasi Kampus* or the Normalisation of Campus Life/the Campus Co-ordinating Body |
| NOVIB | the Netherlands Organisation for International Development Co-operation |
| ORA | *Organisasi Rakyat* or People's Organisation |
| Ormas | *Organisasi Massa* or mass organisations |
| ORNOP | *Organisasi non-pemerintah* or Non-governmental Organisations |
| OTB | *Organisasti Tanpa Bentuk* or formless organisation |
| OXFAM | Oxford Committee for Famine Relief (an international NGO based in the United Kingdom) |
| PAD | *Pendapatan Asli Daerah* or original regional income |
| PAN | *Partai Amanah Nasional* or National Mandate Party |
| Pansus | special inquiry committee in the people's representative body (DPR) |
| PAR | Participatory Action Research |
| PBB | *Partai Bulan Bintang* or Star and Moon Party |
| PDI | *Partai Demokrasi Indonesia* or Indonesian Democratic Party |
| PDIP | *Partai Demokrasi Indonesia Perjuangan* or Indonesian Democratic Party of Struggle |
| Pemda | *Pemerintah Daerah* or local administration |
| Perda | *Peraturan Daerah* or local government regulation |
| Pertamina | *Perusahaan Tambang Milik Negara* or the state oil corporation |
| PIR | *Perkebunan Inti Rakyat* or Nucleus Estate Small-holders |
| PGOs | Primary Grassroots Groups |
| PKB | *Partai Kebangkitan Bangsa* or National Awakening Party |
| PKI | *Partai Komunis Indonesia* or Indonesian Communist Party |
| PKK | *Pembinaan Kesejahteraan Keluarga* or Family Welfare Guidance |
| P3M | *Perhimpunan Pesantren dan Pengembangan Masyarakat* or Association for *Pesantren* and Community Development |
| Polsek | *Kepolisian Sektor* or sub-district police office |
| PPL | *Petugas Penyuluh Lapangan* or Field Extension Workers |
| PPP | *Partai Persatuan Pembangunan* or United Development Party |

## Abbreviations and acronyms

| | |
|---|---|
| PRA | Participatory Rural Appraisal (a method of assessment of rural development problems) |
| PRD | *Partai Rakyat Demokrasi* or People's Democratic Party |
| Prokesa | *Promotor Kesehatan Desa* or the state-formed village health cadre |
| Puskesmas | *Pusat Kesehatan Masyarakat* or the government-run health centre |
| P2W-KSS | *Peningkatan Peran Wanita menuju Keluarga Sehat Sejahtera* or Programme for the Improvement of Women's Role and the Family Welfare |
| Repelita | *Rencana Pembangunan Lima Tahun* or Five-year Development Plan |
| Rp | *Rupiah* (the Indonesian currency) |
| SBPY | *Sekretariat Bersama Perempuan Yogyakarta* or Yogyakarta Women Joint Secretariat |
| SBSI | *Serikat Buruh Sejahtera Indonesia* or Indonesian Union of Prosperous Workers |
| SIP | *Suara Ibu Peduli* or Voice of Concerned Mothers |
| SMID | *Solidaritas Mahasiswa Indonesia untuk Demokrasi* or Indonesian Student Solidarity for Democracy |
| SPSI | *Serikat Pekerja Seluruh Indonesia* or the All-Indonesia Workers' Union |
| SSCI | Small-scale and Cottage Industries |
| Susenas | *Survey Sosial-ekonomi Nasional* or the National Social-economic Survey |
| TNI | *Tentara Nasional Indonesia* or the Indonesian National Armed Forces is the term used by the military circle in the post-Suharto era as a substitute for ABRI |
| UMR | *Upah Minimum Regional* or Regional Minimum Wages |
| USAID | United States Agency for International Development |
| USC | Unity Service Cooperation Foundation (an international NGO based in Canada) |
| UU Ormas | the law on mass organisations (No. 8/1985) |
| WALHI | *Wahana Lingkungan Hidup Indonesia* or Indonesian environment network |
| WID | Women in Development |
| YAKKUM | *Yayasan Kristen untuk Kesehatan Umum* or The Christian Foundation for Public Health |
| YAPPIKA | *Yayasan Penguatan Partisipasi, Inisiatif dan Kemitraan Indonesia* or the Foundation for Indonesian People's Participation, Initiative and Partnership |
| Yasanti | *Yayasan Annisa Swasti* or *Annisa Swasti* foundation |
| YLBHI | *Yayasan Lembaga Bantuan Hukum Indonesia* or Indonesian Legal Aid Foundation |
| YSTM | *Yayasan Sosial Tani Membangun* or Farmers' Social Development Foundation |

# 1 Introduction

## Background

The past two decades have seen a substantial increase in the number, size and scope of the non-governmental organisations (NGOs). These organisations have established themselves in pivotal positions in the social, economic and political landscapes across the globe. In Southeast Asia, as in much of the rest of the developing world, NGOs have proliferated since the early 1980s. In Thailand, in the early 1990s it was estimated that there were 10,000 NGOs, indicating a 250 per cent increase from around 4,000 in the early 1980s (Farrington *et al.* 1993b: 277). In Malaysia, 14,000 similar organisations were registered under the 1966 Societies Act in the early 1990s (Clarke 1998: 26). In Singapore, the number of registered charities and social organisations grew from 656 in 1988 to 4,562 in 1994 (Clarke 1998: 26). In the Philippines, between 1985 and 1995, the number of NGOs increased by 260 per cent from an estimated 27,100 to 70,200 (Clarke 1998: 93). In Indonesia, while there is no accurate data on the exact number of NGOs, it is believed that the number of NGOs has grown significantly from 10,000 in 1996 to around 70,000 in 2000 (BPS 2000: 34).

Commentators argue that the rise of NGOs is an indication of a substantial break from the conventional wisdom that social development is primarily the responsibility of the state and the market (Clark 1991: 43–5; Hulme 1994: 253; De Janvry *et al.* 1995: 4; Edwards and Hulme 1997: 3–5). Falling living standards in many parts of the developing world have raised attention on immediate survival and on the alternative possibilities which NGOs can offer when the state and the market are no longer able to deliver services efficiently (de Janvry *et al.* 1995: 1). Many NGOs are formed as a manifestation of people's dissatisfaction with the failure of both the state and the market to deliver welfare, public goods and jobs. Disenchanted with the state's limited capacity to provide public services, people begin to turn their attention to agencies outside the state which are expected to provide substitutes for the state's welfare programmes, to help the poor overcome the strains of daily economic activities, and to help them generate self-help initiatives (Hudson 1995: 292; Salamon and Anheier 1996: 2). NGOs also grow as a result of what Hansmann (1994: 21) termed a 'market failure', a situation in which consumers are in a poor position to judge the goods and services they are

2  *Introduction*

receiving. NGOs, in this context, are formed to ensure confidence that goods and services are supplied and distributed efficiently and have a high quality.

When one talks about the growing significance of NGOs, one should be able to locate where exactly NGOs settle themselves in the general context of social organisations. In modern societies, there are three clusters of organisations that carry distinct purposes. The first cluster belongs to the so-called 'first sector' whose purpose is to protect, secure and regulate the lives and activities of citizens. The state agencies whose main duties are, among others, to ensure citizens exercise their rights and obligations, to provide services to the people and to supply basic social securities, and these are some of the examples of this sector (Fowler 1997: 21; Turner and Hulme 1997: 52–3). The 'second sector' consists of the private realm whose major purpose is to make a livelihood, create and accumulate wealth. This sector includes private market-oriented agencies, namely, the business and industrial establishments (De Janvry *et al.* 1995: 8–9; Hudson 1995: 34; Fowler 1997: 22). The 'third sector' refers to the private realm whose main purpose is to pursue individual interests or tackle personal or social concerns collectively such as spiritual, social, recreational, and cultural issues (Billis 1993: 158–9; Hudson 1995: 33–4; Fowler 1997: 22). NGOs belong to this sector. As 'third sector' organisations, NGOs are not subject to direct political control from the political elite and are not meant to distribute profits to those who run them (Hudson 1995: 27–9). Operating outside both the state and the market, NGOs are supposed to have a certain degree of independence to determine their own policies and strategies.[1]

## The argument

Current studies on NGOs have been infused with either optimism or pessimism with regard to NGOs' ability to encourage grassroots initiatives, to carry the 'voices of the voiceless', and to induce social and political transformations. The optimist school of thought suggests that NGOs have demonstrated the capacity to design and implement development programmes, using innovative approaches and by-passing long bureaucratic procedures, enabling them to reach the poorest members of society (Aubrey 1997: 25). Some have argued that NGOs are sources of diversity and innovation because they contribute to pluralism by creating centres of influence outside the state and by providing the means through which disenfranchised groups can organise themselves (Clark 1991: 19; Di Maggio and Anheier 1994: 179; Hulme 1994: 261). Others have noted that NGOs have the capacity to make governments more responsive, to get new issues on the public agenda, to provide low-cost services, to raise people's awareness of their social milieu, to focus on humanitarian issues and even (in extreme cases) to overturn governments (Hodgkinson and Sumariwalla 1992: 490–1; Jorgensen 1996: 39; Trivedy and Acharya 1996: 59; Blair 1997: 29). Fowler (1997) identified four factors that have determined the strength and effectiveness of NGOs: (1) their ability to design an agenda linking vision to action; (2) their ability to achieve goals because of the commitment and determination of their staff members and leaders; (3) their capacity to mobilise necessary resources due to the presence of competent and disciplined cadres; and (4) their flexibility in maintaining relations with governments, donors and target groups.

The pessimist school of thought, on the other hand, comes out of a belief that NGOs are 'oversold' since their presumed strength and effectiveness may not materialise in practice (Clark 1991: 63; Aubrey 1997: 26). In the words of Annis (1987), an analyst of NGO performance: '... in the face of pervasive poverty, "small scale" can merely mean "insignificant", "politically independent" can mean "powerless" or "disconnected", "low cost" can mean "under-financed" or "poor quality", and "innovative" can mean simply "temporary" or "unsustainable"...'. Streeten (1997: 196) argued that NGOs may describe in their statute the goal of helping the poorest, but in practice they rarely reach this group because they tend to reinforce the rule of the elite circles and put too little effort in ascertaining whether the beneficiaries are really the poorest. A study by Farrington *et al.* (1993a: 91–100) suggested that the participatory and empowerment rhetoric of NGOs is vulnerable, especially since most NGOs are accountable to donors, not to the beneficiaries of their work. Veltmeyer *et al.* (1997: 85–6), perhaps the most extreme authors of the pessimist school, argued that NGOs have a negative impact on grassroots initiatives because they tend to fragment the social constituency of popular movements and create a new strata of dependent administrators based on exogenous resources who are in direct competition with the activities of the poor.

These two schools of thought represent the current competing development paradigms with regard to the interpretations of the role of agencies in facilitating grassroots initiatives. Although there is a danger of overstating NGOs' successes or failures in each of the schools of thought, I believe the two perspectives contain some elements of truth about NGOs' strengths and weaknesses. The fact that NGOs are formed by concerned individuals, staffed with low-paid but committed individuals, organised on the basis of flexibility, and guided by humanitarian values (justice, equality, democracy, and so on) raises the hope that they must make a difference to the community whom they serve (Hulme 1994: 264). But, it is also important to note that NGOs may face some problems as a result of their limited resources, restricted political space, dilemmas in management, pressures from the political environment, and so on.

This study attempts to examine the 'politics' of NGOs in Indonesia. Although politics has been associated with the study of government and public affairs, nowadays it has come to be understood in a much broader context to include other areas of social life such as gender, race and class (Gamble 1990: 412). Politics can therefore be understood as the exercise of power and authority to influence others that occurs throughout society: from family groups and the voluntary association (clubs, professional associations, social organisations, NGOs, and so forth) to the state (Stoker 1995: 5). In this broader sense, politics, according to Leftwich (1984: 83–4), comprises all the activities of co-operation and conflict, within and between societies, whereby the human species goes about organising the use, production and distribution of human, natural and other resources in the course of the production and reproduction of its social life.

4  *Introduction*

This book is concerned with the question of how NGOs survived under different social and political contexts. During Suharto's government, when the society suffered from serious political constraints and the powerless were too afraid to challenge the powerful, NGOs were forced to adopt strategies and approaches that conform to the political conditions set out by the state. However, since the mid-1990s, when Suharto's political legitimacy was beginning to wane, some NGOs attempted to facilitate grassroots resistance by conducting the pro-democracy campaigns. In the post-Suharto era, the role of NGOs in facilitating the political transition to democracy becomes more significant. Many NGOs conducted activities to facilitate the formation of a strong civil society. This book covers mainly the period between 1990 and 2001 when Indonesian NGOs began to exert influence on the process of grassroots empowerment[2] and the strengthening of civil society.[3] Its main purpose is to examine how complex sets of relationships among various kinds of associations, the state agencies, communities and individuals have had an impact on a specific area at a specific time and how NGOs respond to particular social and political contexts in order to ensure their survival. This raises the following questions: How do NGOs adjust to specific circumstances? How do NGOs contribute to the promotion of democracy? How do NGOs sustain their operation in different political situations? And what is the impact of particular social and political contexts on NGO activities?

## Defining NGOs

Many have attempted to classify and define non-governmental organisations, though to nobody's great satisfaction. Some observers loosely group NGOs under an assortment of headings such as 'voluntary organisations', 'non-profit organisations', or 'intermediary organisations' carrying out various social activities. But this grouping seems to cover too much. It can include hundreds of types of organisations within the society ranging from political action committees to sports clubs. Applying these terms as a general nomenclature for NGOs will force someone to put an international charity organisation such as Oxfam and an exclusive sports club into a single category, since both of them are created voluntarily, carry out non-profit social activities and sometimes play intermediary roles. Such umbrella terms also fail to make a substantial differentiation between political groups demanding the overturn of authoritarian regimes and local neighbourhood associations providing support for the elderly, women, children and the disabled.

Some other observers try to solve this problem by refining the concept of NGOs through the introduction of various specific terms. Carroll (1992), for example, introduced the term 'grassroots support organisations' (GSOs) – namely a civic developmental entity which provides services and support to local groups of disadvantaged rural, or urban, households and serves as an intermediary institution in establishing links between the local people and governments, donors and international financial institutions – which can be differentiated from 'membership support organisations' (MSOs). While MSOs represent (and are accountable to) their base membership, GSOs have no members (Carroll 1992: 11). Both GSOs and MSOs, according to Carroll, can be distinguished from 'primary grassroots organisations' (PGOs) by scope, level of complexity and function. A PGO, he argued, is the smallest aggregation of individuals or households that are regularly involved in joint development activities, while GSOs and MSOs tend to serve, represent and co-operate with one or more PGOs in various development activities (Carroll 1992: 11).

Carroll's attempt to diversify NGOs into several groups does not seem to reduce the complicated nature of NGOs. While one can accept the differentiation between GSOs/MSOs and PGOs, many would equate GSOs with MSOs without further explanation because the two organisations often operate under the same philosophy of self-help and the same organisational framework. The differences between these two types of organisations are in fact subject to local variations. In some societies, especially in Latin America and the Philippines, one can see a clear distinction between GSOs and MSOs; but in other parts of the world, people tend to see them as overlapping organisations working under the same principle of self-management (Farrington *et al.* 1993b; Fisher 1994).

Although definitions may not necessarily reduce complications surrounding the concept of non-governmental organisations, they may help us to determine what type of organisation is included and excluded in this study. The NGOs in this study can be defined as follows:

1  Organisations which serve as advocates of the poor, the neglected and the disenfranchised. They are also advocates for social change. They provide social services, particularly to underserved groups, and in some nations serve as the major vehicle for the provision of social welfare. They provide innovation, are flexible, and can deliver more personalised services to specific groups or in local situations. With their value orientation, they serve in many nations as moral associations. In societies with authoritarian governments, they help to create institutions where citizens can learn to work, play and worship together and where they can they try to become part of a strong civil society (Hodgkinson and Sumariwalla 1992: 486).

2  Organisations sharing the following characteristics: (1) *formal*, in terms of having regular meetings, offices, a set of rules or procedures and some degree of organisational permanence; (2) *private*, i.e. institutionally separate from the government; (3) *non-profit-distributing*, i.e. not returning profits generated to their owners, directors or the governing boards; (4) *self-governing*, in terms of having their own internal procedures for governance and not being controlled by outside entities; (5) *voluntary*, i.e. involving some meaningful degree of voluntary participation either in the actual conduct of activities or in the management of their own affairs; (6) *non-religious*, i.e. not primarily involved in the promotion of religious worship or religious education; and (7) *non-political*, i.e. not primarily involved in promoting candidates for elected office (Salamon and Anheier 1996: 14–15).

These definitions refer to organisations with rules, structures and procedures which perform intermediary roles to achieve at least two common goals: to help the poor to develop self-help management to solve their problems; and to represent the marginalised in their attempt to challenge social and political structures that cause their marginalisation. Consequently, this study will *not* include exclusive sports clubs, religious organisations, peasants' organisations, labour unions and professional associations because their activities are dedicated to promote the interests of their own members rather than speak on behalf of anybody within the category of the 'poor' and the 'marginalised'.

NGOs often involve a wide, sometimes diffused, issue. In developed societies, NGOs may include charity organisations operating globally such as Oxfam, while in developing societies they are usually established by middle-class professionals representing a wide range of goals from charity to advocacy for social and political change. NGOs are often staffed by paid professionals, even though they may also use middle-class volunteers (Fisher 1994: 129). Although many NGOs in developing societies have been promoted and stimulated by external agencies such as the church, foreign donors or international NGOs, they have become increasingly more active on their own. In reaching the grassroots people, NGOs often work with local popular organisations such as co-operatives, neighbourhood associations, peasant groups, fisherfolk organisations, labour unions, students' organisations and the like.

In Indonesia, the term NGOs has a rather complicated interpretation. During the 1970s the term *Organisasi non-pemerintah* (ORNOP) was used as a direct translation for the internationally accepted phrase 'non-governmental organisations' (NGOs). But this terminology was subsequently changed due to the government's objection. In the 1980 NGO seminar in Jakarta, another term, *Lembaga Swadaya Masyarakat* (LSM), which literally means self-reliant community institutions, was introduced as a substitute for ORNOP. This change was made under strong government pressure. Professor Emil Salim, who was then Minister for Population and Environment, explained that 'non-government' was perceived in government circles and in more conservative sections of the urban middle-class as denoting an anti-government connotation. He proposed that the term LSM contained more cultural resonance and political euphemism than ORNOP (Eldridge 1995: 13). The acceptance of the term LSM by the NGO community stemmed at least partly out of a fear among NGO activists that the term ORNOP might provoke government repression, particularly when the New Order government was determined to increase its political control and censorship as a response to the 1978 student protest movements. These activists believed that in order to secure political legitimacy, NGOs should open themselves for co-operation with the government, by which they should '*menjadi bagian dari sistem pemerintah*' (integrate themselves into the government's system) (Setiawan 1996: 36).

But some activists questioned the suitability of the term LSM in the Indonesian context. Ismid Hadad, an activist of a Jakarta-based NGO, for example, observed that the term LSM is more appropriate to describe primary groups with obvious membership such as *kelompok arisan* (credit-and-saving rotation groups), neighbourhood associations, local co-operatives, water-users' associations, and the like whose members work together on the basis of a common goal. The term NGOs, according to Hadad, had more resemblance with what was known in Indonesia as

LPSMs (*Lembaga Pengembangan Swadaya Masyarakat* or self-help community support institutions), that is, those secondary organisations which were formed to provide technical and financial assistance for LSMs (Prijono 1996: 100). However, Indonesian NGO activists have never achieved a consensus as they variously use the terms ORNOP, LSM and LPSM as the translation for NGOs. Some radical activists prefer to use ORNOP, while others use the terms LSM and LPSM interchangably. Even some conservative activists prefer to use their own term, *Organisasi Nir-Laba* (non-profit organisations), to call their organisations. In this study, in order to avoid such complications surrounding concepts and definitions I will use the term NGOs to include all kinds of organisations within the scope of the definitions quoted earlier.

## The research site

When I designed my research proposal, I was tempted to cover Indonesia as a whole in which I could select NGOs from different localities as samples. But then I realised that covering such a huge area where more than 70,000 organisations (in 2000) existed could force me to neglect some crucial matters. First, while taking samples from different areas may be more 'representative' as far as the research population is concerned, it would prevent me seeing interactions or disinteractions between organisations because NGOs in a particular region are more likely to make contacts with one another than those in different regions. Second, while it is true that covering a wider area would give one more opportunity to generalise findings, a wide study area would reduce the accuracy and the detail of information. A focus on a particular region allows a researcher to conduct more intensive interviews and observations. Meetings can be easily arranged and I can always go back to the informants or to the sites whenever I feel necessary to pursue further information gathering. Third, a focus on a particular region also allows a researcher to spend more time to gather information because one does not need to make long journeys to meet the informants. In this way I have more opportunity to look closer at NGO activities without losing too much time and energy.

On the basis of these considerations I decided to carry out my research in a particular region, namely, Yogyakarta, a provincial city where NGO movement has its own dynamics. Yogyakarta is a middle range city and serves as the capital of the DIY (*Daerah Istimewa Yogyakarta* or the Yogyakarta Special Province) with an approximately 487,115 population in 1999. The DIY itself is composed of five districts – Yogyakarta, Bantul, Sleman, Gunung Kidul and Kulon Progo – with a total population of 3,264,942 in 1999 (see Table 1.1). Yogyakarta was founded in 1755 when a conflict in the Mataram kingdom between King Paku Buwono II and his own son, Prince Mangkubumi, was settled by dividing the kingdom into two parts: the eastern part was named Surakarta and led by King Paku Buwono II himself, the western part was named Yogyakarta and led by Mangkubumi who subsequently changed his name to Sultan Hamengku Buwono I (Poerwokoesoemo 1984: 137). The expansion of the city took place in the course of the second half

8  Introduction

Table 1.1 Population distribution and density according to the districts in the Yogyakarta Special Province (1999)

| Name of districts | Land area (in km$^2$) | Number of population | Number of population per km$^2$ |
|---|---|---|---|
| Kulon Progo | 586.28 | 437,930 | 746.96 |
| Bantul | 506.85 | 767,035 | 1,513.34 |
| Gunung Kidul | 1,485.36 | 739,259 | 497.70 |
| Sleman | 574.82 | 833,603 | 1,450.20 |
| Yogyakarta Regency | 32.50 | 487,115 | 14,988.15 |
| Total | 3,185.80 | 3,264,942 | 1,024.10[a] |

Source: BPS 1999. *Daerah Istimewa Yogyakarta Dalam Angka 1999*. Yogyakarta: Badan Pusat Statistik Propinsi Daerah Istimewa Yogyakarta.

Note
a  The average number of population per square kilometer in Yogyakarta Province.

of the eighteenth century when a new principality, the court of Pakualaman, was established in the eastern part of the city. The building of railroads (in 1872) and the installation of electricity (in 1890) and drinking-water pipes (in 1918) stimulated commercial activities that attracted more people to reside in the city (Kartodirdjo 1981: 14).

This city is nowadays renowned as the centre of Javanese culture. In Yogyakarta, one can see people (young and old) speak a refined Javanese language (*kromo inggil*) more frequently than in any other place in Java. They enjoy the traditional Javanese arts – the *wayang kulit* (shadow puppet show), the *ketoprak* (traditional theatre), the *bedoyo* (royal dance), the batik painting, and so forth – and believe in the Javanese concept of harmony[4] in social relations (Kuroyanagi 1990; Sullivan 1992). The monarchy still retains its symbolic, political and cultural roles. The merging of the two courts (Yogyakarta and Pakualaman) was legislated under the *Staatsblad* No. 47/1941. In the post-colonial era, the Indonesian government granted Yogyakarta special province status under the *Undang-Undang Republik Indonesia* (the Republic of Indonesia Regulations) No. 22/1948 in which the region's leaders or governors had to be appointed by the president from the monarchy's family (Poerwokoesoemo 1984: 61). Until the mid-1990s, cultural and political power was shared more or less equally by the two kings. While Sri Sultan Hamengku Buwono X, the King of Yogyakarta, retained considerable symbolic significance of a cultural and spiritual kind, the Sri Paku Alam VIII, the King of Pakualaman, served as the governor of the province. In 1999, however, following the sudden death of Sri Paku Alam VIII, Sri Sultan Hamengku Buwono X was appointed as the new governor.

## Poverty reduction in Yogyakarta

Since the early 1980s, Yogyakarta has experienced a dramatic reduction of poverty and diversification of the rural economy. For example, around 41.50 per cent of the total population of Yogyakarta province lived below the poverty

Table 1.2 Percentage of population below the poverty line in Yogyakarta Province (selected years)

| Year | Urban | Rural | Urban + rural |
|---|---|---|---|
| 1980 | 37.30 | 45.70 | 41.50 |
| 1987 | 16.55 | 8.20 | 12.42 |
| 1993 | 14.35 | 8.85 | 11.77 |
| 1995 | 15.50 | 7.10 | 11.46 |
| 1996 | 11.66 | 8.47 | 10.42 |
| 1999 | n.a. | n.a. | 26.10 |

Source: BPS Daerah Istimewa Yogyakarta. 1997. *Profil Kependudukan*. Yogyakarta: Kantor Statistik Propinsi Daerah Istimewa Yogyakarta; and BPS. 2000. *Statistik Indonesia*. Yogyakarta: Badan Pusat Statistik Propinsi Daerah Istimewa Yogyakarta.

line in 1980, but the figure was reduced to only 12.42 per cent in 1987 and to 10.42 per cent in 1996; yet it declined again – due to the 1997 economic crisis – to 26.10 per cent in 1999 (see Table 1.2). The poverty line is measured on the basis of the total value of per capita consumption of food and non-food items per month at current prices. In the 1990s, the poverty line index in Yogyakarta increased from Rp 19,316 (in 1990) to Rp 35,841 (in 1996) and to Rp 76,773 (in 1999) (BPS 1997: xii; BPS 2000: 597).

Evers (1995: 169) noted three indications of poverty reduction in Yogyakarta. The first indicator was the growth of off-farm employment in which small-scale and medium-sized cottage industries began to reach far into the rural hinterland bringing new income to the villagers. This finding was supported by Maurer's (1991) study in four villages in Bantul district in which he observed that between the 1970s and the 1990s the economy of the villages had been increasingly diversified and transformed into non-farming activities. The number of self-employed artisans and daily workers, according to Maurer, had substantially increased. This expansion occurred in several forms. First, the construction boom – as a result of the expansion of the tourism and hotel industry – had increased demands for brick and tile makers, bricklayers, carpenters, and the like (Kuroyanagi 1990: 50; Maurer 1991: 100). Second, the growing number of souvenir/curio workshops has led to the growth of skilled manpower in batik-processing, wood-carving, silver-making and leather-processing (Maurer 1991: 101; Yamaguchi 1998: 158). Third, the rapid spread of two wheeled motor transport and other intermediate manufactured consumption goods has also increased the number of workshops for bicycles, motorcycles, tyres, radio/TV sets, watches and so on (Evers 1995: 169). Table 1.3 indicates that during 1998–1999 the number of industrial establishments in Yogyakarta has increased from 84,212 to 93,720. It was in this situation that NGOs began to launch commercial projects by providing credit at commercial rates and training on management and marketing skills and by treating rural small entrepreneurs as their customers or business partners.

## 10  Introduction

*Table 1.3* The number of industrial establishments in Yogyakarta, 1998–1999

| Type of industry | 1998 | 1999 |
|---|---|---|
| A  Large and medium scale industries | 259 | 259 |
| Basic metals industry | 104 | 104 |
| Agriculture and forest industry | 79 | 79 |
| Miscellaneous industry | 76 | 76 |
| B  Small scale industries | 83,953 | 93,461 |
| Food manufacturing and processing | 31,276 | 34,747 |
| Leather and clothing | 5,373 | 5,995 |
| Chemicals | 4,337 | 4,888 |
| Handicrafts | 35,404 | 39,329 |
| Services | 7,563 | 8,502 |
| Total number | 84,212 | 93,720 |

Source: BPS 1999. *Daerah Istimewa Yogyakarta Dalam Angka 1999.* Yogyakarta: Badan Pusat Statistik Propinsi Daerah Istimewa Yogyakarta.

*Table 1.4* The number of work force and employment sector in Yogyakarta (1999)

| Sector of employment | Number of employment | Percentage |
|---|---|---|
| Agriculture | 487,096 | 31.47 |
| Mining and quarrying | 8,982 | 0.58 |
| Manufacturing | 207,075 | 13.38 |
| Electricity, gas and water supply | 1,293 | 0.08 |
| Construction | 92,269 | 5.96 |
| Trading | 386,078 | 24.95 |
| Transportation | 60,981 | 3.94 |
| Finance, insurance, real estate | 17,638 | 1.14 |
| Services | 286,218 | 18.49 |

Source: BPS. *Daerah Istimewa Yogyakarta Dalam Angka 1999.* Yogyakarta: Badan Pusat Statistik Propinsi Daerah Istimewa Yogyakarta.

The second indicator was the growth of the working-class both in the formal and informal sectors (Kuroyanagi 1990: 46–7; Evers 1995: 171). Data from the BPS (Centre of the Statistical Bureau) indicate that in 1999 there were 1,547,630 people (47.4 per cent) out of the total population of 3,264,942 employed in various sectors. The rest were either at school or performing domestic work. Table 1.4 shows the number of population aged 10 years and over employed in different sectors. A large proportion of this employment was the agricultural sector (31.47 per cent), which was followed by trading (24.95 per cent), and services (18.49 per cent) (BPS 1999: 107).

The third indicator was the changing lifestyle among middle-income families due to the rise of average income in both rural and urban areas (Evers 1995: 171).

For example, bicycles had been increasingly replaced by motorcycles, while TV sets with satellite dishes that can receive dozens of local, national and international broadcasting stations were also available even in the most remote villages (Evers 1995: 172; Yamaguchi 1998: 158). Newly constructed houses were embellished with Greek columns and equipped with modern, factory-made furniture. People began to enjoy a middle-class lifestyle which led to a steady increase in demand for services such as beauty parlours, dress makers, shoe repairers, photo studios and so on (Maurer 1991: 101; Evers 1995: 170). In the city, families enjoyed a night out at the nearby shopping malls (e.g. Hero Supermarket, Malioboro Mall, and Galleria) with big department stores and multi-national fast-food restaurants such as Pizza Hut, MacDonalds and Kentucky Fried Chicken, and enjoyed American films at one of the many cinemas (Evers 1995: 173). By 1999, there were 23 cinemas, 20 museums, 13 art theatres and 34 other recreational centres in Yogyakarta (BPS 1999: 130).

It appears that the growth of non-farm employment in rural areas has enabled NGOs in Yogyakarta to run their cost-recovery programmes. Tendler (1989: 36) maintained that NGOs' success in micro-enterprise development depends not only on their competence, skill and ability to adopt market principles, but also on the capacity of their target groups to develop businesses out of their saving-and-borrowing activities. Likewise, Sahley (1995: 32–3) argued that NGOs can succeed in their commercial projects if their target groups have sufficient skills to recover costs, develop a market-oriented mentality, and adapt to the complex financial and administrative systems. In Yogyakarta, the expansion of rural small-scale enterprises since the early 1980s has increased the demand for small-credit schemes and the need among the villagers to learn about management and marketing skills which can be provided by NGOs.

## *Ethnicity, religion and the 'Kampung' settlement problems*

The majority of the population in Yogyakarta is ethnic Javanese; but people come to the city from all over Indonesia to attend the fine universities, study arts and crafts, do business, or simply seek work (Sullivan 1992: 114). By far the largest non-Javanese group, however, was the ethnic Chinese who constituted about 4 per cent of the total population. Like many indigenous people all over Indonesia, Javanese people tend to conceive the Chinese (*Wong Cino*) collectively as a foreign enclave to be sharply contrasted to the *pribumi* (the indigenous) in terms of culture, physical characteristics, religion and sometimes language (although most Chinese speak fluent Indonesian and Javanese). Given the long history of this prejudice, the ancient practice of Java's foreign and indigenous rulers of casting the Chinese as scapegoats, and the sad history of Chinese-non-Chinese relations on the island, it was perhaps not surprising that the Javanese used this group to symbolise 'the outsider' (Koyano 1996: 464). The Indonesian Chinese are often subject to indictment by the indigenous population as being aloof, haughty, unsociable, and their success in any field appears to the unsuccessful as 'virtual crimes' or as acceptable ends achieved through nefarious means such as bribery or conspiracy (Sullivan 1992: 115).

Although the Chinese minority are subject to continuous abuse and attack, especially in times of heightened social stress, thus far there has not been any incident of mass violence against the Chinese in Yogyakarta to the degree that has occurred, for example, in Solo, Semarang, Pekalongan, Bandung, Medan or Jakarta. A serious conflict along ethnic boundaries in the city took place in 1973 when a Javanese *becak* (pedicab) driver became involved in an argument with three students from West Sumatra and Central Sulawesi. The dispute ended in the death of the driver which subsequently sparked mass violence against non-Javanese students by a group of Javanese (mostly pedicab drivers). A series of attacks on non-Javanese student quarters killed two West Sumatran students, wounded several other students and destroyed properties. The violence ended only after the security forces intervened. This incident, according to Emmerson, was a result of a complex mixture of ethnic prejudice, a sharp distinction between *pendatang* (migrants) and *penduduk asli* (natives), and the growing 'socio-economic dissatisfactions' of the lower-class that generated hostility against the upper-class (Emmerson 1976: 225).

As far as religion is concerned, people with different faiths seemed to get along relatively well in Yogyakarta. According to the data from BPS, in 1999 the largest group was Islam which constituted 91.98 per cent of the total population, followed by Catholicism (4.99 per cent), Protestantism (2.66 per cent), Buddhism (0.20 per cent) and Hinduism (0.18 per cent) (BPS 1999: 130). Despite the absence of violence against the minority, religious tension – especially between Muslims and Christians – remained a potential threat to the harmony of the population, as manifested in several incidents in which religious leaders accused one another of conducting 'clandestine' activities to proselytise their followers (Sullivan 1992: 116). Perhaps a long discussion is needed to explain the low level of religious conflict in Yogyakarta. Since the main purpose of this section is to provide a brief ethnic, religious and socio-economic background of the people in Yogyakarta, I can only refer to some points made by scholars that may partially 'explain' the low level of religious conflict in the area. Some argue that the strong influence of Javanese culture, focusing on harmony, self-restraint and tolerance, has constrained a possibility of an open inter-religious conflict. Historian Onghokham, for example, noted that a strong tradition of syncretism (i.e. the tendency to integrate different values, norms and beliefs) among the Javanese people has led to a process of 'Javanisation of Islam' (the integration of Islamic teaching to the Javanese culture), which led to a substantial degree of tolerance among the Javanese Muslims (Onghokham 1994: 153).

In a similar vein, Abdurrahman Wahid, former president of Indonesia and former leader of the largest Islamic organisation, the *Nahdlatul Ulama*, argued that Javanese culture has contributed to the rise of a high degree of *tenggang rasa* (tolerance) and *penghargaan* (appreciation) among the Javanese Muslims towards other religious faiths insofar as they accept and integrate aspects of other religions into their own faith as manifested in the acknowledgement of 'Sunday' (a 'holy' day in the Christian tradition) as their 'holy' day, instead of 'Friday'

(Muslim's prayer day), and the preservation of mystical rituals inherited from Hinduism (such as *sekatenan, ruwahan, slametan* and the like), which is well maintained by the *Keraton* (palace) of Yogyakarta (Wahid 1994: 6–7). However, religious sensitivity still remains a difficult problem for NGOs with a Christian origin. Despite some degree of tolerance among the Javanese people, some local Muslim leaders are still suspicious that behind their community development programmes, Christian NGOs may try to achieve their agenda of *Kristenisasi* (Christianisation) by persuading their target groups to embrace Christianity (Budiman 1994b: 164–5; Munawar-Rahman 1994: 115–16). As we will see in Chapter 5, constant accusation of *Kristenisasi* has made some NGOs not only cautious in developing relationships with target groups, but also lead them to seek protection from the local authorities especially when they face an extremely dangerous situation.

Another crucial problem in Yogyakarta was the tension between streetside residents and settlers of the slum riverflat areas. Like other growing cities in developing societies, Yogyakarta has also experienced a rapid urbanisation that brings social problems. The booming of tourism as an industry since the early 1970s has resulted in the growth of new migrants to settle in Yogyakarta. From the early 1970s, more and more people from various poor villages especially those in the Gunung Kidul area migrated to search for employment in the city. According to Koyano (1996: 438), about 49 per cent of the immigrants came from Gunung Kidul district, especially Wonosari, an area vulnerable to famine and drought about 40 km to the southeast of the city. Most of these new migrants lived in the riverside *kampung*[5](slum) areas and developed a lifestyle unacceptable to the rest of the city's inhabitants. In most of the Javanese towns, a *kampung* was renowned as a place for some 'illegal' activities such as receiving stolen goods, drug pushing, gambling, prostitution, smuggling, petty theft, larceny, drinking, and so on (Geertz 1965: 33).

Residents in Yogyakarta showed their disapproval of the lifestyle and occupations of *kampung* residents as they invariably described this population as *nakal* (naughty), *kasar* (crude), *kotor* (dirty) or *ugal-ugalan* (wild) (Guinness 1986: 102). Awed by the occasional violence and bawdiness of the *kampung* inhabitants, streetside residents tended to see the increasing population of the riverside *kampung* as a threat to the city's life, and they often associated an increase in crime rates and violence with the expansion of *kampung* settlements. In 1982, the security forces launched a campaign to cut down crime rates. Known as *Operasi Pemberantasan Kejahatan* (crime-alleviation operation), this action was randomly targeting criminals in which dozens of them were shot dead without trial. These problems had tempted many church-related charitable groups and individuals to set up NGOs with the purpose of resolving problems in the *kampung* settlements and to create a positive image of a *kampung* lifestyle. Efforts by Didit, Willy Prasetyo, Fr Mangunwijaya (a Catholic priest) and the YSS (Sugiyopranoto Social Foundation – a Catholic foundation based in Semarang) to organise and develop solidarity among settlers of the Code and Winongo riverflat areas during the early 1980s were examples of this type of activity.

## The city of education and movement

Yogyakarta, widely known as *kota pelajar* (the city of higher education) – where 159,799 students (in 1999) from all over Indonesia pursued their studies in 63 public and private universities employing 19,400 lecturers (BPS 1999: 129) – appeared to meet the necessary conditions for the rise of social movements as argued by the 'resource mobilisation' theorists.[6] The presence of students, who constituted almost half of the city's total population, has generated social and political activities in the region. Many seminars, discussions and workshops on various topics were organised in various university campuses and research centres in the city. Students played a key role in NGO operations in terms of supplying human resources and stimulating various political discourses among the activists. It is therefore tempting to select Yogyakarta as a research site because one can see enormous activities that can influence the way NGOs and other elements of social movements establish themselves.

Consistent with its status as the city of higher education, Yogyakarta has a high degree of literacy. According to the data from BPS, in 1999 around 96 per cent of the total population above 10 years of age in the city were able to read and write, while in Gunung Kidul (the least developed district in the province) the literacy rates was 71 per cent (BPS 1999: 140). Around 16 national and local newspapers, magazines and tabloids – both in Indonesian and Javanese – such as *Kompas, Suara Pembaruan, Media Indonesia, Pos Kota, Republika, Jawa Pos, Kedaulatan Rakyat, Berita Nasional, Yogya Pos, Suara Merdeka, Jaka Lodang, Gatra, Forum, Kontan* and many others, were sold in the newsstands available on most street corners in the city. Academics, students and NGO activists occasionally expressed their political views and exchanged ideas in the columns made available for them by the local newspapers, especially *Kedaulatan Rakyat* and *Berita Nasional*.

A combination of rapid development in communication technology, the state's successful programme of *Listrik Masuk Desa* (village electrification), a high level of literacy rates and the growing number of private TV and radio broadcasting stations has opened greater access for the population of Yogyakarta to information. If in 1979 there were only 23 villages (5 per cent of the total villages in the province) with electricity serving only 269 households in rural areas, in 1997 the number of villages with electricity had increased to 429 (98 per cent of the total villages) covering 339,531 households (Bappenas 1997a: 2). Meanwhile, data from Susenas[7] (the national social-economic survey) indicated that in 1999 about 65 per cent of the total population above 10 years of age were regular radio listeners, 69 per cent were regular TV watchers, and 32 per cent were newspapers readers (BPS 1999: 128).

Yogyakarta also preserved a long tradition of movements in the areas of education and social welfare. One of the most important organisations was the *Taman Siswa* educational movement, which arose in the early twentieth century as a pioneer of Indonesian national education. Led by Soewardi Soerjaningrat (also known as Ki Hadjar Dewantara), *Taman Siswa* had attempted to build awareness among the indigenous population (whose access to education was denied by the colonial government) of the importance to obtain a formal education in order to free themselves from apathy, ignorance and backwardness (Tsuchiya 1987: 55). Soerjaningrat himself was renowned as one of the pioneers of the nationalist movement in Indonesia and became popular among the nationalists through his article titled *Als ik eens Nederlander was* (If I were to be a Dutchman), published in *De Express* on 13 July 1913, which challenged the justice of the colonial rule. The first *Taman Siswa* school was opened in Yogyakarta offering a kindergarten and a teacher's course. During the 1930s the number of *Taman Siswa* schools continued to grow apace throughout Java, Sumatra and Kalimantan. By 1936, this organisation had established 187 schools across Indonesia with 1,037 classes, 602 teachers and 11,235 students (Tsuchiya 1987: appendix 1). Given the fact that many of its graduates became leaders or active participants in various nationalist study groups, *Taman Siswa* had served as an important organisation in the Indonesian independence movement. In the post-independence period, however, *Taman Siswa* subsided following a rapid expansion of the more modern public and private schools.

Another important voluntary association in Yogyakarta has been the *Muhammadiyah* movement. Established in 1912, the *Muhammadiyah* (literally means 'the followers of Muhammad') adopted, from the beginning, the stance of political non-involvement *vis-à-vis* the colonial authorities and concentrated on the areas of education and social welfare by establishing schools, clinics, hospitals, orphanages, and the like. It was founded by some of the religious officials in the court of Yogyakarta (*abdi dalem santri*) who became critical of the laxity of Islamic faith and practice among their fellow officials. They urged the ruler and the *priyayi* (Javanese administrators) to rectify their behaviour following the standard of Islamic orthodoxy (Nakamura 1983: 45). Kyai Haji Ahmad Dahlan (1868–1923), the founder of this organisation, was one of these critical *santris* in the service of the Sultan of Yogyakarta. Within 20 years of its formation, the *Muhammadiyah* became one of the largest religious organisations in the Dutch colony (Nakamura 1983: 3). It survived the period of the Japanese occupation (1942–1945) and the *revolusi kemerdekaan* (independence revolution) of 1945–1949, and grew larger throughout the 1950s and 1960s to function as one of the largest and most influential Islamic organisations in Indonesia.

In Yogyakarta one can also see a strong concentration of church-related groups such as *Yayasan Kanisius*, *Yayasan Syantikara*, Pelkesi (All-Indonesia Christian Health Service), *Yayasan Purba Danata*, *Yayasan Realino* and so on, most of which were formed during the 1950s and 1960s and run a number of schools, hospitals, clinics, orphanages and other charitable activities. One important organisation with substantial contributions to community development was *Yayasan Realino* (the Realino Foundation). Led by Fr de Blot, and later by Fr Suasso, both Dutch-born priests from the Jesuit order, during the 1970s and 1980s *Yayasan Realino* devised programmes to rehabilitate former political prisoners (*ex-tapol*) – mainly ex-PKI members and affiliates – most of whom lived on Buru island. The first programme concentrated on supplying prisoners with essentials such as clothes, food, blankets, and the like. The second part of the programme

16  *Introduction*

was to encourage self-reliance among the prisoners' families (who were excluded from civil and military services) by teaching them practical skills such as sewing, tailoring, weaving and carpentry. The third programme was the formation of a co-operative named *Koperasi Mandiri* which linked 42 workshops producing furniture, metal products and agricultural tools into a federation (Eldridge 1995: 128). *Yayasan Realino*'s most important contribution to NGO activity, however, was its effort to raise students' awareness of issues concerning poverty and human rights violation. During the late 1960s and early 1970s students were motivated and trained to undertake community works with the prisoners' families. In this way, *Yayasan Realino* had influenced Anton Soedjarwo, an engineering student at Gadjah Mada University, and some others to form a voluntary group which later known as the *Dian Desa* Foundation, one of the biggest income-generating NGOs in Indonesia.

## The cases

Case-based research, according to Creswell (1994: 12), obliges the researcher to explore a single entity of phenomenon (the case) bounded by time and activity (a programme, event, process, institution or social groups) and to collect detailed information by using a variety of data collection procedures during a sustained period of time. The use of cases are essential to illustrate particular propositions or arguments and to provide the details and complexities of how things work or fail to work. In this study, I use case studies to illustrate my arguments regarding the works of local, social and political conditions that may have affected NGOs' attempts to produce greater impact, to develop professional management systems, to serve as representatives of the oppressed, to maintain organisational stability, to develop co-operation with one another and to expand linkages with other elements of social movements.

Four organisations, Bina Swadaya Yogyakarta (BSY) and CD-Bethesda representing development NGOs, the Yogyakarta Women's Joint Secretariat (SBPY) and the Annisa Swasti Foundation (Yasanti) representing movement NGOs, and one local networking body, the Yogyakarta NGO Forum, were selected and researched as our samples. Table 1.5 provides general information on five organisations used as case studies. I selected these organisations not only because they are organisations that come so close to the definitions of NGOs used in this study, but also because they are far removed from Constantino-David's (1992) categories of GRINGOs (government-run, -inspired or -initiated NGOs) and COME'NGOs (fly-by-night NGO entrepreneurs) frequently observed in the Philippines during Marcos dictatorship, which are not included in this study. While GRINGOs refer to organisations formed by politicians or government functionaries to serve as conduits for government and agents for distributing bilateral aid funds, COME'NGOs are paper organisations that never operate or operate only one project and then disappear because they are lacking organisational structures, short of funds, and are highly unsustainable (Constantino-David 1992: 138). The inclusion of GRINGOs is avoided because their heavy reliance

Table 1.5 The profile of NGOs used as case studies

| Name of organisation | Major aims | Area of activities | Target groups | Annual revenue in 2000 (US$)[a] | Year of formation | Number of employees |
|---|---|---|---|---|---|---|
| Bina Swadaya Yogyakarta Foundation (BSY) | Improving the productive activities of the poor | Small-credit and Micro-enterprises development | Poor peasant; small artisans | 146,784 | 1970 | 12 |
| CD-Bethesda (CD) | (a) Promoting alternative medication to the poor (b) Building organisational capacity of poor villagers (c) Democratising rural political life | Primary healthcare; income generation; civic education; facilitating people's organisations | Poor peasants; urban poor communities | 869,873 | 1974 | 78 |
| SBPY (Yogyakarta Women's Joint Secretariat) | Representing women in the informal sector | Organising; mobilising women; gender-equality campaign; and networking | House-keepers; petty traders; women migrant workers | 30,000 | 1992 | 12 |
| Yasanti (Anisa Swasti Foundation) | Promoting gender equality; women's advocacy | Organising; mobilising; networking; and awareness building | Factory workers; load-carriers | 50,000 | 1982 | 11 |
| Forum (Yogyakarta NGO Forum) | Facilitating local NGOs; building local NGO network; promoting democracy | Organisational trainings; organising seminars and discussions; making political statements | Local NGOs; rural and urban poor groups | 13,258 | 1986 | 41 |

Source: Data collected from fieldwork.

Note

a These figures are calculated based on December 2001 exchange rates in which US$1 = Rp 10,000.

18  *Introduction*

on the government in terms of budget, management, staff and other resources puts them into the category of the state sector. COME'NGOs are also not included in this study since the reasons for their short lived operation, lack of innovation, poor commitment, organisational instability and disintegration are obvious, so that no further explanation can be provided.

In Indonesia, some GRINGOs were formed by state officials to achieve different purposes. For example, in the case of Bangdes (village development group), an organisation administered by the Ministry of Home Affairs to distribute annual village development funds, the GRINGO was formed to meet the conditions set by foreign donors suggesting that a portion of development assistance should be channeled through NGOs. In the case of a number of *yayasan* (foundations) related to President Suharto and his family and friends such as *Yayasan Dakab*, *Yayasan Dharmais*, *Yayasan Amal Bhakti Muslim Pancasila* and some others, the GRINGOs were formed to serve as fund-raising agents and to achieve the social and political ambitions of the ruling elites. Meanwhile, COME'NGOs emerged during the late 1980s and early 1990s many of which were founded by a group of concerned, but slightly indeterminate, ex-student activists who formed organisations with vague mission and uncalculated strategies that often suffered from acute financial problem and disintegration. In Yogyakarta, dozens of organisations that might fall into Constantino-David's category of COME'NGOs were formed by students preoccupied with the radical social theories of participatory action research (PAR) and alternative education, but most of them collapsed after running one or two programmes. The reason for their collapse, according to Mohammad Farid, a senior NGO activist in Yogyakarta, was that their formation was more determined by short-lived, emotional excitement rather than rational calculation (Farid, interview, 28/02/1997). Indeed, many of these organisations disintegrated because they had neither a long-term goal nor a clearly stated mission. These organisations are beyond the scope of this research.

While excluding GRINGOs and COME'NGOs, this study tries to focus on those organisations that have passed Anton Soedjarwo's 'passing grade', that is: (1) having a more or less permanent office with sufficient administrative facilities to run programmes; (2) having a stable organisational structure; (3) operating on the basis of a clear mission, purpose and a written constitution; (4) employing both full-time and part-time workers with sufficient knowledge of community development activities; and (5) running a regular (annual) budget whose funding may come from either internal or external sources (Soedjarwo, interview, 21/01/1997). NGOs, according to Soedjarwo, should first pass this 'passing grade' before they can be considered as 'true' NGOs with some degree of seriousness to pursue whatever activities they are enduring (Soedjarwo, interview, 21/01/1997). It appears that only organisations with this kind of 'passing grade' which will receive serious attention from their governments, donors, target groups and observers.

## Data collection procedures

Social research can be divided into two main approaches: qualitative and quantitative. Qualitative research, according to Creswell (1994: 2), is a research activity whose major aim is not to generalise findings, but to form a unique interpretation of events based on a holistic picture which documents detailed views of informants. Meanwhile, a quantitative study, he argued, is a process of inquiry into a social and human problem based on testing a theory composed of variables, measured with statistical procedures in order to determine whether the predictive generalisations of the theory hold true.[8] If in a qualitative study researchers interact with those they study and minimise the distance between themselves and those being researched in order to gather detailed and subjective information, in a quantitative study the researchers should remain distant and independent of those being researched in order to maintain objectivity (Creswell 1994: 159). This study attempts to present a picture of NGOs operating in particular social and political contexts based on information gathered from various sources which puts it closer to the category of qualitative research. Although some data may be quantitative in character, it will be used simply to illustrate the arguments rather than to generalise findings.

I chose NGOs in Yogyakarta which I believe to be broadly representative of both 'development-oriented' and 'movement-oriented' NGOs. My central interest is to describe and analyse the way these NGOs attempt to adjust to particular social and political contexts, to establish relations with their target groups, to develop professional management systems, to improve their performance, and to interact with one another. Consequently, this requires intensive research of a 'qualitative' kind in which I need to minimise the distance between myself and those involved in NGO activities. However, important and quantifiable facts should not be neglected since they can also support arguments developed throughout this study. Thus, although in this study I employ a qualitative data collection procedure, I also use quantitative data from various documents such as NGO reports, official statistical records, interviews and so on to support the arguments or propositions wherever appropriate. By using both qualitative and quantitative data, my generalisations of other NGOs in Yogyakarta, elsewhere in Indonesia and beyond, can be no more than suggestive.

## *The population and sampling procedure*

Data and information were gathered from two stages of fieldwork. The first was 12 months of field research from October 1996 to September 1997 and the second was three months of research from June–August 2001. Research based on fieldwork is indeed an inquiry process of understanding of a social or human problem, based on building a complex, holistic picture, formed with words, reporting detailed views of informants and conducted in a natural setting (Creswell 1994: 12). Because it requires detailed information of facts, events and processes, this type of research must be carried out in a selected research population. In order to avoid complications, information was gathered from a group of samples. Since this study focuses on NGO activities in a particular context with specific programmes involving specific target groups, the sample cannot be randomly selected from the population. Inevitably, I must use a purposive sampling procedure in which informants are selected purposively according to their occupation, authority, capacity and relationships with NGO activities.

## 20  Introduction

I prefer to use the term 'informants' instead of 'respondents' since I carried out unstructured interviews, where interviewees expressed their opinions and views freely without obligation to answer strictly set questions. In this study, I interviewed a number of informants in several categories: (1) NGO activists including directors, staff members and fieldworkers; (2) NGOs' target groups or beneficiaries; (3) staff members of international NGOs who provide financial support for NGOs under study; (4) community leaders, that is, individuals with power and authority to influence the activities of local co-operatives, neighbourhood associations, government-sponsored grassroots organisations, farmers' associations, and so on; (5) government officials at village and provincial levels; (6) intellectuals, that is, academics and religious leaders; and (7) ordinary people who may have both direct or indirect relationships with NGOs: students, workers and small entrepreneurs. Throughout the fieldwork, I managed to interview 87 informants: 31 NGO activists, 24 NGOs' beneficiaries, three staff of international NGOs operating in Yogyakarta, six community leaders, five government officials, seven intellectuals/academics, four small entrepreneurs and nine student activists.

### *Data collection strategies*

My strategy to collect data from the field involved several activities: (1) gathering information through participatory observation in various activities of a selected number of NGOs by visiting several villages where NGO programmes are carried out; (2) carrying out in-depth interviews with a number of informants; (3) document studies on NGO reports, government publications and other visual materials; (4) establishing a protocol to ensure similar questions are asked to different institutions or individuals; (5) using relevant data and information from newspapers, magazines, newsletters, bulletins, official publications and the like. I started my observation by making early visits to a number of organisations while permission from the local authority was still being processed. This was followed by serving as a *pengamat* (observing participant) in various NGO internal meetings and gatherings. This allowed me to make the personal acquaintance of a number of NGO activists, academics, community leaders and NGOs' target groups. Most of the interviews were carried out informally through day-to-day contacts, except those which involved academics, religious leaders, government officials and directors of large NGOs whereby advance appointments were required. Document studies were carried out through a careful examination of various notes, transcripts and unpublished documents whenever available. Other relevant visual materials were also selected according to their content. Whenever appropriate, I recorded information from my interviews by using note-taking and audiotapes. For this purpose, I equipped myself with a protocol, a personal diary and a tape recorder. The protocol or form for recording information was used to note observations in the field and to ensure that I consistently use similar questions to gather information from various sources, while the diary recorded my personal impression of the information I gathered and the events I encountered. All taped information was transcribed accordingly.

Research which involves a number of informants with such a high level of authority and knowledge is always vulnerable to personal biases in which informants can impose their own subjective views on an 'ignorant' researcher to the extent that it could change the whole direction of the research. One major problem was that many NGO staff in Yogyakarta tended to boast about the success of their organisations and understate their limitations or failures. In order to avoid this, I started my fieldwork by interviewing informants with less knowledge of NGO activities and culture, that is, junior NGO workers, volunteers, target groups and community leaders with the purpose of preventing knowledgeable informants from imposing their personal biases. With information from the less knowledgeable individuals in hand, I became more confident and prepared to begin my encounter with well-informed individuals such as senior NGO activists, NGO directors, donors and academics. Also, I used every opportunity to check and recheck the information by asking various informants or referring to different visual materials.

## The structure of the book

This book is divided into eight chapters. Chapter 1 describes the background, the argument, terminology, the research site, the cases and the research procedures. Chapter 2 outlines various issues related to NGO activities. It provides cross-references of NGO activities in other regions. The aim was to provide a comparative perspective of Indonesian NGOs. Chapter 3 discusses the social and political settings that have affected NGOs. It argues that social and political conditions from the Sukarno years to Suharto's government and then the post-Suharto democratic transition had a paradoxical consequence on NGOs. On the one hand, NGOs had themselves to tread carefully in order not to provoke political suspicion from the government as well as the society, but on the other hand, there were also opportunities, especially toward the end of Suharto's government when social resistance began to grow. These conditions have their origins in the politics of the Sukarno years where political leaders were obsessed with the idea of maintaining unity of the 'multi-group' state that led them to believe that tensions in the society followed from ethno-religious conflicts rather than class struggle. I believe that these unavoidably complex social and political settings can affect the way NGOs develop their strategies, approaches and institutions.

Chapter 4 discusses the way Indonesian NGOs respond to the complicated social and political settings discussed earlier. It argues that in order to strike a balance between avoiding political suspicion and pursuing their empowerment agenda, Indonesian NGOs appeared as two distinct organisations: 'development-oriented NGOs' and 'movement-oriented NGOs'. While development-oriented NGOs put much emphasis on community development and income-generation, movement-oriented NGOs focused on advocacy and mobilisation. This chapter will also discuss new opportunities and challenges faced by Indonesian NGOs in the post-Suharto period. Chapter 5 describes the experience of BSY and CD-Bethesda in carrying out their community development and income-generating activities. It argues that although NGOs had been constrained by the New Order government, some of them managed to play an important role in rural development – that is, the agricultural sector, health care and small industries – especially in the last few years prior to the 1997 economic crisis. In the post-Suharto era, when opportunity to include political activities in their agenda arose, CD-Bethesda decided to move beyond its traditional role by conducting political education and by disseminating democratic values to its target groups. In a similar vein, BSY began to change its approach by providing more opportunities for villagers to determine their own development.

Chapter 6 examines the challenges faced by two women's NGOs – SBPY and Yasanti – in their attempt to build constituencies[9] and to institutionalise a movement. Because their major aim was to propose new structures, values and norms that would benefit their constituencies, the two organisations tended to face resistance from those whose interests were threatened by their activities. Moreover, operating in a context where confrontation is not totally acceptable, both SBPY and Yasanti tended to face resistance from the state (most notably during the New Order government), other groups in society or even their own constituencies. As far as management is concerned, the two movement-oriented NGOs tended to set a balance between 'movement' and 'institution'. They tried to minimise institutionalisation in order to maintain flexibility; but at the same time they developed rules and procedures to ensure sustainability. This middle-way approach caused confusion in the relationship between staff and trustee members as manifested in the internal conflicts in both SBPY and Yasanti. Chapter 7 illustrates the dynamics of a local NGO network in developing local democracy. It will focus on the experience of the Yogyakarta NGO Forum amid the growing popular resistance that led to the pro-democracy movements in the 1990s and the subsequent transition to democracy in the post-Suharto era. Despite its success in developing democratic discourse among the grassroots people, the Yogyakarta NGO Forum faced some challenges. Some of them were internal: members were not ready to be governed by structures outside their own organisations, institutionalisation was constrained by members' fear of bureaucratisation, and performance were limited by over-ambitious goals. Another factor was external to the network, that is, the challenges from the New Order government as well as the radical Islamic organisations whose interests were threatened by the NGO network's attempt to establish linkage with grassroots people. Finally, the concluding chapter will summarise the role of NGOs in two different capacities: as development institutions whose main purpose is to alleviate poverty, and as social movements whose main agenda is to challenge social and political structures that have created poverty and injustice. The conclusion will also indicate that changing political context in the post-Suharto era has allowed Indonesian NGOs to move beyond their traditional role as promoters of grassroots-oriented development to become more actively involved in the promotion of democracy and grassroots mobilisation.

# 2 NGOs, community development and social movements

## The role of NGOs

In developing societies, some have argued that although NGOs had their inception during the colonial era when branches of European churches opened charitable organisations in the colonies, the rise of development-oriented NGOs began from the early 1970s (Kandil 1993: 4; Smillie 1995: 62; Wanigaratne 1997: 218–19). During the 1980s and 1990s their activities expanded very rapidly, moving from one type of activity to another and performing different roles. Korten (1987: 147–9), for example, argued that NGOs have moved through a linear evolution: (1) 'first-generation' NGOs focusing on relief and welfare activities; (2) 'second-generation' NGOs addressing the structural context of local self-help action through organisation and the mobilisation of local resources; and (3) 'third-generation' NGOs seeking changes in the institutions and policies at national and sub-national levels that inhibit effective self-help action.[1]

In a similar vein, Elliott (1987) distinguished three different approaches of NGOs: (1) The 'welfare' approach: One that focuses on fundraising activities and delivers services to specific groups (e.g. child-sponsorship or famine relief) but is not particularly concerned with empowerment of local communities. (2) The 'developmental' approach: One in which the programme emphasis is on support of development projects which have as their ultimate goal improvement in the capacity of a community to provide for its own basic needs. (3) The 'empowerment' approach: One that sees poverty as a result of political processes and is therefore committed to enabling (or training) communities to enter those processes. Although the three approaches are interrelated, nowadays there has been a tendency of NGOs in developing societies to move along the spectrum from simple provision of food and health care or education to something that is more recognisably developmental in approach, and then to the empowerment of their constituency (Elliott 1987: 57–9).

When NGOs begin to expand their roles to include Kortens's and Elliot's second and third categories, the challenge is whether or not they are capable of combining development and empowerment approaches. Many NGO staff members realise the importance of a combined approach since they believe that empowerment without production is as futile as production without empowerment (Elliott 1987: 59).

24  *NGOs, community development and social movements*

The merit of a combined approach is that NGOs can have a greater impact on the community with which they are working. While income-generating is important in helping people adapt to market-driven productive activities, empowerment can help increase people's bargaining position in their relations with both the state and the market. In Bangladesh, for instance, NGOs such as BRAC (Bangladesh Rural Advancement Committee) and Proshika are able to work with twin strategies: (1) income-generating to provide non-collateral credit schemes to poor households; and (2) 'conscientisation' designed to develop the potential of poor people to challenge structural inequalities through education, organisation and mobilisation (Lewis 1997: 35). With this combined approach, they have succeeded not only in encouraging people to put more pressure on the government but also in making them more confident to conduct market-driven productive activities in rural areas.

However, NGOs' success in combining different approaches depends on the local political situation. In a situation where the government develops a sympathetic approach, NGOs face fewer obstacles in their attempt to combine development and empowerment. In India, for instance, NGO approaches have evolved from early relief efforts sponsored largely by Christian organisations, through to the 'village uplift' of the Gandhian movement, to a professional development approach stressing sound management planning and to an empowerment approach (Robinson *et al.* 1993: 94). Supported by the government, NGOs in India are able to combine project-based development activities with active organisation of the poor. For example, the AKRSP (Aga Khan Rural Support Programme), an environmental NGO in Gujarat, has been praised by foreign donors, the press and the local government for its ability to combine project-based development with organising activities (Madsen 1997: 262). Local farmers are treated as analysts, facilitators and decision-makers in the process involving Participatory Rural Appraisal[2] and planning for the development of natural resources in the village and the formation of village groups (Sethna and Shah 1993: 124–6).

A similar trend occurred in the Philippines under Aquino. When the government became more accommodating towards grassroots activities, there was a growing realisation of the need to combine sectoral development with the mobilisation approach. Many NGOs believed that institutional mechanisms for information-sharing and lobbying activities are fundamental to foster issue-oriented campaigns, and at the same time, mobilisation was also crucial to ensure participation (Miclat-Teves and Lewis 1993: 235). This combined strategy appeared to be essential in the formation of a special task-force involving NGOs, local people, businessmen and church leaders. For example, the Urban Land Reform Task Force (ULRTF), which was established in 1990 to protect the rights of the urban poor, was more or less able to serve as a grassroots alliance involving a number of NGOs, progressive church-related business groups and leaders of the Catholic church. This task-force successfully lobbied parliament to pass a bill on urban land reform more favourable to the poor. It also strengthened the ability of grassroots organisations to negotiate with local authorities (Covey 1995: 171–2).

However, in situations where governments are less accommodative, NGOs tend to face pressure to limit their approach to sectors that are considered 'safe' to declare. Many NGOs with a strong commitment to fundamental change have to avoid concentrating on political mobilisation and move themselves instead towards relief, welfare and income-generating activities in order to gain the government's recognition and 'blessing'. Failure to do so will risk co-optation, manipulation, intimidation or even dissolution. This may not be a 'backward' move on their part (as Korten's and Elliott's categories seem to suggest), more accurately, it is simply a realistic one that suits the needs of particular political circumstances (Biggs and Neame 1995: 35).

It appears that in the less democratic societies NGOs come to light in two different forms: one of which concentrates in community development activities to promote the idea of people-centered development, since they are not prepared to confront the state, and the other focuses on organising specifically defined constituencies to generate social movements. This has certainly been the case in Indonesia under the New Order. Here, the government's constant threat to suppress grassroots political activities had limited NGOs' choice to combine development with the empowerment approach, which led to the emergence of the two forms of NGOs mentioned above. The democratic transition in the post-Suharto era is therefore seen by many observers as the opening up of new opportunities for Indonesian NGOs to set up a grassroots coalition combining development and empowerment activities as performed by their counterparts in India and the Philippines.

## NGOs and people-centered development

One important item on the NGO agenda in the context of community development is of course poverty alleviation. Initially, poverty was treated as a lack of minimum nutritional intake needed to sustain life, lack of physical assets (land, shelter, clothing and the like), and lack of human capital (education, skill and so on). The response of the aid system – whose projects were carried out by NGOs – was to provide technical assistance and investment in primary health care, water supply and income-generation. In the early 1980s, a call for a people-centered development practice emphasised the need to strengthen institutional and social capacity supportive of greater local control, accountability, initiative, and self-reliance at grassroots level (Chambers 1995: 33). While the conventional view of development, based on transfer of capital and technology, was seriously questioned, a new priority was placed on a process of grassroots empowerment, that is, the imposition of decentralised and self-organising principles in the management of development resources (Nelson and Wright 1995: 8; Chambers 1997: 13–14). This new emphasis grew out of weariness that in the name of development and the national interest, many large-scale projects in developing societies – such as the Mount Apo geothermal construction project in the Philippines or the Kedung Ombo dam project in Indonesia – called for the eviction of the poor from their homes as well as the land and water from which they obtained their livelihoods. Often sponsored by international funding agencies – such as the IMF and the World Bank – these projects represent a persistent pattern of confiscatory dislocation that transfers resources from more or less sustainable uses for the benefit of people who are already better off than those who are displaced (Korten and Quizon 1991: 25). For the proponents of this view, the role of NGOs should be expanded to include attempts to promote people's self-reliance at grassroots level, that is to say, to remove structural constraints hindering the process of autonomous development (Rahman 1995).

A people-centered development approach was built upon two basic assumptions: (1) a belief that the state is part of the problem, and that development must proceed outside and perhaps even against the state; and (2) a notion that community action is essential for autonomous development (Friedmann 1992: 6). In people-centered development, people are encouraged to mobilise and manage their own local resources, with governments and other external agencies in an enabling role only (Korten 1984: 343; Nelson and Wright 1995: 14; Rahman 1995: 159). It is generally believed that international capital transfers to the developing world – carried out by transnational corporations and international financial institutions – have failed to generate productive investments because they are seriously thwarted by corruption, cronyism and patronage if channeled through government institutions (Korten 1987: 146; Bradlow and Grossman 1996: 42–5). Even when they are not bedeviled by these difficulties, they often fail to benefit the poorest group in society. As demonstrated by Marcos in the Philippines (Korten 1987: 146) and Suharto in Indonesia (Bresnan 1993: 257), the instrument of expropriation was determined by those who control state power and their cronies which included 'commissions' on construction and purchasing contracts, padded payrolls, defaulting on personal loans, mining and timber concessions, and crony-controlled marketing monopolies. In these countries, the patronage system was imposed from above by authoritarian leaders at village level, and self-help grassroots initiatives were systematically circumscribed. When corruption and patronage are part of the avenues to advancement, the poor who lack access to these avenues and have no choice but to depend in their day-to-day struggle for survival on their own labour, find themselves subject to often not so subtle scorn.

Moreover, the 'developmental state', once praised for its ability to produce effective development policies, has been increasingly questioned since its legitimacy relies on the use of repression and terror rather than on bargaining and negotiation (Kothari 1993: 64). Nowadays, more and more people in developing societies are no longer willing to accept exploitative or repressive regimes, state structures, and a development paradigm that excludes them in a fatalistic way. NGOs emerge in many nations to make sure that the benefit of development reaches the poorest and that grassroots initiatives are not undermined or manipulated by the patronage arrangement (Korten 1987: 146). However, in carrying out this duty NGOs may face problems regarding how to develop the right size and scope of activity in order to make a greater impact and how to set up a good management system that will ensure performance and sustainability. It is in this context that NGOs are expected to 'correct' the mistakes of the conventional development approaches by allowing the poor to initiate their own advancement (Korten 1987: 147).

## Size and scope

In the mid-1980s, NGOs began to realise that the impact of their activities on the lives of the poor was highly localised and often transitory because their project-oriented small-scale programmes had not produced changes in the structures which determine the distribution of power and resources within and between societies. Small could still be beautiful, but considerations of learning, replicability, sustainability and wider impact became more and more significant (Drabek 1987: ix). The most important challenge for NGOs, according to Edwards and Hulme (1992: 13), was how to make the right linkages between their work at micro-level and the wider systems and structures of which they formed a small part. One way to produce greater impact is to scale up the scope of activities. Clark (1991: 84–5) proposed three types of NGOs' scaling-up process: (1) project replication in which NGOs increase the outreach of their most successful programme(s) and help others to establish similar programmes; (2) building grassroots movement in which NGOs help foster widespread networks articulating popular concerns and striving for changes in systems which disadvantage the poor by using their local knowledge and national or perhaps international contacts; and (3) influencing policy reform whereby NGOs attempt to influence local policies and practices of government to create a more favourable environment to the grassroots-initiated development. Meanwhile, Edwards and Hulme (1992: 15) held that the most important distinction of scaling-up lay between: (1) 'additive' strategies which include an increase in the size of the organisation as well as the outreach of its programmes; (2) 'multiplicative' strategies which do not necessarily imply growth but achieve impact through networking, policy and legal reform, and training; and (3) 'diffusive' strategies where spread is informal and spontaneous, linking the grassroots with lobbying and advocacy.

NGOs' scaling-up process often coincides with the transformation towards Korten's 'third-generation' category in which organisations began to re-examine their strategic issues relating to sustainability, breadth of impact, and recurrent cost recovery. A growing number of NGOs realise they need to exert greater leadership in addressing ineffective aspects of the policy and the institutional setting of the sectors and groups with which they work. Moving to a third-generation strategy also means putting more focus on facilitating more sustainable changes in these settings on a regional or even national basis (Korten 1987: 149). Thus, financial discipline and professional management are necessary if NGOs are to succeed in their scaling-up process. What really matters for many NGOs in developing societies is whether their receipt and utilisation of donors' money will enable them to have greater impact in their operational work (Commins 1997: 141). When donors think that NGO projects should be quickly scaled up in order to produce rapid disbursement and financial sustainability (Edwards and Hulme 1997: 9), some NGOs will consider an increase in their size and scope of activity as synonymous with greater impact (Biggs and Neame 1995: 36). Furthermore, in an era of declining financial resources, donors begin to expect NGOs in developing societies to be more 'efficient', that is, to produce a higher output per unit input.

Consequently, they need to generate more projects, process more paper, and render more accounts (Elliott 1987: 60). In the 1990s, the influence of donors on NGO activities was 'justified' by the so-called 'New Policy Agenda': a new policy direction in which NGO operation is linked with attempts to promote a liberal–capitalist economy and democracy (Moore 1993; Robinson 1993; Edwards and Hulme 1995b: 219). Acceptance of increasing volumes of foreign aid often leaves NGOs in developing societies in a state of disagreement about what is to be done and how it is to be reported and accounted for (Edwards and Hulme 1997: 7). Although in theory they can refuse that pressure – as some organisations occasionally do – the fear of being accused of being dishonest, incompetent, corrupt as well as the possible termination of foreign funding, has forced these NGOs to comply with donors' demands for organisational expansion, accounting procedures and hierarchical chains of command.

Inevitably, NGOs' scaling-up process involves an increase in organisational size, scope of activities, number of divisions or branch offices and the adoption of better management systems. Scaling-up may also involve combining different approaches such as charity, self-help action, mobilisation and so forth. The extent to which an NGO succeeds or fails in its scaling-up process depends on both external and internal factors. In extremely rare cases some NGOs are able to undertake all the aspects of scaling-up depicted by Clark (1991) and Edwards and Hulme (1992). One reason for this success is that these NGOs receive full support from their governments and donors, and secure a high degree of 'acceptability'[3] from their beneficiaries so that they can plan their scaling-up more carefully and expand their approach without facing serious resistance or political obstacles. Their success may also result from their ability to improve their management system through staff development, accountability procedure, financial management, and so on. However, other NGOs (that may constitute the majority) may only be able to carry out 'partial scaling-up' due to the pressure put on them by governments, the lack of human resources, poor management system and an unfamiliarity with the new sector with which they are dealing.

There has been a growing concern that scaling-up will undermine NGOs' flexibility and solidarity with the poor. Bebbington and Riddell (1997: 113), for example, posit that NGOs' rapid expansion risks the possible demise of their effectiveness and the collapse of popular participation. This caution is indeed vindicated in some cases. For example, in India, *Apnalaya* (an NGO working with street children and slum dwellers in Bombay) faces the negative effect of growing organisational size. Its experience suggests that pressures to adopt a system of accountability deriving from 'linear' world views, with targets and sanctions to be imposed in the event of non-achievement, reinforce other pressures for the organisation to transform itself into a routine service provider and reduce its capability to explore new ideas (Desai and Howes 1995: 84). In the early 1990s, amid the growing expectation of NGOs' professionalism and financial discipline, *Apnalaya* developed an 'upward', instead of 'downward', accountability, that is, a system of accountability designed to satisfy donors and the government, rather than the beneficiaries, in project design and evaluation. Moreover, its tendency to develop an accountability mechanism based on individual projects (rather than on the entire spread of the organisation's work) has made *Apnalaya* vulnerable to the criticism that it focuses too heavily on immediate results in its reporting at the expense of longer term effects and impacts (Desai and Howes 1995: 90). In Sri Lanka, the growth of *Sarvodaya Shramadana*, an income-generating NGO, has begun to compromise some of the participatory process inside the organisation and has also weakened the common mission which had previously united its staff members (Bebbington and Riddell 1997: 113). In the early 1990s, the pressure from its consortium of donors, led by NOVIB (the Netherlands Organisation for International Development Co-operation), to adopt a centralised administrative system, financial discipline, and professional expertise, destroyed the flexible and informal character that had been the hallmark of *Sarvodaya*. Perera (1997: 163) argued that *Sarvodaya*'s experience illustrates how an NGO is forced, in its scaling-up process, to serve as a subcontractor of foreign donors and the state rather than a partner to grassroots organisations. *Sarvodaya*'s subordination to the Premadasa government resulted from the political pressures imposed by the Prime Minister to make the organisation concentrate on short-term, quick-yielding development projects (Perera 1997: 164–5).

However, there are other cases in which organisational growth does not necessarily dilute a participatory approach. For example, *Proshika* in Bangladesh is known for its participatory planning process in developing income-generating activities. Although *Proshika* has expanded its activities and has remained dependent on foreign donors, this organisation is able to maintain its participatory approach that begins at grassroots level. Every year its partner groups are invited to set their own plan for the following year. Each group's plan is subsequently taken to the Village Committee (a representative body of NGO fieldworkers and group members) where it is reviewed and approved, and a village plan is developed (Ul Karim 1995: 114). In the Philippines, the experience of *Mag-uugmad*[4] Foundation Inc. (MFI) in Cebu suggests that even a large, professional organisation can maintain its voluntarism and participatory approach. In the late 1980s, with the help from a US-based NGO, World Neighbours, MFI planned its growing scope of operation and projects very carefully. From a concentration on soil and water conservation programmes, MFI subsequently developed a farmer-based extension strategy with the aim of increasing farmers' productivity through the use of appropriate technology and environmentally friendly farming methods. A board consisting of professional NGO staff members and representatives of the local farmers and fishermen was established to implement programmes. Participants were expected to judge for themselves whether the technologies and practices could bring them adequate returns on their investments in time and labour (Cerna and Miclat-Teves 1993: 248–50).

These cases indicate that the impact of scaling-up on NGO activities is more complicated than one would seem to expect. It is difficult to link the success or failure of NGOs' scaling-up process to a single factor. To assume that NGOs' growing relationship with (and dependence on) foreign donors as the only factor that diverts NGOs' flexibility and accountability is erroneous for at least two reasons. First, NGOs in developing societies do not necessarily accept all conditions set out by donors. Some of them may have a significant degree of bargaining power because of their innovative projects (Wils 1995: 60). Second, more and more NGOs in developing societies have attempted to reduce their dependence on foreign funding by running projects on cost-recovery basis. The experience of *Proshika* and MFI suggests that if scaling-up is planned carefully and managed professionally, it will not harm NGOs' ability to respond to their beneficiaries.

## Challenges in the management sector

In the context of management, NGOs can be considered as part of the voluntary sector (Hudson 1995: 25). Handy (1988: 2–4) argued that the voluntary sector appears to contradict the principles of organisation because it tends to emphasise the 'voluntary' aspect and play down the 'organisational' principles. Most of the voluntary sector, according to Hudson (1995), considers management unnecessary because it is generated by commitment and good intentions rather than by rules or procedures. But at the same time, voluntary organisations exist to meet a need and provide assistance to those who require it, and some take pride in being professional, effective and low-cost. Consequently, they need management to ensure that services are delivered properly, professionally and efficiently. Some even argue that the voluntary sector should follow for-profit organisations in developing professional management because greater use of contracts requires skills that have been understood in the private sector for many years (Handy 1988: 3,14; Hudson 1995: 33; Berman 1998: 8).

Others consider that the voluntary sector simply consists of organisations that cannot be classed as either 'private' or 'bureaucratic'. Using Leach's model which differentiates the public/bureaucratic world from the private world (Leach 1976) in the field of social policy, Billis (1993: 134) holds that voluntary organisations occupy an 'ambiguous zone', that is, an overlapping area between the two other spheres (see Figure 2.1). While bureaucracy draws its strength from concepts such as hierarchy, accountability, formality, legality and rationality, the private or associational world is bound together by informality, equality and flexibility (Billis 1993: 160–1). It follows that the voluntary sector operates under the 'management of ambiguity' which requires an understanding of the ground rules of both the bureaucratic and associational worlds. Elected leaders and paid staff must appreciate that bureaucratic organisation means paying attention to issues of managerial authority and accountability, levels of decision-making, career progression, staff development, conditions of service, explicit policy-making and all other essential components of modern bureaucracies. At the same time, they must uphold the essential concepts of association: membership, mission, informality and democracy (Billis 1993: 169).

Operating in this ambiguous zone, the voluntary sector faces complex challenges in its management. Hudson identifies seven management challenges of voluntary organisations: (1) a tendency to develop vague objectives; (2) a difficulty in monitoring performance; (3) a difficulty in accounting due to the plurality of

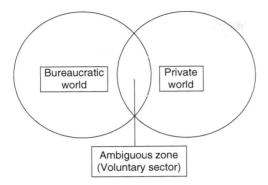

*Figure 2.1* The 'ambiguous zone' of the voluntary sector. (Source: Adapted from David Billis, 1993. *Organising Public and Voluntary Agencies*. London: Routledge, p. 134.)

stakeholders: members, funding bodies, individual donors, staff members, volunteers, governments and beneficiaries; (4) a problem in developing management structures that balance the interests of different stakeholders; (5) a great dependence on voluntarism since they must provide services for small or even no financial reward; (6) values must be cherished from one time to another to ensure that all who are involved share the organisations' purpose and style of operation; and (7) a lack of financial 'bottom line' or framework that would guide future priorities and investments because they rely on negotiations rather than rules (Hudson 1995: 35–7). Meanwhile, Billis (1993: 131–2) focuses on three aspects: (1) unclear goals that may lead to a contradiction between strategy and mission; (2) rapid and unplanned organisational growth due to a flexibility in responding to new challenges; and (3) poor governance because trustees, management committees, staff members, and the like are all too often unclear about their roles.

It is therefore important for NGOs, as part of the voluntary sector, to balance the bureaucratic and associational countenance in their organisations in order to be successful in their attempt to adopt a proper management system and to produce a greater impact. Korten (1987: 155) noted that to ensure a better performance NGOs need to be guided by more than good intentions; they must have a certain degree of technical competence, that is, the technical capacity to obtain the respect of those who control the relevant technologies or resources – whether they be doctors, engineers, lawyers, politicians, administrators or village leaders. Consequently, NGOs need staff members with some degree of competence (the capacity to combine individual behaviour, personality, knowledge and skills in order to achieve particular tasks or goals), which is often critical to the success of any organisations in achieving their targets and in overcoming their problems (Berman 1998: 235). Thus, if NGOs are to succeed in their community development activities, they must be able to develop their own personnel, create sufficient career paths and establish appropriate organisational structures.

## NGOs, social movements and civil society

Since the early 1990s, a growing body of literature has been emerging which views the importance of social movements in the renewed moves towards democracy in developing countries (Foweraker 1994: 218). This view has been based on the assumption that changes are often made at the initiative of citizens, a view that has regained currency in the so-called 'third wave' of democratisation in the 1980s and 1990s. In his book, *The Third Wave: Democratization in the Late Twentieth Century*, Huntington (1991) argued that we are now in the midst of a global democratic expansion in which countries around the world are experiencing a widespread democratic progress, that is, a diffusion of popular demands for political freedom, representation, participation and accountability. The third wave, which began with the overthrow of the Caetano dictatorship in Portugal in 1974, became a truly global phenomenon during the 1980s, doubling by 1990 the number of democracies in the developing countries (Huntington 1991: 26). This emerging euphoria has provided NGOs with theoretical and empirical justifications to play a greater role as facilitators of grassroots initiatives.

### *Social movement theories*

Democratisation has indeed opened up a new opportunity for social movements to play a greater role in society. McCarthy and Zald (1977) defined 'social movements' as 'a collective challenge trying to implement a set of opinions and beliefs in a population which represents preferences for changing some elements of the social structure and/or reward distribution of a society'. Touraine (1981) decried the formation of social movements as a process in which a dominator imposes laws, beliefs, an economic system and a political regime, whereas the people submit to these impositions; but they will revolt against them whenever their physical and cultural existence becomes threatened. This revolt often takes the form of militant struggle since it explodes the contradictions of the social order and destroys the barriers blocking the way for the natural progress of society (Touraine 1981: 78; Blumer 1995: 64–5).

Some commentators see the rise of social movements in the context of state–society relations. Migdal (1988), for example, argued that state–society relations can be understood as a continuous struggle for social control and domination involving different individuals, groups or organisations. For him, the most important agents in state–society relations are in fact 'social forces', instead of social classes. In his view, various social forces – regardless of their class status – endeavour to impose themselves on the political arena, prescribe others their goals and respond to existing problems (Migdal 1994: 21). Their leaders attempt to mobilise followers and exercise power in a situation where other social forces are doing the same. Their aims may vary and may be asymmetrical. Some use social forces to extract as much surplus or revenue as possible; others look for deference, respect or simply power to rule other people's behaviour (Migdal 1994: 22). The meeting grounds between the state and social forces are those in which social and political changes are shaped by conflict, opposition, corruption, co-optation, and coalition. The relationship between the two sides can be mutually empowering if social forces accept the state as the appropriate institution to establish the proper practices for all of society; but it can be conflicting if social forces question and challenge the state's domination (Migdal 1994: 23–4).

Migdal's theory is useful for at least two reasons. First, it describes the dynamics of state–society relations and the possible outcome of different types of relationships. Second, it provides some insights regarding the formation of social movements and resistance against the state particularly in societies where social classes as perceived in the Western world have not yet been formed. Just as this study tries to situate NGOs in the dynamics of Indonesian state–society relations prior the fall of Suharto and during the transition to democracy, so Migdal's theory may explain why NGOs – as a part of society – are involved in conflict and co-operation with the government and why NGOs' activities in organising grassroots people are inevitably political.

Scholars disagree on how social movements emerge and evolve under particular circumstances. Gurr (1970), Huntington (1968) and Johnson (1966) have argued that social movements are generated by the feeling of deprivation among the marginalised people. Dubbed by commentators as the 'relative deprivation' approach, this theory maintains that people develop aggressive behaviour in response to political exclusion, blockage of political channels, system disequilibrium, and so on. Another theory christened the 'resource mobilisation' approach can be associated with, among others, Tilly (1978), Schwartz (1970) and McCarthy and Zald (1977). It argues that collective action is likely to evolve if particular preconditions have been met. These preconditions include: (1) the presence of contenders organised around some specifically motivated core groups; (2) the presence of organisational structures (a pattern of frequent interaction or network, leadership and rules), strategies, and common acceptable symbols and beliefs; and (3) the issues raised gain increasing acceptance at least among potential participants.

Contemporary writers, however, tend to combine these two different approaches. Melucci (1989: 32–3) and Sztompka (1993: 279–80), for example, argue that the formation of social movements can be linked to a number of factors: (1) the 'rise and fall': a situation in which a period of prosperity is followed by a sharp decline in the capacity of a social system to satisfy the needs of its population; (2) the 'rising expectation': after a period of sustained growth, a gap normally appears between expectations and the satisfaction of needs, thereby causing social unrest; (3) the 'relative deprivation': actors compare their position and rewards unfavourably with those of comparable groups thus creating discontent and mobilisation; (4) the 'downward mobility': when actors lose their social position and compare themselves with their previous condition and the position of other social groups; (5) the 'status inconsistency': social actors see an inconsistency between the various elements of their status (income, prestige and power) and mobilise in order to eliminate this discrepancy; and (6) a rapid urbanisation and industrialisation that facilitates greater opportunities for contact, interaction, the elaboration of common purposes, and the articulation of shared ideologies.

According to the historical epoch under which they emerge and evolve, social movements can be divided into 'old' and 'new' paradigms. While 'old' social movements refer to those movements dominating the early phase of modernity, focusing on economic interests in which membership is generally recruited from single social classes, 'new' social movements have emerged in recent decades when societies are entering the phase of late modernity or even, as some authors claim, post-modernity. These groups have raised new issues, new interests and new fronts of conflicts such as the quality of life, group identity, expanded life-space, the championing of civil society, genuine democracy, gender equality and so forth (Touraine 1981: 51–2; Sztompka 1993: 284; Plotke 1995: 117). Although old and new movements are different in some respects, the NGOs (especially in places where grassroots organisations are facing political constraints) seem to enter both categories since they address a wide range of issues (economic interests, group identity, a better quality of life, gender equality, popular democracy and so on) that concerns both old and new movements (Kothari 1993; Wignaraja 1993).

In developing societies, many dominant institutions such as the traditional parties have lost their legitimacy in the eyes of movement participants at least partly because they are no longer able to uphold the interests of the defenseless or prosecuted groups (Alvarez and Escobar 1992: 323; Fals Borda 1992: 306). Thus, social movements emerge in many nations to fill the gap left by disfunctioning parties and other formal political institutions. Through networks and other mechanisms of regional and national co-ordination they begin to propose (or demand) structural changes for society at large. Although they do not seek the seizure of political power, they attempt to promote ways in which ordinary citizens can have a say in and control the acts of those governing them (Fals Borda 1992: 311). Seen in this context, social movements emerge as part of the broader-based response of people to ecological, ethnic, religious or gender conflicts. As a result, their identity appears to be heterogeneous, representing different backgrounds and origins. Some are the result of romantic and idealistic approaches taken by charitable institutions, religious organisations and the 'small is beautiful' advocates (Wignaraja 1993: 17). Others evolve from a conscious resistance to or 'popular upsurge' against the state's domination and authoritarianism (Diamond 1992: 15). They inevitably encompass a wide variety of activities which include protest, confrontation, lobbying and pressuring government agencies and politicians, as well as self-help development projects (Alberoni 1984: 15; Lehmann 1990: 150). At the local level, small human rights and economic subsistence organisations begin to appear. In factories, underground political networks are established, and in universities students defy regulations prohibiting political discussion and organise demonstrations in opposition to the regime (Schneider 1992: 260). At the national level, social movements emerge with the help of intermediary organisations or other external facilitators (e.g. churches, concerned middle-class professionals and so on) which help them to form an institutional and sometimes ideological framework (Schneider 1992: 261; Sethi 1993: 231).

These theories describe two important things. First, they elucidate the social and political background under which social movements emerge and evolve.

Second, they present a range of issues and motivations that generate different types of social movements. They may help us in identifying social and political conditions that generated the rise in popular resistance in Indonesia, and Yogyakarta in particular, especially since the early 1990s. They may also help us in indicating the range of issues, missions and purposes raised by the NGOs in facilitating social movements.

## *NGOs and social movements*

Some argue that NGOs are themselves new social movements formed as a spontaneous response from groups in the society concerned about economic stagnation, political repression, the collapse of a certain way of life, and sectarianism in existing revolutionary vanguard groups (Frantz 1987: 123; Lehmann 1990: 149; Fals Borda 1992: 304; Hellman 1992: 52; Hulme 1994: 253). Others see NGOs as leading actors in a vibrant civil society whose main duty is to widen popular participation and to deepen policy accountability by educating and mobilising citizens, by encouraging previously marginalised groups to participate, by building a complex network of groups, by facilitating a constant influx of citizens to the state, by encouraging all groups to press their agendas on the state, and by representing citizen interests to the state (Biggs and Neame 1995: 35; Blair 1997: 28–9; Fisher 1997: 440).

While putting civil society in the middle ground between communal groups and state structures, Chazan defines 'civil society' as associational groups that can function 'as the key brake of state power (and consequently in constant confrontation with the state), as a benign broker between state interests and local concerns, or as medley of social institutions that interact with each other and with formal structures in ways that may either facilitate or impede governance and economic development'[5] (Chazan 1994: 255). Civil society is different from political parties and their front organisations as well as the institutions of market (e.g. national and multi-national corporations) in the sense that it does not contend for power through regular elections and that its focus is not simply on the attainment of material benefits (Diamond 1992: 7; Tandon 1996: 114). As 'counter-hegemonic' institutions, a civil society carries with it at least three basic components: (1) a material base, that is, private ownership or control over resources that predate the formation of human association; (2) an organisational framework which determines how people organise themselves to do what they want to do with their lives; and (3) an ideology and values which guide collective action (Fowler 1996: 16–17).

Seen in this context, NGOs perform at least two important duties in strengthening civil society: (1) to co-ordinate collaboration and alliances among 'alternative social change groups', namely those movements bound by shared values of solidarity, trust, respect and partnership, blended with progressive and innovative styles of transformational change; and (2) to expand the opportunities for cultural and organisational dialogues among local grassroots initiatives (Lende 1995: 248). By introducing new ideas and meanings, NGOs not only announce to society that a fundamental problem exists but also provide elements for the construction of alternative models and practices (Alvarez and Escobar 1992: 328; Friedmann 1992: 31). By stimulating contacts among such groups and by facilitating their creation where they do not already exist NGOs can play an important role in ensuring the survival, maturation and internal democracy of those organisations (Farrington *et al.* 1993a: 12). In a similar vein, Bebbington and Riddell (1997: 110) maintained that NGOs can help popular organisations in: (1) identifying their members' or social base's main concerns; (2) formulating strategies to meet those concerns; and (3) making them interact more effectively with the market and the state in order to defend and enhance the interests of their constituency. NGOs are also respected for their ability to nurture an alternative ideology used by social movements to counter the state. Lehmann (1990) argued that NGOs had proposed *basismo*, an alternative ideology that proclaims its democratic identity but challenges the formal apparatus of liberal democracy, just as it challenges the formal apparatus of the modern state. *Basismo* is anti-Marxist insofar as it does not accept the idea that the democratic character of a regime has to be judged by its approximation to the objective interests of the proletariat. In the context of *basismo*, Lehmann argues, democracy is a matter of overcoming unwarranted forms of domination and the restoration of communal self-management (Lehmann 1990: 192).

My own view of NGOs as part of social movements may be less optimistic than the views of these commentators. Together with Clayton (1996) and Tandon (1996), I tend to argue that NGOs may just be a small fraction of civil society together with community-based associations, mass organisations, religious organisations, professional associations, consumer groups and other 'social movements'; their survival depends on both external (social and political contexts in which they operate) and internal factors (resources, skill, management, and so on). Although NGOs can and must help strengthen civil society, it is important to note that the extent to which they succeed or fail in achieving their political ambitions depends on the social and political contexts in which they operate and their ability to mobilise their own resources.

## *NGOs and democratisation*

As part of social movements, NGOs are pictured as agents that can stimulate the process democratisation. The expectation that NGOs can foster democracy is premised on, among other things, their ability to strengthen local institutions and to link horizontally and vertically into mass movements that will provide an organised countervailing power against the state (Fowler 1993: 334; Fisher 1997: 441). In this context, NGOs are encouraged to forge alliances with broader social movements (women, peasants, trade unions, environmentalists and the like) nationally and internationally in order to ensure their own legitimacy and to put pressure on governments to embrace alternative development policies (Drabek 1987: x). Edwards and Hulme (1995a: 7) argued that NGOs should be proud of their achievements in helping to cement human and political rights in many societies and in democratising the informal political process by training grassroots activists, in building stronger local institutions, in promoting micro-policy reform and in undertaking education for citizenship. Clarke (1996: 18) noted that NGOs' ideological diversity enables them to play a vital role in facilitating political participation through their involvement in issue-based social movements and through their support of people's organisations.

Others appeared to be less optimistic about NGOs' capacity to foster democracy. Sanyal (1994: 40), for instance, argued that the political impact of NGO projects is less striking than their economic impact, especially when they fail to put pressure on the local elites and the government to institute change. Hirschman (1987: 98) shared this pessimistic view as he maintained that it is impossible to prove a connection between the withering of the authoritarian states in Latin America and the rise of NGOs and grassroots social movements. Meanwhile, Smith (1990: 275) and Fowler (1993: 333) argued that NGOs are unlikely to have made a significant impact on political transformations in both Latin America and Africa during the 1980s and early 1990s. The problem for most NGOs in Latin America, according to Smith (1990: 275–8), is that their scope of activities is too small, their focus too fragmented, their collective effort unorganised, and their existence vulnerable to co-optation by the ruling elites. Moreover, the fact that their staff members are often dominated by the urban middle-class seems to prevent them from fostering a broad pro-democracy coalition. Likewise, Fowler (1993: 334) noted that the main obstacles of NGOs in Africa are that they are weak in organisational structure, seldom truly indigenous or rooted within the mass of the population, incapable of resisting patronage by the political and bureaucratic elites, and lack the capability to collaborate among themselves.

There are a few cases, however, in which NGOs have fostered the process of democratisation. In the Philippines, for example, the rise of 'people power' which contributed to the fall of President Marcos in 1986 can be associated with the activities of various NGOs, especially NAMFREL (National Citizens' Movement for Free Election), EBJF (Evelio B. Javier Foundation), KABATID (*Kilusang Kababaihan na Tumataguyod sa Demokrasiya* or Women's Movement for the Nurture of Democracy) and others. NAMFREL was founded in 1983 to restore popular faith in the electoral process and was capable of mobilising no less than half a million volunteers in pool-watching activities during the 1986 election (Pascual 1992: 58). EBJF was created to promote the values of democracy and to teach the technical and administrative aspects of municipal government. KABATID was founded to serve as a 'school of democracy' for its members, exposing them to free discussions and teaching them respect for accommodation and procedual rules that are intrinsic to democratic politics (Pascual 1992: 59).

Throughout the period of democratic transition in the mid-1980s, NGOs in the Philippines were able to provide an important institutional framework and maintain the spirit of togetherness and solidarity among the Filipinos allowing them to act collectively in challenging an authoritarian regime (Miclat-Teves and Lewis 1993: 231; Clarke 1998: 124). They played crucial roles not only during the pro-democracy campaign to oust President Marcos, but also during the early years of the Aquino government in reconstructing democratic institutions and in implementing the new government's programmes (Diamond 1992: 4–7;

Pascual 1992: 70–1; Clarke 1998: 93). In Bangladesh, despite the risk of confrontation with political parties controlled by the local elites, GSS (*Gono Shahajjo Shangstha* or People's Support Organisation) – an NGO with a conscious attempt to organise the poor – managed to support candidates from the landless and assetless people to win seats in the local election in the district of Nilphamari in North Bengal (Hashemi 1995: 106; Lewis 1997: 63).

The particular historical, social and political settings from which NGOs emerge and evolve appear to have an important impact on the way in which NGOs link themselves to social forces in society. In some societies, NGOs emerge from a 'heroic' effort of concerned individuals. In Bangladesh, the NGOs have their roots in the liberation struggle for independence of 1971. Efforts were made by many concerned young people to render humanitarian services in the refugee camps across the border in India to help war victims. After the war, many embryonic Bangladeshi NGOs recognised that the needs of the landless should be considered as central to an equitable development strategy which did not simply rely upon 'trickle-down' benefits (Lewis 1993: 51). Interactions with the poor in the villages were made which led gradually to the transformation of their charity into participatory development (Ul Karim 1995: 110–12). In such a situation, Bangladeshi NGOs tended to receive a high degree of 'acceptability' from their target groups.

In India, some NGOs began from revolts involving the oppressed landless people against a class of landlords. For example, the *Bhoomi Sena* (Land Army) movement in Maharastra, India, was formed by a group of militant landless people in the Junglepatti Thana district in the early 1970s whose aim was to end the domination of landlords, money lenders, grass traders and forest contractors in the area. With the help from the Indian Communist Party, *Bhoomi Sena* led a militant movement for crop seizure on land that belonged legally to the landless people (*adivasis*) but had been usurped by the landlords (*sawkars*) (Rahman 1993: 35). In order to ensure a more purposeful action, *Bhoomi Sena* created an organisational structure. Some urban social workers were brought in to design its agricultural and small credit programmes. But this organisation did not allow outsiders to dictate what should be done. Its central leadership, called the 'vanguard group', assumed control in spreading village-level struggles to other villages, in organising mass demonstrations, in representing local grievances in government offices and in conducting investigations to identify the nature of injustice and exploitation (Rahman 1993: 36).

## *NGOs and the state*

State sanction is indeed most crucial for NGOs in developing societies. Only after securing what amounts to state 'recognition' can an NGO come into operation (Korten and Quizon 1991: 23). An NGO is considered acceptable to the state if its objectives are not incompatible with those of the state and if its activities do not pose a serious threat to the ruling elite (Clark 1991: 74). An NGO secures sanction when the state recognises its existence, acknowledges its leaders, approves of its programmes and accepts its advice.

However, the relations between NGOs and the state are always ambiguous. On the one hand, interactions arising from service delivery tend to be considered as passive (by the state as well as the NGO community); but the activist, advocacy and protest roles tend to provoke co-optation or repression (Jain 1991: 19). Likewise, clandestine activities tend to be considered as unruly or even subversive; but if NGOs openly declare their goal of empowerment and mobilisation, this transparency will make it easier for the state apparatus to identify what is happening and thwart them (Edwards and Hulme 1995a: 12). Some NGOs, according to Farrington et al. (1993a: 47), deliberately minimise their relations with the state for at least two reasons. First, the fear that co-ordinating with the state may reduce NGOs' effectiveness and capacity to remain close with their target groups since they believe that an association with the state will damage their image of being flexible and egalitarian organisations. Second, collaborating with the state will risk criticism of being an extension of the government or 'public contractors', which is what many governments and donors would like them to be. For some NGOs, developing close relations with the government is almost impossible, and for others it can cause great internal tension.

Democratic governments tend to develop a friendly relationship with NGOs which subsequently allows NGO–government co-operation to surface. Echeverri-Gent (1993: 187), for example, argued that India represents the most significant example of co-operation between state and NGOs in the developing world. In its seventh Five Year Plan (1985–1990), the Indian government channeled Rs 2 billion (US$150 million) through NGOs. By the early 1990s, NGOs in this country had become significant allies of the government in carrying out poverty alleviation projects with an estimated 15,000–20,000 organisations actively engaged in rural development (Farrington et al. 1993b: 92). In the Philippines, NGOs and the state forged one of the closest relationships to be found anywhere in the developing world during the Aquino government (Clarke 1998: 93), in which many NGO leaders were appointed to the cabinet and to other positions in government ministries or agencies.

Authoritarian governments, on the other hand, are always worried about NGOs' ability to work at grassroots level since they believe this could mean that NGO-sponsored activities would disturb their control over society (Jain 1991: 19). In a situation where the political leaders are resisting the introduction of political reforms, NGOs (especially those which show any hint of political opposition) tend to be treated unfavourably by their governments. In the case of Chile under Pinochet (Clark 1991: 77), the Philippines under Marcos (Clarke 1998: 62–3) and Indonesia under Suharto (Sinaga 1992: 5), authoritarian regimes appeared to have imposed a strict control on NGO activities. But at the same time, authoritarian regimes cannot deny the significance of NGOs' community development activities. This seems to encourage the state to tolerate (within reason) NGOs' income-generating activities and recognise their existence. It appears that the chance of government 'recognition' for NGOs operating under authoritarian rules depends on the ability of NGOs to select a particular approach that will not 'threaten' the state too dramatically.

## The significance of networking and coalition

In order to produce a greater impact on the community, it is important for NGOs to develop 'networking' that can be defined as a fluid web of relationships connecting NGO actions to numerous levels and fields (Fisher 1997: 450). There are at least two crucial functions of NGO networks. First, through networks NGOs can bring local and regional issues to national and international attention. It is believed that by forming a network NGOs can carry out their 'mainstreaming' strategy, that is, the incorporation of NGO models (such as institution, methods of work, programmes and so on) into the official policy framework (Wils 1995: 58). Second, networking can also be seen as a process of 'capacity-building' in which NGOs develop a collective consensus on a shared mission, clarify their roles to others, maintain their participatory values, conduct an ongoing learning process (from each other), share their burden, develop strategic links with other institutions, discuss the most difficult questions concerning performance, and expand their horizon of thinking and action (Fowler 1997: 100).

An example of a successful NGO network is perhaps the Caucus of Development NGO Networks (CODE-NGO) in the Philippines. Founded by ten national networks in the early 1990s CODE-NGO represented around 1,300 individual development NGOs throughout the country. Its major aim was to maximise the impact of its members by providing more opportunities to learn from each other, share experience and gain greater access to funds (Constantino-David 1992: 142). This network operated on the basis of similarities in thrust, field of operation and ideology. After several years of operation, CODE-NGO has succeeded in striking a balance between the need to maximise impact and individual flexibility, in encouraging NGOs to share information and expertise, in experimenting with concrete alternatives, in facilitating the formation of regional NGO coalitions, in increasing advocacy, in strengthening partnership with donors and government agencies, and in minimising possible undue harassment of NGO activists in carrying out their work (Constantino-David 1992: 145–6).

According to Fowler (1997: 113), NGO networks can and often do lead to coalitions or alliances. A coalition is normally based on multiple relationships involving a variety of actors: NGOs, governments, international development agencies, constituencies, communities, leaders, elites, municipalities, state institutions and social movements (Fisher 1997: 450). Resistance to a particular development project is often conducted with the assistance of coalitions at national or even international levels. For example, in the case of the Mount Apo geothermal project in the Philippines and the Kedung Ombo dam construction in Indonesia, attempts to pressure the government to change its policy direction were supported by a multi-group coalition involving grassroots organisations, local NGOs, intellectuals, international NGOs and foreign donors. However, the formation of effective networks and coalitions appears to be the most difficult task for most NGOs to achieve. There are at least two sets of obstacles to NGO collaboration. First, the inherent preference of participants to obtain the highest degree of benefit with the lowest cost in terms of resources or reduced autonomy which subsequently leads to a poor level of commitment (Fowler 1997: 112). Second, the lack of willingness among participating organisations or individuals to reach the compromises needed to enable a network to develop a strong institution with the authority and power to achieve its goals (Bennett 1994: 33). Thus, if NGOs are to succeed in their networking or coalition-building, they must first resolve these two challenges.

## The dynamics of NGO activity in Indonesia: critique to Eldridge

Attention on NGO activities in Indonesia began to grow since the early 1980s. Yet, the literature on Indonesian NGOs was hardly sufficient. To obtain data and information on NGO activities in Indonesia, researchers had to rely on a limited number of articles in Indonesian journals, most notably *Prisma*, or on unpublished papers written by domestic as well as foreign scholars. Eldridge's *Non-Government Organisations and Democratic Participation in Indonesia* (Oxford University Press, 1995) appeared to fill the big gap in the literature on Indonesian NGOs. This book was the first attempt to provide a complete description and analysis of NGO activity in Indonesia. Eldridge's extensive fieldwork throughout the 1980s was able to portray NGOs facing constant repression from the New Order government. It was during this period that President Suharto was able to maintain his political grip by putting society under his personal thumb. As a result, the NGO sector found itself in a very difficult position: on the one hand, they were expected to pursue their empowerment and grassroots-mobilisation agenda; but on the other hand, they were forced to adjust their activities to the state's development policies and preferences.

I agree with Eldridge that working under the constant pressure from an authoritarian regime in a situation where room for political manoeuvres was too narrow, NGOs tend to adopt different strategies and approaches. Those who were too afraid to face a possible ban or even suspension by the authorities would understandably adopt a more co-operative strategy by focusing on collaborative development projects involving government agencies. Meanwhile, those with the courage to challenge the government would adopt a confrontational strategy by concentrating on grassroots-mobilisation activities. For these reasons, Eldridge was right in proposing three models of what he termed 'NGO paradigms' in Indonesia, in which he divided Indonesian NGOs into three clusters according to their types of relationship with the government: (1) high-level co-operation – grassroots development; (2) high-level politics – grassroots mobilisation; and (3) empowerment from below (Eldridge 1995: 36–8).

NGOs in the first category showed no interest in changing or intervening in the political process as such, although they were active in promoting their core values of self-reliance and grassroots participation. In any case, NGOs of this kind reflected the values of 'conflict avoidance' which were deeply rooted in many Indonesian cultural systems, most notably among the Javanese. The second stream of NGOs was more explicitly critical of the government's development policy and practice. While promoting consciousness-raising and the capacity of self-management among specific target groups, they sought legal status and protection for them against local officials and other influential people through contacts forged at higher level of government. The third cluster of NGOs put more emphasis on building people's awareness of their rights. Rather than acting as intermediaries in relation to the authorities, they attempted to build up confidence and skills among the people to enable them to conduct their own negotiations. Although Eldridge did not make special reference to the works published earlier by Korten (1987) and Elliot (1987), his classification appeared to follow both Elliot and Korten's categories. Korten's three models – first, second and third-generation NGOs – and Elliot's three types of NGO strategies – welfare, development and empowerment – show a great deal of similarity to Eldridge's three models. This is certainly not a coincidence, but rather indicates a general trend of the expansion of the NGO sector throughout the developing world.

In Indonesia, an indication of transformation of NGO strategies was revealed for the first time in the late 1980s when radical groups began allying themselves with small NGOs and conducted various workshops expressing their critical view toward conservative NGOs. These activities culminated in a meeting at Baturaden, Central Java, on 19 December 1990, in which radical activists drafted a motion of non-confidence called the 'Baturaden Statement'. It was clearly indicated in the statement that the majority of NGOs in Indonesia had lost their vision and sense of mission to pioneer an alternative model of development and to establish an opposing movement to represent the poor. Since their own programmes had become increasingly similar to those of the government they once criticised, they began to enter the world of bureaucracy characterised by hierarchy, centralisation and elitism. The Baturaden Statement also called for an immediate correction of NGO strategy through the adoption of the grassroots-empowerment approach. This development seemed to support Eldridge's argument of a strategic transformation in Indonesian NGOs.

Eldridge was accurate in describing the political and economic backgrounds of the rise of NGO activism in Indonesia. In the early 1980s, the absence of political parties with any real degree of independence had left an obvious vacuum in Indonesian politics. NGOs were certainly not the only independent voices representing the people since students, intellectuals and various religious organisations had also played important role in grassroots mobilisation and in building people's critical stance toward the New Order government. But NGOs appeared to have developed organisational and ideological resilience in the context of the New Order government's constant pressure. While other organisations were strongly curtailed by the government through the imposition of heavy regulations, direct control, threat, ban and even dismissal, NGOs were capable of maintaining their survival. Their ongoing participation in most fields of social and developmental work enabled them to operate flexibly across sectors and secured government's blessing. In the mid-1980s, the fall of state revenues due to declining international oil prices rendered the apparently low-cost alternative offered by NGOs relatively attractive. Within the Indonesian government there was a growing awareness that state agencies could not achieve effective outreach or mobilise sufficient community support without at least assistance from NGOs.

Eldridge could not be blamed for being a little pessimistic toward NGOs' contribution to the democratisation process, although he would have been more optimistic had he carried out his field research a few years later when popular resistance from different quarters began to emerge. Although he had recognised that a mask of activist groups had emerged since the late 1980s, he considered this development not as a chance for NGOs to produce greater political impact. Rather, he contemplated that the emergence of radical activists had reflected the generational conflict within the NGO sector in Indonesia. These student forums or study groups, according to Eldridge, had succeeded in forming coalitions with farmers, the landless, workers, urban squatters, women's groups, and others (Eldridge 1995: 25). But he was worried that these radical factions, which constantly expressed their impatience with the apparent unwillingness of established NGOs to pursue political struggles with some degree of militancy, could disturb the ideological unity of the NGO sector. In his defense of the more established NGOs, Eldridge argued: 'Accusation that most NGOs have lost their vision seem to be based on an incorrect premise that this vision was originally one of mass action to achieve political change. It also perhaps reflects a hope that they will fill the vacuum left by the emasculation of popularly based political parties by the New Order state' (Eldridge 1995: 40–1). The political situation had changed rapidly since Eldridge completed his fieldwork in 1991. Inspired by the 'Third Wave of Democratisation',[6] since the early 1990s Indonesia has experienced a growing popular resistance, involving different groups in society (workers, the urban poor, peasants, students, intellectuals, religious leaders and the like). This new development, which was not recorded in Eldridge's research, seemed to have given a moral impetus for NGOs' radical activists to be more confident in carrying out their pro-democracy campaigns.

I would go along with Eldridge, however, that the failure of Indonesian NGOs to undertake wider roles had to do with factors internal to NGOs themselves which included: (1) the problem of internal communication and factional rivalries; (2) poor structures of accountability; (3) limited understanding, confidence and skills in handling programmes among staff members; and (4) hierarchical patterns of NGO organisations which perpetuate dependence of client groups (Eldridge 1995: 17). He was also right in maintaining that high levels of informality, which NGOs feel obliged to adopt in shaping their organisational structures for purposes of survival, was also a factor in holding back the emergence of accountable organisational structures.

Beside the strong points discussed above, Eldridge's book suffered from some weaknesses. Throughout his work, the issue of NGO management does not seem to receive enough attention. He did not consider NGOs' institutional aspects as an issue. Consequently, he was not interested in the questions of how NGOs operate as institutions, how NGOs recruit and develop staff members, how they manage their annual budgets, how leadership is exercised by NGOs and so on. In my view, management is too important to be omitted in discussing NGOs since NGOs' survival is often determined by factors such as staff development, budgeting and leadership. Although management may not be the major concern of NGOs – as they tend to be guided by commitment and good intention rather than by rules or procedures – gradually, however, NGOs are beginning to think about improvement in their performance, administrative capacity and accountability.

In Indonesia, following the demand from foreign donors of NGOs' professionalism, sustainability and greater impact, many organisations began to devote more serious attention to budgeting, staff development, leadership, strategic management and accountability. Anton Soedjarwo, the Director of the *Dian Desa* Foundation (one of the large NGOs in Indonesia), for example, argued that in a situation where financial scarcity becomes more apparent, NGOs need to 'professionalise' their management system in order to ensure survival (Soedjarwo, interview, 29/01/1997). Even movement-oriented NGOs, which emerge as a pseudo-union for a specifically targeted constituency rather than as a professional NGO, expressed their support of improvement in the management sector, especially in terms of human resources development. As argued by Dian Gayatri, an activist of SPBY (Yogyakarta Women Joint Secretariat): 'Although we serve as a movement rather than an NGO, we still think that human resources development is important in order to improve our performance' (Gayatri, interview, 03/07/2001).

Eldridge was not entirely clear on how social and political contexts had affected NGOs' activities. His only account in this respect was that Indonesian NGOs emerged as an expression of the more general 'culture of silence' (*budaya diam*). This culture, according to Eldridge, had pervaded Indonesian society since the upheavals of 1965–1966, which resulted in mass killings and reprisals against the communists and other leftist organisations followed by systematic depoliticisation of Indonesian society (Eldridge 1995: 2). The reality seems to be more complicated than Eldridge has suggested. The systematic attempt of the New Order government to curtail the leftist activism had affected rural politics in which grassroots political activities were isolated from external influences. Group meetings and gatherings were subject to approval from the local authorities (neighbourhood co-ordinators, village heads, sub-district heads and so forth). Consequently, the presence of NGOs in particular area was also dependent upon the support from the local officials. In many cases, entry points were granted by village heads and programmes were subject to approval from local authorities before they were implemented. As we shall see in Chapter 5, the two NGOs under study – BSY and CD-Bethesda – had to adjust their programmes to the state's preferences and they were forced to work under the patronage of the local elites. Surprisingly, Eldridge neglected to take these issues on board.

Furthermore, Eldridge appears to be inaccurate in saying that the ideological base of Indonesian NGOs was ambiguous, so that their activities will never produce greater political impact. He argued that Indonesian NGOs tended to express ambivalence toward the Western style of political reform (Eldridge 1995: 24). In his view, NGOs tended to sit uncomfortably with the individualistic emphasis which they saw as inherent to liberal democratic ideology. He concluded that the general attitude of Indonesian NGOs to political democratisation was ambivalent. On the one hand, stress was placed on the right to organise and on the creation of greater democratic space. On the other hand, such demands were intentionally dissociated from values of liberal democracy, which was seen as a political project of international capitalism (Eldridge 1995: 39). But this ambiguity should not be seen as a major obstacle for NGOs to conduct the pro-democracy campaigns. In my opinion, Indonesian NGOs should be forgiven for being confused about democracy because democracy itself is an ambiguous concept. These days almost everyone is in favour of democracy. Such a degree of almost universal acclaim makes one suspicious, especially when it is to be found among individuals, organisations, groups and governments better known otherwise for their animosity. Even dictators can profess their faith in democracy while simultaneously banning parties, censoring the press and having opponents tortured in prison. It is therefore unfair to consider NGOs' ambivalence toward democracy as a sign of their lack of democratic spirit.

Some other commentators seemed to contradict Eldridge's argument. Bunnell (1996: 181), for example, argued that Indonesian NGOs had demonstrated their strong commitment to support social democratic values centred on redistributing power from the state to the civil society and from the rich to the poor. At the third INGI[7] Conference, 27–29 April 1987, in Zeist, The Netherlands, Indonesian NGO activists drafted an *aide memoire* in expressing their support toward popular democracy, stating that:

> [The participants]...underline their conviction that a development strategy based on the denial of civil, political, social or cultural rights not only violates international human rights standards but is also a negation of the very concept of development. (They) note that alleviation of 'structural poverty' should be an essential element of every development strategy and stress that structural poverty is indicated by a lack of access to social, economic, political, legal and cultural resources. (They) call attention to the essential role of people's participation in general and women's participation in particular at the community level in the development of objectives and strategies for development.
>
> (Bunnell 1996: 193)

My own observation seems to support Bunnell's contention that NGOs were supportive toward the idea of popular democracy. The need to formulate a clear political platform was expressed in a meeting on 18–19 June 1993 in Cisarua, West Java, during which more than 60 NGO activists from the island of Java demanded a new transforming role for Indonesian NGOs. They fearlessly criticised the state's domination in almost every aspects of society and subsequently demanded NGOs to play a greater role in facilitating the development of a strong civil society (CPSM 1993: 41). In other words, NGOs were expected by their radical activists to form a counter-hegemonic movement against the authoritarian state. As argued by one of the participants of the meeting, Dadang Juliantara: 'We felt it was about time to wake up and to take initiative in making attempts to strengthen Indonesian civil society' (Juliantara, interview, 03/08/1997). I therefore would not hesitate to argue that despite NGOs' ambivalence toward individualism, they had seriously attempted to initiate the process of democratisation in Indonesia long before the fall of Suharto's regime in 1998.

Another serious mistake in Eldridge's work was his generalisation that women's NGOs tended to be low profile, behind-the-scene, and consensus-building rather than stridently asserting their rights (Eldridge 1995: 153). His understanding of women's NGOs appears to be a little out of date. For him, women's NGOs in Indonesia, as in most countries, had been directed towards raising their social and economic status. This interpretation resembles the more widely known women in development (WID) approach initiated by Ester Boserup in 1970, which treated women as active participants in production and household economies. In the 1980s, however, this approach was strongly criticised by radical activists for its failure to address the desire to challenge women's subordination in social relations. A new perspective was introduced in the late 1980s to oppose existing gender relations benefiting men. Widely known as the gender and development (GAD) approach, this perspective proposed the strengthening of women's organisational capacity and critical awareness of their subordination.

GAD has undoubtedly laid a strong foundation for the radical women's movement in developing societies, including Indonesia. Yet Eldridge did not seem to be aware of GAD's influence in Indonesia which was brought in by some radical activists in the late 1980s. I was fortunate to be able to conduct my research six to seven years after Eldridge completed his fieldwork. By coming later I had more opportunity to see women's NGOs working under strong influence from the GAD approach. In both SBPY and Yasanti – two radical women's NGOs used as my case studies – I found that women's NGOs were in fact the most radical and determined in their attempt to effect structural changes among their specific target groups (women market traders, migrant workers and factory workers).

Surprisingly, Eldridge had treated Yasanti as one of the moderate, consensus-building NGOs, although he realised that from the beginning Yasanti had focused on awareness-building among female factory workers in Central Java. He might have mistakenly considered Yasanti's micro-credit schemes as its main programme. The truth was that Yasanti used the welfare approach to win support from the local authorities and to avoid resistance from the conservative target groups. As argued by Amin Muftiyanah, Yasanti's current director: 'Working among the community that preserved conservative views of women's status, we had to use welfare programmes as entry points to attract potential beneficiaries as well as to avoid opposition from the people and the local authorities' (Muftiyanah, interview, 06/08/2001). Although Eldridge had made reference to Berninghausen and Kerstan's (1992) radical analysis of women's movement in Java, it came as a surprise that he should have missed Berninghausen and Kerstan's point that Yasanti was indeed the first women's NGO which attempted to strengthen women's self-motivation, courage and self-confidence in order to increase their sphere of activities within the family and in the community (Berninghausen and Kerstan 1992: 209).

I am not saying that Eldridge's important contribution has been nullified by his miscalculations and misinterpretations of Indonesian NGOs. I do realise that those who observe NGO activities in an extremely dynamic society at a later stage will reap the benefit of having the opportunity to see a more developed picture. To be fair to him, I must admit that his book has succeeded in persuading me to carry out research into Indonesian NGOs. His book has inspired me to raise questions and try to explore what might not have been identified by Eldridge.

# 3 The social and political settings

## Political changes, 1945–1965

On 17 August 1945, the nationalist politicians Sukarno and Hatta proclaimed Indonesia's independence in a brief ceremony in the front yard of Sukarno's private home in Jakarta (Anderson 1990: 99). Feith (1962: 27) called this new republic a 'pluralist society', a 'mosaic society' and a 'multi-group society'. One can easily agree with him. First, a sharp division existed between the *pribumi* (indigenous) and the Chinese, Arabs, Eurasians and Europeans. Second, the *pribumi* segment was itself divided into around 366 self-conscious ethnic groups, the largest of which were the Javanese, Sundanese, Malay, Minangkabau, Batak, Buginese, Madurese and Balinese (Feith 1962: 28; Dahm 1971: 143). Third, a high degree of religious conflict which began as early as the 1940s when Muslim leaders drew up a draft preamble to the constitution according to which the state would be based on belief in God with 'the obligation to carry out the laws of Islam (*syariah*) for the adherents of Islam'. This draft, also known as *Piagam Jakarta* (the Jakarta Charter), was refused by secularists and non-Muslims. For radical Islamic groups, the failure to enact the draft became a painful reminder of the Muslim's defeat (Emmerson 1976: 57; Vatikiotis 1993: 121; Schwarz 1994: 12–14). Fourth, the Muslims (particularly in Java) were divided into a group of *abangan* (nominal Muslims) who share syncretic beliefs combining animism, Islam and Hinduism and *santri* (devout Muslims), namely those who execute all the basic rituals of Islam – the prayers, the Fast, the Pilgrimage and the whole complex of Islamic social and charitable activities; and another group called *priyayi* (the aristocracy), that is, those who share neither the animistic beliefs as do the *abangan*, nor the Islamic doctrine as do the *santri*, but embrace Javanese mysticism (Geertz 1960: 4–6). There was also a division between traditionalist (represented by an organisation called *Nahdlatul Ulama* (NU)) and modernist groups (represented by *Masyumi* and *Muhammadiyah*) (Samson 1978: 198–9; Nakamura 1983: 103). While traditionalists insisted on the domestication of Islam and Arabic into the local (Javanese) culture, the modernists asserted that the Koran means what it says, just that and only that, and that Arabic is the language of truth and rationality and must be directly understood as it is (Anderson 1990: 127–9).

This diversity had a prominent impact on the Indonesian political landscape. In the early 1960s, through the work of Geertz (1960), the term *aliran* (which literally means stream) entered into the discussion of Indonesian politics. *Aliran* invariably represents identity or sentiment along different political, religious and ethnic lines. It may correspond to political parties, where in the 1950s the nationalists were represented by PNI (*Partai Nasional Indonesia* or Indonesian Nationalist Party), the communists by PKI (*Partai Komunis Indonesia* or Indonesian Communist Party), and Muslims by two major parties: *Masyumi* and NU. It also represents religious differences between the *abangan, santri* and *priyayi*. In other words, *aliran* indicates a complex interplay between ideological beliefs and religious sentiments (Kahn 1982: 95). It is commonly believed that in Indonesian contexts, the division according to *aliran* is more significant than class or even political persuasions (Anderson 1990: 149).

Realising the potential danger of this plurality, the post-revolutionary leaders envisaged the formation of *negara kesatuan* (unitary state). They invoked the saying, ascribed to the medieval sage Mpu Tantular: *Bhinneka Tunggal Ika* (unity in diversity), which was brought out in the early 1940s and then adopted as the official motto of the new republic (Dahm 1971: 143). Accordingly, the system of government was highly centralised and the idea of decentralisation was not seriously pursued at least until 1999, except during 1949–1950 when the new sovereign state had to accommodate a demand from the Dutch for the formation of a federal state as a precondition for a full recognition of Indonesian independence at the Round Table Conference in the Hague. In the aftermath of the conference, however, a 'unitarist movement' was promoted by the protagonists of the unitary state, including President Sukarno and Vice-President Hatta, which led to the return to *negara kesatuan* (Feith 1962: 71). Political leaders and theorists tried to formulate the philosophical foundation of *negara kesatuan*. Professor Soepomo, an expert in state law, proposed the idea of 'integralism' (Simanjuntak 1994: 20; Bourchier 1996: 78). While arguing that the task of an integralist state is not to fulfil the interests of either individuals or groups, but rather to protect the interests of the whole society, he spoke of the compatibility of integralism (adopted from the works of Spinoza, Adam Mueller, Hegel and other German theorists) with the basic impulse in Indonesian (or Javanese) culture towards the unity of life which entails a unity between microcosmos and macrocosmos, between servants and lords, between the people and the rulers (Bourchier 1996: 78). Conspicuous in Soepomo's integralistic theory was the spirit of collectivism and a rejection of individualism (Schwarz 1994: 8; Simanjuntak 1994: 23). Although integralism was not totally accepted by Indonesia's founders, this idea has served as a theoretical justification for the centralised New Order state (1966–1998) and the rejection of the concept of genuine opposition, at least until early 1998.

## *The parliamentary democracy 1950–1959*

Despite pressure to establish a centralised, totalitarian state, during 1950–1959 Indonesia carried out a democratic experiment. The great majority of parties, most of which were founded between 1920 and 1948, unreservedly opted for democracy (Dahm 1971: 148). Feith maintained that during that period democracy in the sense of the recognition of popular participation in politics, the freedom of the press, the presence of an independent judiciary, free election, free association, the creation of representative government and the presence of an independent parliament was put in practice (Feith 1962: 38–40). A free general election was held in 1955 and a representative government was established on the basis of a coalition between four major political parties: PNI with 22.3 per cent of the total vote, *Masyumi* (representing modernist Muslims) with 20.9 per cent, NU (representing traditionalist Muslims) with 18.4 per cent, and PKI with 16.4 per cent (Feith 1962: 43; 1970: 7).

However, by 1957 the democratic experiment began to founder. Cabinet ministers were caught in countless and endless arguments which made it difficult for them to devise and implement policies as well as to maintain the coalition (Feith 1962; May 1978: 75–6; Ricklefs 1981: 253–4). Commentators related the collapse of the parliamentary democracy to a number of factors. Feith (1962: 113–22), for example, argued that such a collapse was caused by a devastating intra-elite conflict involving the so-called 'administrators' (leaders with administrative, technical, legal and foreign language skills), on the one hand, and 'solidarity makers' (leaders skilled as mediators between groups of modernity and traditionalism, as mass organisers, and as manipulators of integrative symbols) on the other hand. Each of them, especially the solidarity makers, used ethnic and religious sentiments to attract followers and besmirch their opponents, which eventually led to the collapse of the coalition. Unlike Feith, Lev (1966: 75) held that the parliamentary system was devastated by the increasing unrest of the masses that can be associated with (though it is not necessarily identical to) the rise of PKI and other radical groups during the late 1950s. Historian Ricklefs (1981: 225) linked such a collapse to the fact that the majority of Indonesian people were mostly illiterate, poor, and accustomed to authoritarian and paternalistic rule that made them unable to force politicians to account for their performances. Meanwhile, Mackie (1994) pointed at a combination of political, economic and geographical factors. Using Schmitt's (1963) study of Indonesia's monetary policy during that period, he argued that the collapse was caused by overlapping political–economic–geographic conflicts. In his view, the inflation and the undervalued exchange rates of the 1950s had hurt exporters of primary products – mainly the 'outer' islands (Sumatra, Kalimantan, Sulawesi and so on) which were politically represented by *Masyumi* – but benefited importers (Java and Jakarta in particular which were represented by PNI, NU and PKI). This subsequently generated conflicts between Java and the 'outer' islands and between *Masyumi* and other parties (Mackie 1994: 32).

## The guided democracy 1959–1965

In the late 1950s, crisis in the government was exacerbated by growing ethnic discontent, military rebellion, war-lordism and intrigue (May 1978: 75). Separatist movements in West Java, West and North Sumatra and South Sulawesi became intensified. In Jakarta, political dissatisfaction was widespread as manifested in mob politics and in criticism of the government for being selfish, corrupt and weak (Feith 1962: 600). Political parties, the civil service and the military became torn by ethnic and ideological conflicts, particularly between the PNI-led group of parties and the *Masyumi*-led group (Feith 1962: 601). The parliament was also weakened by a deadlock over the Muslim's plan to reintroduce the Jakarta Charter, which was strongly opposed by secularist groups (Ricklefs 1981: 253).

On 5 July 1959, adopting a proposal from General Nasution, the top army leader, Sukarno dissolved the parliament and restored the 1945 Constitution which marked the beginning of the so-called *Demokrasi Terpimpin* (guided democracy). This system was dominated by the personality of Sukarno, although he shared the initiative of its introduction with army leadership (Ricklefs 1981: 245). But Sukarno was well aware of the potential danger to his own position of reliance on the army. Thus, in addition to exploiting rivalries within the armed forces (especially between the air force and the army), he encouraged the activities of civilian groups – most importantly the PKI – as a counterweight to the army (Crouch 1978: 42). By 1960, Sukarno had come to look favourably on the PKI. Hailing the communists as 'fighters against imperialism', he adopted a Javanese proverb to express his identification with them: 'you are my blood relatives; and if you die, it is I who shall be the loser' (Mortimer 1974: 79). This gave the PKI (with some 27 million members by the early 1960s) the opportunity to carry out a national-based movement (Mortimer 1974: 366). During 1963–1964, the PKI launched the so-called *aksi sepihak* (unilateral action) campaign to implement the land reform laws of 1959/1960. However, as PKI members began seizing land – especially in Central, East and West Java, Bali and North Sumatra – they came into violent conflict with landowners (many of whom were committed Muslims or PNI supporters), bureaucrats and military officers. Brawls, burnings, kidnappings and killings began to spread particularly in East Java, the main stronghold of NU (Mortimer 1974: 262; Crouch 1978: 64). *Aksi sepihak* backfired when an anti-PKI campaign began to spread. In East Java, anti-PKI violence was spearheaded by the NU youth group, *Ansor*. Within the army, the number of anti-PKI officers was also growing fast. By 1964, the PKI was on the defensive and opposition against it became stronger (Ricklefs 1981: 264). Rivalries between the PKI on the one hand and the army, the PNI, and the NU on the other hand eventually brought Sukarno's guided democracy to an end.

In the early hours of 30 September 1965, seven army generals were kidnapped and killed by left-wing military soldiers led by Colonel Untung. On the following day, Suharto (the Commander of Army's Strategic Command) and his army colleagues immediately took the view that the coup attempt had been a PKI plot, and the PKI's many enemies throughout the country accepted this version of events (Ricklefs 1981: 274). What had actually happened on that day was not at all clear. While most Indonesians believed that the event between 30 September and 1 October 1965 was a failed coup by the PKI against Sukarno's government, a document written by Anderson and McVey (1971), known as the 'Cornell Paper', argued that the coup was the result of internal army divisions in which younger officers had acted against those senior officers viewed as decadent and corrupt. The Cornell Paper also denied PKI's role by arguing that it had little motive to launch the coup. Following this incident, between October 1965 and February 1966, while complicated manoeuvres took place in Jakarta to demolish the so-called G-30-S/PKI (the 30 September 1965 movement), in the countryside mass violence against the PKI exploded with the encouragement of the army (Crouch 1978: 224). PKI supporters became targets of attack in the worst domestic massacre of Indonesia's history (Anderson 1990: 109). There were no reliable data on how many people were actually killed, but most scholars accept the estimated figure between 150,000 and 500,000, mainly in rural areas where land-reform conflicts were intense (Crouch 1978: 155; Ricklefs 1981: 274; Mackie and MacIntyre 1994: 10). On 11 March 1966, under pressure from Suharto and some other army generals, President Sukarno issued the *supersemar* (the 11 March letter of order) giving Suharto supreme authority to restore order and impose a permanent ban on PKI and other organisations linked with it. Hundreds of thousands of PKI members and sympathisers who had survived the massacre were detained and imprisoned. It was estimated that about 200,000 prisoners were held immediately after the attempted coup (Crouch 1978: 224).

## The rise of the New Order

In March 1968 the provisional parliamentary session appointed Suharto as the republic's second president. To ensure political stability Suharto began to impose various measures. The first strategy put emphasis on strengthening the role of military in politics. New military agencies were established to restore order and to carry out domestic surveillance. The Operation Command to Restore Security and Order (KOPKAMTIB) was created in 1967 to serve as the government's main instrument of political control, especially in tracking down ex-PKI supporters. Another agency called the State Intelligence Co-ordinating Body (BAKIN) was formed in place of Sukarno's Central Intelligence Board to watch over the internal development of political parties and to prevent a possible communist revival (Crouch 1978: 223). More importantly, in order to justify the role of the military in politics, a doctrine called *Dwifungsi* (dual function) was introduced. According to the *Dwifungsi* doctrine, the Indonesian armed forces should not only defend the country against external or internal enemies, but also play an active role in social and political affairs. In practice, however, the concept was used by the New Order government to justify the appointment of military officers to fill various positions in the public sector from village heads to cabinet ministers (Sundhaussen 1994: 276–7). Adopted from General Nasution's 'middle way' concept, *Dwifungsi* has provided a theoretical backing to expand military influence throughout the government apparatus, including reserved allocation of seats in the parliament and top posts in civil service (Reeve 1985: 269; Schwarz 1994: 30).

The second strategy attempted to impose control on the ideology of the society. While liberal democracy was considered by officials of the New Order 'inappropriate' for Indonesia, communism was seen as a permanent threat to national unity (Ramage 1995: 22). Thus, a state ideology called *Pancasila* (five moral principles) was reenacted as an ideological basis for the culturally diverse but nationally unified Indonesian society. *Pancasila* is a sanskrit-derived term which was stated in the preamble of the 1945 Constitution as the official ideology of the Indonesian state. These five principles include: (1) the belief in one almighty God; (2) a just and civilised humanity; (3) national unity; (4) democracy based on *musyawarah* (consultation) and *mufakat* (consensus); and (5) social justice. Although *Pancasila* originated in the 1940s, it has been implanted to the national education system from the primary school to the university level in the so-called *Pendidikan Moral Pancasila* (*Pancasila* moral education) since the early 1970s (van Langenberg 1990: 123). From the early 1980s, a *Pancasila* indoctrination programme known as P4 (the guidance, understanding and implementation of *Pancasila*) was instituted to create ideological conformity around the official state ideology (Mackie and MacIntyre 1994: 15). This was followed by the enactment of *Azas Tunggal Pancasila* (*Pancasila* as the sole ideology) which obliged all mass organisations (political parties, interest groups, professional associations and NGOs) to adopt *Pancasila* as their sole ideology. The obligation of unreserved allegiance to *Pancasila* had caused further impediments to independent political activities of society because societal groups were not allowed to work under an ideology of their own choice (Vatikiotis 1993: 104).

The third strategy was an attempt to limit political participation in order to ensure political stability. A military-sponsored political party called Golkar (Working Groups) – developed from the army-backed Sekber Golkar (the Joint Secretariat of Working Groups) – was founded to provide political backing for the New Order regime. Formed during Sukarno's government to counter PKI and its affiliates in the mobilisation of workers, since the 1970s this party has served as an important political instrument for Suharto's government to integrate all political organisations (youths, peasants, workers, civil servants, businessmen and so forth) throughout the country in a corporatist[1] mode of representation and to secure grassroots support for the regime (Reeve 1985: 140–3; Vatikiotis 1993: 78).

## *Conceptualising the New Order state*

In order to understand the nature of the New Order government, we need an appropriate definition of the state. A classical definition of the state was provided by Max Weber when he defined the state as 'a compulsory association with territorial base claiming the monopoly of the legitimate use of physical threat in that territory' (Gerth and Mills 1965: 77). Liberal theorists, however, tend to play down the significance of the state. Some even suggest that the liberal democratic society does not need a theory of the state. MacPherson (1989: 17), for example, argued that in a liberal democratic society the state can be treated simply as an agent which does, or should, serve the principles of justice and liberty, that is, the just distribution of 'primary goods', or of 'holdings', or of the allowable amount and kind of individual liberty. For liberal theorists the state is no more than 'a site of conflict between departments that represent a range of interest groups' (Eckstein 1963: 392), 'an interaction of various social elements' (Easton 1967: 172), or 'multiple centres of power none of which is wholly sovereign' (Dahl 1967: 24). Marxist theorists are even more skeptical towards the state as they hold that the state is inherently shaped by classes or class struggles and functions to preserve and expand the dominant mode of production (Milliband 1969; Anderson 1974; Block 1977).

In the late 1970s, scholars reintroduced a concept of the state as an autonomous entity capable of pursuing its own goals and values. Skocpol (1979: 29), for example, argued that the state is not an arena in which socio-economic struggles are fought out or an organisational control of the dominant classes; it is, rather, a set of administrative policing, and military organisations controlled by an executive authority. In a similar vein, Stepan (1978: xii) defined the state as 'a set of continuous administrative, legal, bureaucratic and coercive systems which attempts not only to structure relationships between civil society and public authority but also to structure many crucial relationships within civil society as well'. Evans et al. (1985) defined 'state' as an entity with the autonomy and capacity to implement policies, achieve its own goals, develop stable administration and extract domestic resources for particular purposes. Suharto's New Order state could be understood in this context since it had the capacity (at least until the mid-1990s) to insulate itself from pressure 'from below' (e.g. societal groups), to design and implement effective development policies, to draw ideological, legal and material resources, to devise a techno-bureaucratic institution to produce and distribute goods and services, and to hold the monopoly in the decision-making process (Crone 1988: 256–63; Kothari 1993: 64; Leftwich 1993: 60; 1995: 402).

What model can depict the essential characteristics of the New Order state? Jackson (1978) proposed a 'bureaucratic polity' (BP) model. Based on Riggs' (1966) work on Thailand, he defined the New Order state as a political system in which power and participation in national decisions are limited almost entirely to the highest levels of the highly trained bureaucratic elites (Jackson 1978: 3). Some, however, argued that this model does not fit with Suharto's New Order regime for at least two reasons: (1) Thailand had a more powerful, professional and long-standing civilian bureaucracy than Indonesia; and (2) the Indonesian bureaucratic elites were always under the personal control of president Suharto (King 1982: 110; Feith, interview, 20/03/1997). Crouch (1979) used the concept of patrimonialism in analysing Suharto's authoritarian rule. As a patrimonial state, the New Order's legitimacy, according to Crouch, depended on President Suharto's capacity to win and retain the loyalty of key sections of the political elite. Lacking basic legitimacy to enforce acceptance of his rule, Suharto sought to win 'voluntary' allegiance by satisfying the aspiration (e.g. the material interests) of his supporters through the distribution of fiefs and benefices in exchange for tribute and loyalty (Crouch 1979: 572). However, despite its ability to explain Suharto's dominant role, this model conveyed too little of the government's systematic attempt to eliminate grassroots political activities.

King (1982) proposed a 'bureaucratic authoritarian' (BA) model in his attempt to analyse the New Order Indonesia. This model stemmed from Linz's (1975) work on Franco's Spain and was subsequently elaborated by Latin American scholars (Collier 1979). As a BA state, the New Order, according to King (1982: 110), deliberately cultivated a multiple legitimacy base, that is, a calculated mixture of traditional, charismatic, legal-rational and technical efficiency principles. He argued that the ultimate authority of the New Order government resided in an oligarchy or the military as an institution, rather than exclusively in a group of civilian bureaucrats (as depicted in the BP model) or in an individual ruler (as argued by the patrimonial model), where a group of military officers formed a ruling group and was surrounded by technocratic and bureaucratic elites whose function was simply to provide advice or consultation in policy-making (King 1982: 110–12). A BA regime is 'excluding' and emphatically non-democratic in which the ruling elite eliminates the electoral competition and severely controls the political participation of the popular sector (Collier 1979: 24). In Indonesia, the New Order government used coercion and co-optation to weaken political opposition to the regime (King 1982: 112). Through a corporatist mode of representation, Suharto's government attempted to structure relations between the state and the society as well as between different groups in the society. Under this arrangement, political participation was limited to a network of state-sponsored organisations such as SPSI (All Indonesia Workers' Association), HKTI (Indonesian Peasants' Union), KNPI (National Committee of Indonesian Youth), KADIN (Indonesian Chamber of Commerce) and MUI (Islamic Religious Leaders Assembly), all of which were subject to the state's control, especially in the selection of leaders and in the setting up of strategies (King 1982: 112). This model appeared to be more accurate in featuring the main characteristics of the New Order government.

## *Political control and restriction*

Obtaining an absolute control on the political activities of the society was the main agenda of Suharto's BA regime. In order to bolster Golkar in the 1971 general election, the government and the army carried out an aggressive campaign of *Golkarisasi* (Golkar-isation) in which civil servants were pressed to sign statements of 'monoloyalty' to the government and to Golkar itself; and local government officials – *Gubernur* (governors), *Bupati* (district heads) and *Camat* (sub-district heads) – were assigned 'quotas' of votes to be mobilised for Golkar in the general elections (Crouch 1978: 267). Village officials were prohibited from campaigning for parties of their own choice and were instead obliged to join and work for Golkar, while military officers were appointed as Golkar's local chairmen (Liddle 1985: 83). These policies made Golkar a dominant ruling party capable of securing over 60 per cent of votes in the general elections from 1971 to 1997 (see Table 3.1).

In the early 1970s the government introduced another policy, *fusi* (fusion), in which existing political parties – except Golkar – were forced to merge into two

*Table 3.1* Election results (1971–1997)

|  | Per cent of votes cast | | |
| --- | --- | --- | --- |
|  | Golkar | PPP | PDI |
| 1971[a] | 62.8 | 27.1 | 10.1 |
| 1977 | 62.1 | 29.3 | 8.6 |
| 1982 | 64.2 | 28.0 | 7.9 |
| 1987 | 73.2 | 16.0 | 10.9 |
| 1992 | 68.1 | 17.0 | 14.9 |
| 1997[b] | 75.5 | 22.4 | 3.1 |

Source: Mackie and MacIntyre. 1994. 'Politics'. In H. Hill (ed.). *Indonesia's New Order*. Honolulu: University of Hawaii Press, p. 12.

Notes
a The 1971 figures for PPP and PDI are based on the combined votes of parties which were merged in 1972–1973 into these two groupings.
b The 1997 figures are taken from I. M. Wiratama and N. Hasibuan. 1997. 'Post-Election Political Development'. *The Indonesian Quarterly* **25**(3), 225.

groupings: the PPP (United Development Party) representing Islamic parties, the PDI (Indonesian Democratic Party) representing the nationalist and Christian parties (Liddle 1985: 71; Reeve 1985: 324–5; Mackie and MacIntyre 1994: 13). This was followed by the introduction of the concept of *massa mengambang* (floating mass) which prevented political parties from opening branches or conducting political activities at village level, except during the brief period of political campaign prior to the general elections. This concept rested on the assumption that the vast majority of the Indonesian population was politically unsophisticated and prone to politicking, which could easily lead to social unrest (Vatikiotis 1993: 95). As a result, villagers were cut off from political parties, they had instead to channel their political aspirations to non-party organisations created by the state such as the LMD (village consultative assembly), LKMD (village people's defense council), *Karang Taruna* (village youth groups) or PKK (family welfare guidance) all of which operated under Golkar's guidance.

Social activities such as public gathering, rallies, discussions and so on were strictly controlled under the *Undang Undang Keramaian* (Law on Public Gathering) No. 5/1963, inherited from Sukarno's government, which required formal permission for societal activities involving more than a dozen participants (Kusumah 1996: 17). This legislation was implemented in conjunction with Article 510 of the Criminal Law, inherited from the colonial government, stipulating that the government can cancel or dissolve any 'illegal' activities and has the authority to press charges against or imprison the organisers (Pangaribuan 1996: 34). To ensure the implementation of these laws, the government introduced the concept of 'joint administration' at district and sub-district levels. At the district level, *Kodim* (district military office), *Polres* (district police office) and *Pemda* (district civil administration) shared an equal responsibility in maintaining order under the so-called *Muspida* (District Leadership Consultative Body). At the sub-district level, the joint administration was carried out by *Koramil* (sub-district military office), *Polsek* (sub-district police office) and *Kantor Kecamatan* (sub-district administrative office) (Salim and Wijaya 1996: xv). This security apparatus held the responsibility to ensure order in their territories and have the authority to use coercion against any indisciplined acts of society.

## The state's intervention

Mouzelis (1994: 144) argued that rapid social and economic transformations in most of East Asian countries have been achieved through the formation of an interventionist state that keeps a close watch on capital (indigenous as well as multinational) and controls most important sectors of the society. The characteristics of the New Order state make one believe that it was an interventionist state in the sense that state agencies dominate political and economic activities of the society (Robison 1988; MacIntyre 1990). Because its legitimacy depended on its ability to provide material benefits to the society, the New Order state found it necessary to maintain a rapid economic growth and a steady process of industrialisation (Robison 1988: 56). Liddle (1985: 82) observed that by the early 1980s most Indonesians appeared to have made their peace with the authoritarian rule. Partly, this was a matter of not opposing an irresistible force, and partly it was a product of the material rewards delivered by the government.

### *The role of the state in the economy*

It was believed that the New Order regime defined its success and risked its legitimacy in the eyes of Indonesian people in terms of rapid economic growth (Mayer 1996: 169). Throughout the 1980s and early 1990s, Indonesia's overall economic growth reached 7 per cent annually. Its per capita GNP has grown from a mere US$60 in 1967 to US$900 in 1995 (Ramage 1996: 147). The country's economic achievement and successful social programmes, at least until the early 1990s, were internationally recognised and praised. In 1990, President Suharto received prestigious awards from the United Nations agencies citing Indonesia's success in food self-sufficiency and population control. A few years later, the widely circulated World Bank Report, *The East Asia Miracle* (1993), pointedly identified Indonesia as one of East Asia's consistently 'high performing economies' (Ramage 1996: 147). Even though inequality between the rich and the poor still persisted, there has been a steady decline in the percentage of the population below the poverty line in both rural and urban areas since the mid-1970s. For example, data from Susenas (the national social-economic census) indicated that in 1976 there were 40.4 per cent of the rural population below the poverty line; by 1987 this percentage had fallen to 16.4 per cent. The decline in urban areas was less dramatic, although the percentage was almost halved over the same period (Booth 1992: 342).

From 1967, two powerful state enterprises – Pertamina (the state oil corporation) and Bulog (the food logistics agency) – played crucial economic roles. While Pertamina served as the prominent source for government revenues, generating around three quarters of the country's total export earnings and two-thirds of government revenue (MacIntyre 1990: 56), Bulog held the monopoly in the distribution, storage and pricing of basic items all over the country and therefore mediated social and economic crises (Robison 1985: 310; Mackie and MacIntyre 1994: 8). The state enterprises were also extended to other sectors such as infrastructure, banking, telecommunications, properties, electricity, transport and so on. They played an important role in direct investment in import-substituting production (cement, petrochemical, steel and so forth), often in joint ventures with private domestic or foreign investors, and in construction projects (Robison 1985: 310). Mackie (1990: 76) argued that by the early 1990s no other non-communist state in Southeast Asia had anything like such a prominent state sector as Indonesia.

Robison (1985: 300) argued that the state's domination was a result of the failure of a powerful national bourgeoisie to emerge. During the 1950s and 1960s in Indonesia there was no such bourgeoisie as the one developed in the West, or more comparably, in some other Asian fast-growing economies (Japan, Taiwan, South Korea, Hong Kong and Singapore), in the sense of a business class with the resources for wielding major influence over the general course of government, because the largest chunks of economic power were in the hands of the oligopolistic Western firms, mainly Dutch, which dominated estate agriculture, the oil industry, shipping, aviation, insurance and so on (Feith 1962: 104). A few decades later, when more Indonesian industrial establishments were formed, following an extensive nationalisation of foreign firms in the 1960s, a new group of middle-class (largely of Chinese origin) emerged and began to play more prominent roles in the national economy, especially in the business sector. However, this group did not constitute a bourgeoisie in any useful sense for they shared no common origin of birth or economic base, and therefore no necessary commonality of interest that might transcend the ethnic and religious divisions among them (Lev 1990: 27).

MacIntyre, however, observed that the period of economic slow-down in the mid-1980s had opened up chances for the business class to exert their political influence (MacIntyre 1990: 56). But one should bear in mind that a high proportion of the business class consisted in fact of Indonesians of Chinese origin whose vulnerable social and political positions have circumscribed their opportunities to exert political influence other than on a purely personal basis (Mackie 1990: 84; Mackie and MacIntyre 1994: 41). Some prominent figures such as Liem Sioe Liong, Bob Hasan, William Suryajaya, Prayogo Pangestu, Eka Ciptawijaya, Ciputra, Sofyan Wanandi and some others could exert some political influence over particularistic decisions about the allocation of contracts, licenses, credits and so on; but they had never acted to influence government policies on behalf of the Chinese community as a whole, let alone of a 'class' of bourgeoisie

(Mackie 1990: 84–5). One major problem for most Indonesian Chinese was social hostility of the indigenous population as they often accused the Chinese of making fortunes in collusion with politico-bureaucrats (Robison 1985: 301; Mackie and MacIntyre 1994: 39). During the 1998 economic crisis, the indigenous population blamed the Chinese for causing the financial down-turn.

Throughout the New Order period, an alliance between the military and bureaucrats on the one hand, and foreign, Chinese as well as indigenous businessmen on the other hand, was built largely upon various state monopolies and controls on distribution, marketing and pricing. Licenses and concessions were commonly sold or allocated in order to secure either revenue or political advantage for particular political factions and individuals as well as their families and clients (Robison 1982: 142). The ruling elites provided political patronage, protection, access to state bank credit and state contracts for supply and construction, while in return the client businessmen were expected to pay commissions and other material incentives to the top state officials. In a few cases, businessmen served as financiers for army commanders and individual generals and *de facto* managers for corporations owned by the military (Robison 1988: 62). Since the early 1980s a growing business group associated with Suharto's family usually referred to as 'the palace group' or simply 'the *Cendana*[2] family' has expanded very rapidly. The president's business interests included three of his sons, three of his daughters, his half-brother, his foster brother, his grandson and other relatives, all of whom in only a few years had acquired major interests in a wide range of business including banking, the spot oil market, the clove trade, flour milling, cement, logging, hotels, textiles and fertilizer distribution (Bresnan 1993: 257). In the 1990s, cronyism grew very rapidly. President Suharto's cronies secured exclusive or semi-exclusive rights to import, produce or distribute flour, cement, steel, tin plate, plastics, raw materials, oil, liquid natural gas (LNG), shipping, insurance, cars and foodstuffs (Bresnan 1993: 259). These events appeared to have generated public criticism against corruption, collusion and nepotism.

## *State intervention in rural development*

During the New Order government, the state's intervention in rural development was obvious. Arce *et al.* (1994: 153) argued that an interventionist state attempts to control rural society by establishing powerful agencies to monopolise rural community development activities. The rapid economic growth, especially during the period of the oil boom (1973–1983), enabled the New Order to construct infrastructures and carry out various community development projects in the areas of family planning, health care, agricultural intensification and small credit (Hill 1994: 61). Government revenue was also used to raise the salaries of state officials (Booth 1992: 340). In the agricultural sector, the government was able to improve crop-growing methods, to provide subsidised fertilizers and foodstuffs to the people, to develop high-yielding seeds, and to build irrigation systems under programmes such as *Bimas* (mass guidance) and *Inmas* (mass intensification) (Booth 1992: 340). By the early 1980s, several government-sponsored projects collectively known as *Inpres* (presidential instruction) supplied rural areas with roads, village-halls, schools, health centres, markets, and so on (Liddle 1985: 78; Ravallion 1988: 54). Inevitably, the state played substantial roles in almost every sector of society.

What is the possible impact of the state's intervention in rural development on NGO activities? A study by the Asian Non-Governmental Organisation Coalition (ANGOC) in 1991 suggested that the degree of state intervention correlates with the way NGOs choose their approach and establish relations with the governments (ANGOC 1991). In countries where state intervention in rural development is low or moderate (Bangladesh, India, Pakistan, Sri Lanka and the Philippines), the activities of local NGOs appear to be broad in spectrum, that is to say, NGOs can combine different approaches (relief, development, empowerment or mobilisation) and NGO-government relations tend to be more collaborative based on mutual co-operation and more or less equal partnership. Meanwhile, in a situation where the state's intervention in rural areas is high (Malaysia and Indonesia), NGOs' activities appear to be limited in scope because they have to concentrate in sectors where state agencies have no control (health care, micro-credit and small-enterprise development); and NGO-government relations tend to be unequal where the state plays a dominant role (ANGOC 1991: 12–18). In Malaysia and Indonesia, for example, the state had the financial capacity and power to exert significant control over rural development programmes and to eliminate grassroots activities, leaving NGOs limited space to conduct their development and empowerment programmes (Clarke 1998: 38).

This study raises two important points. First, a low degree of state intervention leaves more opportunities for NGOs to pursue their activities in rural areas, while a high degree of state intervention tends to limit NGOs' activities. Second, governments with less financial and political capacity to intervene in rural activities tend to be more prepared to recognise and develop equal partnership with NGOs, while governments with greater financial and political capacity to control rural development programmes tend to be less co-operative towards NGOs. This view seems to corroborate Nugent's (1995: 202) argument that NGOs are welcome if the state sector shrinks and Clark's (1991: 77–9) contention that NGOs operating under a strong state sector tend to have little opportunity to expand.

Putting ANGOC's study in the New Order context, one may argue that the role of NGOs has been disadvantaged by an extensive state intervention in rural development. Hart (1986: 19) argued that the state's intervention in rural activities during the New Order regime had gone so far to the extent that the rural elites had been transformed into a class of favoured clients of the state in which almost all of their activities were directed from 'above' and they were increasingly treated as implementers of state-sponsored programmes. Using oil revenues, the New Order government ran a number of poverty-alleviation programmes which included small credits, agricultural intensification and income generation, while villagers acted as passive recipients of the government's assistance. Every year the central government – through the Ministry of Home Affairs – allocated a special fund called Bangdes (village development) to villages all over the country and left its implementation to various state-sponsored grassroots organisations such as the LKMD, the PKK, the *Dasawisma* (neighbourhood association) and the *Karang Taruna* (Thamrin 1995: 13). By the late 1980s, the total expenditures passed through the district government, according to Jim Schiller, had increased dramatically to around thirty times compared to what they had been in the late 1960s (Schiller 1990: 397). Because most sectors of rural activities (health care, family welfare, sports activities and so forth) were controlled by the state-sponsored organisations NGOs had to negotiate their entry into rural development, not only with the local authority but also with leaders of various state-sponsored grassroots organisations.

## Political activism: opportunities and challenges

Despite the state's attempt to eliminate grassroots political activities, some sort of political activism had been exercised by different groups in society (Crouch 1994a). Among the middle-class, political activities came from outside the business sector. Politically concerned groups (religious leaders, academics, students, journalists, artists and NGO activists), with a growing desire for a more open and free political system, began to organise and question the state's domination (Schwarz 1994: 235). Meanwhile, among the lower-class, workers and farmers began to instigate local struggles demanding policy changes (Uhlin 1997: 117–18). However, resistance both from the middle-class and the lower-class (at least until 1997) appeared to be too weak. In a number of cases, the state could easily thwart their actions. Not only did they appear to be too small in scale or too sporadic, but they were lacking a strong ideological basis, being unorganised and unsustainable (Lev 1990; Crouch 1994a; Budiman 1994a).

### *Middle-class political activism*

Because the business sector (the majority of which are Indonesians of Chinese origin) suffered from a lack of political power and interest, the political activity of the middle-class was exercised by various professional groups. During the 1970s and 1980s, a number of professional associations such as IKADIN (Indonesian lawyers' association), ISEI (Indonesian association of economists), ISAI (Indonesian association of architects), AIPI (Indonesian association of political scientists), PIKI (Indonesian association of Christian intellectuals), ISKA (Indonesian association of Catholic intellectuals) and so forth were formed to represent the interests of the professional middle-class. One important professional association was indeed ICMI (Indonesian association of Muslim Intellectuals) which was formed in 1990 by a group of Muslim intellectuals. Headed by then Minister for Research and Technology who later became Indonesia's third president, B.J. Habibie, this hybrid organisation included among its membership Muslim leaders, academics, government officials, journalists and NGO activists. It was set up to unify Indonesian muslims and to improve their economic well-being, as well as to ensure that Islamic values would be reflected in government policies (Schwarz 1994: 176). To help formulate and broadcast Muslim views, ICMI launched its own newspaper, *Republika*, its own think-tank, Centre for Information and Development Studies (CIDES) and its own bank, *Bank Muamalat* (Budiman 1994a: 232). By the mid-1990s, ICMI claimed to have 80,000 members throughout the country (*Far Eastern Economic Review*, 18 August 1994). However, despite its success in representing the middle-class Muslims, this organisation had been weakened by internal conflicts, particularly between the bureaucrats and those who were critical of the government. In the post-Suharto era, the role of ICMI began to wane, especially when Habibie lost his interest in politics and left the organisation.

In 1991, a group of intellectuals in Jakarta formed the *Forum Demokrasi* (Democratic Forum). Although its activities had never been glaring due to the absence of a strong institutional framework and the lack of a clear mission and purpose, this organisation was able to unite intellectuals from different religions and ethnic groups and managed to raise awareness among Indonesian intellectuals of the importance of a cross ethnic and religious co-ordination (Budiman 1994a: 233). There were also prominent individuals who used the newspapers, theatres, seminars, discussions and various informal gatherings to express their symbolic criticism of the New Order government. This activity could be associated with individuals such as Abdurrahman Wahid (the chairman of NU), Arief Budiman (an academic), Emha Ainun Nadjib (a poet), George Aditjondro (an academic), Gunawan Mohammad (a journalist and poet), Mohammand Sobary (a researcher at the Indonesian Institute of Science), Riantiarno (a script-writer), W.S. Rendra (a poet) and Y.B. Mangunwijaya (a Catholic priest) whose writings and performances often included critical assessments of Suharto's government. Budiman (1994a: 231) argued that although the impact of this resistance on society in general was limited, it nevertheless conveyed a critical message to the state officials.

Another important group within the middle-class with a desire to challenge the regime consisted of university students. Student activism has always played important role in Indonesian politics (Aspinall 1995: 29; Uhlin 1997: 105). In the colonial era, Western-educated students served as important actors in generating Indonesian nationalism and the struggle for independence in the form of the *pergerakan kaum muda* (youth movement) (Shiraishi 1990: 29–30). In 1966, student movements managed to secure apparent mass support for the overthrow of President Sukarno, and thus gave the new regime crucial legitimation (Crouch 1978: 235). In the 1970s, disillusionment among students with Suharto and what was seen as the circle of corrupt generals surrounding him increased. A series of student demonstrations in Jakarta culminated in the January 1974 riots during a visit of the Japanese Prime Minister, Tanaka. In 1978, the re-emergence of student protest in Jakarta, Bandung and Yogyakarta was marked by a hardening attitude towards the New Order regime reflected in the call for Suharto not to stand for re-election which led to the government's systematic attempt to thwart student activism (Aspinall 1995: 30). In those incidents, student activists such as

Hariman Siregar, Sjahrir, Marsilam Simanjuntak, Indro Tjahjono and Heri Achmadi were charged with subversion and jailed.

In the late 1970s, the government adopted an uncompromising approach towards students. Student councils were frozen and existing student associations such as HMI (Islamic Student Association), GMNI (Indonesian Nationalist Student Movement), PMKRI (Indonesian Catholic Student Association), GMKI (Indonesian Christian Student Movement) and PMII (Indonesian Muslim Student Movement) were prohibited from conducting activities on university campuses (Sinaga 1994: 74). University bureaucracies were given greatly extended rights to intervene in student activities (Aspinall 1995: 29). Taken together, these policies were known as NKK/BKK (*Normalisasi Kehidupan Kampus/Badan Koordinasi Kemahasiswaan* or Normalisation of Campus Life/Body for Co-ordination of Student Affairs). Under NKK/BKK it was virtually impossible for those students critical of the government to form organisations openly on campus (Aspinall 1995: 30). Frustrated with this political control, students became active in community development activities by working with various NGOs. Others created their own *kelompok studi* (study groups) which from the early 1980s began to mushroom around major campuses (Bunnell 1996: 181). In these kind of groups, students re-evaluated activism of previous generations, searched for new strategies and studied a broad range of critical theories including dependency theory, the writings of the Frankfurt school, and Latin American liberation theology (Aspinall 1995: 30; Uhlin 1997: 106).

In the early 1990s, a new and protracted wave of organised student protest emerged pressing a very broad range of issues including the demand for 'campus autonomy', for the abolition of restrictions over mass organisations, for the protection of human rights, for the ban on the national lottery believed to be run by Suharto's family, for the reduction of the electricity tariff, and for the prevention of irregularities in land dispute cases. Some campaigns – such as those concerning major land disputes in Kedung Ombo (Central Java), Rancamaya (West Java) and Badega (West Java), the trials of student activists in Jakarta, Bandung and Yogyakarta, as well as the ban on the news magazines *DeTik, Tempo* and *Editor* in mid-1994 – were particularly intense and massive in scale involving thousands of students from different campuses. Aspinall (1995) and Juliantara (1996b) identified some important characteristics of Indonesian student movements of the 1960s/1970s and the 1990s. In terms of regional distribution, student activism was spread more widely. If in the 1960s/1970s outbreaks were concentrated in Jakarta and Bandung, in the 1990s the new wave of activism emerged in most university towns in Java (Yogyakarta, Solo, Semarang, Salatiga, Purwokerto, Bogor, Surabaya, Malang, Jombang and Jember) as well as outside Java such as Medan (Sumatra), Ujung Pandang (Sulawesi), Denpasar (Bali) and Mataram (Lombok) (Juliantara 1996b: 106). Unlike the 1960s/1970s, when students from elite state universities (the University of Indonesia in Jakarta and the Bandung Institute of Technology) were regarded as 'pace-setters' of the movement, in the early 1990s new groups involved more students from smaller and less prestigious private campuses (Aspinall 1995: 32).

In terms of organisational form, student activism in the early 1990s had increasingly moved from the legal and officially recognised student organisations to informal and *ad hoc* action committees operating on and off campuses. These action committees usually served as an alliance of less publicly visible groups based on particular campuses. The prototype was a group called FKMY (Yogyakarta Student Communication Forum) which in 1990 claimed a membership of 1,500 students from some 20 different campuses. Similar groups such as BKMJ (Jakarta Student Co-ordinating Body), BAKOR (Bandung Student Co-ordinating Body), FKMS (Surabaya Student Communication Forum), FAMI (Indonesian Student Action Front) and SMID (Indonesian Student Solidarity for Democracy) were formed in other cities (Juliantara 1996b: 104). In 1998, more groups were created including KAMMI (Indonesian Islamic Student Action Group) and FORKOT (City Forum). Unlike students in the 1960s/1970s who had taken up 'elite' issues concerning corruption and leadership in national politics, the new movement of the 1990s was more concerned with struggling for the rights and interests of the underprivileged and demanding an immediate end to state repression. Their slogans stressed that they were interested in the basic empowerment of the poor (Aspinall 1995: 32).

## *Lower-class politics*

Among the lower-class, factory workers are the major force that can generate a movement because factory work gathers men and women together, allowing them to share their common experience and form collective action (Piven and Cloward 1977: 21). In Indonesia, during the colonial period, it was European workers who introduced the spirit of unionism to the Indonesian workers. The first labour union was formed in 1905 by European workers of the state railways in Bandung (West Java). Known as the *Staatsspoorbond* (SS Bond or State Railway Union), this organisation was initially restricted to the European members but later included Indonesian constituents and expanded to Central Java (Ingleson 1986: 62). The forming of SS Bond was followed by the formation of similar unions for pawnbrokers, postal workers, journalists and sugar factory workers whose branches spread all over Indonesia, especially in major cities in Java. These unions effectively took up individual and collective grievances incorporating the Europeans and Indonesians and conducted spontaneous strikes in situations where the management failed to comply with the unions' demands. Between 1906 and 1910, there was an average of 137 labour strikes per year demanding better working conditions, wage increases and better housing (Ingleson 1986: 63). Political repression imposed by the colonial government failed to eliminate these organisations.

In the years immediately following Indonesian independence, the most prominent organisation which was occasionally involved in numerous protests and strikes was the Indonesian Workers Front (BBI), established in 1945 and later changed into the Federation of Indonesian Trade Unions (GABSI). This organisation evinced the spirit of labour unionism instituted earlier during the colonial era. Another workers' organisation was the communist-affiliated All Indonesia Workers Organisation (SOBSI) established in 1946. During the Sukarno era, these two organisations represented a large number of militant, politically oriented workers in major cities, particularly in Java (Hadiz 1994: 192).

During Suharto's government, however, labour movements faced a serious setback. The only trade union allowed to operate was the state-sponsored All Indonesia Workers Federation (FBSI) formed in 1973. In the 1980s, a further repressive measure was taken when the government arbitrarily changed FBSI into All Indonesia Workers Union (SPSI) and the concept of HIP (*Hubungan Industrial Pancasila*) or Pancasila Industrial Relations) was put in place. Under the HIP, the state had the authority to denounce any labour strikes if it found such actions had transgressed the harmonious, family-like social relationships contained in the state's ideology, *Pancasila* (Hadiz 1994: 193). In the 1990s, labour movements began to reappear. Militant workers formed their own union called SBSI (Indonesian Union of Prosperous Workers) and a number of co-operative groups. Labour strikes became more frequent, from 19 (1989) to 61 (1990), to 110 (1991) and to 177 (1992) (Budiman 1994a: 232). However, their actions subsided with the government's use of coercion in thwarting them. Following a series of labour strikes which turned into riots in Medan, Tangerang, Bandung and Surabaya, security forces intervened and many labour activists were intimidated and their leaders were jailed (*Far Eastern Economic Review*, 27 October 1994). Moreover, the lack of a strong ideological basis, vulnerability to violence, poor organisation, concern about short-term goals and the focus on local issues appeared to limit the capacity of labour movements to produce significant changes (Juliantara 1994: 5–6; Soewito 1994: 18; Budiman 1994a: 232). In the post-Suharto era, the number of independent workers grew very rapidly. Dozens of new organisations – most of them local in character gathering members from one or two factories – are formed to express concerns for low wages, poor working conditions and lack of adequate compensation in many redundancy cases. In June 2001, for example, thousands of factory workers in Bandung – many of whom being members of the newly formed organisations – turned violent protesting against what they considered as an unfair redundancy law introduced by the Ministry of Manpower a month earlier.

Peasant movements also suffered from the lack of organisational competence which contributed to a sustainability problem. In the colonial era, far from being a series of simultaneous eruptions touched off at some central point of control, peasants' movements in Indonesia, according to Kartodirdjo (1973: 1), tended to be short-lived in duration, each breaking out in response to local initiative; and in most cases these movements were combining Islamic revivalism – triggered by millenarian hopes of the coming of *Ratu Adil* (the Just King) who would come to restore a golden age – with demand for material benefits. In the post-independence period, peasants – rich or poor – failed to play substantial political roles. Land ownership did not constitute a strong political platform because the majority of farmers were petty owners and only a few of them had more than 3 hectares of land (Feith 1962: 105; Mackie 1990: 75). During the New Order era, peasants'

66   *The social and political settings*

political activities were subject to a strict government control. The only institution through which peasants could channel their aspiration was the HKTI (the Indonesian Peasants Association), a government-sponsored peasants' organisation whose leaders were appointed by the government and recruited from military officers, civil servants or ex-servicemen. It operated under the auspices of the ruling party, Golkar (Eldridge 1995: 49; Juliantara 1996b: 98–9; YLBHI 1997: ix). During the 1980s and 1990s, a number of incidents in Lampung (South Sumatra), Kedung Ombo (Central Java), Badega (West Java), Rancamaya (West Java) and Nipah (East Java) indicated peasants' revolts against local authority. However, these cases were too local, sporadic, small in scale and unsustainable (Budiman 1994a: 230). In the post-Suharto era, peasants become more radical in expressing their political interests and claims. In West Java, Central Java, East Java and Sumatra thousands of peasants flocked to plantations, shrimp ponds, vacant real estate, teak forests, golf courses – including Suharto's Tapos ranch – and harvested the produce or ploughed the soil to signal their new claims. It was estimated that during the first six months after Suharto's resignation there were no less than 30,000 hectares of the reclaimed land (Sangkoyo 1999: 172).

*Ideology and class struggle*

Why did both the middle-class and the lower-class fail (at least until 1997) to establish a more co-ordinated and sustainable collective resistance that might have brought about more pressure for radical social and political changes? One possible explanation is the absence of an ideological framework that would generate a movement. Johnson (1966: 82–3) argued that groups or individuals will act when an ideology that offers alternative values or structures is available. Ideology, in this context, can be seen as a hierarchy of values and beliefs that guides human action whose effectiveness is contingent on the degree to which it is internalised by individuals or groups (Moaddel 1995: 237). In most developing societies, political transformations and popular movements are often triggered by the activities of groups disseminating radical ideology. In the Philippines, for example, the Communist Party of the Philippines (CPP), with its armed wing, the New People's Army (NPA), and its united front, the National Democratic Front (NDF), has long been an important force in shaping NGOs' radical activities (Clarke 1998: 113). During the Marcos period, the CPP became a formidable political and military force. It was claimed that by December 1984, over 30,000 Filipinos were members of the party and that the NPA had 20,000 troops with 10,000 high-powered rifles active on 59 guerilla fronts in 50 provinces (Kessler 1989: 28). In the late 1970s, the triumvirate (CPP–NPA–NDF) had influenced existing NGOs, established new ones and used NGO funding to support its armed struggles. Leading underground leftist activists such as Ed de la Torre, Gerry Bulatao and Edgar Jopson helped establish important NGOs. With close church and social democrat connections, they brought the idea of institution to the underground that could operate legitimately and secure foreign funding (Clarke 1998: 114).

*The social and political settings* 67

In the Philippines, NGOs' history is closely related to the evolution of radical leftist ideology (Davis 1989: 37). In 1919, the National Union of Peasants directly addressed problems faced by the rural poor and forced the colonial administrator to deal with them. After the Second World War, organised groups of peasant guerillas, especially the Hukbalahap[3] (*Hukbo ng Bayan Laban sa Hapon* or People's Anti-Japanese Army) forced the newly independent government of Manuel Roxas to focus on the plight of the peasantry in Luzon, the main victims of insecure tenancy and poverty (Steinberg 1986: 23; Clarke 1998: 56–7). The role of the Catholic church in organising the poor and in helping them nurture a strong ideological basis was also crucial. In 1947 the Jesuit order founded the Institute for Social Order (ISO), followed by the Federation of Free Workers (FFW), a labour organisation founded in 1950, and the Federation of Free Farmers (FFF) in 1953. In 1966, the Catholic Bishops Conference of the Philippines (CBCP) organised the National Secretariat for Social Action (NASSA) to co-ordinate social action centres in every diocese with the responsibility to maintain justice and peace. In 1970, an organisation called Basic Christian Communities (BCC) was founded by foreign missionaries as an instrument for the provision of an organisational basis and political education for the poor (Kessler 1989: 46–7).

By the mid-1980s, a relatively strong ideological basis at the grassroots level had provided a conducive environment for the emergence of popular resistance in the Philippines. It was at this point that NGOs were able to carry out their pro-democracy campaign and generate support from other groups within the society, that is, church leaders, university students and academics, salaried middle-class workers, women's organisations, and the lower class to form 'people's power' (Miclat-Teves and Lewis 1993: 230; Rocamora 1995: 35). Under these circumstances, institutional and emotional links between NGOs, opposition groups and other pro-democracy supporters became more feasible. For example, the assassination of Evelio B. Javier (the provincial chair of the opposition alliance led by Corazon Aquino) in 1986, while he was watching over ballot boxes in the town plaza of San Jose, Antique, had accelerated the massive popular protest that contributed to the fall of President Marcos (Diamond 1992: 4).

In the New Order Indonesia, radical ideology has always been under suspicion. Following the attempted coup of 1965, the state carried out a systematic elimination of Marxist–Leninist ideology. Between 1966 and 1968 hundreds of thousands of writers, intellectuals, civil servants, workers and peasants, who were either members of the PKI and its supporting organisations or merely sympathisers, were arrested and classified by their degree of involvement with the organisations. Many ended up on Buru island, a remote prison camp in Maluku (Vatikiotis 1993: 34). In order to prevent a possible revival of communism, the government imposed a strict administrative control on the society. A special letter of non-involvement with the PKI (*Surat Keterangan Bebas G-30-S/PKI*), issued by the local police, was required for school and job applications either in the public or private sectors (Mundayat 1994: 42). Applicants for positions in the civil service and the military were asked to produce a special letter called *Surat Keterangan Bebas Lingkungan* (literally letter of 'clean environment'), also known as 'Sampul-D', issued by the sub-district military office which traced a possible involvement of their extended families or associates with the PKI. Members of parliament, party officials and leaders of mass organisations were obliged to follow a special screening procedure (*penelitian khusus*) to make sure that they had no communist background or had not been endorsing ideologies other than *Pancasila* (Djiwandono 1997: 95).

The New Order government also obliged all social organisations to accept the official ideology, *Pancasila*, as their sole ideology as stipulated in the Law on Mass Organisation No. 8/1985 (Lubis 1993: 215). By promoting *Pancasila* as the sole ideology the New Order government hoped to sever the connection between *aliran* and mass political behaviour. Officials of the New Order were worried about the revival of 'old ideological issues'; and they were determined to impose a policy invariably termed as 'de-politicisation', 'de-ideologisation' or 'Pancasila-isation' with emphasis on ensuring that grassroots politics conform to the state's idology (Ramage 1995: 186). To many organisations, this law had effectively ended their hope of operating under an ideology of their own choice.

The problem with *Pancasila* was not that it is an anti-democratic ideology since it carried four basic principles: humanitarianism, nationalism, democracy and social justice (Darmaputera 1988: 174). The controversy was propagated by the fact that *Pancasila* was open to a 'self-transformation' in the sense that people could interpret it in different ways. For example, Sukarno saw *Pancasila* as a manifestation of Javanese syncretism capable of integrating Indonesian nationalism, religion and communism under the slogan of *Nasakom* (*Nasionalisme-Agama-Komunisme*) (Darmaputera 1988: 164). In the New Order period, *Pancasila* was initially understood as a middle-way solution (combining liberalism with socialism, authoritarianism with democracy and nationalism with internationalism) to maintain harmony and balance between groups in the society (Darmaputera 1988: 165); but it was increasingly used as an ideological justification for Suharto's regime to repress the 'political' Islamic groups and leftist movements. Due to the past experience in dealing with the *Darul Islam* (an armed separatist Islamic group) and the PKI, the Indonesian armed forces thought that their legitimacy stemmed from their role as the 'defender' of the *Pancasila* state: a non-communist, non-Islamic, unitary state (Ramage 1995: 22).

Thus, unlike social movements in the Philippines, complicated social structures and the New Order's firm policy of 'de-ideologisation' have eliminated the chance for a radical ideology to evolve at the grassroots level in Indonesia. Even the pro-democracy groups, whose number has increased since the mid-1990s, were unable to operate on the basis of a solid ideology to the extent that Latin American grassroots organisations profess *basismo*.[4] For these groups, working under a radical ideology of their own choice appeared to be too dangerous because the government would use various 'political labels' (branding them as communists, Islamic extremists, anti-nationalist, anti-development and the like) to stigmatise its critics and opponents (Heryanto 1997: 109). In the late 1980s, for example, activists in many politicised, environmentally-oriented organisations were cautious of being labeled 'watermelons' (*buah semangka*), that is, green (symbolising the environment) on the outside, but red (symbolising Marxism) within, by military leaders. Activists, vividly remembering the bloody anti-communist campaigns during 1965–1966, were alert to the dangers of such a label (Mayer 1996: 184).

The impact of the absence of a strong ideological framework on the political activities of the lower-class in Indonesia was evident. Despite the growing number of labour strikes in the early 1990s, workers' movements could only manage to stage sporadic, intermittent and unsustainable protest actions bringing local issues and short-term interests such as demand for the rise of UMR (regional minimum wage) and better working conditions (Budiman 1994a: 231; Hadiz 1994: 192). Most of their activities subsided when employers met part of their demands. Even if they managed to develop a certain degree of militancy, their action was vulnerable to military repression because their protests could be easily diverted into anti-Chinese mass violence as manifested itself in a number of incidents in Medan, Tangerang and Sumedang.

One reason for the lack of coherence of the political activity of the lower-class is the low degree of class struggle in Indonesia. It will certainly be much easier to envisage a movement in places where class struggles are intense. In India, for example, conflicts between a group of dominating landlords and the marginalised landless peasants appeared to have created the necessary condition for the emergence of social movements (Byres 1989: 46). While some landlords (in their capacity as landowners and money-lenders) tried to keep the rent as high as possible, landless peasants asserted their right to self-determination, which created a high level of exploitation that constituted a condition for a class struggle. The introduction of new agricultural technology in the early 1970s had widened the already substantial gap between the rich farmers and poor peasants because rich farmers had far greater access to the new input, greater knowledge, more capital, and better storage capacity that made them more capable of bearing risks in growing quick-yielding crops. They were also far better placed to acquire the high-yielding seeds, fertilizers and canal-irrigated water which were crucial for agricultural intensification (Dasgupta 1977: 232–4). As a result, the new agricultural technology tended to accelerate the process of rural proletarianisation in which small peasants and tenants had been increasingly pushed out of self-employment into wage labour (Byres 1989: 53). It was in this situation that NGOs such as *Bhoomi Sena* in India and GSS (*Gono Shahajjo Shangstha*) in Bangladesh could play an important role in generating social movements. By exploiting class struggles in society these organisations were able to build a more or less solid constituency, develop a radical ideological basis, and serve as representatives for the oppressed.

In the Philippines, the commercialisation of agriculture in the late eighteenth century had also caused the alienation of poor peasants from their land. With the growing involvement of the country's economy in world commodity tradings, land ownership gradually became concentrated in large estates known as *haciendas*, many of which grew export crops. By the late nineteenth century, land tenure (with concentration of ownership in *haciendas*) had become the major source of conflict in rural areas. Kessler (1989: 8) characterised the years between 1890 and 1914 as disastrous for the peasantry because of epidemics among man and beast, wars, banditry and general economic depression in which landowners reacted to the threats to their economic interests by squeezing tenants harder. The society in the Philippines has therefore had a long tradition of popular activation and mobilisation. Throughout the twentieth century, peasant and trade union movements challenged economic and political systems biased against the interests of the poor through a combination of mass protest and armed struggles. These movements were typically broad, class-based and ideologically cohesive; during the 1980s and 1990s they became increasingly focused, pursuing more concrete objectives, more organised, and more sectoral or issue-oriented (Clarke 1998: 123).

In Indonesia, class struggle has been uncommon. Geertz (1963: 97) observed that the pressing need for more land and resources – due to a rapid population increase (especially in Java) – did not seem to bifurcate rural society into a group of landlords and a group of oppressed landless peasants. He went on to argue that rather than demanding more land and resources, Javanese peasants tend to maintain social harmony and economic homogeneity by dividing the economic pie into a steadily increasing number of minute slices, a process to which he referred to as 'shared poverty'. This process was particularly apparent in wet-rice cultivation, with its ability to maintain levels of marginal productivity by always managing to employ one or more people without a serious fall in per-capita income (Geertz 1963: 80). Thus, in the delicately muted vernacular of peasant life in Java, there were only groups of *cukupan* (just enough) and *kekurangan* (not quite enough) rather than the 'haves' and the 'have-nots' (Geertz 1963: 97). Contrary to what had happened in the Philippines, the commercialisation of agriculture in Indonesia did not generate conflict between export-oriented agricultural estates and rice growers because of the mutual integration between crops, that is, sugar and wet-rice growing. The expansion of sugar plantations, according to Geertz (1963: 57), brought with it the expansion of wet-rice growing because both sugar and rice could be grown under relatively similar conditions (better irrigated terraces, the use of part-time labourers, and land-processing skills). Thus, sugarcane and wet-rice could be grown alternately without causing serious disturbances. If terracing was improved or extended, the peasant food production and commercial cultivation could both be increased, and landless peasants could contribute their labour to both sugar and non-sugar cultivation (Geertz 1963: 57). Although the situation in rural Java has been much more dynamic since the introduction of the new agricultural technology in the 1970s (White 1983), Geertz's proposition has nevertheless illustrated that the chance for peasants' radicalisation in Indonesia appeared to be smaller than in the Philippines or India.

Some observers agreed with Geertz that the level of class struggle in Indonesia is curiously low (Mortimer 1982: 55; Robison 1985: 300; Mackie 1990: 73). Mackie (1990), for example, argued that land ownership in Indonesia did not generate class struggle for at least two reasons. First, the ownership of land was very widely dispersed, not concentrated in the hands of a few, in nearly all regions of the country that made land ownership less meaningful and the class of landlords insignificant. Second, the tenancy system was rare, while the traditional share-cropping (a complex two-way type of transaction) could not be seen as an instrument of class exploitation due to its flexibility (Mackie 1990: 75). One important traditional share-cropping system was certainly the *kedokan* or *ceblokan* (in East Java known as the *gogolan*) system, a traditional arrangement between land owners (*pemilik*) and tenants (*penggarap*) where particular pre-harvest tasks were paid in kind with shares of output at harvest time rather than cash (Papanek 1985: 25; Hart 1986: 179). Under this system, non-labour input costs were shared by land owners and tenants on the basis of two-thirds to the land owners and one-third to the tenants, which appeared to minimise the sense of exploitation among the tenants. Hart (1986: 188) argued that although by maintaining the *kedokan* system a wealthy land owner may lose popularity by being condemned as greedy or anti-social by his/her fellow villagers, he or she may still face less hostility than those big landowners who must face uprisings from their tenants as happened in India and the Philippines.

Thus, rather than evolving along class lines, conflicts and struggles in Indonesian society tended to develop along the line of *aliran* cleavages in which antagonism between various social forces was divided according to a complicated, overlapping set of ethnic, religious, cultural, political and geographical boundaries (Jay 1963: 96–7; Kahn 1982: 96; Mortimer 1982: 57; Mackie 1990: 73). In the 1960s even the PKI was unable to exploit class conflict to generate resistance at grassroots level (Robison 1982: 136). Its unilateral action backfired because of the strong *aliran* conflicts in rural areas (Mortimer 1982: 57). In reality, during the 1950s and 1960s the PKI operated under the 'protection' of Sukarno and in return it had to moderate its class appeals and endorsed the 'revolutionary' ideas dictated by the Sukarnoists (Mortimer 1982: 61). It appeared that the PKI was forced, to a large extent, to work through patron–client structures and therefore reinforce rather than transform the character of elite-dominated political contest (Mortimer 1982: 61; Robison 1982: 136). Operating in a situation in which radical ideology is repressed, class struggle is weak and the society shares a high degree of apathy, NGOs are faced with a paradox. On the one hand, their presence is needed because they can help the powerless organise among themselves and build their consciousness of their social milieu. On the other hand, NGOs must adjust their radical orientations to the local situation by avoiding activities that will put themselves or their target groups at risk of direct confrontation with the state.

## The growing political uncertainty and the fall of Suharto

From the mid-1990s, the feeling of dissatisfaction with Suharto's government in society increased. The judiciary became a target of public anger and derision following a series of misconduct which included, among others, the escape of convicted tycoon Eddy Tanzil from a Jakarta prison, the escape of suspected drug dealer Zarima, the controversial trial of Sri Bintang Pamungkas (who was accused of insulting the president), the Supreme Court's overruling of both the District

72  *The social and political settings*

and High Court decisions declaring the 1994 banning of *Tempo* magazine illegal, and the Supreme Court's reversal of its own decision to set free Muchtar Pakpahan (a convicted leader of SBSI) (Heryanto 1997: 123). Rampant corruption and misdemeanour within the bureaucracy and the security apparatus were also targets of growing public criticism. The media frequently published corruption cases involving top state officials. In 1996, for instance, people were stunned by reports over corruption involving the Minister of Transportation, Haryanto Danutirto (*Kompas*, 21 July 1996). A few months later the media accused the Minister of Mining and Energy, I.B. Sudjana, of receiving illegal payments from foreign mining companies and of distributing concessions among his own cronies (*Forum Keadilan*, 12 November 1996).

Suharto family's business interests were also subject to public scrutiny, albeit less in the limelight. One important controversy was the Presidential Decree No. 2/1996 and No. 42/1996 granting Timor Putra Nusantara (TPN) Limited, a company owned by Hutomo Mandala Putra (Suharto's youngest son), an exclusive status as producer of the 'national car'. This status exempted TPN from both import tariffs and luxury good taxes. The decree also allowed TPN to import 45,000 cars tax-free from South Korea for a period of one year while the domestic production site was still in preparation (Heryanto 1997: 122). Resentment came from both domestic and foreign parties. The public (notably the government's existing critics) objected to Suharto's flagrant favouritism towards his own son. Meanwhile, foreign countries such as the United States, European Union and Japan accused Indonesia of violating the principle of fair trade; and they subsequently brought the case to the World Trade Organisation (WTO) (*Kompas*, 26 February 1997). Just as Suharto's popularity was beginning to wane, popular groups became more determined in expressing their opposition against the government.

### *The growth of the pro-democracy and human rights groups*

From the early 1990s, people began to express their dissatisfaction more openly. A new generation of pro-democracy and human rights groups – such as INFIGHT (Indonesian Front for the Defense of Human Rights), LPHAM (Institute for the Defense of Human Rights), Aldera (Alliance for People's Democracy), GENI (a human rights group based in Salatiga, Central Java), PIJAR (Information Centre and Action Network for Reform), PIPHAM (Centre for Human Rights Information and Education) and PRD (People's Democratic Party) – were formed and had become increasingly active in facilitating anti-government street demonstrations and protests (Uhlin 1997: 113–14). Describing the New Order state as 'totalitarian' and 'fascist', these groups attempted to unite all forms of pro-democracy movements and increase pressure against Suharto's government. Some of them – Aldera, LPHAM and PRD – tried to form a strong alliance with workers and peasants (Uhlin 1997: 110). PRD openly declared its radical commitment and started to recruit radical students and workers. Apart from its active involvement in workers' and peasants' movements, PRD called for, among others, the 'return to civilian supremacy', the 'review of *Dwifungsi* and security approach', the 'removal of restrictions on the formation and operation of political parties', and the 'return of the civil rights of the ex-political prisoners' (Aspinall 1995: 34). In 1998, PRD changed itself into a political party although it failed to win a single seat in the 1999 election. Another organisation called PUDI (United Democratic Party) was formed by some senior politicians. Led by Sri Bintang Pamungkas, an academic and former prominent member of the opposition party, PPP, this organisation claimed to be an alternative opposition political party. It took advantage of the absence of a clear rule on presidential elections by nominating its leader as the next president, even if the chance of winning was slim (*The Jakarta Post*, 12 October 1996). In 1998, Pamungkas re-established PUDI and turned it into a political party although he failed to win seats in the 1999 election. As expected, the government subsequently declared these organisations illegal and their leader were jailed (*Kompas*, 12 May 1997).

Senior military officers were disturbed by growing calls for democratisation from these groups. In October 1995, Lieutenant General Suyono, the Army Chief of Staff, issued a strongly worded warning that OTBs (*Organisasi Tanpa Bentuk* or formless organisations) using communist tactics and associated with 'known' communists were attempting to destabilise the country through various acts of agitation (*The Jakarta Post*, 17 October 1995). This was followed by a statement by Lieutenant General Syarwan Hamid, then the Assistant Chief of Social and Political Affairs, stipulating the danger of ex-PKI who 'colluded with idealistic extremists, utopian humanists and moralists and were active in the areas of legal aid, NGOs, human rights, environment and other political activities' (*Forum Keadilan*, 6 November 1995). Most outside observers believed that Indonesian military officers were over-zealous in ascribing social and economic unrest to the declining communism. Despite the appeal from the democratic leaders at home and abroad not to confuse legitimate social protest with the insidious threat of resurgent communism, military leaders continued to raise the spectre of communism in their warning against indiscipline and instability (Hanseman 1997: 131). Invoking the communist threat, according to Heryanto (1997: 110), was part of the political aim of the New Order regime to stigmatise political enemies, enhance eroding legitimacy, invent convenient scapegoats, deflect public anger, mobilise public support and improve internal cohesion. Tougher restrictions on societal activities were soon imposed. Between January and September 1995, for example, it was estimated that around 12 seminars/discussions, eight public gatherings and seven theatrical performances were either banned or dissolved by the security forces in major cities such as Jakarta, Bandung, Yogyakarta, Solo and Surabaya on the grounds that they failed to follow a proper procedure of permission or contained sensitive political issues (Forum 1996: 154–8).

The most scandalous affair was the government's attempt to depose the elected leader of the PDI, Megawati Sukarnoputri. The government saw Megawati as a threat not only because she is Sukarno's daughter but also because she openly declared that she would contest the election for president, a deliberate challenge to Suharto. Military leaders and officials within the Ministry of Home Affairs

## 74  *The social and political settings*

succeeded in exposing internal conflicts within the PDI and in a government-sponsored extra-ordinary congress in Medan, Suryadi (a pro-government politician defeated by Megawati a year earlier) was appointed as the party's new chair (*Suara Independen*, 20 July 1996). A few weeks later, angry supporters of Megawati occupied PDI's headquarters in Jakarta. On 27 July 1996, riots started to spread in some areas in Jakarta when troops, anti-riot police forces and followers of Suryadi brutally attacked Megawati followers. Scattered confrontation between the angry masses and security forces ensued leaving 40 buildings (government offices, banks and shops) burnt or damaged, five people killed instantly, 149 people (mostly Megawati followers) seriously injured and 74 others missing (*Kompas*, 13 October 1996; YLBHI 1997: 4).

This incident received serious attention from the international community. Human Rights Watch, an NGO based in New York, condemned the government's atrocities against Megawati followers and other pro-democracy activists and demanded that the US Congress take firm action against Suharto's government including the cancellation of bilateral aid to Indonesia (YLBHI 1997: 32). Amnesty International, a London-based NGO, expressed regret over the government's handling of internal tension within the PDI, condemned the use of force in the take-over of the party's headquarters, and demanded the unconditional release of Megawati followers detained by the security apparatus (YLBHI 1997: 32). Likewise, in Washington DC, President Clinton expressed his deep regret at the use of violence in handling what he called 'a peaceful action at PDI's headquarters' and demanded a thorough investigation of the incident (*Suara Pembaruan*, 3 August 1996).

Despite these criticisms, the government went on with its vigorous campaign against Megawati followers and other pro-democracy activists. It used radical students' groups, PRD and SMID, as scapegoats by openly accusing them of being reincarnations of the banned PKI (YLBHI 1997: 33). In many cities (especially Jakarta, Bogor, Solo and Yogyakarta) young Indonesians in their early twenties were arrested and charged with subversion for their involvement in the 27 July incident and for their roles in both PRD and SMID (Heryanto 1997: 110). In August 1996, the government organised a public gathering, as part of its counter-mobilisation strategy, involving around 30,000 people from around Jakarta. Supported by a few pro-government organisations, the gathering condemned PRD's involvement in inciting riots in Jakarta and declared an oath of loyalty to the government. Among the crowd there were several top military officers such as Lieutenant General Syarwan Hamid (Assistant Chief of Staff for Social and Political Affairs), Major General Sutiyoso (the Greater Jakarta Regional Military Commander), Major General Hamami Nata (the Greater Jakarta Regional Police Chief) and Major General Suryadi Sudirdja (the Governor of Greater Jakarta) (*Kompas*, 12 August 1996). In October 1996, the Co-ordinating Minister for Political and Social Affairs, General Soesilo Soedarman, publicly accused 32 NGOs of conducting activities that threatened political stability and must therefore face 'disciplinary action' which included an obligation to allow a special committee under the Ministry of Home Affairs to check on their ideological orientation and to carry out a special screening on their employees to make sure that no one had any connections with the banned PRD, SMID and PKI (INFID 1997: 5). Some argued that the 27 July incident was used by the government as a precedent to thwart the growing pro-democracy and human rights groups, notably PRD and SMID, whose attempt to link themselves with the lower-class was seen by the government as a major threat (Heryanto 1997: 116; YLBHI 1997: 33–6).

## The politics of violence

In the mid-1990s, resistance in urban areas had become increasingly sectarian. A number of mass violent actions were directed towards the minorities (Chinese and Christians). Conflicts on the basis of SARA (*Suku, Agama, Ras, Antar-golongan*) – an Indonesian acronym for ethnic, religious, race and inter-group conflicts – became intensified between 1994 and 1997 (Hanseman 1997: 129). In a number of incidents in major cities in Java and Kalimantan, urban popular protests turned into anti-Chinese and anti-Christian mass violence. Anti-Chinese sentiment grew out of objection against the economic domination of Indonesians of Chinese descent who in 1993 constituted 247 of the top 300 tax payers, and 129 of the 162 companies listed on the Jakarta stock exchange (*Info Bisnis*, 23 November 1993; Crouch 1994b: 143; Schwarz 1994: 105–6). While their collusion with state bureaucrats was increasingly criticised, reports that several Chinese conglomerates were investing in China had increased anti-Chinese feeling among the indigenous population (*Sinar*, 17 October 1994). This was made worse by the highly publicised corruption case involving Eddy Tanzil, an ethnic Chinese businessman, who in 1994 was found guilty of having manipulated a large amount of credit from a state bank, Bapindo (Indonesian Development Bank) (Rasyid 1995: 159). In May 1998, the Chinese in Jakarta, Solo, Medan and Surabaya became a target of mass violence following accusations that Chinese businessmen had actually caused the economic downturn. It was believed that the May violence might have been orchestrated by rogue elements within the Indonesian armed forces (Walters 1999: 61).

Meanwhile, the growing anti-Christian sentiments seemed to be generated by at least two factors: a perception that the Christian minority (most Indonesian Chinese are Christians) has disproportionately controlled the national economy (Budiman 1994b: 168) and a growing accusation brought by sectarian Muslim leaders against Christian groups or organisations of proselytising poor Muslims (Wahid 1994: 9). Mass violence against Chinese and Christians broke out during 1996–1997. On 9 June 1996, 10 churches in Surabaya, East Java, were attacked and looted by a group of youths following rumours of a Christian making a mess at a mosque (YLBHI 1997: 76–7). On 10 October 1996 in Situbondo, East Java, a mass protest against the district court's verdict on a Muslim found guilty of insulting a highly respected local *kyai* (Islamic leader) turned into anti-Christian and anti-Chinese violence in which a state court, 25 churches, four schools and four shops were looted and damaged (*Kompas*, 13 October 1996; YLBHI 1997: 54–74). On 26–27 December 1996, riots exploded in Tasikmalaya, West Java, which were ignited by an incident that had no connection with the Chinese or the Christians.

76  *The social and political settings*

The incident began when three Islamic teachers were beaten up in police custody; and for an inexplicable reason the uproar developed into racist and sectarian sentiment which stimulated a massive mass violence causing the lives of four civilians, 13 churches, 16 local police stations, 84 shops, four factories, four schools, six banks, three hotels and dozens of houses and cars to be destroyed or burnt, most of which belonged to the Chinese minority (*Forum Keadilan*, 30 December 1996; Legowo 1997: 103). On 30 January 1997, mass violence erupted in Rengasdengklok, a town about 40 km to the East of Jakarta, where two temples, four churches, 79 residential houses, four factories, two banks and 72 shops were burnt following a quarrel between a Chinese woman and a group of Muslim youths (*Kompas*, 31 January 1997). Sukma (1998: 105) argued that such violent actions were the result of an accumulation of social frustrations, political powerlessness and economic injustice. Meanwhile, Abdurrahman Wahid offered a 'conspiracy theory' in which he believed that the riots (especially those which occurred in Situbondo and Tasikmalaya, two areas known as basic strongholds of the NU) were engineered by certain parties in order to defame his organisation and its leaders (*Forum Keadilan*, 10 February 1997).

In 1997 as the general election was approaching, violence tended to increase. Many consider the 1997 general election as the 'worst' election in terms of violence and manipulation in the history of the New Order government (Sukma 1998: 108). The government's attempt to ban rallies by party supporters during the political campaign period was ignored and mass violence involving supporters of rival parties continued to occur, causing the loss of hundreds of lives. A number of campaign-related riots took place in several places in Jakarta, Solo, Yogyakarta, Bali and Ujung Pandang, leaving 310 people dead and 500 injured (*Tiras*, 28 May 1997). The government estimated that five police stations, two military offices, 26 sub-district and village head offices, six political party offices, 110 resident houses, three churches and four mosques were damaged in the first two weeks of the political campaign (*Kompas*, 21 May 1997). The most serious incident occurred in Banjarmasin, South Kalimantan, on 23 May 1997, when angry supporters of the opposition parties incited riots across the city leaving more than 200 people dead and a significant number of government buildings, shops and banks either damaged or burnt down (*Media Indonesia*, 27 May 1997).

In the 1997 general election, it appeared that the government's attempt to incapacitate the opposition party, PDI, was successful. Golkar received a landslide victory winning an absolute majority of 325 (out of 425 seats) in the DPR (People's Representative Body), followed by PPP with 89 seats and PDI with 11 seats (*Kompas*, 24 June 1997). PDI's debacle at the polls (losing 45 seats in the parliament) was a result of government-sponsored coup against Megawati. This poor result, the party's worst performance since its formation in 1973, was an indication of a 'punishment' by the party's constituencies who regarded Suryadi (PDI's chair) as a pro-government political opportunist (Wiratama and Hasibuan 1997: 226). He himself lost his seat in the parliament. Djiwandono (1997: 95) noted that the 1997 general election was simply a *dagelan politik* (political joke) in which people were mobilised to vote for fun and not to express their democratic rights.

Indonesian NGOs were caught in the middle of growing political and social uncertainty. On the one hand, some of them regarded street demonstrations and other protest actions as effective in putting pressure on the New Order government for political openness; on the other hand, they were also aware that mobilising people to the streets might provoke mass violence that would invite military intervention. Some activists expressed their fear that NGOs' activities in advocating workers' and peasants' peaceful protest actions might be diverted into mass violence against the minorities. Juliantara (1994: 4) argued that the security apparatus may play its role in turning peaceful protest into mass violence. In a number of incidents, the security forces deliberately encouraged the protesters to turn violent in order to justify the use of coercion. It appeared to be too risky for NGOs promoting social justice and equality to expose the issue of economic exploitation because it could easily provoke primordial sentiments. As Budi Santoso, a staff member of a legal aid NGO in Yogyakarta, put it: 'In a situation where religious and ethnic conflicts become more apparent, NGOs need to be more careful in carrying out their human rights campaigns by avoiding issues that may generate violence' (Santoso, interview, 06/08/1997).

## *The fall of Suharto*

The political situation in Indonesia has changed dramatically since the 1997 election. Suharto's legitimacy was dependent upon his success to deliver economic development. But when the economy began to deteriorate in 1997, Suharto became increasingly unpopular, particularly among the students. In May 1998, ongoing student demonstrations in some major cities in Java and riots in Jakarta (to which many Indonesians refer as the 'May 1998 Revolution') had led to the resignation of Suharto as Indonesia's second president. Kimmel (1990: 9) argued that resistance turns into revolution if there are the right triggers: that is, immediate historical events which can spark off the entire revolutionary process.

In 1998, the precipitous fall of the Indonesian currency, the *rupiah*, to only 20 per cent of its value on the year before was followed by the soaring prices of basic items, the collapse of the national banking system and the devastation of the industrial sector. On 4 May 1998, the government announced rises in electricity and fuel prices which led to violent demonstrations throughout the country (*Berita Nasional*, 5 May 1998). What seems to have triggered the 'May 1998 Revolution' was the economic crisis that seriously damaged the state's capacity to sustain its legitimacy. The currency crisis which spread across the East and Southeast Asian regions during 1997–1998 dealt a fatal blow to the New Order government, which was already facing harsh criticism from students and opposition leaders for its vulnerability to KKN (*Korupsi, Kolusi dan Nepotisme* or corruption, collusion and nepotism).

Students had begun their protest a few weeks earlier at the end of the parliamentary session on 11 March 1998, in which the ageing Suharto was reappointed as president. Large protest meetings occurred sporadically on major campuses in Surabaya, Yogyakarta, Semarang, Bandung, Solo, Malang, Manado, Ujung

Pandang, Denpasar and Padang, even spreading to smaller regional centres like Kudus, Jombang, Purwokerto and Jember (*Forum Keadilan*, 23 March 1998; *Gatra*, 18 April 1998). From the start these demonstrations explicitly rejected Suharto's reappointment as president, a sentiment expressed most vividly by the burning of an effigy of the president at the University of Gadjah Mada demonstration on 11 March 1998 (*Ajinews.com*, 12 March 1998). They also called for a reduction in prices of basic items, rejection of KKN and emphasised the need for *reformasi* (reform) in all political spheres: the abolition of *Dwifungsi*, a stronger role for the DPR/MPR (people's representatives and consultative bodies), press freedom, the recognition of citizens' rights to organise, free elections, and so on (*Gatra*, 12 April 1998). On 18 May 1998, after the student occupation of the DPR/MPR building had begun, the DPR/MPR chief, Harmoko, announced that the people wanted President Suharto to resign and gave him a deadline of three days to make an announcement to this effect (*Kompas*, 19 May 1998). On 21 May 1998, in a short ceremony in the Merdeka Palace, Suharto announced his resignation and appointed B.J. Habibie, the Vice-President, as his successor (*Kompas*, 22 May 1998). Habibie's appointment as Indonesia's third president marked the end of the New Order government.

## The post-Suharto politics: volatile transition to democracy

B.J. Habibie was a German-educated aeronautical engineer working at *Messerschmitt-Boelkow-Blohm* (MBB) in Hamburg before he returned to Indonesia at Suharto's request in 1974. While serving as the Minister of Research and Technology between 1978 and 1998, he was assigned to develop an Indonesian aircraft-manufacturing industry. He did this at enormous (and irrecoverable) expense to the state budget which made him unpopular among the country's leading economists.

His failure to consult other state officials before making major decisions (including the purchase of military equipment) also alienated him from most senior military leaders (Liddle 1999: 98). However, despite his numerous failings and enemies, his personal relationship with Suharto and his ability to use ICMI – an organisation he chaired – to mobilise support from Muslim intellectuals, enabled him to rise to the vice-presidency. Article 8 of the Constitution of 1945 states that: 'If the president dies, resigns or cannot carry out his responsibilities during his period in office, he is succeeded by the vice-president until the end of the term' (Wahjono 1982: 145).

### *Habibie's presidency*

Shortly after becoming president, however, Habibie agreed to make some radical political changes. Heckled and harassed by students and opposition leaders for his close association with Suharto, Habibie promised a new general election within one year, allowed new political parties to be formed, guaranteed more freedom of expression and association among the people and freedom of the press (van Klinken 1999: 60; Young 1999: 73). On 10–13 November 1998, the People's Consultative Assembly (MPR) held a special session (*sidang istimewa*) and made several historic decisions including decrees limiting future presidents to two terms, revoking presidential emergency powers, reducing the military's dual-function (*Dwifungsi*), ending the compulsory *Pancasila* indoctrination programme, and promising a more equitable centre–region fiscal balance (Liddle 1999: 116). It appeared that the military agreed to submit to civilian authority. For example, in early September 1999, the plan to legislate a new emergency law, which would have given the armed forces the power to control the state, was rapidly withdrawn following the widespread protests from students and other human rights activists (*Suara Pembaruan*, 2 October 1999).

Habibie's government introduced a new political regulation that allowed a number of political parties with their own constituencies to reappear at centre-stage, after they had been suppressed by both Sukarno and Suharto for more than four decades. There are now 48 parties ready to compete in the general elections. The largest new parties are Megawati's PDIP (the Indonesian Democratic Party of Struggle), Abdurrahman Wahid's PKB (the National Awakening Party), and Amien Rais's PAN (the National Mandate Party). PDIP, which was formed by Megawati supporters in the PDI, is the successor to the PNI of the 1950s. Its main supporters are the nationalist and secular Muslims, Christians and other non-Muslim minorities. PKB, which was formed by members of the biggest Islamic organisation, the NU, represents the traditionalist, syncretic Muslims, especially in Java and parts of Sumatra and Kalimantan. PAN was formed by the second biggest Islamic organisation, the *Muhammadiyah*, although it claims to be a non-religious party loosely based on economic populism. Unlike their predecessors during Suharto's government, these parties appeared to be more accommodating to NGOs and popular organisations because they were formed to represent the interests of grassroots people.

On 7 June 1999, a fair general election to elect 462 members of the DPR (People's Representative Body) was held. Predictably, Golkar lost its majority of votes because people were allowed to vote according to their own choice and voters had been sickened at Golkar's domination during Suharto's government. Megawati's PDIP secured 33.3 per cent of votes (153 seats in the DPR), which was followed by Golkar with 25.9 per cent (120 seats), PPP with 12.7 per cent (58 seats), PKB with 11 per cent (51 seats) and PAN with 7.5 per cent (34 seats) (*Suara Pembaruan*, 15 July 1999).

## Gus Dur's election as Indonesia's fourth president

Because the president was not directly elected by the people and none of the existing political parties managed to win a convincing majority, none of the contenders for the presidency could secure his or her position. The election of Abdurrahman Wahid – more popularly known as Gus Dur – as Indonesia's fourth president occurred in such an unpredictable situation. The process of forming a government was complicated by the requirement that whoever is chosen a president must command the support of a majority not just 500 members of parliament but the broader 700-member MPR. This top legislative body includes members of parliament alongside appointed representatives of the regions, civil society and the military. This seemed to open the opportunity for political horse-trading as presidential candidates seek to outbid one another for the support of key constituencies (ICG 1999: 3).

The front-runner in the presidential race was Megawati Sukarnoputri whose party controlled 30 per cent of seats in the parliament. This followed from Habibie's withdrawal as a contender after the MPR decided narrowly (355 votes against 322) to reject his performance in office (*The Guardian*, 20 October 1999). Despite support from radical Islamic groups and a number of political groups in the eastern parts of Indonesia,[5] Habibie was criticised for his reluctance to prosecute Suharto and his family, his failure to reduce corruption and his poor handling of the East Timor case. At the end of his term, Habibie's chance to remain in power was seriously damaged by at least there events: the court's order to stop investigation on Suharto's corruption case, an attempt by him to protect his close associates in the Bank Bali corruption scandal,[6] and the problem in East Timor which led to the cancellation of the much needed financial help from the International Monetary Fund (IMF) and the Asia Development Bank (ADB).

Earlier on, Megawati had been led to believe that Gus Dur would support her bid for the presidency but she was considered too secular by *Poros Tengah* (the Central Axis) – a loose grouping of Muslim parties led by Amien Rais (now speaker of the MPR) – which supported Gus Dur as the lesser evil. When the incumbent president B.J. Habibie withdrew, many of his supporters in the Golkar party also transferred their support to Gus Dur, thus securing his victory. This had allowed a candidate, whose party – the PKB – secured only 11 per cent of the votes in the national election, elected as the president which in turn led to its vulnerability.

Although initially Gus Dur and his party were not taking his own nomination seriously (given that he was widely separated from Rais in terms of Islamic teaching and political views), he became interested in running for the presidency just a few weeks before the MPR session. On 3 October 1999, Gus Dur was elected as Indonesia's fourth president, defeating Megawati by 60 votes – 373 against 313 (*The Times*, 21 October 1999). The shocking defeat of Megawati provoked violence in Jakarta, Solo and Bali where Megawati supporters destroyed public facilities and set fire to government offices.

A compromise was reached when Megawati was rewarded with the vice-presidency, after defeating another candidate, Hamzah Haz, the leader of PPP, by 112 votes – 396 to 284 (*The Guardian*, 22 October 1999). Two other serious contenders, Akbar Tanjung (the chair of Golkar who was considered Wahid's initial choice), and General Wiranto, the Armed Forces Commander (http://www.detik.com, 22 October 1999) withdrew to pave the way for Megawati. This move proved to be effective in preventing Indonesian society from plunging into more disastrous political turmoil. Many believed that the Wahid–Megawati pair would be an ideal combination, not only because Wahid had been Megawati's close friend, but also because they brought together the two new forces of the post-Suharto era: a revitalised Muslim voice and a strong secular political orientation (*Suara Pembaruan*, 22 October 1999). Wahid represents the moderate stream of Muslim thinking. Having spoken out against efforts to inject Islamic doctrine into Indonesian politics, he argued that if Islam became institutionalised it would raise religious tension and increase the risk of national disintegration. But many see his biggest disadvantage to be his poor health. Though only 59, he is nearly blind and had just recovered from a serious stroke. This indicates that Megawati's position as number two is much more than a consolation prize. If the president is incapacitated, the Vice-President takes over until the end of the five-year term.

## Gus Dur's presidency: political impasse

The election of Gus Dur in Indonesia's first competitive presidential election was widely welcomed as the opening-up of further path towards democracy. During the last few years of Suharto's regime, Gus Dur himself was among those who struggled for democratisation in Indonesia. Together with Arief Budiman, Marsillam Simanjuntak and several others, he formed a pro-democracy coalition, *Forum Demokrasi* (the Democratic Forum), with the aim of building a democratic discourse at least within the intellectual circles.

The president, despite some inconsistency, had seriously engaged in the promotion of Indonesia's democracy. He involved himself in public debates and regularly emphasised that differences of opinion are normal. He often reiterated his philosophy of religious tolerance and was a determined enemy of narrow Islamic orthodoxy (ICG 2001a: 2). With regard to separatist movements in Aceh and Irian Jaya, he had adopted an accommodating approach. He also took an important step to end official discrimination against Indonesians of Chinese descent and against those previously associated with the banned Communist Party. His important contribution to democracy was his drastic reduction of the military's political role. He cleverly appointed an admiral – instead of an army general – as the top military commander to reduce the army's strong political influence. His brave moves to dismiss most influential military officers – including General Wiranto, a chief military commander under Suharto – indicated his determination to control the military, which raised discontent among senior military officers. The market initially responded positively to Wahid's presidency as the value of the *rupiah* against the US dollar began to increase.

But this promising situation was short-lived. The value of the *rupiah* started to collapse again within less than six months of Gus Dur's presidency. While the process of democratisation remained sluggish, President Wahid himself was caught in wrangles with cabinet ministers and the DPR which had weakened the whole political structure. His alleged involvement in scandals such as *Bruneigate*[7] and *Buloggate*[8] and his failure to bring corrupt officials and investors to justice had raised doubts of the seriousness of his commitment to fight corruption. Fierce critics such as Amien Rais, the speaker for the MPR, for example, even expressed his fear that Gus Dur might not be fit to serve his term until 2004. Among the elite and middle-class circles, the continuing conflicts in Aceh, Maluku, and Kalimantan, the collapse of the *rupiah*, the ongoing corruption among the state and party officials, public disorder, and the soaring prices of basic items had generated frustration. Some even blamed democracy for bringing disorder and uncertainty to Indonesian politics.

Although Gus Dur had in some respects been an inspiring leader, he had shown himself to be lacking the managerial skills needed to run a modern state. His knowledge of the way in which economies work, how state bureaucracy is to be co-ordinated, and the proper procedure of the legal process was clearly inadequate. From time to time he made public statements, which were not necessarily based on accurate information. Unable to read, Gus Dur relied heavily for information on what his friends and personal aides tell him. Even in the eyes of his close friends, Gus Dur was lacking the managerial skills necessary to run the state. As Arief Budiman put it: 'He has a good heart. He is not a bandit or a criminal – he is erratic. Basically, he could not govern' (*Far Eastern Economic Review*, 2 August 2001).

In less than two years after his election, Gus Dur's popularity had begun to wane. He seemed to have disappointed those who had hoped that democratic reform would be accompanied by reform in other fields. Despite government rhetoric, little had been done to curb the corruption that permeated the Suharto regime. Although former President Suharto was charged, his trial had not taken place and none of his family members nor his cronies but one[9] had faced trials. Suharto's son, Tommy, was convicted but managed to escape.[10] The government had also failed to guarantee security. Ethnic and religious violence was still common, and virtual civil war broke out sporadically in Maluku. A corrupt and ineffective police force seemed incapable of preventing violence throughout the country. Most of the attention of the people, however, was focused not so much on policy failures but on Gus Dur's impulsive and erratic style of leadership. The president had become famous for what were called 'controversial statements' that were contradictory, erratic and sometimes based on wrong information (ICG 2001a: 3). These statements often caused much confusion about the government's intentions.

The most crucial incident that had halted the promotion of democracy was the conflict between the president and the legislature. Gus Dur, whose own party held only 11 per cent of the seats in the DPR, needed allies to form an effective coalition government. After securing support from the leading party PDIP by offering the vice-presidency to Megawati, his initial solution was to form a 'rainbow' cabinet which included members of seven leading parties. However, unable to accommodate all interests, in less than six months, Gus Dur was under pressure to reshuffle his cabinet. Three ministers – Hamzah Haz from PPP, Laksamana Sukardi from PDIP and Jusuf Kalla from Golkar – were dismissed, which led to the deterioration of the president's relationship with the DPR (ICG 2001a: 6–7).

At the annual session of the MPR in August 2000, Gus Dur became the target of sharp criticism. Amien Rais, the speaker of MPR and leader of the Central Axis who had nominated Gus Dur as president, took an extreme position by indicating the possibility of an impeachment process. Pressure from the main parties compelled the president to delegate to the Vice-President the tasks of carrying out day-to-day technical details of running the government, preparing the cabinet's working agenda and determining the government's policy priorities. But Gus Dur himself did not act according to the compromise as he went on making another cabinet reshuffle without consulting the Vice-President. Interestingly, in his new cabinet Gus Dur did not include any representatives from either PDIP or Golkar.

In September 2000, another case emerged which caused further damage to the relationship between the president and the DPR. Sensing that the president may have been involved in the Bulog (the food logistics agency) case more than he had admitted, the DPR voted 356 to 4 (with 45 absentees) to establish a special inquiry (*Pansus*) into the *Buloggate* and *Bruneigate* scandals. During the next few months, the *Pansus* hearing dominated news headlines as indication appeared that Gus Dur might be implicated. In its report presented to a plenary session of the DPR at the end of January 2001, the *Pansus* concluded that it was 'reasonable to suspect' (*patut diduga*) that the president had been involved in the Bulog affair. With the support of 8 out of 10 factions in the DPR – including the military – the session accepted the report and issued a warning – known as the First Memorandum – stipulating that the president had truly violated the constitution and the national will in two respects: (1) he had violated his oath of office to hold firmly to the constitution and fully implement all laws and regulations; and (2) he had failed to implement the MPR Decree No. XI/MPR/1998 on 'clean government', free of corruption, collusion and nepotism (ICG 2001b: 4–6; *Kompas*, 2 February 2001). The president reacted by insisting that the formation of *Pansus* was illegal and the report should therefore be ignored.

President Wahid's chances of retaining office suffered another blow when the DPR issued a 'Second Memorandum' on 30 April 2001. Having sensed that the president had failed to respond adequately to the First Memorandum, the DPR declared that if the president fails to satisfy the DPR within one month, the DPR has the authority to call a special session of the MPR to consider his dismissal. The warning received support from all major parties except the president's own, the PKB. The adoption of the Second Memorandum meant that the president must reach some kind of compromise with the main political parties before 30 May 2001 if he was to avoid the MPR special session (ICG 2001b: 3–7 ). But instead of supplying a satisfactory answer to the DPR, the president maintained that six provinces in Indonesia would announce their independence if he was to be dismissed by the MPR. He also insisted that Indonesia's constitution is presidential in character, not parliamentary, and therefore the president could not be dismissed by a parliamentary vote of non-confidence.

Having lost the support of the DPR, the president increasingly turned to 'the people', whom he was convinced would continue to support him. As resistance against the president among students and radical Muslim groups became stronger, Gus Dur seemed to turn his attention to his supporters, especially from his party's stronghold in East Java. In February 2001, immediately after the DPR's adoption of the First Memorandum, the president's supporters in the rural-based traditional Muslim organisation, the NU, had disrupted traffic along major highways in East Java, burnt down Golkar's offices in the provincial capital Surabaya and other cities. Attacks were also directed against buildings associated with the rival 'modernist' Islamic organisation, the *Muhammadiyah*. Although the president did not explicitly endorse this behaviour, he did not publicly condemn it either. In April 2001, as the DPR session to consider the Second Memorandum approached, his supporters in East Java formed a 'Front to Defend the Truth' which registered thousands of volunteers to join what they called the 'Ready-to-Die Force' (*Pasukan Berani Mati*) to defend the president. On Sunday, 29 April, the day before the DPR session, the NU itself organised a mass prayer attended by 100,000 people from all over Java. In June 2001, following the DPR's call for an MPR special session to impeach the president, violent clashes between the security forces and the president's supporters took place in Pasuruan, East Java, which caused one dead and 20 injured by gun-shots. The president blamed the police for taking improper measures, which led to the dismissal of the Chief of National Police, General Bimantoro. Wrangles between the president and the Chief of National Police began to spread in the media since General Bimantoro – who had secured support from hundreds of senior police officers and the DPR – refused to step down (ICG 2001b: 3).

Spending so much time and energy to deal with various attacks from the legislature and other institutions, Gus Dur's government had become increasingly poor in its performance. The government's inconsistency in making monetary policies and its slack action in dealing with corruption scandals had led the IMF to postpone its promised US$400 million loan. This rescheduling has caused a further deterioration of the *rupiah*'s value from US$1=Rp 6,800 in the first month of Gus Dur's presidency to US$1= Rp 11,200 (in June 2001). New forms of corruption and fraud were also rampant. For example, in the case of IBRA (Indonesian Bank Reconstruction Agency), despite the fact that it had failed to accomplish its main duty to recapitalise the problematic banking sector and to repay the private sector's international debts, IBRA was susceptible to corruption and fraud. Moreover, poor distribution and inability to control smuggling to the neighbouring countries had caused serious disturbances to the supply of petrol in major cities, especially in Java. The fact that in less than two years Gus Dur had already replaced 16 ministers in his cabinet seems to reflect the president's nervousness in dealing with the country's grave economic and social problems. While the economic crisis was still going out of control, local parliament members in West, Central and East Java were demanding higher salaries and better cars for their private use. In March 2001, frustrated by the government's poor handling of the current economic crisis, three student organisations – the Islamic Student Association (HMI), the Indonesian Muslim Student Action Group (KAMMI) and the *Muhammadiyah* Student Association (IMM) accused Gus Dur's government of being insensitive to the country's crisis and subsequently demanded his immediate resignation (*http://www.tempointeraktif.com*, 1 March 2001).

These political problems clearly brought uncertainty to the future of Indonesia's democracy, particularly when certain members of the society began to blame democracy for failing to end political wrangles among the elite circle. Commentators, however, argued that the political uncertainty was a reflection of the ongoing sectarian conflict involving the nationalists, the 'modern' Islamic groups and the radical Muslims on one side, and the traditional Muslims on the other side. Daniel Lev, an American political scientist, argued that the conflict between the president and the legislature had nothing to do with the constitutional debate on the role of the democratic political institutions (the presidency, the vice presidency, the People's Representative Body, the People's Consultative Assembly, and so on), but it simply reflected the sectarian conflict embedded in Indonesian pluralist society that has its origin in the early twentieth century (*Tempo*, 1 April 2001). In the end, Lev argued, most Indonesians who had hoped for democratisation were frustrated by the inability of the political elites to place the priority on constitutional and institutional reforms much needed to cope with the democratic practices.

Frustration and fear that political squabbles within the elite circle would damage the agenda of democratisation had indeed raised concern among different groups in society. In June 2001, a number of NGOs in Jakarta – the Urban Poor Community (UPC), the Indonesia Legal Aid Foundation (YLBHI), the Institute for Policy Research and Advocacy (ELSAM), and many others – urged the political elites to stick to the democratic agenda by proposing three proposals: (1) the prevention of a possible military come-back to politics; (2) the implementation of legal procedures in handling corruption and human rights violations; and (3) the need to build a strong commitment to curb nepotism and other kinds of power abuse. They also expressed their doubt whether Megawati would share the same commitment to democracy if she were appointed as the new president (*Kompas*, 7 June 2001). Their suspicion was not entirely unfounded, given that Megawati showed her reluctant support for both a substantial reduction of the military's political role and an instant introduction of the concept of regional autonomy.

What can be considered as the most serious threat to democracy during Gus Dur's presidency was probably the possible popular support of new militarism. Frustrated by the government's inability to maintain order and to ensure political confidence, people began to talk about a possible come-back of Suharto-like government, most notably among the middle-class. There had been a growing confidence that the threat of violence as a result of intra-elite conflicts should be dealt with firm military action. Immediately after the dispute between President Wahid and the National Chief Police in early June 2001, for example, there were no fewer than 14 NGOs who strongly criticised the president's intervention in police affairs. This group – who formed the 'Red-and-White Network' (*Jaringan Merah Putih*) – also expressed their firm support of the way the police and the military had handled riots involving Gus Dur's supporters in Pasuruan (*Far Eastern Economic Review*, 7 June 2001, 17; http://www.tempointeraktif.com, 4 June 2001).

86  The social and political settings

## The fall of Gus Dur and the rise of Megawati

In July 2001, President Gus Dur's controversial acts caused greater resistance from the people. A poll conducted by *Kompas*, a leading national newspaper, revealed that 80 per cent of the 723 respondents selected from the main cities in Java, Sumatra and Sulawesi described the president's controversial acts as disgraceful and 49.4 per cent of them agreed that Gus Dur's removal would be the only solution for the political problems in Indonesia (*Kompas*, 9 July 2001). Gus Dur's controversial acts began as early as 26 October 1999 when he dismissed the Department of Information and the Department of Social Affairs without consulting parliament. Table 3.2 compiles the president's controversial acts that led to his impeachment.

The biggest controversy that had encouraged the MPR to bring the special session ahead of schedule was indeed the president's removal of Bimantoro as the

*Table 3.2* President Abdurrahman Wahid's controversial acts, November 1999–July 2001

| Date | Issues or controversies |
| --- | --- |
| 23 November 1999 | The president calls the parliament 'kindergarten' referring to its sessions. |
| 5 January 2000 | The president declares his intention to remove the Governor of Indonesian Central Bank, Syahril Sabirin, breaking his own promise to keep the Central Bank autonomous. |
| 12 January 2000 | The president's personal masseur takes US$4 million from the state logistics agency, Bulog. In the same month, the president allegedly receives a US$2 million personal donation from the Sultan of Brunei. Months later the public learn of the two scandals, known respectively as 'Buloggate' and 'Bruneigate'. |
| 24 April 2000 | The president sacks two Cabinet ministers – Laksamana Sukardi (Minister of Foreign Investment) and Jusuf Kalla (Minister of Trade and Industry) – on corruption charges despite lack of evidence. |
| 24 August 2000 | The president reshuffles Cabinet, handling top jobs to his allies, neglecting both the Golkar party and Megawati's PDIP. |
| 18 September 2000 | The president removes the Chief of National Police, Rusdihardjo, without consulting parliament although the MPR's decree No. VII/MPR/2000 stipulated that the president must consult the DPR on the appointment or removal of the National Police Chief. |
| 27 January 2001 | The president refuses to co-operate with the special committee (*Pansus*) that investigates Buloggate and Bruneigate scandals. |

*Table 3.2* (Continued)

| Date | Issues or controversies |
|---|---|
| 22 February–8 March 2001 | While Dayak tribesmen massacre Madurese immigrants in Central Kalimantan province, president Wahid goes abroad for state visits and pilgrimage to Mecca. As the murders mount he rejects to return to Indonesia. |
| 19 May 2001 | Rumors spread among the president's circles that the president might declare a state of emergency, dismiss the DPR and demand a new election if the MPR continues with their plan to impeach him. The Armed Forces express their refusal to support the president's plan. |
| 1 June 2001 | The president reshuffles Cabinet, sacks top Security Minister Susilo Bambang Yudhoyono, Attorney General Marzuki Darusman, and suspends the Chief of National Police Suroyo Bimantoro, again without consulting the DPR. |
| 1 July 2001 | The president appoints Chaeruddin Ismail as a caretaker Police Chief, following the refusal of Bimantoro (the Police Chief who was sacked a month earlier) to step down. |
| 23 July 2001 | The president announces the state of emergency, suspends the DPR, dismisses the former ruling party, Golkar, and demands a new election. |

Sources: Compiled from *Kompas*, 9 July 2001 and *Time Magazine*, 6 August 2001.

National Police Chief. As mentioned earlier, the president had sacked the National Police Chief, Bimantoro, following riots in Pasuruan involving Gus Dur's followers. In his televised announcement, the president argued that the dismissal was recommended by the people. While demanding for more clarification from the president, Bimantoro refused to step down. On 4 June 2001, approximately 100 police officers declared their refusal of the president's intervention in police affairs. They also implicitly expressed their support to Bimantoro. The dispute continued until 12 July 2001 when the president – through his personal aide – announced his order to arrest Bimantoro on the charge that he had disobeyed the president's order to step down (*Pikiran Rakyat*, 14 July 2001). Most Indonesians appeared to be behind Bimantoro. A poll conducted by the Bandung-based newspaper *Pikiran Rakyat*, for example, indicated that 371 (74.2 per cent) of 500 respondents in the city agreed that the president's dismissal of Bimantoro was both improper and illegal (*Pikiran Rakyat*, 14 July 2001).

The MPR expressed their concern on the matter and explicitly showed their support for Bimantoro. The assembly fell short by a week because it was spurred into premature action by Gus Dur's decision to swear in a caretaker National Police Chief. On 1 July 2001, the assembly held a meeting and agreed to put the special session to impeach the president ahead of schedule. Amien Rais, the speaker of the assembly, argued that the president had seriously violated the MPR's decree No. VII/MPR/2000 stipulating that the president's appointment or dismissal of the National Police Chief is subject to approval from the DPR. This was seen mainly by Gus Dur's supporters as Rais's deliberate attempt to launch a final blow in his haste to get rid of Gus Dur, the bitter rival he had helped to power in October 1999, because Megawati – at least at that moment in history – was not acceptable to Muslim parties.

As the final impeachment hearing was drawing near, Gus Dur warned that tens of thousands of his followers – including the 'Ready-to-Die Force' formed a few months earlier – might storm Jakarta and block the MPR/DPR building in Senayan. But the fanatics stayed away. Gus Dur's advisers said that he had ordered his supporters to stay home in order to avoid a massacre by the 40,000 soldiers and police guarding Jakarta during the showdown (*Time Magazine*, 6 August 2001). Realising that his time was up, the president made a final effort to impose his will on the military he constitutionally controls. On Sunday night, 22 July 2001, the president summoned Security Minister Agum Gumelar and Armed Forces Chief Admiral Widodo Sucipto to the palace and sought their help to implement a state of emergency. The two men refused (*Time Magazine*, 6 August 2001). Had it worked, he would have blocked the assembly and staved off the impeachment. However, on Monday morning at 1 a.m. Gus Dur continued to announce the decree suspending the DPR, freezing the Golkar party, and demanding immediate new elections. The move's ineffectiveness became apparent when the generals sent for the tanks to surround the presidential palace.

Barely 12 hours after Gus Dur's decree, the Supreme Court Chief Justice Bagir Manan declared the president's decree unconstitutional. This was sufficient to encourage 591 MPR members to commence a special session to end Gus Dur's 19-month presidency and install Vice-President Megawati Sukarnoputri as the fifth president (*Far Eastern Economic Review*, 2 August 2001). Support for Megawati had been declared one day earlier. On Sunday 22 July 2001, the leaders of the major political parties met at Megawati's private home in Kebagusan, South Jakarta, to provide necessary support on her way to the presidential seat. Amien Rais, who is also the MPR's speaker, said the meeting was aimed at creating a sense of togetherness among the leaders of the major political parties to support Megawati. As he put it: 'We agree to give our moral support to Megawati, so that her government will be stable, just, productive, and be able to restore confidence to the people, which has now faded from the current government' (*The Jakarta Post*, 23 July 2001).

Megawati's lack of political ideas and her limited political experience had raised doubt whether she will be able to serve out her term until 2004, let alone drag the country out of crisis. Foreign as well as domestic observers have the bigger fear that after two years of messy, often volatile transition, the pendulum will swing back in favour of conservative forces and that Megawati is beholden to them. That would mean that reform will slow down, corruption go unpunished and unchecked, and business confidence be even harder to restore. Juwono

Sudarsono, a former Defense Minister and respected academic, for example, argued: 'Wahid may have had a point when he said Megawati is a prisoner of the New Order type of government' (*Far Eastern Economic Review*, 2 August 2001). Nevertheless, the market welcomed the change. Gus Dur's removal saw the *rupiah* strengthening significantly from US$1 = Rp 11,300 (on 22 July 2001) to US$1 = Rp 8,470 (on 15 August 2001). There is no guarantee whether this situation is sustainable, yet the positive sentiment from the market seems to indicate that people have been sickened by political uncertainty under Gus Dur's presidency. Although most Indonesians may not get a full guarantee of an immediate economic recovery from Megawati, yet they may have been satisfied with the end of bickering among the elite circles that have brought uncertainty to Indonesian politics.

# 4 NGOs in Indonesia
## Strategies and approaches

### NGOs and the New Order government

For a long time self-reliant activities have been developed in Indonesia, particularly among the rural people, as a form of 'collective action' that can be defined as the conditions in which people act together in pursuit of common ends (Kartodirdjo 1988: 97). They have been rooted deeply in the tradition of *gotong royong* (mutual help) in which people carry out voluntary activities to help each other in building houses, digging wells or in a situation of emergency (death, illness and so on) (Koentjaraningrat 1961: 3–4; Kartjono 1988: 30; Prijono 1992: 440). These activities were exercised through a number of self-help groups such as *arisan* (credit-and-saving rotation groups) *lumbung paceklik* (food security groups), *kelompok kematian* (burial associations), *selapanan* (weekly meeting groups), *beras perelek* (burial insurance groups), and the like whose activities continue to survive, especially in rural areas (Tjondronegoro 1984: 16; Sinaga 1994: 59).

In the colonial era, voluntary activities were often associated with organisations such as *Budi Utomo, Taman Siswa, Sarekat Islam, Nahdlatul Ulama* and *Muhammadiyah* (Sinaga 1994: 81). Two organisations (*Budi Utomo* and *Taman Siswa*) were devoted to the promotion of education among the indigenous people who had no access to the Dutch formal schools (Rahardjo 1988: 11). *Sarekat Islam* was established by Muslim traders to challenge Indonesian Chinese domination in the production and distribution of batik (Shiraishi 1990: 41). Two other organisations (*Nahdlatul Ulama* and *Muhammadiyah*) were active in the nurture of *pesantren*,[1] education and the provision of health care to the poor (Nakamura 1983: 3; Barton 1997: 327). In the post-colonial era, some of these organisations survived and continued to play a community development role. Some new groups were formed during the 1950s and 1960s to represent the interests of grassroots people. These groups can be associated with a number of PKI-affiliated organisations such as the BTI (Indonesian Peasants Group), *Pemuda Rakyat* (People's Youth) and GERWANI (Indonesian Women's Movement), which operated at the village level (Mortimer 1974: 366; Hainsworth 1983: 46). Despite their success in mobilising grassroots support, these left-wing organisations were dissolved following the New Order government's policy to demolish the PKI and other left-wing mass organisations.

## NGOs in the 1970s and early 1980s

Although self-help grassroots organisations have been active in Indonesia for generations, development-oriented organisations became more visible only in the late 1960s and early 1970s. A new wave of self-help initiatives followed from a period of attrition at the aftermath of 'the events of 1965' when a complicated conflict on the basis of ideological, political and *aliran* (streams) differences devastated the social fabric of Indonesian society (Kartjono 1988). The mutual hatred and killings among villagers had substantially increased fear among the state leaders that uncontrolled grassroots activities would generate violent conflicts. Under the New Order, villagers were precluded from political activity and no political party was permitted to form village level participatory groups amid the state's suspicion that organisational activities and cadre-forming at grassroots level would nurture the very 'subversive' idea that prosperity did not depend on state guidance (Hainsworth 1983: 46; McVey 1996: 24). As a result, grassroots organisational activities had become increasingly replaced by state-sponsored organisations such as KNPI (Indonesian National Youth Committee), SPSI (All Indonesia Workers' Union), HNSI (Indonesian Fishermen's Association), HKTI (Indonesian Farmers' Association), LMD (Village Consultative Assembly), LKMD (Village Defense Council), *Karang Taruna* (youth groups) and PKK (Family Welfare Guidance).

In the early 1970s, a number of organisations, such as *Bina Swadaya*, LP3ES (Institute for Social and Economic Research, Education and Information), LSP (Development Studies Institute), YLKI (Indonesian Foundation of Consumers' Organisations), P3M (Association for *Pesantren* and Community Development), YIS (Indonesian Welfare Foundation), *Sekretariat Bina Desa* (Village Development Secretariat), *Dian Desa* (a community development NGO based in Yogyakarta) and many others, were formed and dedicated entirely to community development and the promotion of self-management activities at village level (Hadad 1983: 3). By concentrating on community development, these organisations were able to convince the New Order government that they would not engage in grassroots political activities as the banned left-wing organisations had done in the early 1960s. Most of these organisations were initiated by concerned middle-class (ex-student activists, lawyers, academics, researchers and religious leaders) and various religiously inspired groups, notably Christian churches and Islamic groups, to develop a capacity for co-operation and organisation among community groups (Billah and Nusantara 1988: 16–17; Sinaga 1994: 54; Saragih 1995: 12–13). Although they started their operation in Java, many of them extended their activities to include some parts of Sumatra, Kalimantan, Bali, Lombok and Nusa Tenggara Timur. In order to control their activities, the New Order government issued a special decree No. 81/1967 which authorised the Committee of Foreign Technical Assistance (whose members were appointed by President Suharto) to monitor and administer all organisations receiving foreign assistance (Sinaga 1994: 220). This decree was implemented in conjunction with the government's regulation on Overseas Technical Co-operation and Assistance, issued by the Ministry of Home Affairs on 7 September 1973, which required foreign agencies to sign agreements covering general objectives and operation procedures with relevant state departments before they would start their co-operation with local NGOs (Eldridge 1989: 6).

However, having realised that NGOs could be a useful adjunct in the official campaign to overcome rural poverty and to enhance life opportunities for villagers, government officials often turned a blind eye to these regulations by allowing NGOs to bypass bureaucratic procedures in establishing contacts with foreign agencies (Hainsworth 1983: 47). This move arose from the belief that various development programmes in the areas of health care, nutrition, rural credit, non-formal education, community development, small-scale industries, environmental protection, appropriate technology and drinking water had, in general, been successfully achieved through experiments pioneered by NGOs which received foreign assistance (Hadad 1983: 7). One most plausible explanation for the positive government–NGO relations was the decline of state revenues (as a result of the fall in oil prices in the international market) which made development programmes more dependent on initiatives from the local society, especially the NGO sector. Throughout the 1980s, central government expenditures decreased, while the state's debt burden increased dramatically. As a percentage of total expenditures, debt charges jumped from 6.7 per cent in 1980 to 33.2 per cent in 1988 (see Table 4.1). The three components of the budget which had been squeezed to make room for the heavy burden of debt servicing were: (1) non-debt routine expenditures (salaries, wages and recurrent expenses on items such as office supplies), which decreased from 42.8 per cent in 1980 to 29.7 per cent in 1988; (2) non-aid development expenditures, which included capital expenditures by state departments and other government agencies, development grants to regional governments and *Inpres* (presidential instruction) allocations from 38.3 per cent in 1980 to 13.0 per cent in 1988; and (3) government subsidies including those on fertilizer, seeds and pesticides and government equity participation in public enterprises from 18.5 per cent in 1980 to 3.0 per cent in 1990 (see Table 4.1).

The decline in domestic revenues rendered the apparently low-cost alternative offered by NGOs relatively attractive (Hannam 1988: 12). There was a growing realisation within the government that its own agencies would not achieve effective outreach or mobilise sufficient community support on their own to implement official programmes aimed at the urban and rural poor, without at least some assistance from intermediary organisations (Eldridge 1995: 30). Thus, despite the fear that NGOs might somehow disturb the state's attempt to de-politicise society, the government invited NGOs to play greater roles in community development activities as stipulated in the *Ketetapan MPR* (parliamentary decree) on GBHN (the general outline of state policies) No. II/MPR/1983 which called for more attention to *pemerataan* (distribution) of welfare in which the government must 'create a basic framework which would allow people to develop through their own strength' (Hadad 1983: 3–5). A more explicit recognition of NGO activities was granted by the government in the environmental sector in which the *Undang Undang Lingkungan Hidup* (Law of the Protection of the Environment) No. 4/1982 guaranteed a greater role for NGOs and society in

*Table 4.1* Trends in major components of central government expenditures, 1980–1990

| Fiscal year beginning | Percentage of total expenditures | | | | |
| --- | --- | --- | --- | --- | --- |
| | Non-debt routine | Debt servicing | Development expenditures of non-project aid | Development expenditures financed by aid | Total subsidies[a] |
| 1980 | 42.8 | 6.7 | 38.3 | 12.2 | 18.5 |
| 1981 | 43.4 | 6.7 | 37.9 | 12.0 | 19.6 |
| 1982 | 40.2 | 8.5 | 37.9 | 13.4 | 14.3 |
| 1983 | 34.5 | 11.5 | 32.9 | 21.1 | 12.5 |
| 1984 | 34.3 | 14.3 | 33.8 | 17.6 | 10.6 |
| 1985 | 37.8 | 14.6 | 32.3 | 15.3 | 7.4 |
| 1986 | 38.8 | 23.1 | 20.7 | 17.3 | 4.9 |
| 1987 | 34.4 | 30.4 | 15.0 | 20.1 | 6.4 |
| 1988 | 29.7 | 33.2 | 13.0 | 24.1 | 3.3 |
| 1989 | 32.5 | 31.3 | 14.2 | 22.1 | 3.1 |
| 1990 | 31.4 | 30.3 | 18.2 | 19.6 | 3.0 |

Source: Bank Indonesia. 1990. *Indonesian Financial Statistics*. Jakarta: Bank Indonesia.

Note
a Includes subsidies in both the routine and development budgets. Subsidies for foodstuff and petroleum products are included in the routine budget; those for fertilizer, seeds and pesticides government equity participation are included in the development budget.

general in the protection of the environment (Hardjasoemantri 1985: 155). Even President Suharto himself appealed for the 'assistance and participation of the whole Indonesian people because development could no longer be delivered by the state sector alone' (Pinney 1983: 40). Various regulations on NGOs were not fully implemented and government officials at various levels often offered their personal guarantee to allow NGOs to have a certain degree of freedom of operation (Hendrata 1983: 28; Kusumohadi, interview, 25/07/1997). A monthly dialogue involving NGO leaders and state officials as well as military leaders was held at both provincial and national levels to share information regarding community development activities and state development policies (INGI 1991: 3–4). During the 1970s, NGOs and the state were able to develop a relatively amiable relationship to the extent that state agencies often sub-contracted parts of their projects to NGOs and invited them to serve as consultants and training agencies for local bureaucrats, village heads, cadres, co-operative managers and community development volunteers (Hainsworth 1983: 48).

## *NGOs in the mid-1980s and 1990s: 'de-ideologisation' and 'de-politicisation'*

From the mid-1980s, however, Indonesian NGOs entered a new era in which the state sought to co-opt or in some ways neutralise NGO activities through some combination of 'sticks' and 'carrots' (Eldridge 1989: 5). The New Order government's stiffer approach towards NGOs was a manifestation of Suharto's attempt to impose the 'de-ideologisation' and 'de-politicisation' strategies in which no organisations were allowed to pursue any ideology other than *Pancasila*; they were not allowed to carry out any activity without the government's consent (Lubis 1993: 214). Some argued that this changing policy direction was prompted by the growing anti-Suharto campaign in the late 1970s and the early 1980s whereby students and radical Islamic preachers in Jakarta, Bandung, Yogyakarta and Solo expressed their anti-government sentiments in various seminars, discussions, *pengajian* (Koran readings) and publications.

In 1985, the government issued *Inpres* (presidential instruction) No. 32/1985 which authorised the newly formed *Biro Kerjasama Teknik Luar Negeri* (Overseas Technical Co-operation Bureau) – supervised by the Minister of Cabinet Secretariat – to administer all projects financed by foreign agencies. This bureau held responsibility to issue permissions for international NGOs operating in Indonesia. Permission was issued if NGOs had fulfilled two requirements: (1) approval from BAKIN (State Intelligence Co-ordinating Board), which usually carried out investigations and decided whether or not the corresponding organisations were idologically and politically 'safe' for the Indonesian government and society; and (2) an Memorandum of Understanding (MoU) with the relevant state departments – that is, those carrying out environmental activities must sign an MoU with the Ministry of Population and Environment, religious activities with the Department of Religious Affairs, agricultural activities with the Department of Agriculture, and so forth (Lubis 1993: 225; Sinaga 1994: 222–3).

The most important and controversial regulation, however, was the *UU Ormas* (an Indonesian acronym for the law controlling mass organisations) No. 8/1985 which was originally designed to govern the activities of all mass organisations (political parties, interest groups, trade unions, professional associations and grassroots organisations), but was later extended to include NGOs (Karebet 1986: 31). Under this law, all organisations already in existence were required to give written notice or re-register with the Ministry of Home Affairs. More importantly, the law contained the concept of *Azas Tunggal Pancasila* (*Pancasila* as the sole ideology) which all organisations were obliged to accept. Some of its articles indicated the government's attempt to control, depoliticise, and impose a corporatist mode of representation that can be summarised as follows:

- Articles 2, 3 and 4 stipulate that all mass organisation must adopt the state ideology, *Pancasila*, as their sole ideology.
- Articles 8 and 12 oblige all mass organisation with similar activities to form an umbrella organisation in order to allow government to carry out its main 'duties' of *pembinaan* (guidance) and *pengembangan* (development).
- Article 13 authorises the government to dissolve the board of trustees of any organisation which: (1) conducts activities that disrupt public law and order; (2) receives foreign assistance without the government's consent; and (3) helps foreign organisations whose activities pose serious threats to Indonesia's national interests.

- Articles 14, 15 and 16 authorise the government to ban or dissolve any organisations which fail to comply with all conditions set in the law or disseminate communism or any other idology that contradicts *Pancasila* (Billah and Nusantara 1988: 19–20).

A key area of controversy in *UU Ormas* was related to the definition of 'mass organisation' and whether or not NGOs were included in the term. Some commentators were misled by the *ormas* acronym. On the one hand, assuming that it referred only to mass organisations (*organisasi massa*), they assumed that such a term did not fit with the general characteristics of NGOs which have no membership base and operate as representatives of the general interests of the society rather than as professional, religious or politically oriented organisations. On the other hand, the government insisted that the term used in the law was *organisasi kemasyarakatan* (societal organisations), namely those organisations 'formed voluntarily by Indonesian citizens on the basis of similar activity, profession, function, religion and purpose' which clearly covered a far broader community context including NGOs (Karebet 1986: 31; Eldridge 1989: 7). Confusion was apparent within government circles to the extent that the then Minister of Home Affairs, Suparjo Rustam, leaned towards the first interpretation, while other agencies such as ABRI's Directorate of Social and Political Affairs, the Ministry of Political and Security Affairs, and the Department of Defense followed the second interpretation (Lubis 1993: 234).

In order to eliminate the confusion, the government issued other regulating devices. In 1986, the government regulation (*Peraturan Pemerintah*) No. 18/1986 was introduced in conjunction with *UU Ormas* which obliged NGOs to: (1) register and report their constitution, activity, funding sources and the composition of their organisational structures to the Ministry of Home Affairs; and (2) co-ordinate their activities with relevant state departments (Sinaga 1994: 214). Another regulation, the Instruction of the Minister of Home Affairs (*Inmendagri*) No. 8/1990, was enacted to monitor and control NGO activities at the provincial and district levels. This regulation gave the authority to provincial governors and district heads to: (1) make an inventory of the number of NGOs and monitor their activities in respective provinces or districts; (2) make sure that NGOs co-ordinate their activities with the relevant government agencies; and (3) present a regular detailed report of NGO activities under their jurisdictions to the Ministry of Home Affairs (Sinaga 1994: 215). In 1995, the government issued a joint decree (SKB/*Surat Keputusan Bersama*) involving the Ministry of Home Affairs and the Department of Social Affairs. While using the term *mitra pembangunan* (development partner) to describe NGO-government relations, the SKB obliged all NGOs to accept government supervision which included: (1) *pembinaan politik* (political supervision) to be carried out by the Ministry of Home Affairs; and (2) *pembinaan teknis* (technical supervision) to be exercised by the relevant state departments: NGOs carrying out agricultural activities must be supervised by the Ministry of Agriculture, legal aid NGOs by the Ministry of Justice, environmental NGOs by the Ministry of Population and Environment, and so forth (Kusumohadi *et al.* 1997: 48).

The impact of these regulations on NGOs' general activities was obvious. First, as a result of the imposition of *Azas Tunggal Pancasila*, NGOs suffered from a serious 'de-ideologisation'. There was no room for NGOs to nurture a strong ideological basis which would have been crucial in guiding their attempt to generate a movement (Billah and Nusantara 1988: 20). Second, in order to escape from the government's control, many NGOs felt it necessary to register with the notary as a foundation (*yayasan*).[2] For both political and practical purposes, a notary's certificate could provide the necessary legal basis for NGOs' existence. More importantly, registration as *yayasan* would make NGOs 'exempt' from *UU Ormas* because, together with private business institutions, *yayasan* were regulated under *Kitab Undang Undang Hukum Dagang* (the commercial law) and were relatively 'immune' from government intervention (Eldridge 1989: 7–8; Bunnell 1996: 198). Third, the government's attempt to put NGOs under its umbrella organisation or amalgamate them in ways which would render them more subject to control had reinforced the need to form networking groups. In encouraging organisations to merge, the *penjelasan* (elucidation) of *UU Ormas* offered examples of corporatist organisations such as KNPI and HKTI, both of which were under Golkar's control. NGOs sought to counter this danger by establishing their own networks and forums with or without government involvement (Lubis 1993: 220). This was a difficult task since NGOs had to make sure that such networks would not threaten the government's interests and, at the same time, maintain unity amid the conflicting interests and approaches among their members (Kartjono 1986: 2; Setiawan 1986: 3; Lubis 1993: 219). Moreover, smaller NGOs tended to resent what they saw as a growing concentration of power and resources in the hands of larger NGOs, which subsequently led them to resist co-ordinating structures promoted by large NGOs (Eldridge 1989: 8). Fourth, in order to ensure freedom of operation in the face of these excessive regulations, NGOs tended to nurture strong leadership with the capacity and power to lobby and negotiate with government officials at various levels to exempt the organisations from obligation to report their activities, funding sources and 'accept' government supervision. Indeed, the presence of strong leadership was crucial for most NGOs to ensure their survival and room to manoeuvre (Billah and Nusantara 1988: 22). This situation persisted at least until May 1998 when the New Order government eventually collapsed. In the post-Suharto era, the introduction of a new political law by President Habibie – which allowed political parties and mass organisations to nurture their own ideologies – had granted Indonesian NGOs the political freedom much needed to facilitate the democratic transition. How Indonesian NGOs respond to this new situation will be discussed later in this chapter.

## *Growing NGO–government tension in the 1990s*

Throughout the 1990s, relations between NGOs and the Indonesian government tended to deteriorate. Factors such as the change in the state–society relations (in which popular resistance began to grow) and the change in the regime itself (in which political leaders started to feel threatened by NGOs' mobilisation activities) seemed to have contributed to the decline. Suspicion of NGOs' clandestine activities among state officials and military circles began to arise. They saw NGOs as potential subverters of the de-politicised village stability and submissiveness or as interlopers in the domain for which the government felt primarily or exclusively responsible (Juliantara 1997: 18–19). This view developed as a result of the growing popular resistance in the 1990s. Military leaders were particularly disturbed by NGOs' tendency to organise at the grassroots level and they assumed NGO activities at village level masked political agitation (Billah 1996: 172–3). Consequently, the personal guarantee of some freedom of operation from various state officials was no longer available and the regular NGO–government dialogue was subsequently terminated (Kusumohadi, interview, 25/07/1997). Neither the Minister of Home Affairs, General Yogie S. Memet, nor the military Chief of Staff for Social and Political Affairs, Lieutenant General Syarwan Hamid, showed any interest in maintaining the dialogue as they believed that NGOs had 'betrayed' the state by telling the international community about the Indonesian government's incompetence, corrupt behaviour and other misdemeanours (INFID 1994: 13; Kusumohadi *et al.* 1997: 178). State officials were always ambiguous in their view of NGO activities. For example, Emil Salim, the then Minister of Population and Environment, on one occasion, recognised and praised NGOs' contribution to the official development programmes on which he commented:

> Ever since they first emerged, NGOs in Indonesia have demonstrated a positive role. They are able to identify problems in society even before the government has thought about them. Family planning is a clear example in which PKBI (an NGO specialised in the family planning) has taken the initiative in devising a family welfare programme, while in the area of environmental management *Dian Desa* (an income-generating NGO) has thought about conservation long before the government does.
> 
> (Salim 1983: 71)

But at the same time, he stressed that the government would not tolerate those NGOs pursuing ideologies other than that of the state. As he put it:

> As long as the differences (between NGOs and the government) only concern problems of project implementation, the NGOs' right to exist is guaranteed. But if the differences concern more 'philosophical' matters, that is, differences in ideology or national interest, then clearly NGOs with this type of differences will not have the right to exist.
> 
> (Salim 1983: 71)

For Salim, and indeed many other government officials, NGOs should be both encouraged and restrained. They had to be encouraged as long as they concentrated on welfare programmes; but they should be restrained when they failed to comply with the state's ideology (Prajitno 1986: 2; Saragih 1995: 21–2).

The most important factor which had caused the decline of NGO–government relations in the 1990s, however, was the change within the NGO community itself, that is, the growing number of radical organisations with a deliberate attempt to challenge government policies. Charges that NGOs have become increasingly 'political' followed in which government officials invariably accused NGOs, especially those which attempted to organise the poor, of: (1) encouraging a split between the people and the government; (2) encouraging religious extremism and disunity; (3) confusing the people about the aims of the government's development policies; and (4) exposing the government's mistakes and shortcomings that often cause officials to lose face (Nusantara 1996: 20–1; Kusumohadi *et al.* 1997: 161–2). NGOs, on the other hand, accused the state of being crippled by corruption, nepotism and inefficiency. Many of them believed that there is no way government programmes can effectively reach the poor if implemented through a bureaucratic and 'top-down' approach (Mahasin 1996: 3–4; Fakih 1996: 72–3). Civil servants were often considered by NGO activitists as playing elaborate games whereby unrealistic instructions received from the top were subverted or misapplied; and glowing reports of success were sent back up the line according to the principle of *asal bapak senang* (an attitude of chronic sycophancy) (Lay 1996: 24).

The first direct confrontation between NGOs and the New Order government was manifested in the so-called 'Brussels incident' of 1989 in which a number of NGOs were 'punished' for jeopardising Indonesia's national interests by telling the international community of the government's misdemeanours. This incident was followed by other open conflicts. Between 1990 and 1998, NGOs became increasingly active in pursuing their anti-corruption, human rights and environmental campaigns. In most of their campaigns, the government was often accused of being incapable of fighting corruption and superficial in protecting human rights.

## *INGI and the 'Brussels incident'*

In June 1985, a network called INGI (International NGO Group on Indonesia) was formed by several Indonesian NGOs – YLBHI, WALHI and *Sekretariat Bina Desa* – in co-operation with a number of Dutch NGOs such as NOVIB (the Netherlands Organisation for International Development Co-operation), CEBEMO (Catholic Organisation for Joint Financing of Development Programmes), HIVOS (Humanistic Institute for Co-operation with Developing Countries) and ICCO (Inter-Church Co-ordination Committee for Development Projects). Initially, this network was aimed at providing the IGGI (Inter-Governmental Group for Indonesia), an international aid consortium for Indonesia led by the Dutch government, with advice and information on IGGI-sponsored development projects; but later it expanded its activity to include attempts to form joint action to influence the Indonesian government's development policies through international advocacy and lobbying (Eldridge 1995: 195).

A secretariat was established, one in the Hague and another in Jakarta, to administer its daily activities. A dialogue was held annually between INGI's appointed delegations and IGGI's officials mostly outside Indonesia. International advocacy was carried out through regular gatherings of INGI's participating organisations and delegations from IGGI's members as well as other relevant agencies such as the World Bank, the Asian Development Bank and the IMF. Each conference produced an important *aide memoire* summarising INGI's recommendations which was presented to IGGI's member countries, e.g. Australia, Belgium, Canada, France, Germany, Italy, Japan, the United Kingdom and the United States (INGI 1991: 7–10). Formal letters were sent on an occasional basis to particular governments of the developed countries and international development agencies to raise issues or problems entailing various development projects in Indonesia. INGI also participated in the hearing conducted by the US Congress in Washington, DC reporting possible misconducts committed by Indonesian state officials in the implementation of US-sponsored development projects (INGI 1990: 14). With these activities, INGI has gained international recognition as a network capable of synthesising understanding of participatory and sustainable development with broader concerns for democracy and human rights within the Indonesian NGO community and of communicating these ideas to wider domestic and international audiences (Eldridge 1995: 201).

The New Order government began to worry that NGOs' greater access to the international community might increase international pressures on Suharto's authoritarian rule and boost demands for democratisation. It was particularly disturbed by INGI's tendency to distribute information about frequent abuse of power, corruption and atrocities committed by state officials to the international community. The conflict between INGI and the Indonesian government erupted in the so-called 'Brussels incident'. In April 1989, the fifth INGI conference (held in Brussels) highlighted the environmental damage resulting from the World Bank-sponsored development projects in the areas of mining and dam constructions in Indonesia. Particular criticism was directed against the Kedung Ombo dam project in Central Java in which the government was severely criticised for its use of political intimidation and its failure to provide adequate compensation to the dispossessed villagers (Sinaga 1994: 172; Eldridge 1995: 198). The conference further demanded a full social impact assessment before projects similar to Kedung Ombo could be implemented in Indonesia.

In July 1989, following a cabinet meeting in Jakarta – which concluded that the Brussels INGI conference had resulted in several European countries announcing their intention to withdraw funds from various 'problematic' development projects in Indonesia – the government started to launch its attack on NGOs (Eldridge 1995: 198). General Try Sutrisno, the Armed Forces Commander, issued various statements condemning NGO activists for jeopardising Indonesia's national interest when conducting activities abroad, while Emil Salim, the then Minister of Population and Environment, warned environmental activists against playing a political card and suggested a 'my country, right or wrong' approach in their dealings with foreigners (*Kompas*, 21 July 1989). A number of vocal NGO activists attending the Brussels INGI conference were subsequently banned from travelling overseas (*Kompas*, 18 August 1989).

100  *NGOs in Indonesia: strategies and approaches*

The government's irritation with INGI and IGGI culminated in April 1992 when President Suharto announced the dismissal of IGGI. Moved by its antipathy to liberal democratic values, as well as an enduring nationalist sensitivity, the New Order regime abruptly rejected all further official governmental assistance from the Netherlands (IGGI's co-ordinator), which it accused of infringing upon Indonesian sovereignty by attaching political strings to its assistance (INFID 1994: 19). This incident subsequently made the existence of INGI irrelevant. A few months later, when CGI (Consultative Group for Indonesia) was set up as a replacement for IGGI, INGI was also transformed into INFID (International NGO Forum for Indonesian Development). Although this alteration did not bring much change to INGI/INFID's general operation, except that the Dutch government's position in regular consultation activities was taken over by the World Bank, it had nevertheless affected official aid channelled through Dutch NGOs to Indonesian NGOs, particularly the YLBHI (Indonesian Legal Aid Foundation), whose funding came almost entirely from NOVIB (INFID 1994: 4). Even if it was unclear whether IGGI's dismissal was deliberately meant to incapacitate NGOs' activities, this incident produced a serious blow for YLBHI and many other local NGOs funded by Dutch NGOs (Bunnell 1996: 184).

*The growing NGO-sponsored protest action*

By the mid-1990s, with more complex problems in the areas of human rights, economic exploitation, alienation and repression, NGOs began to increase their 'empowerment' and 'mobilisation' activities. From their experience NGOs learnt that although some progress had been made in their community development programmes (as target groups increased their income and skills), the structures that caused poverty still persisted; and the state showed no interest in adopting policies that would favour the poorest (Billah 1996). Rather than providing short-term or temporary relief for the poor, a new group of activists proposed a more progressive role for NGOs in generating mass-based resistance and collective action to challenge norms, values, structures and institutions that had been causing injustice and oppression (Rahardjo 1985: 80; Billah 1996: 173). This function was carried out by organisations active in legal aid, human rights, environment, women's movement and street children advocacy such as YLBHI, WALHI, SBPY, Kalyanamitra, Yasanti, Humana and many others. These NGOs increased their resistance and attempted to forge popular collective action by linking with various grassroots organisations and associations. They demanded the elimination or reduction of the damaging impacts of large state-licensed logging, mining, plantation and manufacturing activities on the local people and environment in Sumatra, Java, Kalimantan and Irian Jaya (Mayer 1996: 203).

Resistance was also conducted in the form of legal battles against the state agencies. In September 1994, for example, eight Jakarta-based NGOs, led by WALHI, filed a case against President Suharto for issuing *Keppres* (presidential decree) No. 42/1994 allowing IPTN (the Indonesian Aircraft Industry) to use a US$200 million reforestation fund collected from logging companies which was supposed to finance forest conservation projects (*Kedaulatan Rakyat*, 23 September 1994). A number of protests and street demonstrations were also initiated by NGOs demanding an immediate end of the use of *rekayasa politik* (polical engineering) and coercion by the government in repressing labour movements, in intimidating peasants in land settlement cases, in stigmatising opposition parties and in imposing censorship on the mass media and other publications (Billah 1994: 5–7; Tjajo 1994: 25; Munir 1996: 124–8; Fauzi 1996: 11). In December 1994, a group of NGO activists protested in the DPR (People's Representative Body) demanding the abolition of the military's dual function. They also called for a more active role of the legislative body in handling human rights violation cases such as the banning of the three leading weekly magazines, *Tempo, Editor* and *DeTik*, the Kedung Ombo land resumption case, the dissolution of a number of mass gatherings, and the unlawful detention of labour activists (INFID 1995: 2–3). While criticising the DPR of being the 'rubber stamp' of Suharto's policies, they also demanded the withdrawal of military representatives appointed directly by the president (*Republika*, 26 December 1994).

Other NGO-sponsored protests followed. On 3 May 1995, 30 activists representing different NGOs drafted a petition demanding the cancellation of government regulations controlling social gathering – especially the laws No. 5/1963, No. 20/1982 and parliamentary decree No. II/1993 – which obliged every organisation or institution to follow a complicated permission procedure involving *Kelurahan* (village administration), *Kecamatan* (sub-district administration), *Polsek* (sub-district police office), *Koramil* (sub-district military office) and *Ditsospol* (the local directorate of social and political affairs) (*Berita Nasional*, 4 May 1995). On 12 January 1996, NGO activists from Jakarta, Surabaya, Malang and Yogyakarta demonstrated outside the parliament demanding a just and fair election and the formation of an independent committee to supervise the electoral process (*Yogya Post*, 13 January 1996). These protests and many other similar activities had undoubtedly caused further deterioration in NGO–government relations which culminated in 1996 when the government started their campaign to systematically thwart radical NGOs in which activists were detained, interrogated and threatened (YLBHI 1997: 20).

## The rise of 'development' and 'movement' NGOs

One of the immediate effects of the New Order government's 'de-ideologisation' and 'de-politicisation' policies was that Indonesian NGOs had become increasingly divided between those who endorsed and those who challenged the state's regulations. Lubis (1993: 239–42) noted that in their response to the *UU Ormas*, Indonesian NGOs were divided into two groups: (1) the 'co-operative' group which agreed to endorse the law and to be co-operative with the government; and (2) the 'non-co-operative' group which decided to reject the law and confront the government. This division showed a great deal of similarity with the attitudes of the pro-independence Indonesian voluntary groups towards the colonial government in the early twentieth century, in which they were divided into the 'co-operative' and the 'non-co-operative' groups. While the co-operative party agreed to restrain themselves from developing anti-colonial feeling, the non-co-operative decided to promote anti-colonial sentiment which led to the imprisonment of their leaders (McVey 1996: 23). NGOs in the New Order government were divided because not all of them were prepared to face the risks of a confrontational strategy. Some of them, due to their religious backgrounds, ideological orientations and political perceptions, decided to 'play safe' by complying with the conditions set down by the New Order government and by limiting their activities to sectors that will not arouse political controversies. Others, due to their political ambitions, radical orientations and insistence on being part of social movements, decided to challenge the government. This division became more institutionalised, especially when NGO activists used various theoretical and ideological propositions to justify their political position, mission, purpose and type of activity.

Fakih (1996) divided Indonesian NGOs into three different clusters. First, 'conformist' NGOs which show a great deal of similarity with Korten's 'first-generation' or Elliott's 'welfare' NGOs. According to Fakih (1996: 125), this type of organisation prefers to 'play safe' by focusing on charity-based activities (child care, nursery, disaster relief programmes and the like) in order to provide temporary relief to those who need help. Most of these NGOs operate under various religious groups and carry out projects as a manifestation of their faith and belief. Rather than speaking about structural changes, these NGOs tend to accept the existing social–political structures. Second, 'reformist' NGOs which focus on attempts to increase the productive activity of the poor. Just as they believe that poverty is caused by the absence of productive mentality and the lack of spirit to achieve progression, these NGOs attempt to produce changes by injecting the principles of entrepreneurship and achievement motives through a variety of programmes such as training of particular skill areas (handicrafts, food processing, prawn farming and the like), small credits, management and marketing expertise, micro-enterprise development, and so on (Fakih 1996: 128). Rather than expecting people to resist current social and political structures, this group of NGOs prefers to help people increase their capacity to perform proper small-scale business activities. This category is similar to Korten's 'second-generation' or Elliott's 'developmental' NGOs. Third, 'transforming' NGOs. Believing that poverty is a result of a political process and that NGOs should help the marginalised people to remove structural factors that cause their marginalisation, this type of NGO appears to be similar to Korten's 'third-generation' and Elliott's 'empowerment' NGOs. In Fakih's view, the main duty of these NGOs is to organise popular groups, to build people's awareness of their economic and political rights, to mobilise them to challenge structures that cause their destitution and to represent them in their conflicts with institutions of the state and of the market (Fakih 1996: 132).

Meanwhile, as has been mentioned in Chapter 2, Eldridge (1995) classified Indonesian NGOs into three categories. The first category is known as the 'high-level co-operation-grassroots development' approach. It follows from a two-pronged strategy of (1) pursuing small-scale programmes directly at village level, specifically targeted towards disadvantaged groups which are encouraged to manage their affairs on a self-reliant basis; and (2) seeking to enhance community participation in official development programmes (Eldridge 1995: 36). NGOs in this category show no interest in changing the political process as such, although they are active in promoting their core values of self-reliance, participatory development and entrepreneurship. This non-political approach is designed not only to safeguard their own freedom of operation from government intervention, but also to reflect the values of 'conflict avoidance' which are deeply rooted in many of Indonesia's various cultural systems, most notably among the Javanese. The second category, the so-called 'high-level politics-grassroots mobilisation' approach, refers to NGOs which are more critical of the New Order government's development philosophy and practice. While promoting awareness-building and the capacity of self-organisation among specific target groups, this type of NGOs seeks legal status and protection against local officials and other influential people through contacts forged at higher levels of government (Eldridge 1995: 37). In recent years, these NGOs have become increasingly involved in areas such as legal aid, environmental management and informal sector advocacy. The third category is known as the 'empowerment from below' approach. It puts more emphasis on building awareness of rights and on attempts to generate social and political changes (Eldridge 1995: 38). Rather than acting as intermediaries which link the authorities to the people, these NGOs seek to develop confidence and skills among the people to enable them conduct their own negotiations with various agencies. These NGOs are also active in local group formation by forming grassroots constituencies. Women's and street children organisations are examples of this type of NGOs.

This study indicates that on the basis of their role, organisational philosophy, mission and objective, area of activity, view of poverty, relationship with their target groups and attitude towards the state, NGOs in Yogyakarta can be divided into at least two groups: 'development' and 'movement' NGOs. NGO activists whom I interviewed tended to describe their organisations either as '*LSM Pembangunan*' (development NGOs) or '*LSM Gerakan*' (movement NGOs). While the first type of NGO attempts to search for a more equitable and participatory development with an emphasis on small-scale enterprises, professional management and partnership with the government, the second type acts as social movements focusing on the formation of grassroots constituency, mobilisation and popular resistance. Although they share the ideal of helping the poor, the two types of NGOs differ in their solutions of poverty. On the one hand, development NGOs believe that the provision of education, capital and skill will solve the problems of poverty. Movement NGOs, on the other hand, suggest that grassroots resistance is the most important, if not the only, way to produce social and political transformations that will guarantee more justice and security for the underprivileged.

These NGOs are also separated by differences in their general views of development. On the one hand, development-oriented NGOs subscribe to a holistic theory of development by incorporating both 'individualism' and 'collectivism' which suggests a kind of syncretism required by NGOs to respond to the political flux of the 1990s. Movement-oriented NGOs, on the other hand, share the radical social analysis of Freire and critical theory as manifested in their continuous resistance to the New Order's use of the national creed of *Pancasila* to construct a hegemonic corporatist state ideology (Bunnell 1996: 191). In their attitudes towards the government, development NGOs appear to match Fakih's 'conformist' or Eldridge's 'high-level co-operation' categories in which they agree to fulfil all obligations stipulated in government regulations. Meanwhile, movement NGOs firmly reject any regulation and chose to confront the government instead. For these organisations, *UU Ormas* was not only a clear denial by the government of the principle of *kebebasan berserikat* (freedom of association), as stipulated in article 28 of the 1945 Constitution, but also an indication of the New Order's attempt to dominate society (Lubis 1993: 240). It was not surprising that facilitating grassroots resistance and challenge against the state should be the main agenda of movement NGOs. Table 4.2 summarizes the different roles and approaches of Indonesian NGOs in carrying out their activities.

*Table 4.2* Different orientations of 'development' and 'movement' NGOs

| Orientations | Development NGOs | Movement NGOs |
|---|---|---|
| The role of NGOs | As professional development institutions | As organised social movements |
| Organisational philosophy | Professional management, formal organisational structures, low profile, syncretic | Anti-bureaucracy, informal management, internal democracy, cracy, assertiveness, boldness |
| Missions and objectives | Improving production, management and marketing skills of target groups | Facilitating a countervailing force, democratisation and empowering civil society |
| Areas of activity | Health care, micro-enterprise development, small credit, animal husbandry, handicrafts production and trading, agriculture, and management training | Grassroots organisation, mobilisation, advocacy, training, popular education, seminars, discussions, workshops, protest and demonstration |
| View of poverty | Poverty is caused by the lack of skill, shortage of capital, poor health and lack of entrepreneurship | Poverty is caused by social injustice, political domination, economic exploitation and manipulation |
| Relationship with target groups | Unequal: NGO staff provide facilitation and guidance, while target groups act as recipients | Relatively equal: NGO staff provide advice, target groups act as active participants |
| Relationship with the government | Partnership, selective co-operations, conflict-avoidance | Critical collaboration, direct confrontation, opposition |

## From development to empowerment

Commentators argued that the role of development NGOs is that of 'mediator' or 'go-between', that is, linking various government agencies to potential target groups in a situation where state agencies are unable to reach out to the poorest due to geographical limitations (remoteness, inaccessibility and so on) or bureaucratic obstacles (hierarchy, formality, long procedures and so forth) (Hadad 1983; Kartodirdjo 1988: Setiawan 1996). As 'go-between', NGOs provide auxiliary means for implementing various official programmes at grassroots level, possibly by introducing perspectives and suggestions which might not otherwise have been considered by the government and by offering a flexible framework for experimentation in the search for workable solutions (Hainsworth 1983: 61). Using their target groups, NGOs are expected to help distribute the government's assistance and to ensure that such assistance is accessible to villagers in remote areas. The role of *Bina Swadaya* in non-collateral small-credit disbursement schemes involving state banks and village-based small enterprises and CD-Bethesda in providing low-cost health care to the poor in Yogyakarta and Central Java are examples of this type of role.

For many development NGOs, the only way to accommodate both the international appeal of participatory development and the demand by the New Order government policy of *Azas Tunggal Pancasila* was the imposition of a 'syncretic' view of development (Bunnell 1996: 192). In his attempt to outline the syncretic ideological basis of his organisation, Paulus Santosa, the former director of CD-Bethesda, for example, stated:

> A holistic development is not a kind of development that focuses simply on the achievement of material growth, it is an attempt to develop *kemandirian* (self-reliance) and *pemerataan* (equal distribution) in which everyone must act independently and receive an equal share of material benefits... In a holistic development, emphasis must be put on the preservation of both individual and community identities in which everyone must recognise his/her own rights and duties and respect those of others ... Thus, a holistic development must strike a balance between individual liberty and community welfare.
>
> (Santosa 1986: 89)

Whatever the risks and limitations, Santosa's cultural syncretism was at least suggestive of the process by which multi-cultural societies can forge a minimal cultural consensus (Bunnell 1996: 191). This syncretic view also showed a great deal of concurrence with the state's ideology, *Pancasila*, focusing on a balance between unity and diversity, individualism and collectivism, as well as democracy and dictatorship. Indeed, many NGO leaders whom I interviewed – especially Anton Soedjarwo (*Dian Desa*), Aleks Wiyarto (*Bina Swadaya*) and Sigit Wijayanto (CD-Bethesda) – expressed their support of Santosa's syncretic view of development as they believed that too heavy a concentration on Western concepts of individual liberty may provoke the accusation of being *anti-Pancasila*.[3]

There was also an issue of religion behind this syncretic view. In Indonesia, a high proportion of development NGOs were founded by Catholic and Protestant groups or individuals. Mohtar Mas'oed, an academic and NGO observer at Gadjah Mada University, Yogyakarta, argued that Christian groups and individuals dominated Indonesian voluntary activities in the areas of health care, education and income-generation because they had more of both the spirit of charity and the resources (manpower, money, organisations and international support) than any other religious groups to sustain their community development activities (Mas'oed, interview, 03/08/1997). However, Indonesian Christians have historically been experiencing great difficulties in determining the proper relationship between religious and political spheres. Given their minority status, they are bound to exercise a great deal of caution in expressing their social and political activism as well as in establishing links with people at grassroots level. Operating in a predominantly Islamic society, NGOs with Christian roots have tended to follow a conformist or accommodating approach to the extent that they must co-operate with the government whenever possible to ensure 'protection' against a possible accusation from radical Islamic groups of proselytizing the poor people through the distribution of material benefits (Eldridge 1995: 170).

This syncretism should therefore be seen as a strategy through which NGOs must avoid the most sensitive and explosive encounters by devising an ideology that would somehow enfold their Christian values in secular idioms that resonate in Java and do as little as possible to draw the criticism of the government (Bunnell 1996: 195). Syncretism will at some point prevent Christian NGOs from being associated with Latin America's liberation theology or Christian evangelism. As Sukur put it: 'Indonesian NGOs are just like a chameleon capable of changing colours in order not to be easily spotted by their enemies' (Sukur 1987: 23). However, some Catholic NGOs (strongly influenced by liberation theology) did attempt to organise the poor (squatters, street children and landless peasants). For example, the activities of the late Fr Mangunwijaya in organising squatters in Terban (Yogyakarta) and in advocating poor peasants in Gunung Kidul (Yogyakarta) and Kedung Pring (Central Java) in the 1980s and Fr Sandyawan with his ISJ (Jakarta Social Institute) in organising street children in Jakarta, had combined a non-violent approach to popular empowerment with a high-degree of sensitivity to local culture and context. As expected, these organisations had to face a great deal of resistance both from the government and the Islamic groups. While in the early 1990s Fr. Mangunwijaya decided to shift to a less risky activity in the field of education for the poor by establishing YDED (Primary Education Foundation), Fr Sandyawan continued his street children advocacy with great difficulty.

Operating as '*lembaga pembangunan profesional*' (professional development institutions) has been the main identity of most development NGOs, not only because they realise that involvement in more complicated programmes requires a high degree of professionalism, but also because foreign donors have begun to expect a certain degree of discipline in NGO administration (Fakih 1996: 171). Some NGOs began to design more bureaucratic-like hierarchical organisational structures in which directors are appointed on the basis of their capacity and specialisation, jobs are distributed formally (every position is defined by a fixed and clear description of tasks), programmes are implemented or evaluated according to a standarised operating procedure and informal job exchanges among staff members are not encouraged. But the extent to which NGOs can adopt professional management depends on the availability of human resources, capital and skill. Because not all NGOs have adequate human resources, funds and skills, developing a professional management is something that most NGOs in Indonesia still have to struggle with.

Financial security was also the main concern of development NGOs. Since the 1980s, NGO leaders have come to realise that running commercial projects – which was initially considered as a 'sin' for most NGOs – is the only way to ensure financial stability in the face of growing financial scrutiny imposed by foreign donors and of the difficulty to mobilise local financial resources (Maryono 1996: 63). By running commercial projects, development NGOs have expected to transform their target groups into small business enterprises capable of carrying out their own productive investments (Wardani 1995: 20). NGO leaders believe that distributing free services and grants to the poor is no longer effective because it could increase people's dependence on external help and could kill their spirit to fight for their own survival.[4] No longer treating villagers as beneficiaries receiving services free of charge, some NGOs began to develop a contract-based 'profit-and-risk' sharing activity with their target groups in running small enterprises in the fields of chicken breeding, handicrafts, crop growing, prawn farming, small-credit and the like. In these activities some charges or commissions were imposed (Sugiyanto and Wahyuni 1994: 31). This new approach has been implemented with such a high degree of confidence that villagers could cope with the new terms set by NGOs. As Aleks Wiyarto, the director of the Yogyakarta branch of *Bina Swadaya*, put it:

> It is wrong to assume that villagers are too poor or unsophisticated to perform effective small business activities. The success of the New Order government in improving the general condition and in providing education to the rural population has made them more capable of carrying out more productive activities and therefore pay for the services they get from us. In general, villagers are now potential business partners for NGOs.
> (Wiyarto, interview, 20/01/1997)

For him, and indeed some other NGO leaders in Yogyakarta, NGOs should no longer simply act as providers of basic services (sanitation, housing, health care and the like) but should also act as partners for the rural small enterprises in order to enable them to compete in a market-oriented economy both at the local and the national levels.

With regard to their organisational philosophy, development NGOs have tended to adopt a 'low profile' approach in which political controversies and strong words that may arouse suspicion from the government are avoided. In Eldridge's words:

> [D]evelopment NGOs... steadfastly avoiding political controversy in their public communications, and preaching a consistent message about helping poor people to form their own groups and define their own needs and solutions... If structural problems are mentioned, they are never confronted with any degree of precision or depth.
>
> (Eldridge 1995: 62)

Although development NGOs often use terminology that may associate them with radical activities such as *pemberdayaan* (empowerment), *pengorganisasian kaum tertindas* (organising the oppressed) and *memerangi kemiskinan* (alleviating poverty), they prefer to offer solutions by focusing on welfare and economic aspects, that is, helping the poor to get better access to education, health care, appropriate technology, managerial skills, marketing strategies and capital (Ismawan 1985: 4–5; Billah and Nusantara 1988: 17; Prijono 1996: 103). Consequently, development NGOs tend to develop an unequal relationship with their target groups in which NGO staff act as trainers or sometimes teachers, while target groups act as passive recipients of NGOs' services.

Having in mind that poverty is caused by the lack of capital, inadequate skills, poor knowledge of management and lack of motivation, staff members of development NGOs believe that their organisations can help alleviate poverty through the dissemination of the spirit of entrepreneurship, competition, innovation and book-keeping as well as the provision of small-credit schemes, appropriate technology, and marketing advice to their target groups (CPSM 1993: 9; Fakih 1996: 104). During the 1970s and 1980s, for example, NGOs' training programmes were based on Max Weber's description of the spirit of capitalism and David MacClelland's 'need for achievement' theory. Fakih recalled: 'Max Weber's *Protestant Ethic and the Spirit of Capitalism* and MacClelland's *The Achieving Society* had become *bacaan wajib* (compulsory reading) for many activists of development NGOs. These two books had undoubtedly shaped the view of many activists about human development' (Fakih, interview, 22/12/1996). Many activists are convinced that society's collective behaviour of 'capital accumulation' and of 'the need for achievement' are the key factors behind rapid economic development and modernisation in the Western world; and that such processes can be replicated in Indonesia (Fakih 1996: 73; Maryono 1996: 62).

In their relations with the government, development NGOs tend to adopt what Eldridge terms 'high-level co-operation' in which they develop selective co-operation with various state agencies in implementing official programmes, although they remain skeptical about the government's top-down approach. While critical comments and language – which may generate conflict – are avoided, constructive suggestions are only made whenever the opportunity arises (Eldridge 1995: 57). Some considered this 'conflict avoidance' approach as an indication of political compromise of Indonesian NGOs operating under the New Order government which regarded open criticism and protest as rebellious and therefore illegal (Dhakidae 1993: 4; Juliantara 1997: 12). Mahasin (1996: 6) noted that this type of approach reflects the tendency of most Indonesian NGOs to adopt *pendekatan jalan tengah* (middle-way approach), that is, to serve as implementers of various official development programmes when required, and secretly maintain relationship with target groups through their networks of cadres. Success is often judged on the basis of short-term achievements. Fakih (1996: 128–30) noted two common indicators of success in NGOs' project evaluation. First, tangible indicators in which NGOs consider a certain programme successful if their target groups secure more income, employ more people, increase their saving-and-borrowing activities, extend their sale and expand the number of outlets in the distribution of products. Second, intangible indicators whereby NGOs measure successful programmes on the basis of the capacity of target groups to adjust to modern business principles, to use appropriate technology, to perform proper business relations with commercial banks, to develop a proper book-keeping, and to master an effective marketing skill. But commentators were questioning the use of such indicators in measuring NGOs' performance. Billah and Nusantara (1988: 18), for example, argued that by focusing on economic indicators such as level of income, employment and the capacity to adjust to modern business practices, development NGOs had failed to touch on more structural problems such as economic exploitation, social injustice and government manipulation of popular participation. In a similar vein, Prijono (1996: 103), Ibrahim (1996: 11) and Setiawan (1996: 40) maintained that too heavy a concentration on economic aspects will reduce NGOs' role to become simply *pengrajin masyarakat* (social artisans) which means that their work demands a high degree of commitment or attention, but has no meaningful, long-term impact on society because structural problems that have caused poverty and destitution (social injustice, economic exploitation, political domination and marginalisation) remain untouched.

Since the late 1980s, self-criticism from activists towards NGOs' 'co-operation' with the Indonesian government have begun to appear in various writings, seminars and discussions held by radical activists. This self-criticism corroborated McVey's observation that NGO activists began to address much the same questions the *werkwilligen* (namely, the pro-independent activists who were willing to co-operate with the colonial government) had to ask themselves in the early twentieth century: whether their effort merely served to support the state's ends, and whether any freedom of action they appear to have won is simply a temporary indulgence rather than a real gain (McVey 1996: 24). One important self-criticism came from a meeting in Baturaden, Central Java, on 19 December 1990. The meeting was organised by activists who belonged to the 'non-co-operative' group. Assuming that 'partnership' with the government had separated NGOs from the underprivileged, these activists drafted a statement, known as *Deklarasi Baturaden* (the Baturaden declaration), proposing six corrective measures in which NGOs were expected to: (1) reassess their role in defending the interests of the marginalised people; (2) dissociate from the global capitalist mode of production in devising their poverty-alleviation programmes; (3) establish democratic and just internal structures; (4) treat target groups as key actors in project design and develop a system of accountability; (5) put more emphasis on advocacy, information sharing and the provision of political education based on the principles of *anti-kekerasan* (non-violence) and *solidaritas* (solidarity) with the oppressed; and (6) seek out their own resources and reduce their dependence on foreign funds (INGI 1991: 15–16; Billah 1996: 35). Eldridge (1995: 39) argued that the Baturaden declaration marked the new awareness, on the part of the NGO community in Indonesia, of the need to reposition their role in the new dynamics of state–society relations in which mobilisation, democratisation and self-sufficiency have become the important items on the agenda of action.

On 18–19 June 1993, another meeting in Cisarua, West Java, was organised by radical activists to declare their commitment to grassroots empowerment. Initiated by a group called Circle for Participatory Social Management (CPSM), this meeting addressed four important points. First, NGOs must help strengthen civil society and challenge the state's attempts to atomise, manipulate and dominate the society. Second, NGOs must free themselves from the state's policy of *kemitraan dari atas* (partnership from above) and serve as a 'counter-hegemonic' force in defending society from the state's domination. Third, NGOs should mobilise their resources and become more active in promoting democracy, social justice and the protection of human rights. Fourth, NGOs must increase their *daya transformasi* (transforming capacity) by developing critical thinking, political sensitivity and the ability to assess social and political problems (CPSM 1993: 17–18, 66–8). This meeting indicated a strong desire for transformation into what they called '*gerakan sosial terorganisir*' (organised social movements),[5] although it seemed rather peculiar that they did not mention any plan to establish their own constituencies or develop relations with other elements of movements such as students' groups, trade unions, professional associations and so forth. These proposals were reaffirmed in another meeting at Cepogo, Central Java, in August 1993. An action plan, called the 'Cepogo Plan', was drafted to drive NGOs further towards a social movement which included proposals to: (1) establish 'political education' programmes for NGO activists guided by a curriculum designed together to improve their capacity to assess current social, economic and political problems in society; and (2) prepare a practical guide for NGO activists with regard to the ways advocacy and mobilisation activities should be pursued (Mahmudi *et al*. 1994: 10). This meeting proposed a new role for NGOs, that is, to serve as a 'dynamic force' or 'facilitator' for the people whom they serve which included two crucial activities: (1) organising, that is, stimulating the motivation and awareness of target groups about the problems they face, identifying available resources, and endorsing their prospects for building a better future on the basis of their own self-reliant efforts; and (2) representing, that is, speaking on behalf of specific target groups and channeling their needs and aspirations to influence public policies (Billah 1996).

NGOs' move towards empowerment approach in the early 1990s was prompted by several reasons. First, the radicalisation of students' movements. Commentators noted that many student activists who were frustrated by the New Order government's tight control on campus activities, particularly the introduction of NKK/BKK in the late 1970s, began to channel their aspirations to the NGO sector (Aspinall 1995: 30; Bunnell 1996: 181; Uhlin 1997: 106). Setiawan (1996: 42) argued that students' groups have served both as major 'suppliers' of NGOs' human resources and 'providers' of radical political discourses since many of the repressed student activists joined existing NGOs or formed their own organisations. In the mid-1980s, a wave of radical groups, mostly based on student forums or study groups, emerged and formed coalitions with farmers, the landless, workers, urban squatters, women's groups and the informal sector to take specific grievances to the government. These groups expressed impatience with the apparent unwillingness of development NGOs to facilitate popular resistance (Eldridge 1995: 25). These radical groups had attempted to offer alternative solutions for social and development problems by making direct complaints about society's political rights (the rights to organise and to express their aspirations) which had been severely repressed by the New Order government (Fakih 1996: 5). Uhlin (1997: 183) argued that international events had a crucial impact on the radicalisation of Indonesian students since their pro-democracy campaigns were inspired by events such as the 'people's power' movement in the Philippines (1986–1987), the students' demonstrations in South Korea (1986–1987), the introduction of the idea of *glasnost* (openness) by Gorbachev in former Soviet Union (1986), the pro-democracy students' movement in China (1989), the massive pro-democracy movements that led to the fall of communist regimes in Eastern Europe (1989–1990) and the protest against military-backed government in Thailand (1992). In many seminars and discussions, student activists analysed the democratic transition in these countries and compared them with their own experience.

Second, the role of intellectuals was also instrumental in the radicalisation of NGO activities. In the 1970s, prominent figures such as Sritua Arief, Adi Sasono, Ismid Hadad, Aswab Mahasin and Farkhan Bulkin brought a radical perspective to the NGO community. Through a series of publications, seminars, workshops and discussions they introduced the Dependency Theory adopted from the works of Latin American scholars such as Theotonio dos Santos, Andre Gunder Frank, Osvaldo Sunkel, Gonzalez Casanova and others. They suggested to many activists that the key factor behind the deprivation in the periphery was a process of 'underdevelopment' in which profit was repatriated from the periphery to the centre states, the domestic resources of the periphery were expropriated by world capitalists through their domestic *compradores*, and the domestic labourers were exploited by foreign corporations (Arief and Sasono 1981; Fakih 1996). In the 1980s and 1990s, with more graduates from overseas working as academics and researchers, the opening of the theoretical outlook became more possible. Another group of intellectuals such as Arief Budiman, Ignas Kleden, Fr Mudji Sutrisno, Fr. Bonowiratmo, George Aditjondro and Ariel Heryanto, to name but a few, introduced some radical versions of social theory, notably Paulo Freire's theory of participatory action, the critical theory of the Frankfurt school, liberation theology and, at a later stage, post-modernism to the NGO community. Although most activists, due to their lack of interest and insufficient educational background, did not comprehend these theories – they often jokingly called various seminars discussing particular theories '*arisan kebingungan*' (confused gatherings) (*Kompas*, 24 September 1993) – they nevertheless agreed that poverty can only be solved if grassroots people are organised and trained in their basic rights in order to challenge structures that have caused their suffering and destitution (Thamrin 1993: 11).

Third, the growing repression, exploitation and marginalisation of the lower-class (peasants, workers, the informal sector and so on) had also contributed to the radicalisation of NGO activities. Nasikun (1995: 66) argued that the need for industrial expansion had generated a conflict of interests between the industrial and the agricultural sectors, particularly in Java, because land had been increasingly 'taken away' from peasants for factories and many other industrial establishments. In many cases, land confiscation (either by the government or by the private sector) was not followed by adequate compensations to the peasants due to the rampant corruption within the local authority and resistance was often met with intimidation and physical threats (Ismanto 1995: 124). Workers had also been increasingly exposed to exploitation and coercion in which their attempts to demand for higher salaries and better working conditions were often responded to terror and intimidation (INGI 1991: 25; Juliantara 1994: 4). Activists felt it necessary that NGOs establish grassroots constituencies to represent the interests of the oppressed in their protest and negotiation for better dealings.

Grassroots empowerment was undoubtedly the main agenda of many movement-oriented NGOs. Their activists were obsessed with the idea of participatory action research (PAR). Karlsen (1991: 47) defined PAR as a method of inquiry in which some of the people in the organisation or community being studied actively participate with the professional researcher throughout the research process from the initial design to the final presentation of results and the discussion of the implications of the action taken. PAR can be associated with Paulo Freire's idea of conscientisation, that is, a process of learning to perceive social, political and economic contradictions and to take action against the oppressive elements of reality (Thomas 1992: 136). Freire's writings, particularly *The Pedagogy of the Oppressed* (1972), set out clearly his revolutionary ideas on the liberating potential of education which combined learning to read and write with looking critically at one's social situation. He constantly placed the human search for freedom and justice in the context of oppression as he argued that to be fully human implies being active and reflective; and the fact that people may be passive and unthinkingly accepting of their situation is the result of their being oppressed (Freire 1972: 21–3).

Freire's ideas had been used by the proponents of PAR, notably Orlando Fals Borda, Robert Chambers, William Whyte and Anizur Rahman, to promote a 'science of the proletariat' with which the masses could conduct their own struggle for social transformation (Whyte 1982: 3; Rahman 1993: 81). They believed that the domination of masses by elites is rooted not only in the control over the means of material production but also over the means of knowledge production including the power to determine what is valid or useful knowledge (Fals Borda 1981: 48;

Chambers 1983: 145). In order to liberate the people, it is therefore important – according to the PAR method – to allow people to develop their own endogenous process of consciousness-raising and knowledge generation (Rahman 1993: 83).

Since the late 1980s PAR has been increasingly used by some radical NGO activists in Indonesia as a method of generating awareness among their constituencies of their social situation. The late Fr Mangunwijaya, a Catholic priest and NGO activist, was considered by many activists as one of the gurus of PAR. His idea of *pendidikan alternatif* (alternative education) was much influenced by Freire's idea of conscientisation. He argued that people's awareness is more than learning about knowledge of how to do things properly, it also includes people learning to think critically and independently (Mangunwijaya 1997: 1). In the early 1990s, Mansour Fakih, a radical NGO activist, together with some young activists, organised a series of seminars in Yogyakarta, Bandung and Salatiga aimed at disseminating the idea of PAR to the NGO community. They invited a selected number of NGO activists from all over the country to discuss the detail of the PAR method. They believed that the major aim of knowledge production is to increase people's understanding of their own situation and their ability to use such knowledge to generate changes for their own good, while the aim of generating knowledge that benefits the researchers is only secondary (Mahmudi *et al.* 1994: 33).

As far as the relationship with the government is concerned, movement-oriented NGOs tend to adopt a critical stance. Unlike development-oriented NGOs, they believe that democracy and justice can only be achieved through struggles rather than persuasion and that the government should be confronted in order to produce changes (CPSM 1993: 17). Movement-oriented NGOs also feel it necessary to dissociate from the New Order state's ideology and practice as they assume that the national slogan of *Bhinneka Tunggal Ika* (unity in diversity) – embedded in the *Pancasila* ideology – has been used and manipulated by the government to undermine the rise and maturation of Indonesian civil society (Aditjondro 1993: 20). With this idea in mind, leaders of movement-oriented NGOs propose a new 'political role' for NGOs, that is to say, to create an organisational platform and to rebuild solidarity among grassroots people to enable them to pursue collective action in challenging state domination and in influencing public policies (Fakih, interview, 22/12/1996; Mangunwijaya 1997: 24–6).

## NGOs in the post-Suharto: new opportunities, new challenges

In the post-Suharto era, the removal of all regulations controlling organisational activities has led to a substantial increase of the number of Indonesian NGOs to approximately 70,000 (in 2000). Both development and movement-oriented NGOs continue to exist, particularly after the 1997 financial crisis. Many of them are formed to distribute loans and grants from various international development agencies – the World Bank, IMF, USAID and so on – to the urban and rural poor, especially those who are badly affected by the financial crisis (urban workers, peasants and the like). Others are established to facilitate the democratic transition initiated since the beginning of Habibie's government. A few years after the fall of Suharto's regime, the presence of both development and movement-oriented NGOs is still relevant for at least two reasons. First, the growing poverty in both urban and rural areas as a consequence of the implementation of the structural adjustment policies[6] which generate unemployment, the removal of government subsidies on basic items and the collapse of the social security system. Poverty has opened up new opportunities for development NGOs to expand their charity, self-help and micro-enterprise activities to help the underprivileged. Second, an indication of conflict and public disorder throughout Indonesia during the transition period, which generates disillusion towards democracy. At the end of Gus Dur's presidency, for example, there was a growing demand among the conservative middle-class people of a possible return of an authoritarian regime. Having enjoyed a relatively stable political situation during Suharto's authoritarian rule, this group of people is convinced that more thorough control of political activities of the society will engender order and stability. This development has alarmed NGO activists of a possible disruption in the democratisation process. In order to keep the democratic transition going NGO community feels it necessary to scale up and replicate their democratic education and training programmes.

However, increased quantity does not necessarily mean higher quality. Among the newly formed NGOs, there must be some overnight operators which are established just to tap development funds for their own benefits. In Garut, West Java, for example, the staff of a newly formed NGO called Hipalapa was arrested and charged with skimming two billion *rupiah* (US$220,000) from a nation-wide farmers' credit programme (*Far Eastern Economic Review*, 20 September 2001). Similar cases are still awaiting trial in other places in East Java, Central Java, and North Sumatra. These cases highlight the impasse confronting Indonesia's vast NGO community. Once the backbone of *Gerakan Reformasi* (the reform movement) and a potential force for change, it now faces charges of corruption, incompetence and lack of discipline. Thus, although democratisation in the post-Suharto era has opened a new opportunity for NGOs, it also raises new challenges regarding NGOs' capacity to facilitate the democratisation and to maintain the trust once put in them by their beneficiaries, donors and the public.

Facilitating a democratic transition is one possible role for Indonesian NGOs in the post-Suharto era. Their access to grassroots organisations and their commitment to empower the marginalised groups have generated optimism that NGOs will contribute to the strengthening of Indonesian civil society much needed to generate demand for a more accountable, clean and transparent government. But the NGOs' position during the political transition appears to be more complicated than one might have thought. Studies by Mainwaring (1989) in Brazil and Canel (1992) in Uruguay showed that NGOs' activities during the democratic transition tended to decline because people were increasingly attracted to political parties which can provide stronger symbolic and ideological identities. In Indonesia, although there is still demand for NGOs' activities in facilitating a further process of democratisation, it is important for NGOs to redefine their roles since many of their previous roles (political communication, interest articulation, political representation and so forth) have been increasingly taken over by the newly formed political parties. Indeed, prior to and during the 1999 general election the existing 48 political parties were active not only in building their own constituencies but also in carrying out voters' education programmes. This new development has encouraged many NGO activists to consider a new role for NGOs. If in the past Indonesian NGOs were directly involved in building political awareness of society, they now need to become involved in a broader political context which include at least three things. First, an attempt to draw political and ideological boundaries within the existing groups in society. Second, an effort to develop a common political platform that should lead to the formation of a collective action involving different social and political groups. Third, a more serious attempt to form a network and coalition in the society in order to build a strong civil society (INFID 2000: 64). Thus, contrary to Mainwaring and Canel's arguments, Indonesian NGOs are still needed to facilitate a further process of democratisation.

## Political reform and grassroots response

Indonesian NGOs had undoubtedly contributed to the fall of the New Order government. Their endless pro-democracy campaigns and political education programmes since the mid-1990s had generated a feeling of being oppressed among the people, especially those in the marginalised spectrum both in urban and rural areas. More importantly, notwithstanding the New Order government's systematic attempt to control all types of organisation in society (students, workers, peasants, professionals, women and so on), Indonesian NGOs were able to preserve the idea of people's sovereignty (*kedaulatan rakyat*) and conveyed it to the grassroots population. Thus, when the opportunity to launch a collective action to challenge President Suharto arose in 1998, people at the grassroots level were already familiarised with the idea of people's sovereignty and were prepared to defend it at all costs.

As mentioned earlier, the situation in the post-Suharto era seems to have provided ample opportunity for Indonesian NGOs to escalate their activities. A Jakarta-based NGO activist, Setiawan (2000: 302), for example, linked this new opportunity with a number of factors. First, a substantial decline of the military's political role which provides greater space for political activities. Second, the collapse of the New Order's corporatist mode of intermediation which allows pluralism to prevail. Third, the introduction of a new political law which guarantees freedom of expression and organisation. Fourth, the introduction of an anti-corruption law which ensures more accountability and transparency in both public and private organisations.

The impact of these new developments on NGOs' activities is obvious. If during the New Order government NGOs had to compromise their radical ideologies to avoid a possible ban or dissolution, in the post-Suharto era they can openly disclose their radical identity without the risk of being repressed. One important organisation which later became a political party, PRD (People's Democratic

Party), has openly declared their leftist leanings since early 1999. By doing so they managed to attract thousands of radical students, workers and peasants throughout Indonesia. Other organisations, however, become increasingly involved in partnership with the government. Thousands of NGOs were involved in the disbursement of the government's *Jaringan Pengaman Sosial* (social safety-nets) programme during 1998–2000. Moreover, the lessening of the military's political control of societal activities has increased NGOs' acceptability among the rural poor. Beneficiaries are no longer demanding approval from the local authorities prior to NGOs' operation in their neighbourhood (Setiawan 2000: 303).

However, NGOs need to be more careful in dealing with the new developments in society. Soon after the fall of Suharto, political opportunists began to emerge. Many of them rely on thugs to subvert peaceful rallies and instigate rioting for their own personal benefits. In Jakarta and many other cities such as Makassar, Medan, Surabaya, Solo, Yogyakarta and Bandung, many political opportunists joined forces with radical groups and spent substantial amounts of money on 'political' investments. They used an increasing number of urban unemployed people to turn peaceful rallies into riots. As one of the street protesters in Bandung put it: 'These days you can easily find someone who is willing to pay you no less than 25,000 *rupiah* (US$2.8) just to wave banners on the streets for several hours; you may even get more if you are prepared to throw stones and destroy properties' (Agus, interview, 23/07/2001). In places where jobs become increasingly scarce, becoming 'professional' protesters may serve as a temporary refuge for many urban unemployed people.

In rural areas, society responded to the democratic euphoria by attempting to regain their land once sacrificed for development purposes during the New Order government. Peasants conducted campaigns to reclaim their land in many places in Java and Sumatra. They also stormed the local forests which were strictly protected by the government and looted the trees. A study by Lucas and Bachriadi (2001) indicated that from 1998 to 2001 in the district of Kedu (Central Java) alone, there was an estimated number of 270,676 trees looted from the local forest constituting a total loss of around 42.8 billion *rupiah* (US$4.2 million).

Another important political development in the post-Suharto era was indeed the resurgence of Islam as a political force. One factor which seemed to have contributed to the rise of Islam in Indonesia during the transition to democracy was the emergence of a Muslim middle-class. Mostly well-educated, this group established many new organisations to promote Islam as both a cultural and a political force. Culturally, Islam tries to develop values among Muslims through winning hearts and minds; and politically it attempts to establish a traditional Islamic state or at least implement Islamic teachings in and through the state (Jamhari 1999: 184; Rais 1999: 200). The new trend, however, draws much attention to the substantive aspect of Islam and the new generation is interested in establishing inclusive and pluralist political parties. Soon after the introduction of a new political law in September 1998, there were no less than 20 Islamic-oriented political parties in Indonesia. Among these groups, there were four of the biggest political parties: PPP (the United Development Party), PKB (the National Awakening Party), PAN (the National Mandate Party) and PBB (Moon and Star Party).

But the rise of Islam as a political force is weakened by internal conflicts between traditionalists vs modernists and between moderate vs radical groups. Since the 1950s conflicts have tended to increase when one particular group holds power at the expense of the other. Towards the end of Gus Dur's presidency, conflicts between PKB on the one side, against a loose coalition involving PPP, PAN and PBB on the other side, tended to escalate. While PKB – which represents the moderate and traditionalist Muslims – tried to secure Gus Dur's presidency, the other Islamic parties attempted to force Gus Dur to step down. With the support from the biggest party, the PDIP (Indonesian Democratic Party of Struggle), the loose coalition finally succeeded in calling for the People Consultative Assembly's special session, which led to Gus Dur's dismissal. Although many would agree that Gus Dur's dismissal had been caused by his controversial leadership style, one should not dismiss the fact that his removal had been precipitated by conflicts within the Islamic political forces. To many NGO activists, this conflict is an indication of a lack of unity in Indonesian civil society. While unity is much needed to sustain democracy, NGOs' contribution appears to be crucial in order to reduce conflicts within the existing political forces, including the Islamic parties (Taufiqurrohman, interview, 07/07/2001). Seen in this context, it is important for Indonesian NGOs to remain politically neutral. As one staff of a Jakarta-based NGO, Enceng Shobirin, put it: 'In order to serve as the facilitator for the development of a strong civil society, Indonesian NGOs should be able to avoid sectarian conflict that prevails during the transition to democracy' (INFID 2000: 219).

## *Facilitating democracy and maintaining trust*

What can be done by Indonesian NGOs during the transition to democracy? How should they respond to the greater political space they have enjoyed after the fall of Suharto? Harper (1996: 127) argued that during the democratic transition NGOs should be able to contribute to the evolution of new forms of civil society. This includes attempts to increase their legitimacy and an expansion of their links with the community and other relevant groups. In a similar vein, Vene-Klasen (1996: 222–3) argued that during the transition period NGOs should perform at least four important duties: (1) to stimulate political consciousness among grassroots groups; (2) to strengthen civil society's analytical capacity of common development problems and solutions; (3) to develop skills in strategic – as opposed to project – planning; and (4) to strengthen organisational capacity of the society in order to increase political leverage in policy and political changes.

These ideal functions have become the main concern of Indonesian NGO activists after the fall of Suharto. In October 1998, a number of activists gathered at a national NGO conference in Bogor, West Java. Organised by a national NGO network, the International NGO Forum on Indonesian Development (INFID), this conference attempted to consider a new role for Indonesian NGOs. This national gathering featured a workshop titled 'Repositioning Indonesian NGOs in the Empowerment of Civil Society', in which NGO representatives from Java, Sumatra, Kalimantan, Sulawesi, Bali and Lombok agreed to incorporate two important tasks: to facilitate the democratic transition and to develop a strong civil society (INFID 2000: 303). Furthermore, the national NGO conference encouraged NGOs all over Indonesia to expand their actions to include activities such as: (1) effecting changes in the public policy-making in order to accommodate voices from the grassroots; (2) developing collaborations with other elements of civil society (students, workers, peasants, the media and so forth) in order to produce greater impact; (3) devising and implementing political education programmes in order to develop political awareness among the grassroots people; and (4) establishing a more steady NGO network in order to facilitate project replication and information sharing (INFID 2000: 304–5).

This conference clearly addressed a new demand from Indonesian NGOs to scale up their operations which includes lobbying, partnership, mobilisation and networking. In his inspiring article, Korten (1987: 154–5) argued that NGOs' scaling-up requires a combination of technical and strategic competence. By technical competence he means that NGO staff must have adequate social, political and managerial skills and should be grounded in the methods, approaches, and values of the new development professionalism, while strategic competence refers to NGOs' ability to position their resources to gain power in the larger system and to deal with strategic issues such as exploitation, oppression and racism. NGOs with high quality human resources and a good management system can certainly scale up their activities with ease. But those NGOs with limited human resources and modest management system will find this difficult. In Indonesia, notwithstanding the strong appeal for NGOs to scale up their activities in the post-Suharto era, many NGOs are not prepared to do this due to their lack of human resources with adequate social, political and managerial skills. For this group of NGOs the only choice is to continue with their previous activities; and a combination of welfare, development and empowerment activities is certainly out of question.

Maintaining the trust put in them by their beneficiaries, donors and government is another challenge currently faced by Indonesian NGOs. When NGOs grow in number, overnight operation and fraud also multiply. The case in Garut (West Java) and many other similar cases mentioned earlier are examples of this growing practice of corruption and fraud in the Indonesian NGO community. It is therefore not surprising if public trust suddenly begins to wane. Since then donors are becoming more precautious in selecting applications for funding. This seems to be the case in the post-Suharto Indonesia, especially after a US$2.4 billion government social safety-nets programme backed by multinational donors was widely accused of misuse by the time it ended in mid-1999. Many seasoned development workers are notorious for their expertise in 'creative' accounting. Double book-keeping and data manipulation become a common practice among the overnight operators. H.S. Dillon, head of an anti-poverty task force at the Bappenas (the National Development Planning Board), for example, argued: 'When (NGO) officials are accused of skimming, they say it is overhead for the institutional support they provide' (*Far Eastern Economic Review*, 20 September 2001).

Although Indonesian NGO activists realise that corruption will engender a bad reputation and a possible loss of trust, they cannot do much to discipline their community members. Binny Buchori, chief of INFID, for example, argued that NGO community cannot do more than imposing social sanctions, that is, shutting out NGOs with bad reputations from the national coalition (*Far Eastern Economic Review*, 20 September 2001). The effectiveness of such an exclusion is questionable since disreputable organisations always find it easy to relocate by switching causes and run other projects. This is possible, given the fact that the supply of funding provided by foreign donors is currently abundant and that the supervision appears to be lax. Maryanto, an NGO activist of Hipalapa charged with corruption, for example, recounts how his colleagues stacked *rupiah* notes worth hundreds of thousands of dollars at his organisation's Bandung head office with little supervision. Donors, however, have taken more aggressive measures against corruption. In April 2001, the World Bank cancelled the second round of a US$600 million social safety-nets for the poor after it found poor performance in the previous year. Moreover, the World Bank's fraud unit is currently investigating 30 cases all over Indonesia, aiming to blacklist suspected contractors. Many advisers to the KDP (the Sub-district Development Projects) – a nationwide development project sponsored by the World Bank – have been fired; and without them costs dropped 20 per cent (*Far Eastern Economic Review*, 20 September 2001).

What should be done by Indonesian NGOs in the post-Suharto era? From our discussion we can now identify at least two crucial duties awaiting. First, NGOs should serve as a safeguard of Indonesian democracy by maintaining the reform movement agenda. Endless rallies and riots during the democratic transition have generated frustration among most Indonesians. Having enjoyed political stability under Suharto's authoritarian rule, many Indonesians began to blame democracy for causing political instability and disorder. The conservative middle-class people appear to be pessimistic about the future of Indonesian democracy as they fear that democratisation may lead to the collapse of Indonesian national unity. At the end of Gus Dur's presidency, many Indonesians began to think of a possible return of a Suharto-like government. This group even demanded Megawati's government to be harsher in dealing with popular protests and demonstrations. What NGOs can do in this context is to expand their democratic education programmes by involving more target groups in both urban and rural areas. Second, in order to maintain their reputation and the public trust put in them, NGOs should work harder in fighting internal corruption and fraud. The incidents of fraud in many places in Java discussed earlier also reflected the concern expressed by many observers in the early 1990s that most NGOs in developing societies tend to be lacking seriousness in developing transparency and accountability (Edwards and Hulme 1995a). For this reason, Indonesian NGOs have to make more serious efforts in improving their accountability system and in providing transparent information to their target groups, donors, government and the general public. As Andreas Subiyono, the new director of CD-Bethesda – an NGO based in Yogyakarta – put it: 'With the growth of overnight operators in the NGO sector in the post-Suharto era, we must be more accountable and transparent in carrying out projects funded by external donors' (Subiyono, interview, 06/07/2001).

# 5 Development, empowerment and professionalism
## The case of development NGOs

### State intervention in rural development

As has been discussed in Chapter 3, the New Order state can be best understood as a set of administrative, legal, bureaucratic and coercive systems that attempted to intervene in the activities of its own society. An activist, interventionist state, according to De Jouvenal (1962) is committed to and is capable of generating far-reaching changes in its society and environment. Applying this concept to the Indonesian context, Schiller (1996: 17) defined the New Order as a 'power-house state', that is, a state which had the power and capacity to influence more and more areas in its society's everyday life; its presence tended to stimulate changes that enabled the society (or parts of it) to adapt to, or even to thrive, in the presence of overwhelming bureaucratic and financial control in the hands of the central government. This definition may underscore the New Order's characteristic as a 'bureaucratic–authoritarian' state (King 1982; Robison 1985). By any measure, the capacity of the New Order government to mobilise financial resources had been remarkable. Whereas at the beginning of the First Five Year Plan (Repelita I) in 1969/1970 the total government revenue from exports of the oil and non-oil products and foreign aid was around Rp 300 billion, at the beginning of Repelita VI in 1995/1996 this figure jumped to Rp 72.3 trillion (Bappenas 1997b: 33). This had enabled the government to increase its development budgets. Between 1973/1974 and 1995/1996, for instance, the provincial governments' development budgets grew substantially from Rp 156.5 billion to Rp 11.3 trillion, indicating an increase by 72 times (Bappenas 1997b: 35). This trend continued until 1998 when the state suffered from enormous budget deficit due to the 1997 financial crisis.

Provincial governments relied on the substantial financial contribution from the central government in carrying out their rural development programmes. Data from Bappenas (National Development Planning Board) indicate that from 1973/1974 to 1995/1996 the proportion of PAD (*Pendapatan Asli Daerah* or original regional income) to the total APBD (*Anggaran Pendapatan dan Belanja Daerah* or regional development budget) at the provincial level in Central Java and Yogyakarta provinces was set between 8.96 per cent and 21.18 per cent, and between 18.66 and 34.07 per cent at the national level. This indicates the domination of central government in providing development funds where it supplied between 78.82 and 91.04 per cent of development funds in the case of Central Java; and between 78.95 and 85.49 per cent in the case of Yogyakarta. In the post-Suharto era, however, the state began to reduce its domination in determining regional development budgets. Law No. 22/1999 on regional autonomy states that district and provincial governments have the autonomy to manage and control their own budgets. The law has substantially reduced regional contribution to the central government and has allowed district and provincial governments to use their own regional income (PAD). However, given the fact that not all regions in Indonesia are self-sufficient, the central government is still predominant in supporting regional budgets.

## State-sponsored rural development programmes

Rural development[1] was the area in which the New Order government played a major role. Commentators argued that the role of the state in rural development is to ensure a balance between the production and the distribution of local resources and commodities. Thorbecke (1995: 142), for example, noted that the state's attempt to remove obstacles in commodity production and distribution in rural areas often includes: (1) the provision of markets for such items as insurance, credit and land; (2) the policy to provide more complete, perfect and symmetrically shared information about production and distribution of commodities for different sectors in the rural community; and (3) the policy to remove disparity in the distribution of human resources (labour) and physical resources (land and capital). In Indonesia, the New Order government had attempted to increase production and distribution of commodities in rural areas from the late 1960s by concentrating on three crucial aspects. First, the provision of guidance on agricultural intensification through state-sponsored extension programmes. Second, the promotion of village grassroots organisations to help implement the official development programmes. Third, the provision of markets for credit and saving to the rural households in order to enable them to run small-scale businesses.

### Agricultural guidance

In 1969, the government launched a programme called *Bimas* (mass guidance) aimed at modernising the rice production in order to achieve *swasembada pangan* (food self-sufficiency). Although the programme started as a pilot project in 1963, it was the New Order government which turned it into a nationwide campaign. Administered jointly by the Ministry of Agriculture and the Ministry of Home Affairs, *Bimas* provided farmers with a package of services which included the provision of high yielding varieties (HYVs) seeds, operating credit, guidance from the PPLs (extension workers) stationed in each village, fertilizer and pesticides at subsidised rates (Thorbecke and van der Pluijm 1993: 251). The credit was provided by the village units of the Indonesian People's Bank (*BRI Unit Desa*) that had been established in every *kecamatan* (sub-district) to handle credit for farmers participating in the programme. The amount of credit distributed in this programme increased from Rp 300 million in 1970/1971 to Rp 21.3 billion in 1980/1981 (Martokoesoemo 1994: 294). The PPLs provided advice on land preparation, pest control, the selection of HYVs and the application of fertilizers.

However, in the course of the late 1970s and early 1980s, *Bimas* programme faced a steady decline. If in 1973/1974 the number of participants had reached 3.6 million farming households, in 1978/1979 it dropped to around 2 million and to about 1 million in 1981/1982, which led to its abolition in 1984 (Thorbecke and van der Pluijm 1993: 252). One of the reasons for this decline was the poor repayment rates that prevented the *BRI Unit Desa* from serving new applicants. In 1970/1971, for instance, the default rate was recorded at 3.5 per cent, in 1980/1981 it rose to 60.0 per cent (Martokoesoemo 1994: 294). Some argued that the poor repayment performance of *Bimas* was caused by two factors: (1) the low interest rates (12 per cent per annum)[2] and the small amount of the average loan (between Rp 18,000 and Rp 100,000 for each borrower) which made borrowers feel less obliged to pay, as many of them tended to regard the credit as a kind of incentive for their participation in the extension programme; and (2) the lack of information and staff required for screening small rural borrowers and for monitoring the use of the loan which subsequently caused a poor repayment rate (Martokoesoemo 1994: 295; Moll and Palallo 1994: 315).

In 1984, the *Bimas* extension programme was integrated into *Inmas* (mass intensification), a programme providing technical guidance on HYVs introduced in 1973. During the late 1980s other programmes – such as *Insus* (special intensification), which provided guidance on pest control to group rather than individual farming, the NES (Nucleus Estate Smallholders), or PIR in its Indonesian acronym, which tied small-scale producers (called *plasma*) to large-scale farming enterprises (called *nucleus*) and many others – were introduced to co-ordinate rice cultivation around the village in order to reduce pest damage and to ensure an increase in rice production throughout the country (Thorbecke and van der Pluijm 1993: 252–4). Unlike *Bimas*, these programmes did not contain small credit disbursement to their participants. They survived because the government was able to mobilise farmers to participate through various state-sponsored grassroots groups and co-operatives.

*The promotion of village grassroots groups*

As has been mentioned earlier, the government formed a number of grassroots groups in order to implement its programmes more effectively. Through the Law on Co-operatives No. 12/1967 the New Order government formed village co-operative groups called BUUD (village unit enterprises), subsequently referred to as KUD (village unit co-operatives), charged with the task of handling rice processing, marketing and the distribution of inputs (Moll and Palallo 1994: 318). From 1978, however, under Presidential Instruction No. 2/1978 the BUUDs/KUDs at village level were encouraged to merge into bigger co-operatives operating at the *kecamatan* (sub-district) level and their functions were also expanded to include the provision of credit and agricultural inputs to the farmers as well as the purchase of rice on behalf of Bulog. By the late 1970s, it was estimated that

BUUDs/KUDs had collected more than 50 per cent of the total rice production all over Indonesia (Thorbecke and van der Pluijm 1993: 266). At the end of Repelita I in 1973/1974, there were 19,975 KUDs all over Indonesia, while in the first year of Repelita VI in 1994 the number of KUDs rose to 44,294 (Bappenas 1997b: 25). In 2000, it was estimated that the number of KUDs had risen to 60,000 (Wiyarto, interview, 03/07/2001).

Other important state-formed grassroots groups operating at village level were the LKMD (village people's defence council), LMD (village people's consultative assembly), *Karang Taruna* (youth groups), PKK (family welfare guidance), *Kontak Tani* (farmers' groups), *Apsari* (family planning groups) and *Kelompencapir* (radio listeners' and newspaper readers' group), each of which charged with the task of mobilising villagers to participate in various official development programmes (Yamaguchi 1998: 153). Since village officials played a major role in selecting members, in appointing leaders and in making decisions, these organisations had failed to function as representatives of grassroots interests (Rahardjo 1985: 76–7). For example, village heads were normally leaders of both LKMD and LMD, while their wives led the PKK and *Apsari*. Other village officials and their families were also appointed as leaders of *Kontak Tani*, *Karang Taruna* and *Kelompencapir* who subsequently selected membership from their own peers. These arrangements were common in several villages in Yogyakarta and Central Java, especially during the New Order government.

*Small credit schemes*

When the *Bimas* credit scheme was terminated in 1984, funds for rural lending were integrated into a scheme called KIK (small investment credit) or KMKP (permanent working capital), created in 1974 to cover small enterprises in all sectors of the economy. Thorbecke and van der Pluijm (1993: 263) noted that in the late 1980s about 50 per cent of KIK/KMKP credits went to services (trade and transport), while 30 per cent were channeled to agriculture and 10 per cent to industry. The maximum loan amount was set at Rp 15 million with collateral requirement of assets and up to 50 per cent of the amount of loan. The total amount of loan under this scheme increased from Rp 57.1 billion in 1975/1976 to Rp 349.1 billion in 1986/1987. Like other state-sponsored lending schemes with highly subsidised on-lending rates, the KIK/KMKP programme encountered serious problems caused by the lack of expertise to assess credit liability which led to high default rates and the confusion of eligibility criteria which failed to distinguish good and bad borrowers (Roeloffs 1989: 20; Martokoesoemo 1994: 296–7). In 1990, the KIK/KMKP programme was discontinued as a result of the escalating losses suffered by the state banks and the government's effort to rationalise and cut back on subsidies on credits (Yamaguchi 1998: 157).

Having learnt from its failure in administering *Bimas* and KIK/KMKP, BRI realised that the new programme should be financially more viable and more demand-driven, that is, based on the financial needs of the rural community (Martokoesoemo 1994: 298). In order to cover costs and make a reasonable

124  *Development, empowerment and professionalism*

profit, lending rates needed to be set higher than for loans offered to the urban population, where the average loan was substantially larger. In 1984, following the new banking regulations of 1983, which eliminated most subsidies to government banks, BRI and its village banking units rationalised its lending practices by introducing a new rural lending programme called *Kupedes* (village general lending). Unlike *Bimas, Kupedes* made credit available to merchants, small-scale industries, builders as well as farmers, both in rural and urban areas (Thorbecke and van der Pluijm 1993: 264). Despite the absence of subsidies that made lending rates higher (around 30 per cent per annum), *Kupedes* turned out to be a successful programme. For example, by June 1994 loans outstanding reached Rp 2,193 billion, spread over nearly two million borrowers; the cumulative total number of loans during a decade of operation was close to Rp 14,000 billion; and the annual growth of the loan portfolio had been very high, indicating the rural community's strong demand for village unit loans. The significant increase over time in average loan size from only Rp 268,000 in 1984 to Rp 1.69 million by 1994 appears to indicate the growing size of rural economic activities which subsequently enabled BRI to lower its administrative cost per *rupiah* loaned. In the post-Suharto era, a new small-credit scheme called KUT (*Kredit Usaha Tani* or Farmers' Enterprise Credit) has been introduced to replace *Kupedes*. The arrangement of KUT is very similar to that of *Kupedes*, although in KUT the loan is distributed to groups whose members have the power to decide the amount of money to be disbursed to each recipient and the responsibility to control the use of the money by each individual.

On top of these rural credit schemes, the government also provided villagers with development grants. Since the early 1970s, the Ministry of Home Affairs distributed grants called *Bandes* (village development assistance) to villages. In 1973/1974 the amount of *Bandes* was Rp 100,000 per village, which was later increased to Rp 1.25 million in 1983/1984 and to Rp 5.5 million in 1993/1994 (Bappenas 1997b: 30). In 2000, the amount of *Bandes* was increased to Rp 10 million per village. Another programme called IDT (less-developed village assistance) was introduced in 1993 to increase the economic productivity of poor villages as stated in *Inpres* (presidential instruction) No. 5/1993. A so-called revolving fund was distributed to villagers through LKMD and PKK to be used as seed capital to run animal husbandry and small village enterprises (petty trading, handicrafts, food preparation and so on). Technical assistance for enterprise development was also provided by the government through trained *tenaga pendamping* (accompanying agents) placed in the village. In 1996/1997 there were 22,054 *desa tertinggal* (less-developed villages) all over Indonesia each of which received Rp 20 million from this revolving fund (Bappenas 1997b: 31). After six years of operation, however, IDT had been increasingly criticised for its complex bureaucratic procedures that confused the recipients and for its vulnerability to manipulation and corruption by village officials who controlled the fund distribution.

In the post-Suharto era, despite a serious attempt to reduce the state's domination in rural development, the role of the state remains crucial, especially in mitigating the impact of economic crisis on the rural population. High inflation rates

Table 5.1 The social safety-nets programme funding allocation, 1998–2000 (in million rupiah)

| Area of activities | 1998/1999 | 1999/2000 | Sources of fund |
|---|---|---|---|
| Food security | 633 | 125 | Govt. of Indonesia and the JBIC |
| Education | 2,923 | 3,120 | Govt. of Indonesia, the World Bank and the ADB |
| Health care | 2,270 | 2,962 | Govt. of Indonesia and the ADB |
| Temporary employment | 2,045 | 1,441 | Govt. of Indonesia |
| People's empowerment | 1,701 | 1,242 | Govt. of Indonesia |
| Subsidies for basic items | 5,450 | 6,235 | Govt. of Indonesia |
| Total | 15,022 | 15,125 | |

Source: Bappenas. *Menatap Ke Depan Perekonomian Nasional*. Jakarta: Bappenas, 2001.

and the deterioration of popular income have brought many rural small-scale business establishments on the brink of bankruptcy. Many small businesses are forced to terminate their operations due to the substantial increase of the price of raw materials and the decline of market demand. The closing down of many rural business establishments has created a large number of unemployed people in rural areas. The burden of the rural community is even greater, especially when migrant workers who lost their jobs in urban areas are forced to return to their villages to join the unemployed group. In 1998, with the help from the World Bank, the Asian Development Bank (ADB) and the Japan Bank for International Corporation (JBIC), the Indonesian government introduced a social safety-nets programme (*program jaringan pengaman sosial*) focusing on a two-pronged strategy: (1) a rescue plan (*rencana penyelamatan*) which includes attempts to help the poorest group of the population by providing basic items (rice, sugar, cooking oil and the like), primary health care, education and temporary employment; and (2) a recovery plan (*rencana pemulihan*) which is aimed at allowing villagers to reopen their small businesses through the provision of low-interest credits, training and marketing advice (Nandika 2001: 194). Table 5.1 illustrates the allocation of funds in the social safety-net programme based on different sector of activities during 1998–2000.

## NGOs and the villages

Despite the state's domination in the most important aspects of rural development, villages in Indonesia are still open to NGO activities. However, the way NGOs contribute to the process of rural development depends on the local politics in the villages: how village officials exercise their power and influence, how villagers encounter the politics of the past (especially the events of 1965–1966), and how sensitive the issue of *Kristenisasi* (Christianisation) appears to be in the village. The way NGOs pursue their programmes also depends on the backgrounds which constituted their formation. It is therefore essential to briefly discuss the backgrounds of the two NGOs under study and the social and political settings of the villages where the two NGOs carried out their programmes. My observations of two villages in Central Java – Wedi (January–February 1997 and July 2001) and Donorojo (June–July 1997 and June 2001) – allowed me to record the local politics of the villages and NGOs' interaction with their target groups. While in Wedi BSY carried out its small-credit schemes and grassroots empowerment activities, in Donorojo CD-Bethesda was involved in health care and grassroots mobilisation programmes.

## The NGOs

It must be noted that both BSY and CD have strong ties with Catholic and Protestant organisations, respectively. Although they employ a secular style of management to the extent that their organisational structures are not related to any church and that their missions are separate from any 'missionary' duties, the two NGOs are nevertheless regarded by many Indonesians as representatives of Christian organisations. While accepting that many individual Christian social activists are not carrying out missionary activities, most Indonesian Muslims are unable to readily accept that the pattern of institutional structures within Christian organisations can guarantee the separation of social activities from missionary duties (Eldridge 1995: 177). Thus, the main challenge for Christian NGOs is to convince the public as well as target groups that their activity has no link with the Christian missionary agenda.

BSY was originally operating as a branch of *Bina Swadaya* which was founded in Jakarta in 1967. *Bina Swadaya*'s history goes back to 1958 when Bambang Ismawan, its long-time executive director, and Fr Chris Melcher, a Jesuit priest, founded ITP (the *Pancasila* Farmers' Association). Initially, this organisation provided training for farmers on legal issues. When the New Order started to disband independent farmers' organisations, the ITP's leadership decided to adopt a two-pronged strategy. First, they formed YSTM (Farmers' Social Development Foundation) of which *Bina Swadaya* became its operational arm. As a foundation, YSTM functioned as a self-help group and service institute rather than a mass organisation (van Tuijl and Witjes 1993: 204). Second, they merged ITP into HKTI (Indonesian Farmers' Association), a peasants' organisation operating under Golkar's influence, of which Bambang Ismawan became secretary general. Although Ismawan's role in HKTI would cause his association with Golkar, *Bina Swadaya* continued to operate as an independent organisation carrying out its own agenda of poverty alleviation and managed to dissociate itself from Golkar's political agenda (Eldridge 1995: 67).

For more than two decades BSY had served as the *satwil* (regional representative) of *Bina Swadaya*. From 1992 onwards, however, BSY became fully autonomous and was responsible for its own budgets, management and programmes. BSY was targeting farmers, artisans and small entrepreneurs in rural areas. Preoccupied with the idea of grassroots-oriented development, this organisation specialised in income generation which included non-collateral small-credit schemes, animal husbandry, cash crop growing, handicrafts and management training. In carrying out these activities, BSY focused on four main objectives: (1) to form and develop the local community groups; (2) to educate and train members of the newly formed local community groups to become productive farmers, craftsmen, petty traders, tailors and so on; (3) to link target groups with public and private financial institutions to enable them run their own businesses; and (4) to improve the production and distribution of agricultural commodities to the benefit of poor peasants (BSY 1996: 2).

BSY's main contribution to rural development was the disbursement of small-credit through groups called KUBs (joint-effort groups), which later became KSMs (self-reliant groups), most of which were crucial actors in the rural economy. By 2000, BSY claimed to have formed and worked with 182 KSMs, each of which has a membership of between 20 and 45 households (BSY 2001: 1). Compared to other development NGOs in Yogyakarta, BSY was relatively small, running an annual budget of around 1.46 billion *rupiah* (US$146,000) (in 2000) and employing 28 staff members. BSY's activities covered six districts (Gunung Kidul, Bantul, Sleman, Kulon Progo, Kotamadya Yogyakarta and Klaten), 25 subdistricts, 52 villages and approximately 6,000 households (BSY 2001: 2).

Meanwhile, CD-Bethesda (CD) was formed in 1974 as a community service unit of the Christian-owned Bethesda Hospital in Yogyakarta. Founded by Yakkum (the Christian Foundation for Public Health), CD began with primary health care activities designed to assist poor patients with limited access to hospital treatments. Although CD's Protestant affiliation does reflect the Christian motivation of at least some of its staff members, political and cultural constraints preclude any theological colouring of CD's development strategy and political view (Bunnell 1996: 184). Indeed, both participant observation and many informal interviews underscored CD's caution in exhibiting any missionary agenda in their operation. By setting up programmes such as *Rumah Sakit Tanpa Dinding* (hospital without walls) and *Rencana Sehat Dari dan Untuk Rakyat* (health plan by and for the people), this organisation created and trained KKDs (village health cadres) – which later turned into ORAs (people's organisations) – in many villages and which are charged with the duty of providing primary health care for their neighbourhoods (Santosa 1986: 11–12). By 2001, Andreas Subiyono (CD's executive director) claimed that his organisation has recruited and trained around 3,200 KKDs in Yogyakarta and Central Java (Subiyono, interview, 06/07/2001).

Compared to BSY, CD operated on a bigger scale, running an annual budget of around 8.69 billion *rupiah* (US$869,000) (in 2000) and employing 78 well-trained staff members. Its *Rumah Sakit Tanpa Dinding* and *Rencana Sehat Dari dan Untuk Rakyat* programmes were spread beyond Yogyakarta, or even Java, to cover 230 villages and 26,000 households in East Nusa Tenggara, West Timor and East Timor (Subiyono, interview, 06/07/2001). Through these programmes, CD received national and international recognition. The Indonesian government awarded CD the prestigious *Kalpataru* Prize, while the Society for International Development (SID) awarded the organisation the Paul Hoffman Award for its innovative approach in providing low cost primary health care (Siebert 1986: xvi).

From 1994, following a major organisational shift which separated CD from Bethesda Hospital, CD began to run income-generating programmes. The role of KKDs were subsequently expanded to include activities in the area of handicrafts, animal husbandry and saving-and-borrowing. Judging from the number of employees, the number of target groups, the scope of activities and the amount of annual income they raise, BSY appears to be a representative of small NGOs, while CD is a representative of large NGOs, at least according to Indonesia's standard.[3]

## The village setting

Many argued that village administration in Java during the colonial era and the Sukarno government had been organised in a more or less 'democratic' setting in which the intervention of a central administration was minimal, village heads were elected directly by villagers and some kind of 'free interaction' between village communities took place (Tjondronegoro 1984: 69). However, grassroots participation was hindered by the growing state intervention since the early 1970s. An autocratic leadership of village administration was introduced by the New Order government as stipulated in the Law on village government No. 5/1979. Although the law provided villagers with the opportunity to elect a new *Lurah* (village head) every eight years, after his/her election, the village head was granted status as *penguasa tunggal* (the sole power) in the territory where he/she appointed village officials as well as members of the two advisory bodies, the LKMD and the LMD (van Tuijl and Witjes 1993: 199). According to the law, village heads were not accountable to villagers who elect them; rather, they were accountable to the *Camat* (sub-district heads) who were subsequently accountable to the *Bupati* (district heads). This law appeared to complement the New Order's 'floating mass' policy[4] in which village leaders were assigned to ensure their 'control' of popular participation (Oepen 1988: 123). Hart (1989: 33) argued that village heads were, in essence, political agents of the state in the countryside as they were often forced by their superiors to ensure villagers' allegiance to Golkar, the ruling party.

Village heads usually belong to long-established rural elites as only these who can raise the financial means (for campaigns, buying votes, bribes and so on) needed to win an election. Once chosen, they usually take their cut from the development funds spent in their villages and are mostly unable or unwilling to act as intermediaries to bring the wishes and concerns of their populace to the attention of their superiors (van Tuijl and Witjes 1993: 199). Due to their lack of interest and limited comprehension of development priorities, many village administrators leave the filling-in of the required forms for project proposals to their superiors, the *Camat* (sub-district heads), who are eager to secure the grant for at least a cluster of villages in their administrative region (Tjondronegoro 1984: 25).

In the New Order era, the state's domination in rural activities had caused further impediments to people's participation in development whereby grassroots initiatives had been increasingly superseded by the state's extension workers and organisations. First, villagers had become more dependent on the state's intervention (in terms of guidance and credit) as manifested in the *Bimas, Inmas, Insus*, NES/PIR and *Kupedes* programmes. In these programmes, the PPLs tended to implement extension package formulated by the Ministry of Agriculture, while villagers acted as passive recipients of their assistance, which signified a top–down development model (Rahardjo 1985: 76). Second, the role of the traditional rural institutions such as *jimpitan* (food emergency group), *arisan* (credit and saving rotation group), *selapanan* (weekly meeting group) and *kumpulan* (village gathering) had been increasingly overtaken by state-sponsored organisations such as LKMD, LMD, PKK, *Apsari, Kontak Tani* and *Kelompencapir*. By joining the state-formed organisations, villagers could gain access to low-interest rural credits, HYVs and various kinds of technical assistance from the government (Tjondronegoro 1984: 15–16). Although some traditional rural groups managed to survive, they were increasingly co-opted and used by the state officials and the PPLs to mobilise villagers to implement official programmes (Lowa 1985: 172). In these circumstances, popular participation was almost non-existent.

*Wedi village in Klaten*

Wedi is located in the district of Klaten, about 25 km to the east of Yogyakarta city. It is easily accessible since the village is just 7 km from the main road connecting Yogyakarta and Solo. In Wedi, Muslims constituted the majority (77.9 per cent of the total population), about one-third of which are *abangan* (nominal Muslims) while Protestants and Catholics constituted 17.1 per cent, followed by Buddhists (3.8 per cent) and Hindus (1.2 per cent).[5] In a nutshell, the economic indicators of the village can be described as follows: there are 73 hectares of irrigated land (*sawah*); 48 per cent of total households are landless; 23 per cent of the men and 49 per cent of the women are employed in rice farming; around two-thirds of the rice-growing is reaped using the *tebasan*[6] system; and 36 per cent of the men and 22 per cent of the women are engaged in non-farming small-scale activities (petty trading and cottage industry) (*Kantor Kelurahan Wedi*, 2000).

My interviews with villagers underscored a previous study stating that the occupational situation in many villages in Klaten had moved towards non-farming jobs (Schweizer 1987: 50). One villager commented that he had given up his farming job and had started a *mie ayam* (noodle-soup) business which was more profitable in the *kecamatan* town (Parno, interview, 23/06/1997). A worker in an umbrella manufacturing unit said that she had decided to work in the non-farming sector due to the scarcity of farming jobs in her village (Amah, interview, 23/06/1997). All in all, the employment structure in Wedi has been changed not only by land shortage but also by the growth of local industry, trade and services. Since the late 1980s, Klaten, in general, has become increasingly known as one of the centre of rural small industry in Central Java in the areas of metal processing (*cor logam*), *soun* (vermicelli),[7] batik, furniture, weaving, roof tiles (*genting*) and handicrafts, most of which (roughly 85 per cent) were small-scale cottage industries employing 5 to 35 workers (Schweizer 1987: 42; Sandee *et al.* 1994: 116). In 2000,

130  *Development, empowerment and professionalism*

18 KSMs with 30–45 members under BSY's supervision were active in small enterprises in the areas of food preparation, vermicelli and roof tile production, petty trading, weaving and handicrafts, receiving a total amount of Rp 171.5 million credit (BSY 2001: 4).

In the New Order government, awareness of local politics was important for BSY before it established contact with villagers. In most cases, some kind of tacit understanding with local authorities had to be reached in order to avoid the possibility of any direct rivalry or confrontation. Eldridge (1997: 212) noted that in the Solo, Klaten and Yogyakarta region of Central Java, which has been regarded as 'politically sensitive' since the upheavals in 1965 and 1966, NGOs must be extremely careful in getting involved in mediating conflicts between local people and the authorities. In 1965, the BTI (Indonesian Peasants' Front), a peasant organisation under PKI's control, claimed to have up to three million members of whom about 70 per cent resided in the Central Java region including Klaten. In Wedi, there were a number of ex-political prisoners who received assistance from BSY.[8] For most villagers, the 1965–1966 was a period of *ontran-ontran* (political upheaval) in which leaders were executed, party members were sent to a prison camp (Buru island) and those who were only followers (*ikut-ikutan*) were asked to report regularly (*wajib lapor*) to the Koramil (sub-district military office) (Pak Jazimin, interview, 21/04/1997). The main challenge for BSY was therefore how to devise programmes that would be acceptable to the local authority and to avoid using strong words (revolution or class struggle) that might open the old wounds in the community.

*Donorojo village in Jepara*

Donorojo is located in the district of Jepara, Central Java. Two features of Donorojo community stand out: (1) it is an overwhelmingly Muslim-populated village (99.5 per cent of its total 4,924 population are Muslims, mostly members or sympathisers of the *Nahdlatul Ulama*);[9] and (2) it is an agricultural village in which about 668 households (64 per cent) of the total 1,037 households in 2000 were engaged in agricultural activities (*Kantor Kelurahan Donorojo*, 2000). Being believers in Islamic teaching, people in Donorojo show a great deal of respect for learned religious teachers called *kyai* and for those who have made the pilgrimage to Mecca, addressed as *haji*. Most of these *kyai* or *haji* are from the large landowning or successful entrepreneurial families. They served as informal community leaders (commonly referred as *alim-ulama*), funding and leading regular *kelompok pengajian* (Koran-reading groups), administering *infaq* (mosque funds), running *pesantren* (traditional Islamic boarding school), building and maintaining mosques and *madrasah* (religious schools) and organising *zakat* (charities). The influence of these Islamic leaders was strengthened because they frequently acted as patrons for villagers seeking employment, credit or education of a spiritual kind (Schiller 1996: 48). Operating under these circumstances, it was necessary for CD-Bethesda to assure the local authority and target groups that its programmes do not contain any elements of the Christian missionary agenda.

A great deal of irrigated land belonged to the village officials, apart from a small number of *kyai* and *haji*. The *petinggi* – the Jepara term for elected village heads – received the biggest share (17 hectares) of land control called *tanah bengkok* from which he generated his main income, while other officials – *sekdes* (village secretary), *modin* (religious official) and *kamituwo* (hamlet head) – received their share in the range of 5–8 hectares (Pak *Sekdes*, interview, 15/06/2001). The rest of the villagers own land between 1/2 and 6 hectares. Although agricultural intensification (which was considered the main factor for commercialisation in rice growing and marketing) had been introduced since the late 1960s in Donorojo, the traditional sharecropping, namely *kedokan* or *ceblokan*,[10] was still used by around two-thirds of land-owners (*Kantor Kelurahan Donorojo*, 2000). Most farmers sold their harvest to the KUD in the nearby *kecamatan* town. Meanwhile, most of the landless villagers performed non-farming activities, especially chicken breeding. Donorojo was also known as an important supplier of broiler chicken in Jepara. In 1999, for instance, the village supplied around 1,800 broiler chickens per month to the local markets (*Kantor Kelurahan Donorojo*, 2000).

In 2000, there were 42 KKDs or ORAs trained by CD in Donorojo, each of whom provided primary health care to around 30–40 households in his/her neighbourhood. CD also worked with 24 small business groups with 10–18 members carrying out various economic activities such as animal husbandry, chicken breeding, petty trading, handicrafts and saving-and-borrowing. The most important activity was chicken breeding in which groups (each receiving one million *rupiah* and technical assistance) produced around 9,000 broiler chickens per month (about 57 per cent of the village's monthly supply of broiler chicken) sold to the wholesale traders or the middlemen in the nearby towns (Subiyono, interview, 06/07/2001).

*New dynamics in the post-Suharto era*

In the post-Suharto era, *Gerakan Reformasi* (reform movement) can also be found in rural areas. The main target of this movement is the village heads and their functionaries who actively collected votes for Golkar during the New Order government. In June 1998, when the anti-Suharto movements in the cities began to subside, reform movements emerged in rural areas. Wearing headbands with *reformasi* written on them, village activists were involved in a series of demonstrations demanding corrupt and authoritarian village officials – whom they called 'local Suhartos' – to resign from office (*lengser keprabon*). In some areas in East Java this movement degenerated into violence as they burnt and destroyed the properties of those who refused to bow to their demand. In turn, village officials vainly attempted to defend themselves, calling on higher ranking officials to maintain the state's control on political activities in their villages. In Jombang District, East Java, for example, 306 village heads staged a counter-demonstration at the district government office to demand protection against the 'reformers' (Kammen 2001: 43). In Kebumen District, Central Java, 406 village heads accused the *Bupati* (district head) of failing to halt reform movements in their areas, which posed a serious threat to their occupations (Soetrisno 1999: 167).

132  *Development, empowerment and professionalism*

This new development conveys a message from the villagers that they want a democratic political life. In response to this new development, the government introduced a new law on regional autonomy, No. 22/1999. This law devolves most authorities, functions and services to the district government and urban municipality, while providing for a separation of power on all levels, including the village, which is also provided with a measure of autonomy. Antlov (2001b: 2) considers this legal framework to be a radical transformation of governance in Indonesia from a highly centralised system of governance to a decentralised one with more focus on the distribution of power.

As has been discussed earlier, Law No. 5/1979 on village government outlines the position of the village as an instrument of central government. Under the law, village affairs were brought under the supervision and close control of higher authorities. Village heads owed their power to higher authorities and could do nothing without the approval of sub-district and district governments. This was the situation over the two decades between 1979 and 1999. The condition has dramatically changed with the introduction of Law No. 22/1999. The new law clearly states that the basis for regulation on village government is diversity (*keanekaragaman*), participation (*partisipasi*), real autonomy (*otonomi asli*), democratisation (*demokratisasi*) and people's empowerment (*pemberdayaan masyarakat*). Table 5.2 outlines the transformation of village government in the post-Suharto era.

In order to implement these principles of village government, the new law authorises the formation of the so-called village representative bodies (BPDs). The authority of the BPD is far greater than that of the former LMD. There are at least four major roles for the BPD. First, it has the right to draft village legislation (*peraturan desa*). Second, it approves of village annual budgets. Third, it monitors and evaluates the implementation of village development projects. Fourth, it has the authority to call on a special meeting when it feels it is necessary to question the village head. There is no screening of candidates for the membership or chairmanship of the BPD, although candidates must still meet certain criteria including minimum level of education, amount of influence and maximum age (Antlov 2001a: 34).

This new arrangement has significantly changed the accountability system of village government. While Law No. 5/1979 stated that village government consists only of the village head, the new law provides for a separation of powers. The reformed village government consists of the head and his staff, and the BPD. The village head has a double accountability: he/she is responsible to the village population through the BPD and he/she must also submit each year an accountability report to the district head (*bupati*) (Antlov 2001a: 33). For the first time in Indonesian history, the village head is not primarily oriented upwards, but can be held accountable by the village population and must answer questions at BPD meetings. Because political parties are mainly urban-based, the politics of village government generally involves the village head and his/her functionaries as well as BPD members. In Wedi and Donorojo, BPD meetings are marked with long debates involving village heads and their functionaries on one side, and BPD members on the other side. Having decided all village development programmes

*Table 5.2* Village government in 1979 and 1999

|  | Law No. 5/1979 | Law No. 22/1999 |
|---|---|---|
| Definition of village | A territorial entity | A legal community |
| Village institutions | Appointed Village People's Assembly (LMD) and Village Defense Council (LKMD) under the authority of village head. No other institutions allowed | Elected village representative body (BPD) with far-reaching rights and autonomy, and other institutions that the village sees fit to establish |
| Village government | Village head | Village head and the BPD |
| Village head appointment and accountability | Village head is appointed by and accountable to district government for a maximum of 16 years | Village head is appointed by and accountable to the BPD, after approval from district government; and serves for a maximum of 10 years |
| Dismissal of village head | Proposed by sub-district government, approved by district government | Proposed by the BPD, approved by district government |
| Village legislation | Drafted by village head, approved by sub-district government | Drafted and approved by the BPD together with village head |
| Village budget | Drafted by village head and the LMD, approved by district government | Drafted and approved by the BPD together with village head |

Source: Hans Antlov. 2001. 'Village Governance and Local Politics in Indonesia'. Unpublished paper.

by themselves for such a long period of time, village heads and their staff members of the two villages find it difficult to accept suggestions from BPD members. Meanwhile, realising its role as an opposition to village government, the BPD is always eager to challenge attempts by the village head to control the meeting. In Donorojo, the meeting between BPD members and village officials has failed to reach agreement on how to spend the village budget of the year 2000/2001 because of BPD's refusal to approve the proposal of the village head. This stand-off happens because BPD's membership is dominated by supporters of candidates who had just lost the previous village head election.

The future of village democratisation in Indonesia becomes more obvious when in 1998 President Habibie reduced the role of the military in villages. The village soldiers (the *Babinsa*), who often used their power in village politics during the New Order government, were being withdrawn. The pull-out was planned to take place over a 10-year period of time. During such a long period there can be many policy changes, but at least the reform has been publicly announced and the *Babinsa* can be expected to no longer hold the same power in village government.

## 134  Development, empowerment and professionalism

Another important development in village life after the fall of Suharto is an increase of the use of money in the election of the village head. Standing for election as village head in Java was (and remains today) extremely expensive. Each prospective candidate is required to pass a preliminary test, requiring payment of official fees as well as bribes paid to the district electoral committee. Further payments are commonly necessary to help defray the cost of the election itself. In Brebes, Central Java, for example, despite a policy stating that the fee was only 3.5 million *rupiah* (US$390), candidates were charged up to 15 million *rupiah* (US$1,670) to stand for election (Kammen 2001: 54). Further pay-offs to the electoral committee are usually made to prevent a particular competitor from also standing for election. More money is needed by candidates to treat potential voters with snacks or drinks prior to the election day. On the day of the election, candidates still need to pay extra expenses to provide transportation for their supporters and to run *Operasi Fajar* (dawn operation), a euphemism for vote-buying, which could range from 10,000–25,000 *rupiah* (US$1.1–2.8) per vote. All in all, the cost of running for village head could range from 50–100 million *rupiah* (US$5,500–11,000) or more (Kammen 2001: 54).

In this situation, the competition for village head is limited to the local elite. The position of village head therefore remains largely the prerogative of land-owning peasants and, in some cases, villagers engaged in business or with connections among the state apparatus. It is therefore common for family dynasties to control the position of village head for years or even decades (Kammen 2001: 54). This argument is supported by another researcher, Kana. Based on his research in three villages in Central Java, Kana argues that there are at least three important factors that enable candidates to win a village head election. First, candidates must be part of the *trah lurah* (the village head dynasty). This means that they have to be descendants of former village heads although they do not necessarily come from the same village. Second, they must be wealthy and capable of mobilising financial support (from relatives and friends) to pay all expenses needed to collect votes. Third, they must have proper connections to the state apparatus in order to receive their blessing (Kana 2001: 13–14).

In both Wedi and Donorojo, village head elections which were held in October 1998 (in Wedi) and February 2000 (in Donorojo) were also subject to money politics. Candidates had to spend between 50 and 75 million *rupiah* (US$5,000 –7,500) to pay the official fees and other expenses. Interestingly, in these two villages *trah lurah* was not the only requirement for the candidacy since candidates must also attract two important Islamic organisations, the *Muhammadiyah* and the *Nahdlatul Ulama*. In Wedi, the candidate finally won the election, not only because he is the son of a former village head, but also because he is a teacher of a secondary school that belongs to the *Muhammadiyah*. In Donorojo, the elected village head is the son-in-law of a village head from a neighbouring village. Although his *trah lurah* is from another village, he received a considerable support from members of the *Nahdlatul Ulama* because he is a relative of a local *kyai* (traditional Islamic teacher).

## Involvement in rural development

In what sectors can NGOs contribute to rural development? What can NGOs do in their attempt to promote community development programmes in rural areas? As has been discussed in Chapter 3, the decline of the state revenues due to the collapse of oil prices in the early 1980s had opened up some areas in which NGOs can participate in rural development. One particular area was the health sector, in which the government could not rely on its own resources in providing adequate health care to the entire population, especially those in rural areas. Another area was the micro-enterprise development in which the government's programmes suffered from a serious deficiency and a lack of capacity in reaching the growing number of small-scale rural industries. The NGOs' flexibility to swap localities easily without facing serious bureaucratic obstacles, their innovative character and ability to raise funding from foreign sources were so tempting that even though most leaders realised NGOs' capacity to disturb political stability in rural areas, they could not deny NGOs' important contribution in sectors where the government was unable to act effectively (Hainsworth 1983; Riddell and Robinson 1996).

### *The health sector*

In the early 1980s, NGOs' involvement in the health sector received a warm welcome from the government. Despite the government's capacity to expand health care services by increasing the number of health centres (Puskesmas) from 1,058 in 1970 to about 5,000 in 1981, the health sector was still suffering from two major challenges. First, the government's health care facilities could not reach the entire population. Data from the World Bank indicated that in 1980 the ratio of doctors to the population in Indonesia (5.5 per 100,000) was far below that of the Philippines (32 per 100,000), India (24 per 100,000) and Thailand (12 per 100,000) (World Bank 1982). By the mid-1980s, maternal and health care provided by Puskesmas reached only less than half of babies born and about 11 per cent of infants under five (Bimo 1985: 116). Meanwhile, the government's attempt to train 100,000 primary health care workers (Prokesa) to serve at village level, each responsible for the basic health needs of about 100 people in their neighbourhood and supervised by 22,250 primary health nurses (*mantri*) based at the Puskesmas, could only reach 6 per cent of the total population (10 million out of a total 150 million in 1983) (Santosa 1986: 143).

Second, the villagers' poor knowledge of modern health care had caused the underutilisation of existing health care facilities. It was estimated that in the early 1980s average bed occupancy in hospitals was around 50 per cent nationwide, while at least 25 per cent of the population sought no medical attention at all when suffering from sickness and only 50 per cent of those who sought assistance utilised health centres and hospitals (Hainsworth 1983: 51). The reason for this problem was twofold: (1) the tendency of villagers to seek 'supernatural' methods of healing provided by *dukun* (traditional healers) or spiritual leaders rather than modern medication available in the local Puskesmas or clinics; and (2) villagers'

136  *Development, empowerment and professionalism*

lack of awareness of a healthy lifestyle (Kushadiwijaya 1985: 107). Thus, in order to optimise the use of health care facilities in rural areas, villagers had to be persuaded to seek assistance from the Puskesmas or hospitals whenever they suffered from any particular sickness and they needed to be taught a healthy lifestyle.

For these reasons, the government had to turn its attention to the NGO sector. NGOs' capacity to provide a low-cost health care delivery system could be crucial in replicating the government's primary health care programmes such as Puskesmas and Prokesa in order to reach the villagers (Hainsworth 1983: 52; Haliman 1997: 232). According to Bimo (1985: 121), NGOs, due to their flexibility (*keluwesan*) and sensitivity (*kepekaan*), could persuade villagers to develop a more healthy lifestyle and organise a bottom-up health plan for themselves through existing self-help community groups, especially in the areas beyond the reach of hospitals or Puskesmas. Although there was no policy or law that guarantees NGOs' participation in the health sector, the government's recognition of NGOs' contribution was expressed openly by state officials at various levels. For example, the head of the regional health office (*Kakanwil Depkes*) in Yogyakarta commented: 'NGOs are the most important partner (*mitra*) for the government in developing primary health care in rural areas that cannot be reached by Puskesmas or Prokesa' (Kushadiwijaya 1985: 104). It was at this point that some NGOs began to make their way into rural development by introducing various low-cost health care programmes.

## *Micro-enterprise development*

Since the early 1980s, the small-scale and cottage industries (SSCIs)[11] have received serious attention from state agencies. According to the data from the Ministry of Industry, no less than 1,878,015 SSCIs all over Indonesia were active in the manufacturing of food, beverages, textile, wearing apparel, leather, wood products, handicrafts, chemicals, metal processing, floor tiles, transport, printing and publishing in the mid-1990s (Husaini *et al.* 1996: 11). Their activities were encouraged and supported by the government for several reasons. First, because SSCIs are characterised by a high labour input per unit of output, they are often considered as a key sector for employment creation. According to the 1999 population census, about 70 per cent of the industrial labour force in Indonesia was employed in the SSCIs (BPS 2000: 127). Second, the SSCIs are capable of providing an additional source of income to a substantial part of the labour force from low income households (Sandee *et al.* 1994: 117). Third, their small size and use of 'appropriate' technology have made SSCIs capable of operating in a situation of surplus labour and scarcity of capital.

Throughout the 1980s and 1990s the government introduced various programmes with regard to the development of the SSCIs. First, the foster parents programme (*Program Bapak Angkat*) which encouraged large industrial firms to buy inputs domestically from SSCIs instead of importing or making these themselves. Regulated under the Law on Small-enterprises No. 5/1984, the programme also included training and other technical advice by large firms to their adopted SSCIs. Second, the allocation of profits from the state-enterprises to develop SSCIs (*pemanfaatan keuntungan* BUMN) in which a particular state enterprise was required to spend one to five per cent of its net profits on assistance to SSCIs and co-operatives as stipulated in decree No. 1232/1989 of the Ministry of Finance. Activities in this area included managerial training, marketing advice, technical guidance and small credits. Third, the KUK (small-enterprise credit) programme in which participating banks were required to allocate 20 per cent of their total credit funds (not including liquidity credit from Bank Indonesia) to the development of SSCIs. Fourth, the selling of shares to SSCIs and co-operatives in which large firms were obliged to sell shares to co-operatives including industrial co-operatives such as KIK (small industry co-operatives) and *kopinkra* (people's handicraft co-operatives) to improve their capital base. Fifth, the BIPIK (guidance and development of small industries) programme in which the Ministry of Industry acted as the 'foster parent' for the SSCIs, that is, co-ordinating education and training in the area of marketing and management.

However, in promoting the SSCIs, the government achieved only little success. Most of the SSCIs were still facing four crucial problems. First, they were lacking productivity and efficiency. One explanation for this was that while most SSCIs paid low salaries that make them unable to recruit skilled workers, the medium and large-scale enterprises were able to attract skilled workers and used modern equipments to increase productivity (Tambunan 1992: 92). Second, many SSCIs, especially those in rural areas, were dependent on middlemen (*makelar*) and financiers (*juragan*) who provided the input, working capital (with a high lending rate) and bought the products at a low price. This illustrates the ongoing process of marginalisation of the rural SSCIs and points to the need for greater financial assistance and more extensive management advice (Sandee *et al.* 1994: 126). Third, due to their poor knowledge of technical standards for production at a larger market, SSCIs tended to produce poor quality outputs. Sandee and Weijland's (1989: 95) study of the roof tile industry in Boyolali, Central Java, for example, suggested that extensive technical guidance and financial assistance to use klins (*mesin press*) were necessary to enable the SSCIs to meet the technical standard for urban markets. Fourth, the SSCIs' marketing strategy was unnecessarily passive as they simply waited for customers or middlemen to buy or make orders of their products at the offered prices. Had they taken up a more active attitude, they would have been able to sell more at higher prices (Sandee and Weijland 1989: 96; Maryono 1996: 194).

For these reasons, the role of NGOs in micro-enterprise development is required. Jackelen (1989: 133) argued that the rural economy usually suffers from the 'unbankability of micro-enterprises', in which formal banking institutions are reluctant to provide credits for small enterprises due to their lack of sufficient collateral, lack of productivity and expensive overhead costs in running a small amount of credits. NGOs are expected to solve the problem by serving as an intermediary in linking the informal small enterprises to the formal banks. Carr (1989: 167) noted that NGOs have more advantages in making direct linkages with rural small enterprises because they use fieldworkers who can easily move

138  *Development, empowerment and professionalism*

between localities, have greater capacity to understand the needs of micro-entrepreneurs, and are more capable of inducing trust and co-operation. NGOs also tend to be more flexible, willing to take risks and are less subject to political control and intervention than public development institutions (Maryono 1996: 196). NGOs' capacity to develop small enterprises was acknowledged by the head of the regional development planning board (*Ketua Bappeda*) of the Yogyakarta special province. As he put it:

> NGOs have a relatively long experience in a diverse range of service delivery, skill enhancement, and income-generation. Their successful programmes in improving farming skills, health care, animal husbandry, handicrafts and other means of livelihood enhancement and community self-help can be extended and replicated at village level and run on a more continuous basis.[12]

It was under these circumstances that NGOs were allowed to carry out their income-generating programmes in rural areas, especially in promoting small-scale rural enterprises.

### *The role of BSY and CD in rural development*

BSY was formed to teach villagers to use resources more productively for their own advancement and to provide them with capital, skill and technical guidance (Ismawan 1985: 4). In the 1970s, BSY began its activity by forming KUBs (joint effort groups or pre-co-operatives) and provided them with guidance on income-generation. Since KUBs as pre-co-operative groups had no legal status, they were not eligible for credit from the government. This might have been the reason why the government 'invited' NGOs to help these groups to develop their management and productive activities. With a membership of around 10–35 households, KUBs mainly served as saving-and-credit groups. Members paid an entrance fee of between Rp 1,000 and Rp 5,000. Thereafter they were obliged to save between Rp 500 to Rp 1,000 a month. Once a year KUBs put part of their collective savings into BSY's central solidarity fund (KSK). They were also given the right to draw credit from the KSK, after fulfilling certain conditions, such as book-keeping, having a permanent organisational structure and active members (BSY 1996: 12).

From the early 1990s, BSY expanded the role and function of KUBs. No longer functioning simply as saving-and-credit groups, KUBs were transformed into the so-called KSMs (people's self-reliant groups) which run small-scale business activities in the areas of petty trading, handicrafts and small cottage industries (BSY 1994: 3). In order to increase the financial capacity of the KSMs, BSY introduced the so-called HBK (groups and banks relationship) programme in which the NGO acted as the guarantor for KSMs in obtaining non-collateral credits from the banks. Guidance on the entrepreneurial skill, management system, the use of appropriate technology and more aggressive marketing strategy was provided. For example, in the vermicelli production, BSY helped KSMs to gain

## Development, empowerment and professionalism 139

access to good quality raw materials at prices to allow producers to remain competitive, while in the case of the roof tile industry, BSY provided producers with access to non-collateral credit used to finance the adoption of new technology, that is, the use of klins (*mesin press*) to improve the quality standard (BSY 1995: 23). BSY's fieldworkers checked the book-keeping of each enterprise regularly in order to ensure that any financial problem could be identified at an early stage to allow enough time to remedy it. The biggest difference between KSMs and KUBs was that while KUBs served as passive recipients of credit by focusing on saving-and-borrowing activity, KSMs served more as BSY's business partners whose relationship was based on a formal contract. Moreover, they had to pay some 'accompanying service' (*jasa pendampingan*) charges[13] (Sugiyanto and Wahyuni 1994: 31).

Meanwhile, CD entered into rural development through the health sector. In order to provide low-cost health care for the poor villagers, CD attempted to replicate the state's Prokesa and Puskesmas programmes by forming KKDs, that is, the village volunteers responsible both for providing services and promoting community control over its own health affairs (Santosa 1986: 211). Volunteers were selected both by local election and by direct appointment by *Lurah* and then trained at CD's training centre. The training focused on two aspects. First, trainees were equipped with basic knowledge of health, fundamental medical science, herbal preparation, acupuncture and interpretive techniques to associate symptoms with major diseases (Santosa 1986: 212; CD-Bethesda 1995: 15). Second, cadres were taught a participatory learning process approach to community development in which each of them were obliged to visit the homes of 8–10 families in his/her neighbourhood to gather data for a village health assessment carried out at CD's office (Santosa 1986: 213). Once trained, KKDs joined with CD's staff members in making decisions about programme priorities and design in their village. With their skills, they were also entitled to the modest charge of services they provided to patients. They were also given the task to distribute medicine and herbs supplied by CD's health clinics at low prices. Contact was maintained through regular visits by CD's fieldworkers, and along with district meetings every three months, there was an annual workshop at Bethesda Hospital's conference centre to remedy problems (Bunnell 1996: 188).

Following its organisational expansion in the early 1990s, the role of KKDs had been extended to include small-enterprise development. Cadres were encouraged to form and co-ordinate groups which were divided into three categories: farming, small-industries and saving-and-borrowing groups (CD-Bethesda 1996a: 18). With a membership of around 10–32 households, these groups carried out various income-generation activities (cattle and chicken breeding, crop growing, bamboo weaving and wood carving) under the guidance from CD's field staff. Each member of the groups was entitled to subsidised credits with three to five per cent of monthly lending rates after putting away compulsory saving of between Rp 2,000 and Rp 10,000 per month. In 2000, the amount of loans to group members was between Rp 200,000 and Rp 1,800,000 (CD-Bethesda 2001: 13). Unlike BSY, information on borrowers' assets (land and animals), their

140  *Development, empowerment and professionalism*

economic enterprises and their reliability was obtained from the KKDs and village officials. Technical assistance and advice were provided which included management training, introduction to larger formal marketing outlets and suppliers, the supply of raw materials and the use of modern equipment (Subiyono, interview, 07/07/1997).

## The role of local politics

How do social and political settings in the village affect NGO activities? How do NGOs respond to these social and political settings? In order to ensure legitimacy[14] in their relations with villagers, in the New Order period NGOs need to establish a close relationship with village officials, especially the village heads as the 'sole power' in the village. In Wedi, for instance, BSY had to ask for a blessing (*kulo nuwun*) from the *Lurah* before it could begin its activity (Wiyarto, interview, 20/01/1997). This seems to corroborate Widaningrum's study stating that by approaching village leaders, NGOs can ensure 'acceptability' *vis-à-vis* their target groups who tend to develop an uneasy attitude towards 'outsiders' (Widaningrum 1988: 14). This arrangement will certainly affect the way in which NGOs carry out their activities, especially in the selection of target groups. Village officials would not only try to make sure that NGOs' programmes would not bring instability to their village, but also use NGOs' programmes to benefit their own peers. In what follows I will recount the experience of BSY and CD in working under the 'patronage' of village officials.

### *BSY's experience in Wedi*

BSY's commitment to poverty alleviation was based on the view put forth by the founder of *Bina Swadaya*, Ismawan, who stated on one occasion that poverty can only be reduced through *pembangunan dari dalam* (development from within), that is, 'a process of developing the confidence, potential and capacity of the poor to enable them to organise among themselves and to proceed according to their own goals' (Ismawan 1985: 10). While criticising the government's top–down approach in rural development, Ismawan proposed an alternative solution which included a conscious attempt by NGOs to help the powerless organise themselves and solve their own problems. In reality, however, it was difficult for BSY to implement Ismawan's idea of *pembangunan dari dalam*. Working with its target groups, BSY had to bow to the conditions laid down by village officials who did not have the knowledge, or willingness, to let villagers organise independently.

In Wedi, as a result of their dreadful experience in the 1960s, villagers tended to develop a 'careful' attitude towards outsiders.[15] Amid the government's phobia of '*bahaya laten komunis*' (the communist threat), villagers were occasionally reminded by the local authorities to remain alert against a possible come-back of PKI. For the villagers, it was important to be careful towards outsiders. As one of them put it:

> In the 1960s we had been deceived by *orang luar* (outsiders), using fine words, flattery and promises to make us become PKI members, and we were fighting with one another like dogs struggling for a piece of bone (*asu nggrayah balung*). Now we have to be more careful in dealing with outsiders, as we were told (by the authorities) to report any presence of individuals or organisations making promises.
> (Pak Mujiyo, interview, 21/02/1997)

It was therefore impossible for BSY to make direct contact with the villagers without the village head's consent. Widaningrum's (1988: 67) study in a nearby village found that many villagers asked whether BSY had been granted *ijin* (permission) by the village head to form KUBs in their village.

Having realised that his organisation operated in a 'politically sensitive' region, Aleks Wiyarto, BSY's executive director, tried to adjust to the local politics in Wedi by combining Ismawan's view of 'development from within' with the government's idea of development focusing on growth and productivity. This combined approach contained three basic components: (1) a view that BSY serves as both facilitators and catalysts for the poor people to find practical and immediate solutions for their problems; (2) a focus on the provision of information on effective management, skill and appropriate technology; and (3) a commitment to promote growth and productivity in rural areas by encouraging target groups to generate working capital through saving-and-borrowing activities (Wiyarto, interview, 22/01/1997). Wiyarto asked his fieldworkers to use terms commonly used by state agencies – *pembinaan* (guidance), *penyuluhan* (extension), *kemitraan* (partnership), *swadaya masyarakat* (community's self-reliance) and the like – and avoid the use of strong terms – *revolusi sosial* (social revolution), *perjuangan kelas* (class struggle), *demonstrasi* (demonstration) and so forth – in order to make sure that village officials accept BSY's presence in their village (Wiyarto, interview, 20/01/1997). The reason for this approach was not only that he wanted to avoid confrontation with the local authority, but also because he realised that *Bina Swadaya* had been founded by the ITP to counter PKI's class struggle campaign in the early 1960s (Eldridge 1995: 67).

In selecting target groups, BSY had to accept suggestions from the *Lurah* who preferred to appoint his own loyal supporters, many of whom were leaders and members of state-sponsored grassroots organisations. Consequently, the newly formed KSMs were full of people who were already members of state-formed organisations such as the LKMD, LMD, PKK, *Apsari, Kontak Tani* and *Kelompencapir*. A fieldworker commented that about two-thirds of the total KSM members in Wedi were 'recommended' by *Pak Lurah*, while only one-third were appointed without *Lurah*'s intervention (Mas Pur, interview, 17/07/1997). My research in Wedi revealed that more than 70 per cent of 38 KSM members were also members of various state-formed organisations (Table 5.3). In the post-Suharto era, despite the liquidation of many state-formed grassroots organisations,

*Table 5.3* Backgrounds of KSM members in Wedi (*N*=38)

| Occupation | Linked with state-formed organisations (LKMD, PKK etc.) | Not linked with any state-formed organisations | Total membership based on occupation |
|---|---|---|---|
| School teachers | 7 | 1 | 8 |
| Civil servants | 7 | — | 7 |
| Small entrepreneurs | 6 | 3 | 9 |
| Craftsmen | 4 | 2 | 6 |
| Farmers | 3 | 1 | 4 |
| Without occupation | 1 | 3 | 4 |
| Total | 28 | 10 | 38 |

Source: Own data collection.

KSM's membership is still dominated by former members of these organisations. Table 5.3 also indicates that 24 out of the 38 KSM members have already had relatively secure jobs (school teachers, civil servants and small entrepreneurs). This seems to support early studies stating that the majority of BSY's beneficiaries are not from the poorest groups, but those who have already got other jobs as teachers, lower level government officials, small traders or wage labourers for whom BSY activities provide supplementary income (Siregar 1987: 107–8; Eldridge 1989: 15; van Tuijl and Witjes 1993: 205).

It also appeared that BSY's programmes run the risk of being manipulated by village officials, especially during the general elections. There were many examples of officials promising villagers that they would be supplied with water, electricity, a bridge or a tarmac road if they helped Golkar to win the elections in their village, *kecamatan* (sub-district) and *kabupaten* (district) (van Tuijl and Witjes 1993: 198). Given the fact that all village officials in Wedi were Golkar's cadres, it was not surprising that they used BSY's programmes to please Golkar voters. For example, a few months before the 1997 general election, one of BSY's fieldworkers claimed that one village official in Wedi manipulated the HBK programme by promising that those who vote for Golkar would be guaranteed a low-interest credit from BSY (Mas Pur, interview, 13/02/1997). Unfortunately, I was unable to confirm this allegation to the village official concerned; however, some villagers said that access to credit in the HBK programme was more open to the friends of the village officials and Golkar voters than to those outside these circles. In the 1999 general election, Golkar was accused of tapping money from Bulog to buy votes from the poor population.

As far as religious tension is concerned, BSY had never faced serious constraint. Two reasons may explain why BSY did not face any religious challenge in Wedi. First, the fact that in Wedi about 20 per cent of the total population are non-Muslims, and about 70 per cent of the Muslim population are *abangan* (nominal Muslims), appears to have yielded some degree of tolerance towards the presence of a Christian-run NGO. Second, although BSY was founded by individuals from a Catholic background, its independence from any influence of any Catholic churches or organisations has made it possible to establish itself as a secular organisation.

## CD-Bethesda's experience in Donorojo

Like BSY in Wedi, CD's entry into Donorojo village was also established through village officials, especially the village head. In recruiting the KKDs, CD had to comply with the values and preferences of local elites in selecting cadres (Bunnell 1996: 186). CD's goal of democratising the election of new KKDs through 'open' election by the community had to give way to the political interests of the village officials who preferred to choose from among candidates of their own choice. The common practice of cadre selection was therefore the village head, in consultation with the heads of each *dusun* (hamlet), directly appointed the cadres. As a result, many KKDs were in fact the relatives or friends of the village officials (Subiyono, interview, 02/07/1997). This arrangement was not only applicable to CD's health cadres, but also to health cadres in the official programmes such as the Prokesa and the Apsari. There were 22 out of 26 health cadres in the village who admitted that they were appointed directly by the village head (Table 5.4). This seems to confirm an early study by Bunnell arguing that CD sees little choice but to bow to the political reality of the entrenched power of village elites (Bunnell 1996: 187). The fact that KKDs were allowed to impose a small amount of service charge and to sell medicine to the patients appeared to have encouraged village officials to intervene in the recruitment of KKDs. This can be seen as a kind of favour from the village officials to their relatives, friends and Golkar's voters. One of CD's fieldworkers, Julius, commented: 'Our attempt to increase the welfare of KKDs by allowing them to impose service charges and earn income from the distribution of our low-cost medicine has increased the village head's influence in appointing new cadres. Many more relatives and friends of the village head were appointed as KKDs' (Julius, interview, 12/07/1997).

CD's close association with the widely known Bethesda Hospital has made it difficult to conceal its Christian identity. Local Muslim leaders and organisations were always suspicious of CD's activities in their area. In 1995, an incident which provoked anti-Christian feeling in Donorojo had landed the organisation in

Table 5.4 Methods of appointment of health workers in Donorojo (N=26)

| Type of health cadres | Appointed by the village head | Elected by the community | Total member of each type of cadres |
|---|---|---|---|
| KKD | 13 | 3 | 16 |
| Prokesa | 6 | 1 | 7 |
| Apsari facilitators | 3 | — | 3 |
| Total | 22 | 4 | 26 |

Source: Own data collection.

serious trouble. On 21 August of that year, dozens of Muslim leaders protested in front of CD's field office in Jepara, accusing the organisation of conducting activities to proselytise the poor Muslims by distributing money and other assistance.[16] The problem started when a few days earlier a group of militant Christian evangelists from Jakarta had come to the nearby village to preach and play a video about Christianity, which raised concern among Islamic leaders in the area. The group was subsequently expelled from the village. However, rumours spread among the villagers implying that those evangelists were related to CD's activities. Islamic leaders in Donorojo reacted by protesting directly against CD's fieldworkers in the village. The resistance increased when Islamic leaders were able to convince villagers (including CD's beneficiaries) to believe that CD's programmes in their village were: *'ada embel-embelnya, yakni ingin meng-Kristenkan masyarakat Donorojo'* (containing a hidden purpose, that is, to Christianise the people of Donorojo).[17] They subsequently held a protest action in the village administration office calling for CD's withdrawal from their village.

Before the situation got out of hand, local authorities intervened. On 24 August, an emergency meeting was held at the village administration office at which CD's representatives, Muslim leaders, KKDs, *Camat* (sub-district head), *Danramil* (sub-district military commander), and village officials were present. The problem was finally settled when the authorities guaranteed that CD had no connection with the evangelists. More importantly, in that meeting the *Camat* and the *Danramil* insisted that CD's presence in Donorojo was to implement the government's community development programmes, especially in the health sector and that people must co-operate with the organisation.[18] The people soon apologised for the misunderstanding and CD's activity was back to normal. Subiyono, the head of CD's branch office in Jepara, recalled:

> Villagers were angry and asked us to pack up and leave their village because they thought those evangelists were related to our organisation. We escaped from a total disaster when the village head, the sub-district head and the sub-district military commander convinced them that our organisation had no connection with the evangelist group. They also guaranteed that our programmes were supported by the government and threatened the protesters that any attempt to disrupt our organisation would be dealt with by the security apparatus. The sub-district and village officials were willing to do so because they relied on our programmes, especially in their attempts to eradicate tuberculosis, to rehabilitate the lepers, and to provide low-cost health care in the village. One official, who was a Muslim, said to me that as long as our organisation continues to help the poor people he does not care whether it is run by Christians or Muslims.
>
> (Subiyono, interview, 31/01/1997)

This incident illustrates two things. First, religious sentiment has always been a threat for a Christian NGO operating in an overwhelmingly Muslim community. The fact that Jepara is one of the major strongholds of the devout Muslims in

Central Java has led to a situation where the Muslim community appears to be less tolerant of other religions. Thus, unlike BSY in Wedi, CD had to work harder to convince the community that its activities are purely social and non-religious. Second, being a Christian organisation operating in a potentially hostile community, CD relied on the 'protection' from the local authorities. Consequently, CD had to maintain its 'close' relationship with the sub-district and village officials. This closeness can only be preserved if CD continues to please the officials by accepting their suggestions and by concentrating on health care and income-generation.

But working under the 'protection' from the local authorities appeared to leave CD with a very limited choice in pursuing their activities in the village. This was obvious in the case of the chicken-breeding programme. In Donorojo, there were 28 small enterprises working with CD, all of which bred broiler chickens. Since the early 1990s, the market networks for broiler chicken in Jepara have been dominated by a number of poultry shops and their middlemen. These poultry shops sent their middlemen to the villages to supply the farmers with poults, chicken-feed and vaccines, while the farmers bred the chicken. Every 35 days (the time needed for breeding broiler chickens) the middlemen went back to the farmers to purchase the grown-up chickens and distribute them in the nearby markets. This arrangement appeared to have disadvantaged the farmers because the prices of poults, chicken-feed, vaccines and chickens were determined by the poultry shops and the middlemen. The middlemen normally bought the chickens at a very low price. In 1997, for example, the price of chickens in the market was set at Rp 2,900 per kilogram, while the middlemen bought from farmers at Rp 1,500 per kilogram. Ironically, this arrangement was regulated under the *Keppres* (presidential decree) No. 22/1990 on *tata niaga ayam ras* (broiler chicken trade regulation), which encouraged big enterprises to develop partnership (*kemitraan*) with small enterprises (*Kompas*, 23 May 1997).

In order to attain a fairer deal for the farmers, CD formed its own small chicken-breeding enterprises in Donorojo and some other villages (Sumber Urip, Telaga Wungu and Gembong). It served as providers of inputs and helped farmers to sell their chickens at higher prices. CD's intervention appeared to be effective, at least in Donorojo, because farmers could get input at a lower price and managed to sell their chickens directly to individual buyers at a higher price (Pak Kosim, interview, 12/07/1997). However, this provoked a retaliation from the poultry shops and their middlemen as they began to boycott the supply of input and the purchase of output from farmers outside their own networks. This action landed CD in a difficult situation. On the one hand, it had to listen to the farmers who wanted to conduct a protest action against the poultry shops in Jepara; but on the other hand, it had to maintain its close relationship with the local authorities who objected any protest or demonstration. After some internal debates among staff members, CD decided to rule out the farmers' demand for protest action. Subiyono, CD's Central Java area manager, commented: 'We do not want to jeopardise our good relationship with the local authorities by supporting the villagers' plan to protest against the poultry shops. We realise that with this growing anti-Christian feeling, we may need a kind of protection from sub-district and village officials' (Subiyono, interview, 31/01/1997). One fieldworker told me that the village head had apparently asked CD to prevent farmers from conducting any protest because such actions might jeopardise the government's attempt to encourage partnership (*kemitraan*) between big and small enterprises regulated under the *Keppres* No. 22/1990 (Julius, interview, 12/07/1997). This incident illustrates the importance of an NGO to build a close 'relationship' with the local authorities.

## New trends in the post-Suharto era: from development to empowerment

As has been discussed in Chapter 4, the situation in the post-Suharto has opened up a new opportunity for Indonesian NGOs to scale up their activities, that is, combining welfare, development and empowerment activities. The lessening of state's control of societal activities has allowed NGOs to become involved in areas that can be considered political. In rural areas, however, the democratisation of village government has not produced an immediate result. Although the BPD has been formed to serve as a control mechanism on village government, this institution cannot really monitor the direction of village government due to some limitations. First, the lack of a clear procedure of recruitment which leads to a poor standard of aptitude of the BPD members. In many places, members are taken from the liquidated village people's consultative assembly (LMD) or the village defense council (LKMD) who were appointed by the village head. Second, poor knowledge of democracy and lack of organisational skill among the BPD members which have made it more difficult for BPD meetings to produce important decisions or policies. In most cases, BPD meetings are marked with endless debates which bring the whole process to a virtual standstill because villagers have very limited skills in lobbying and bargaining. Third, the BPD can be co-opted by village head. Law No. 22/1999 states that the BPD 'sits on the same level and functions as a partner to the village government'. This could be interpreted that BPD might not criticise the village head. There are cases in which the village head provides salaries to BPD members, who feel obliged to support him.

The need to empower BPD members has inspired many development-oriented NGOs to devise a programme which combines education, training and mobilisation. This programme is aimed at enabling grassroots people to control the direction of village government. In Yogyakarta, CD-Bethesda attempts to form new organisations which serve as a control mechanism of village government. Activists of this organisation consider village democratisation in the post-Suharto era as an opportunity to transform their own KKDs into the so-called ORAs. While KKDs were mainly responsible for the provision of primary health services and the promotion of small-scale economic activities in rural areas, ORAs are designed to influence policy and decision-making in villages. Although welfare and development activities are still maintained, ORAs are expected to be more actively involved in village decision-making processes. This transformation signifies CD's new commitment to train villagers to develop more democratic political activities.

In the meantime, BSY responds to the new developments of the post-Suharto era in a slightly different way. Although its activists realise that village democratisation has enabled them to carry out political mobilisation, they are not interested in forming new organisations to influence the village decision-making process. Instead, they are more interested in working with the existing KSMs (people's self-reliant groups) to remedy the impact of the economic crisis on the rural population. BSY, however, is aware of the need to increase people's capacity to decide on their own development. In 1999, this organisation launched a new programme called 'Project Support to Home Workers' Response to the Economic Crisis'. Using the participatory rural appraisal (PRA) method, this project was aimed at enabling KSM members to identify and analyse problems in the small-scale business activities during the economic crisis. The experience of both CD and BSY in conducting empowerment activities in the post-Suharto era will be illustrated below.

### *CD-Bethesda: from KKDs to ORAs*

The situation in the post-Suharto era has indeed influenced CD's decision to combine welfare, development and empowerment approaches. The formation of BPDs – which reflects the will of villagers to embrace democracy – has inspired CD to increase the villagers' involvement in village politics. The appointment of the new executive director, Andreas Subiyono, in January 2001 has made it more possible for CD to include mobilisation in its agenda. Subiyono was a former student activist in Yogyakarta who came to CD in 1992 as the Central Java field coordinator. During his career at the organisation he has become renowned among his colleagues for his hard-work and dedication to grassroots empowerment activities. He is also one among CD's young staff members who consistently demands for a more radical approach to CD's daily activities. According to one of CD's staff members, Budi Santoso, CD owes much to Subiyono in devising most controversial programmes such as the project that challenges President Suharto's decree on chicken-trade regulations and more recently the transformation of KKDs to ORAs (Budi Santoso, interview, 05/07/2001).

The idea of transforming KKDs to ORAs was put forward by Subiyono for the first time when he served as an area manager for CD's Central Java office in 1998. Although the central office approved his idea, the formation of ORAs became CD's official programme only after Subiyono's appointment as the executive director. Asked what he had in mind when transforming KKDs to ORAs, Subiyono commented: 'In the post-Suharto era, I realise that NGOs must respond to the desire of villagers to democratise and to preserve the idea of *kedaulatan rakyat* (people's sovereignty) by providing institutional help to allow them to exert more influence on the rural decision-making process' (Subiyono, interview, 06/07/2001). He asserted that although KKDs have been successful in motivating a community-based development, they have failed to build a 'critical mass' in rural areas. Thus, their transformation to ORAs is expected to enable CD to establish a critical group consisting of the rural population which serves as an opposition to the village government.

148  *Development, empowerment and professionalism*

In 1999, it was estimated that there were only 26 ORAs in Central Java and Yogyakarta. Two years later, the number of ORAs has grown to 173 covering Central Java, Yogyakarta, Lombok, Sumbawa and West Timor (CD-Bethesda 2001: 48). Initially, Subiyono wanted to keep the name KKD to refer to his new organisations. However, the fact that their focus of activity has been changed to include political education, negotiation and bargaining has encouraged him to search for a more appropriate name. It was agreed later that ORA – an acronym for *organisasi rakyat* (people's organisation) – should be used as a new term for KKD. Subiyono estimated that by July 2001, around 90 per cent of the total number of KKDs in Central Java and Yogyakarta should have been changed to ORAs (Subiyono, interview, 06/07/2001). ORAs were formed to achieve four targets: (1) to encourage villagers to control the direction of their own development; (2) to check the power and authority of village head in order to create a democratic village government; (3) to facilitate the promotion of economic democracy in rural areas; and (4) to serve as a catalyst and a mediator for settling differences and conflicts in the village (CD-Bethesda 2001: 3–4). In order to achieve these targets, CD provides training in ideology, organisational skills, democracy, negotiation techniques and conflict resolution methods to ORA's members.

Initially, villagers respond to the formation of ORAs with hesitation. But when they realise that ORAs can affect village policy-making, they begin to welcome KKDs' transformation to ORAs. In order to optimise ORAs' activities, new members are brought in. Subiyono realises that he cannot rely on the KKD members who automatically become ORA members because not all of them have interests in local politics or are prepared to serve as an opposition to the village government. He therefore encourages ORAs to recruit new members, especially those who are critical of the village head and his/her functionaries. There is no special requirement for ORA's membership, except that they have to be nominated and elected by KKD members. Compared to the KKD, the election of ORA members is more open and independent. While the majority of KKD members are appointed by village heads, all members of ORA are elected by villagers. In Donorojo, for example, in 1997, 13 (81.25 per cent) of the total of 16 members of KKD were appointed by the village head. In 2001, all of 37 members of ORA were elected by villagers after being nominated by KKD members.

Improvement in bargaining and negotiation skills has allowed ORAs' members to control the village representative bodies (the BPDs). In Gunung Kidul District, Yogyakarta, for example, it was estimated that ORAs have secured between 60 per cent and 80 per cent seats in the BPDs. This domination has allowed ORA to control the direction of village development. As argued by Puji Astuti, a member of ORA in Semin, Gunung Kidul: 'Through ORA we have succeeded in changing the village government's plan to build a dam in the prosperous northern part of our village. After long debates at the BPD meetings we finally succeed in moving the dam to the less prosperous southern part of the village' (CD-Bethesda 2001: 11).

Influencing policy-making at village level, however, does not seem to be the only target of ORA. Subiyono expects that in the future ORA should become an independent partner of CD-Bethesda not only in devising and implementing development programmes, but also in disseminating the idea of people's sovereignty to the grassroots population (Subiyono, interview, 06/07/2001). One possible way to achieve this target is through the formation of a network involving different ORAs. For this purpose, on 25–27 January 2001 CD organised a meeting for ORA representatives from all over Indonesia. Held at CD's central office in Yogyakarta, this meeting was attended by 71 representatives from Yogyakarta, Central Java, Lombok, Flores, Sumba, Alor and West Papua.

Three major issues seemed to have dominated the meeting. First, programme evaluation in which ORA representatives sat together and evaluated every programme they had carried out in their respective villages. The delegates were divided into eight groups: (1) the Kulon Progo region; (2) the Central Java region; (3) the Flores region; (4) the Sumba region; (5) the Alor region; (6) the health workers group; (7) the professional group; and (8) the handicrafts group. Each delegate presented his/her organisation's programme implementation, while others made comments or asked questions. All conversations were taped and documented. Most delegates agreed that despite their successful experience in implementing various programmes, they felt that ORAs still need to improve their human resources, especially in the area of organisational skills and knowledge of democracy (CD-Bethesda 2001: 27). Second, the renewal of vision and mission. Since many ORAs were formed before the introduction of Law No. 22/1999 on regional autonomy which allowed the formation of BPDs (village councils), they felt it necessary to respond to the new development by reviewing their vision and mission. The session was divided into four groups consisting of 15–20 delegates. Each group discussed new visions and missions to be adopted by ORAs. A final decision was made in the plenary session. In their renewed vision, ORAs focused on law enforcement, anti-corruption and self-reliance. They also put more emphasis on civil society formation and empowerment at village level in their revised mission. Third, problem identification. With the help of CD's facilitators, delegates were asked to identify current social, economic and political problems in their respective areas. They were also asked to make recommendations of the possible solution to the problems. Table 5.5 outlines ORAs' problem identification and recommendations drawn from the January 2001 meeting.

What has been achieved by ORA after three years of its formation? My interviews with villagers and staff members of CD indicate that ORA has contributed to village democratisation in at least four different ways.[19] First, ORA has increased villagers' assertiveness in expressing their criticism to village government. At many of ORA meetings, villagers openly discuss their problems through which they express their direct criticism to the village head and his/her subordinates. Second, villagers have become more active in the village decision-making process. As ORA tends to dominate BPD's membership (at least in Central Java and Yogyakarta), villagers have more power to counter the influence of the village head in determining the direction of development in their village. Third, ORA has made villagers more aware of democracy. Through a series of training sessions and civic education, ORA has taught villagers how to develop the idea of tolerance,

*Table 5.5* Outline of ORA's problem identification and recommendations

| Problems identified | ORA's recommended actions |
| --- | --- |
| *Political problems* | |
| Lack of law enforcement | Training in state laws, rules and regulations |
| Poor knowledge of democracy among grassroots people | Political education and training |
| Power abuse by the ruling elite | Serving in opposition to the village government |
| Collusion, corruption and nepotism | Demanding more accountability and transparency of village government |
| Poor quality of public services | |
| *Economic problems* | |
| Decline of per-capita income due to economic crisis | Facilitating rural micro-enterprises |
| Unequal access to economic resources and capital | Opening up new access of villagers to local resources |
| Lack of government support to village co-operatives | Supporting local co-operatives |
| | Organising regular management training |
| Poor human resources | Disseminating the spirit of entrepreneurship among villagers |
| Poor knowledge of market mechanism | |
| *Social problems* | |
| Social inequality | Organising training and simulation in conflict resolution techniques |
| Deterioration of norms and values | |
| Increasing primordial conflicts | Disseminating the concept of tolerance and pluralism |

Source: Compiled from CD-Bethesda. 2001. *Laporan Hasil Pertemuan Organisasi Rakyat dan Organisasi Profesional Mitra CD-Bethesda.* Yogyakarta: CD-Bethesda, pp. 23–25.

pluralism, political bargaining, and so forth. Fourth, the involvement of ORA members in BPD consultative meetings with the village head seems to have increased accountability and transparency of village government. Because BPD has the power to approve or disapprove of village legislation and budget, the village head becomes increasingly obliged to be more transparent in running various development projects. Whether or not ORA can be sustained for a long period of time is not clear. But the enthusiasm of its members and the conducive political environment after the implementation of the law on regional autonomy have raised optimism among the villagers about the future of ORA.

### *BSY: implementing the PRA method*

Unlike CD, BSY is not interested in political mobilisation. According to its current director, Aleks Wiyarto, there are at least three reasons which have prevented his organisation from getting involved in village politics. First, BSY tries to maintain its original function as a development-oriented NGO focusing on community development activities as stated in its constitution. Second, BSY has very limited human resources. All of its existing staff members are trained to help villagers to run small-scale business activities and to discourage them from getting involved in local politics. Third, the majority of its KSM (people's self-reliant groups) members are women who are not disposed to get involved in village politics (Wiyarto, interview, 03/07/2001).

However, the lessening of the village officials' tendency to 'patronise' NGOs has encouraged BSY to be more concerned with attempts to build villagers' awareness of their social and political situation. No longer thinking that they have to adjust their concept and approach to the state's development programmes, BSY's staff members begin to realise that villagers have to be encouraged to determine the direction of their own development without any intervention from village officials. As argued by BSY's vice-director, Sudarman: 'In the post-Suharto era, when we have more freedom to design and run our own programmes in villages, we can ask people to be more responsible for their own development' (Sudarman, interview, 03/07/2001).

For this purpose, BSY adopts the PRA technique, a method of assessment of rural development problems in which villagers carry out their own appraisal, analysis, planning, action, monitoring and evaluation, while outsiders facilitate, sit down, listen and learn. PRA has been developed and spread since the first half of the 1990s as a method to enable rural people to share, enhance and analyse their knowledge of life and conditions (Chambers 1997: 103). This method has often astonished facilitators and surprised local people who have found themselves doing things they did not know they were capable of.

Widely used in Latin America, Africa and Asia, PRA has contributed to the rise of a new understanding of the role of outsiders and local people in rural development. This new interpretation consists of five important views: (1) outsiders should reflect critically on their concepts, values, behaviour and methods; (2) they should learn through engagement and committed action; (3) they have roles as convenors, catalysts and facilitators; (4) the weak and marginalised can and should be empowered; and (5) the poor people can and should do much of their own investigation, analysis and planning (Chambers 1997: 108).

In order to allow local people to play a greater role in identifying and in analysing local problems, PRA uses a number of approaches that can be classified into six different categories. First, mapping and modeling: people draw a map with chalks, sticks, seeds, powder, pens and so on to describe the social, economic, health or demographic situation of their respective village. Second, time lines and trend analysis: people describe chronologies of events with approximate dates in order to show ecological histories, changes in land use and cropping patterns, rates of migration, fuel uses, level of education and so on. Third, linkage diagramming: people make diagrams indicating the flow, connection and causality of events. These versatile diagrams have been used for the analysis of sequences, marketing, nutrient flows on farms, social contact and impacts of interventions. Fourth, wealth ranking: people arrange and rank households starting from the richest to the poorest according to local criteria (land ownership, level of income and so on). The purpose of this method is to show the livelihood of the whole households in the village. Fifth, analysis of difference: people analyse experiences of different groups (by gender, social grouping, wealth/poverty, occupation and age) in order to identify differences between groups, including their problems and preferences. Sixth, shared presentation and analysis: maps, models, diagrams and findings are presented by local people and/or by outsiders, and checked, corrected or discussed in group meetings.

In 1998 BSY began to pay serious attention to the PRA technique by sending four staff members to study the PRA method in a two-month course at *Bina Swadaya*'s Jakarta central office. In June 1999, this organisation devised a pilot project called 'Project Support to Home Workers' Response to the Economic Crisis' to assess current problems and challenges faced by some of their KSMs. About 13 KSMs from different villages in Yogyakarta were selected as target groups. Using the PRA method, this programme was carried out to achieve two targets: (1) to enable villagers to identify and analyse factors that have caused the decline of average household income as a result of the 1997 economic crisis; and (2) to enable villagers to find their own solutions to the problems (BSY 1999: 4).

The project was launched in Sendangsari village, Bantul District, Yogyakarta, involving 44 KSM members, the majority of which are women. In this village, all of the KSM members are running small-scale business activities such as food stalls, petty trading, processed-food home industries and so on. After the 1997 economic crisis, all businesses in the village fell off due to several problems: (1) the substantial increase (between 200 and 300 per cent) of the prices of raw materials; (2) the decline of market demand as a result of income deterioration; (3) higher production costs due to the high inflation rates; and (4) the scarcity of raw materials as a result of the poor distribution system. Sendangsari village was selected as a pilot project by BSY because in this village KSMs were most seriously affected by the economic crisis. Many of KSM members are unable to repay their debts because their businesses are on the brink of total collapse.

In carrying out the project, BSY has assigned nine of its staff members to play different roles. Setya Utama and Mugiyo serve as facilitators who lead the discussions, encourage villagers to express their views, provide necessary information, and create a stimulating environment for brainstorming. Kusmartono and Kristin Indarjati serve as observers who monitor the whole process and make sure that all procedures are followed. Sasongko, Yosephus and Kristanto serve as notetakers who record the whole process. Hartoyo and Cecillia serve as supervisors who monitor the project and give feedback to all participants. In Sendangsari, the whole process was carried out from June to December 1999. Initially, BSY activists carried out preliminary research to gather information with respect to the problems faced by KSMs after the 1997 financial crisis.

The programme itself was divided into three important stages. First, mapping, in which villagers were asked to draw a map using a boardmarker on a piece of paper describing the whole situation of the village: roads, river, houses, school, rice-fields, village enterprises and so on. The purpose of this method was to enable villagers to give a detailed description of their village. A general description of directions, main roads, river and so on was provided by facilitators. Villagers were asked to locate strategic places (the local market, rice-fields, river, fishponds and so on) and the households on the map. They were also asked to locate large, medium and small-scale business activities in their area according to their own estimation. Second, problem identification which included attempts to encourage villagers to detect problems that had caused the decline of small-scale businesses in their area. At this stage, local people were asked to make diagrams indicating the connection or causality of events. The meeting was divided into smaller groups consisting of seven to eight participants, each of which were required to name factors that had contributed to the economic decline in the village. All identified factors were discussed at a plenary meeting at the end of the session. Third, problem analysis and solution in which all maps, diagrams and tables were checked, commented on and discussed at a plenary meeting. Guided by facilitators, participants were required to propose solutions for each problem. In order to avoid over-generalisation, problems were classified into different categories based on social grouping, gender, age, occupation, income and so on. At this session, villagers were also asked to devise a collective action plan to solve the identified problems.

In December 1999, at the end of the whole session, KSM members in Sendangsari began to realise that they actually had have a mental capability to describe their own village in detail, to detect problems, to propose solutions and to devise a collective action plan. After they had shown their houses, resource maps and models, linkage diagrams, wealth ranking and other findings they began to gain confidence that through planned collective action they were able to solve their problems. As argued by Suro Utomo, one of the participants of the programme: 'Initially, we are not sure whether we can draw maps or diagrams about our village accurately. But, with the help from facilitators we eventually gain confidence (*keyakinan*) that we can find alternative solutions to our problems' (BSY 2001: 27). It appears that BSY's facilitators played an important role in stimulating the discussion. After pointing the direction, facilitators demanded the more informed participants to draw main roads, footpaths, river and trees on the map; and they asked all participants to locate their own house, stall, land, cattle and so forth. Discussions started to take place when participants began to get involved in debates determining the precise location of their properties (BSY 2001: 18).

Since most participants were running small-scale food production and trading, the discussions were dominated by attempts to identify problems that had caused the decline of their earnings and efforts to devise a solution to problems in their processed-food business activity. They agreed that their businesses had gone down due to several reasons. First, the growing competition in the food business sector due to growing number of new competitors. Villagers believed that the close-down of many factories and other business establishments in the city of Yogyakarta had driven people who subsequently opened small businesses as a temporary refuge back to their villages. Second, they agreed that the price increase of raw materials used in production had led to a subsequent decrease in their earnings. In this growing competition, they felt that increasing the sale price of their products was totally out of the question because it could diminish their competitiveness. Third, the scarcity of raw materials due to the poor distribution system. As a result of a growing political uncertainty and instability in the post-Suharto era, the distribution of goods has become increasingly problematic, especially when the government is no longer able to control the distribution networks. Fourth, a steady decline of demand for processed food due to the deterioration of popular income. The villagers realised that when the whole population suffered from income reduction, the tendency to cut down on the consumption of processed food became more obvious.

At the end of the programme, participants made several recommendations all of which were subsequently implemented with the help from BSY. These recommendations included: (1) an attempt to form village business associations (*persatuan wirausaha desa*) in order to avoid tough competition in different sectors of activities; (2) a collective purchase of raw materials in which BSY provides soft loans for KSM members who need extra money to buy a large number of raw materials; (3) an effort to encourage KSM members to purchase a large amount of raw materials and establish a collective storage system in order to avoid scarcity; (4) an attempt to encourage villagers to produce half-processed foods and sell them to a number of outlets outside Yogyakarta. In September 2000, BSY began to help KSM members in Sendangsari to implement all of their planned actions. Several business associations were formed and organised according to different types of businesses which included the cassava-crackers producers association, the food-stall runners association and the *geplak* (coconut-cake) traders association. BSY also provided soft loans for these associations in order to enable them to organise a collective purchase of raw materials. With the help from BSY's fieldworkers, KSM members began to produce half-processed foods and sold their products to a number of outlets in other cities such as Semarang, Surabaya and Jakarta. The establishment of a common storage system was attempted, but villagers failed to agree on how to manage this and on who should look after the storage. However, villagers are generally satisfied with their actions. Although the slow recovery of the national economy has made their businesses remain uncertain, they are convinced that their collective actions have prevented their businesses from total collapse. As argued by Marsiyam, a member of the food-stall runners association: 'Although we cannot recover our business to the situation prior to the economic crisis, we can still avoid total bankruptcy because we have worked together to solve our problems' (BSY 2001: 36).

In general, BSY activists think that their pilot project in Sendangsari has succeeded in achieving its main targets. In his personal account of the programme, Aleks Wiyarto (BSY's current executive director), argues:

> The PRA experience has led to insights and discoveries. I was surprised that local people have largely unexpected capabilities for appraisal, analysis and planning. Diagramming and visual sharing are popular and powerful in expressing and in analysing complexity. All in all, villagers are always enthusiastic in taking part in the whole process. I strongly believe that our competent staff members have succeeded in enabling local people to analyse their own problems and to devise their own actions.
>
> (Wiyarto, interview, 03/07/2001)

The use of PRA seems to have reversed BSY's approach to running community development programmes. Whereas in the past BSY, like other development-oriented NGOs, tended to put emphasis on how to set up pre-determined development programmes to be implemented by villagers, nowadays this organisation is prepared to give villagers more freedom to carry out their own assessment and to propose their own solutions to the existing problems as manifested in the Sendangsari pilot project. Indeed, the situation in the post-Suharto era – in which grassroots people have more freedom and the autonomy to express their will – has encouraged BSY to involve villagers in the design and implementation of its village development programmes. Thus, although BSY does not respond to the new development by conducting political mobilisation in rural areas, it nevertheless takes the opportunity by encouraging villagers to determine their own development.

## Developing professional management and institution

As has been discussed in Chapter 2, as part of the voluntary sector NGOs tend to face problems of ambiguity with regard to the way they set their objectives, determine their approach, mobilise financial resources, carry out planning and budgeting, monitor performance and develop a professional management system. Although institutional development[20] and management have not been the major concern of NGOs (as they tend to focus more on programmes and relations with target groups rather than on their own administration), gradually, however, NGOs have begun to think about improvement in their institutional performance and management system (Sahley 1995: 49; Smillie 1995: 152).

Professionalism, according to Fincham and Rhodes (1996: 283), refers to a set of character and method which links services and activities performed by a particular organisation with a code of ethics, extensive skills, technical knowledge and competence. Professional management, therefore, is a kind of management which is based on ethics, skills, knowledge and competence to achieve goals. In the past, professional management was not a term people used when talking about the NGO sector because management was seen as part of the culture of business and was not considered to be appropriate for value-led organisations. However, nowadays NGO staff begin to see professional management as a key factor that will determine the success of the organisation (Hansmann 1994; Rose-Ackerman 1994; Hudson 1995; Salamon and Anheier 1996; Fowler 1997). In their attempt to professionalise their management, NGOs normally concentrate on the questions of how to mobilise financial resources to ensure stability, how to devise effective planning, how to pursue sufficient staff development, how to adopt appropriate leadership and management style and how to develop an accountability system. Some NGO writers suggest that there are at least five important aspects of NGO management: (1) financial management or budgeting; (2) staff development; (3) strategic management; (4) leadership; and (5) system of accountability (Handy 1988; Drucker 1990; Steinberg 1990; Billis 1993; Oster 1994; Hudson 1995; Salamon and Anheier 1996; Fowler 1997; Berman 1998; Suzuki 1998).

## Financial management or budgeting

Fowler (1997: 153) noted that there are at least three major components of NGOs' financial structure: (1) external financing which includes grants or revolving funds from foreign funding agencies and governments; (2) local financial resources which include fund-raising from the general public (mailing, appeals, campaigns, special events and so forth), grants from local government, corporate support and contribution from local charities; and (3) self-financing which includes sale of products and services that used to be free, consultancy fees and commissions. Nowadays, funds generated by market-driven activities have become increasingly crucial in ensuring NGOs' financial stability because they are more predictable and reliable in the sense that they can be accessed or paid out when needed; they are free from stringent conditions imposed by the contributors and ensure long-term impact because they are allocated according to programme instead of project (Sahley 1995: 23; Fowler 1997: 134).

In Indonesia, between the 1980s and 1990s, self-financing became more important for NGOs following the withdrawal of foreign donors (as they saw less justification for their activities in this fast-growing society). Meanwhile, the lack of support from the government (except occasional contribution to joint projects) and the difficulty to raise funding from society have also contributed to NGOs' decision to run cost-recovery projects. Conscious of the government's tendency to patronise the voluntary sector, NGO leaders were reluctant to receive regular financial assistance from state agencies because of the fear that such grants would allow the government to impose financial control and a possible take-over of their organisation (Ibrahim 1997: 105). Attempts by Indonesian NGOs to raise money from society are undermined by a number of factors: (1) the fact that NGO activities are not familiar to the public in general; (2) the limited amount of personal economic surplus in society; (3) the tendency of most Indonesian people to donate money directly to the poor;[21] and (4) the absence of a tax rebate system to individual donors that would encourage local well wishers to donate their money (Kusumohadi *et al.* 1997: 121). Thus, for many development NGOs, running commercial projects is the only solution to ensure financial stability.

### BSY's financial mobilisation

BSY's self-financing resources come from three major sources. First, the *jasa konsultasi* (consultancy) in which BSY serves as a consultant for other institutions (usually state agencies and other NGOs) on various community development projects, especially the saving-and-credit activity. For example, since the early 1990s BSY has been acting as a consultant for the Yogyakarta district government in forming and in developing co-operative groups in various traditional markets (*pasar*) throughout the city. It also provided regular training programmes for other NGOs on the operation of small-credit disbursement. This sector constituted 12.08 per cent of BSY's total income in 2000 (Table 5.6) in which state agencies served as BSY's major clients. Second, the *usaha ekonomi* (economic

*Table 5.6* BSY's revenue from internal and external financial sources (2000)

| Sources of income | Amount of revenue (Rp) | Amount of revenue (in US$)[a] | Percentage of total revenue (%) |
|---|---|---|---|
| 1  Internal financing | 1,237,583,000 | 123,758 | 84.32 |
| Consultancy | 177,241,000 | 17,724 | 12.08 |
| Economic Enterprise | 40,847,000 | 4,084 | 2.78 |
| Accompanying Service | 1,019,495,000 | 101,949 | 69.46 |
| 2  External financing (Grants from CEBEMO, ILO and P-to-P) | 230,260,000 | 23,026 | 15.68 |
| Total (internal + external) | 1,467,843,000 | 146,784 | 100.00 |

Source: Bina Swadaya Yogyakarta. 2001. *Laporan Kinerja Tahun 2000.* Yogyakarta: BSY.

Note
a These figures are calculated at October 2001 exchange rates in which US$1 = Rp 10,000.

enterprise) which includes trading, animal husbandry, crop-growing and handicrafts. Trading includes the sale of fertilizers, concentrate and pesticides. Animal husbandry and crop-growing are based on the traditional sharing arrangement in which BSY pay all non-labour input costs, while villagers contribute their labour to livestock feeding, land preparation, ploughing and hoeing. Handicrafts were purchased directly from KSM members and sold to international buyers such as Oxfam and Fair Trade. BSY's income from this sector, however, decreased from a total of Rp 22.5 million in 1993 to Rp 21.6 million in 1994, to Rp 13.9 in 1995 and to Rp 9.5 million in 1996; but increased to Rp 25.3 million in 2000.[22] In 2000, this sector constituted just a small fraction of BSY's financial source (2.78 per cent of the total revenue) (Table 5.6). One reason for this small proportion is the fact that BSY has become increasingly specialised in small-credit disbursement programme. Third, the *jasa pendampingan* (accompanying service) in which BSY acts as a credit guarantor and a business consultant for small-scale enterprises in their relations with formal banking institutions and private firms. Working capital, management consultation and technical advice are provided with a specific amount of service charges. In 2000, this sector appeared to be the most important financial source for BSY in which 69.46 per cent of the organisation's total revenue was derived from this sector (Table 5.6).

From these three activities BSY managed to earn a relatively large amount of revenue. By 2000, this organisation had already become a self-sufficient organisation in which 84.32 per cent of its total revenue (Rp 1.22 billion out of a total Rp 1.46 billion) came from its commercial activities (Table 5.6). The data in Table 5.6 also suggest that the majority of BSY's internal financing comes from credit disbursement (69.46 per cent of the total revenue). Some argued that BSY's success in small-credit had to do with its ability to minimise costs by allowing KSM members themselves to evaluate credit liability of potential borrowers[23] (van Tuijl and Witjes 1993: 204; Eldridge 1995: 71). Rural small-credit programmes usually run high costs per *rupiah* spent because of the relatively low amount of the average loan, long administrative procedures and the need for investment to evaluate numerous small applicants (Roeloffs 1989: 20; Timberg 1989: 230). Commercial banks tend to resist small loans because of these high unit costs and the impossibility of making character judgements about applicants with whom they are not familiar (Tendler 1989: 38). By shifting much of the cost of processing loan applications from the bank to borrower groups, NGOs can avoid high administrative costs in their rural lending programmes. Tendler's study on SEWA (Self-employed Women's Association) in India and the Grameen Bank in Bangladesh confirmed that control over borrowers by peer groups has contributed to the high repayment rates and the more effective use of the money (Tendler 1989: 38).

In the case of BSY, KSMs decide who should receive a loan based on character judgements about the borrowers, rather than on an evaluation of their business proposals. Because they have better information about borrowers' attitudes, their assessment of borrowers' reliability is often accurate. Moreover, since BSY insists that further technical assistance and advice to the KSMs are dependent on the repayment rates of their members, KSMs tend to be more careful in deciding who should receive the loan. This mechanism contributes not only to the reduction of administrative costs but also to a more disciplined attitude of the borrowers which subsequently generates higher repayment rates. BSY's current director, Aleks Wiyarto, claimed that in 2000 his organisation had linked 183 KSMs with 11 banks distributing around Rp 582 million (US$58,200) in 41 villages to 5,000 households with repayment rates of 95 per cent (Wiyarto, interview, 03/07/2001).

*CD's self-financing*

CD began its commercial activities from the early 1990s. It focused on four main programmes. First, handicrafts in which various items made of ceramic, bamboo, rattan and leather were collected from craftsmen and sold to foreign buyers. CD supplied the raw materials, working capital, product designs, equipment and technical advice on quality standards, while villagers contributed their labour. In 2000, CD secured around Rp 810 million (9.32 per cent of its total revenue) from this sector alone (Table 5.7). Second, health care services in which CD runs several polyclinics in Yogyakarta, Central Java, East Timor, Alor and West Papua. In 2000, this sector served as an important financial source for CD, which secured Rp 2.4 billion (28.65 per cent of the total revenue). Third, training sessions and courses on health care targeting the public to be trained as paramedics. A number of courses on alternative medication (herbal preparation, acupuncture, traditional massage and reflexology) are conducted on a regular basis. While KKDs are trained in a shorter period (3–4 weeks) free of charge, other participants have to take longer courses (three months) and are asked to pay Rp 2 million (in 2000) for the course. In 2000, this sector constituted just a small fraction of CD's total revenue (2.43 per cent of the total revenue). Fourth, micro-enterprise development which included animal husbandry, small-credit and agricultural commodity trading. In 2000, this sector generated only Rp 104 million (1.20 per cent of CD's total revenue).

*Table 5.7* CD's revenue from internal and external financial sources (2000)

| Sources of revenue | Amount of revenue (Rp) | Amount of revenue (US$)[a] | Proportion of total revenue (%) |
|---|---|---|---|
| 1  Internal financing | 3,618,369,715 | 361,837 | 41.60 |
|     Handicrafts trading | 810,698,511 | 81,070 | 9.32 |
|     Health services | 2,492,671,141 | 249,267 | 28.65 |
|     Training and Course Fees | 210,465,624 | 21,047 | 2.43 |
|     Micro-enterprise devt. | 104,534,439 | 10,453 | 1.20 |
| 2  External financing | 5,080,362,047 | 508,036 | 58.40 |
|     Foreign donors[b] | 4,001,670,448 | 400,167 | 46.00 |
|     Bethesda Hospital | 1,078,691,599 | 107,869 | 1.40 |
| Total (Internal + External) | 8,698,731,762 | 869,873 | 100.00 |

Source: CD-Bethesda. 2000. *Laporan Pelaksanaan Program Tahun 2000.* Yogyakarta: CD-Bethesda.

Note
a Calculated at October 2000 rates of exchange, US$1 = Rp 10,000.
b CD's foreign funds come mainly from EZE (Germany), Simavi (The Netherlands) and ICCO (The Netherlands).

The data on the financial structures of the two NGOs suggest that bigger size does not necessarily mean a higher degree of financial self-sufficiency. While in 2000 BSY generated more than 80 per cent of its revenue from its own market-driven activities, at the same time CD secured only 41.60 per cent. Compared to BSY, CD appeared to be less self-sufficient because 58.40 per cent of its total revenue came from foreign donors – EZE (Germany), Simavi (The Netherlands) and ICCO (The Netherlands) – and its patron, the Bethesda Hospital. However, these figures indicate a high proportion of self-financing compared, for example, to another NGO such as BRAC in Bangladesh which raised only 31 per cent of its turnover from commercial activities (Fowler 1997: 145). One explanation of BSY's determination to become financially self-sufficient was the financial pressure in 1992 following its 'separation' from *Bina Swadaya*. Aleks Wiyarto, the director of BSY, recalled: '*Bina Swadaya*'s decision to make our organisation independent by allowing just one year period of transition has made us think and work harder in pursuing activities that would generate income' (Wiyarto, interview, 29/01/1997). Similarly, CD's commercial activities also emerged from a desperate situation following organisational restructuring in the early 1990s, which made CD a semi-independent organisation by no longer operating as a community development arm of the Bethesda Hospital (Wijayanto, interview, 07/06/1997). Another factor that might have contributed to the 'success' of both BSY and CD in mobilising their internal financial sources was the growing number of SSCIs in rural areas as a result of the state's active promotion of this sector. It was estimated that between 1970 and 1990, the number of SSCIs all over Indonesia had doubled from around 900,000 to 1,800,000 (Tambunan 1992: 89). This rapid expansion has enabled BSY and CD to establish links with the growing rural micro-enterprises and run their commercial projects.

160  *Development, empowerment and professionalism*

Like many other NGOs, both BSY and CD wanted people to believe that they are productive at a minimum cost. One way to measure NGOs' efficiency is by looking at the ratio of administrative costs to total income (Fowler 1997: 155). The absence of a standard accounting procedure has made it difficult to determine the extent to which an NGO is efficient. Moreover, NGOs may apportion their overhead costs to projects so that they may look highly efficient. Some NGO observers, however, argued that an efficient NGO should have a ratio of administrative costs to the total revenue of around 5–20 per cent (Smillie 1995: 152; Fowler 1997: 156). This means that in order to be considered efficient, an NGO should not spend more than 20 per cent of its total income on administrative costs (salaries, rent, electricity and so on). In 2000, BSY paid administrative costs of Rp 101 million (6.9 per cent) of its total revenue of Rp 1.4 billion (BSY 2001: appendix 1), indicating an efficiency rate far below the 20 per cent limit set above. Meanwhile, CD allocated Rp 1.1 billion (12.8 per cent) of its total revenue of Rp 8.6 billion (CD-Bethesda 1997: 59), indicating its status as an efficient NGO.

## *Staff development*

Fincham and Rhodes (1996: 112) argued that job satisfaction among the employees of a particular organisation is determined by two factors: (1) 'motivators' which include recognition, status, achievement, advancement and promotion; and (2) 'hygiene factors' that can be associated with working conditions, salary, job security, company policy and interpersonal relations. In terms of both motivators and hygiene factors, BSY did not seem to be attractive to most university graduates. The fact that BSY could only offer a low level of salary, few career prospects[24] and a low employment status appeared to have limited its capability to attract workers with specialised skills, experience and high educational background. Even if it managed to employ workers with some qualification, as it did in the late 1980s, they moved as soon as they had found better jobs elsewhere. As a result, BSY suffered from a high employment turn over. For example, only four of its total twelve staff members have been working with the NGO for more than four years, five have been working between for 3–4 years, and three have been working between six months and two years (Wiyarto, interview, 03/07/2001). In 2001, the monthly salary of BSY's staff members ranged between Rp 450,000 and Rp 1,500,000 which was slightly lower than that of the private sector in Yogyakarta (Rp 600,000–1,800,000) or other NGOs such as PKBI (Rp 700,000 – 2,000,000) and *Dian Desa* (Rp 650,000–3,000,000); but it was approximately the same level as the salaries of civil servants. Given that most BSY's staff members consider the level of salary as an important factor in their decision to accept a particular job, the organisation cannot avoid a high level of employment turn over.

In terms of educational background, most of BSY's workers have completed one or two-years of university education, but only two have actually completed their university degrees. This seems to substantiate an early study stating that BSY suffers from a serious lack of professional skills, which subsequently limits its capacity to maintain and expand programmes (van Tuijl and Witjes 1993: 215).

Many of BSY's programmes in the economic enterprise sector (rice-hulling, trading, handicrafts, animal husbandry and crop-growing) had to be reduced or cancelled because of the absence of competent staff or because experienced workers had moved elsewhere. However, BSY benefited from *Bina Swadaya*'s excellent community development training programmes in Sawangan, Bogor. Staff members are sent regularly to attend those programmes free of charge.

Meanwhile, CD adopted a totally different approach to staff development. Its ability to offer higher salaries (compared to other NGOs), better fringe benefits (housing, health insurance, pension fund and other bonuses) and career promotion has certainly made this organisation more attractive to university graduates or workers with specialised skills and experience. In 2000, the monthly salary of CD's workers ranged between Rp 1,000,000 and Rp 6,000,000. On top of that, workers received bonuses equal to the monthly salary paid over during Christmas and the Muslim New Year (CD-Bethesda 2000: 14). In the case of illness, workers and their families are entitled to free treatment at the Bethesda Hospital. Since 1995, CD has also provided its employees with an interest-free housing loan. A housing estate consisting of 36 houses was built in Besi, about 15 km to the north of Yogyakarta to house its workers. Priority was given to those in desperate need of housing and payment is deducted from their monthly salary (CD-Bethesda 1996a: 147).

Working on a larger size, CD is able to create a hierarchy of power which allows some kind of career paths. CD's top managerial position is in the hands of an executive body (*badan pelaksana*) consisting of an executive director, two vice-directors and seven area managers who directly supervise 16 section heads (*kepala bagian*). Its current director has just been promoted from the position of area manager. In terms of skills and technical knowledge, CD regularly sends workers to various short courses, workshops, seminars and conferences both at home and abroad. By 2001, about 75 per cent of CD's staff members (59 out of 78) held university degrees, 12 of whom held Master's degrees (CD-Bethesda 1997: 41). Most talented staff are given opportunity to pursue degree courses in a specialised field of study. With a relatively high level of education and intellectual capability, some of CD's workers are able to win scholarships offered by domestic and foreign institutions. Internal scholarships are provided for those who pursued studies in Yogyakarta or in the nearby cities. In 2000, one staff member completed his doctorate from a university in Malaysia and six others had just finished their master's courses in Australia, Malaysia and the Philippines (Subiyono, interview, 06/07/2001). Without doubt, CD is able to develop relatively strong human resources and create a stable organisation. More than two-thirds of its workers have been working for four to eight years and only seven (about 10 per cent) of them have been working for less than four years (CD-Bethesda 1997: 37), which indicates a low level of employment turn over.

## *Strategic management*

For the NGO sector, through which people with different aspirations need to be integrated to share common missions, objectives and values, the adoption of strategic management[25] is important in order to avoid contradiction between action and mission (Billis 1993: 132). A strategic management can also help organisations respond to new challenges and make all staff members and stakeholders clear about their roles (Hudson 1995: 89; Fowler 1997: 45). One most important component of strategic management is strategic planning whose objective is to make long-term choices in terms of concrete goals and resource allocations, which are likely to maximise impact without compromising identity, autonomy and viability (Hudson 1995: 133). Some NGO commentators argued that when NGOs grow in size, the pressure to adopt strategic planning is greater because the separation of tasks, hierarchy of authority and less intensive interpersonal relations among staff members would lead to a great deal of confusion over vision, mission and objectives (Smillie 1995: 147; Fowler 1997: 46; Berman 1998: 119).

Operating on a small-scale basis, in which workers had a great deal of opportunity to establish interpersonal relations, BSY had no intention to develop a strategic plan. As Wiyarto put it:

> Our small (*ramping*) organisation has allowed interpersonal communication and interaction to flow smoothly between different sections. Every problem is always settled through deliberation (*musyawarah*). For us, developing a family-like management style (*manajemen kekeluargaan*) is more important than strategic planning.
>
> (Wiyarto, interview, 20/01/1997)

CD, on the other hand, regarded strategic planning as the only way to internalise its 'core values' to staff members and to focus its skills and energies on what it could do best. Sigit Wijayanto, CD's former executive director, argued that a strategic plan should be adopted in order to guarantee better performance because the organisation's vision and mission need to be shared by all staff members at all levels (Wijayanto, interview, 31/01/1997). With 78 staff members, many of whom worked in different localities (Yogyakarta, Central Java, Flores, Alor, West Papua and East Timor), while mechanisms for an extensive interpersonal dialogue were not in place, CD considered strategic planning as priority. Thus, with the help from two international NGOs operating in Yogyakarta – Oxfam (UK) and USC (Canada) – CD began to implement its strategic planning activity in July 1995.

This process involved four stages.[26] First, preparation which included data collection, identification of critical issues and the setting of development priorities. It took three to four weeks to complete. Second, reappraisal and revision which included the process of redefining beliefs, values and identity, revision of original strategies, identification of policy options and analysis of strengths, weaknesses, opportunities and threats (SWOT). This was carried out through a series of discussions and brainstorming under the guidance of external facilitators from Oxfam and USC. The whole process lasted approximately three weeks. Third, the drafting of a strategic plan document called the *buku putih* (the white book) which documented CD's mission, vision, budgeting, assessment of current social and political situations, prediction of future direction of the organisation and identification of challenges and opportunities. The first draft was discussed and revisions were made on the basis of feedback from staff members which took more than eight weeks to complete. Fourth, implementation in which the final version of the 'white book' (completed by December 1995) was distributed to staff and field-workers in different localities and necessary adjustment of field operation to the new mission, goals and objectives were made (CD-Bethesda 1996b: 4–5). It was difficult to measure the immediate impact of the strategic planning on CD's performance because performance is determined by many factors. One of CD's staff members in Central Java, however, commented that the 'white book' has enabled workers to develop a clear picture of the NGO's main objectives (*tujuan utama*) and 'core values' (*nilai dasar*), which guide their action (Sarjono, interview, 02/07/1997).

## *Leadership: the 'power' and 'role' cultures*

Leadership is always important for NGOs. Externally, a strong leadership will enable NGOs to deal with other agencies and stakeholders in their fund-raising, lobbying and negotiation activities. Internally, leadership is also required to overcome bureaucratic rigidities and resistance from lower managerial positions who may be in fear of losing control or power (Berman 1998: 20). Fowler (1997: 75) argued that in most Southern NGOs, leadership tends to be highly personalised: a leader or manager is appreciated by staff in terms of how he/she establishes linkages in the wider context within society. No matter what the formal position and job description may specify, the individual occupying it is often expected to make a qualitative difference and guidance on how things are to be done and how relations with external agencies should be established. Consequently, NGO managers are often leaders of the organisations too; and they need to set agendas and mobilise followers by appealing to their inner convictions, often other instruments of guidance – either coercion or incentives – whenever available or culturally appropriate. The problem of NGO leadership is that while a strong leader is necessary to ensure sustainability and greater impact, heavy reliance on prominent leaders tends to dilute internal democracy and responsiveness toward grassroots demands (Constantino-David 1992: 140–1; Billis 1993: 180–1; Hudson 1995: 241–2).

Handy (1993: 184) differentiated between what he called 'power culture' and 'role culture' in NGO leadership. In a 'power culture' organisation, leadership depends on a central power source, with rays of power and influence beaming from that central figure. A 'power culture' organisation is therefore a 'political' organisation whose faith is determined by a personal ruler with a habit of direct intervention rather than by the purely logical procedures or rules (Handy 1988: 86; 1993: 184). This type of leadership is particularly apparent in small organisations where a dominant individual leader makes most decisions (Handy 1993: 184). Meanwhile, in a 'role culture' organisation, the exercise of authority is determined by a set of rules and procedures. The main characteristics of a 'role culture' organisation seem to follow Weber's description of a bureaucracy in which: (1) authority and responsibility of staff are clearly defined; (2) positions are organised into a hierarchy of power; (3) staff members are selected on the basis of technical qualifications and competence; (4) officials are to be appointed rather than elected; and (5) staff members are subject to strict rules, discipline and controls regarding the official duties (Handy 1993: 129). Larger-sized organisations opt for this type of leadership because it will offer the chance of specialist expertise and because it will ensure more security and predictability (Handy 1988: 89; 1993: 185).

Judging from the way in which authority is exercised, BSY seems to follow Handy's category of 'power culture' where the fate of the organisation depends entirely on the presence of Aleks Wiyarto, its long-term director and co-founder, who controls almost all of the organisation's decision-making and operation (programme planning, proposal writing and fund-raising). His long association with the organisation and long experience in community development activities (longer than anyone else in the organisation) have made staff members hold him in such high esteem that they grant him the privilege of determining BSY's strategy and action. Moreover, its small size and family-like management style have prevented BSY from developing procedures of operation. Rather than functioning as a bureaucracy, BSY operates instead on the basis of guidance from its director. As one of its staff members puts it: 'We cannot imagine BSY's sustainability without the presence of Aleks (Wiyarto), who knows every detail of community development activities better than anyone else (in the organisation)' (Sudarman, interview, 03/07/2001). Although as a 'power culture' organisation BSY can move quickly between localities or programmes, it suffers from a low morale because workers are frustrated by the absence of a career path and because of the domination of the top leader. This seems to have disturbed BSY's organisational stability as illustrated by the high employment turn over discussed earlier.

Meanwhile, since the early 1990s CD has moved closer towards Handy's category of 'role culture'. Operating on a larger scale, CD relies on rules and procedures which distribute jobs and authority among workers. Its executive director and the two vice-directors (one in charge of health care programmes and another in charge of micro-enterprise development) carry the tasks of meeting main objectives (i.e. making villagers responsible for their own health, economic and political activities), making the best use of resources, providing direction to subordinates, developing teamwork, making decisions, monitoring performance and resolving problems (CD-Bethesda 1996b: 16). Its seven area managers (two in Yogyakarta, one in Central Java, one in Flores, one in Alor, one in East Timor and another one in West Papua) are assigned to implement programmes, resolve problems within their territory, write proposals and reports and supervise fieldworkers (CD-Bethesda 1996b: 16). Its section heads are assigned to provide support to area managers and fieldworkers regarding specific issues under their jurisdiction (training, research and development, women's issues, handicrafts, animal husbandry and so on) (CD-Bethesda 1996b: 17). Individuals are selected based on satisfactory performance of a role and their performance is judged on the basis of their knowledge, skill and ability to carry out tasks (Subiyono, interview, 07/07/2001). A 'role culture' seems to offer more security and predictability both to the organisation and the workers. While the organisation benefits from a relatively stable environment, the workers enjoy relative security and are less confused in carrying out their activities. For example, the transition from Paulus Santosa's leadership to Guno Samekto, from Guno Samekto to Sigit Wijayanto, and from Sigit Wijayanto to Andreas Subiyono did not cause a serious problem because most workers already knew their roles and followed the organisation's rules and procedures. Although as a 'role culture' organisation CD has become less flexible than BSY, it enjoys a greater stability, which enables the organisation to sustain programmes.

## Performance and accountability

Measuring NGOs' overall impact on rural development is a risky business. First, NGOs' attempt to alter human behaviour depends on many external historical, cultural, social and political factors. Second, the timescales needed to assess impact are usually much longer than the ones needed to assess output or outcome of particular programmes (the number of wells installed, the amount of money distributed, the number of patients cured and so forth). Third, the impact on poverty does not occur only through NGOs which make it difficult to decide whether progress is related to NGO programmes or other factors (Fowler 1997: 161–2).

However, both BSY and CD have their own way of judging their performance. For BSY, success is determined by three factors: (1) the amount of money distributed to the KSM members: the larger the amount of money disbursed, the greater the impact on the community; (2) the number of KSMs formed; and (3) the capacity of KSM members to repay their debts on time (Widaningrum 1988: 26–7; Wiyarto, interview, 03/07/2001). While no one would question BSY's ability to increase the number of borrowers in the HBK programme, some argue that the high repayment rates might not indicate KSMs' productivity, but rather a result of villagers' practice of 'management of risks' in which they take money from overlapping rural small-credit schemes (provided both by the government and NGOs) and use it to repay their debts elsewhere (Hiemann 1997: 17; Rahardi 1997: 8).

CD attributes its performance to three aspects: (1) the number of KKDs – which later become ORAs – created in the villages; (2) its capacity to convince the government of the significance of alternative medication (acupuncture, reflexology and traditional massage) for the rural poor; and (3) the capacity of villagers to carry out sustainable income-generating activities (Wijayanto, interview, 31/01/1997; Subiyono, interview, 06/07/2001). With respect to ORAs, CD set a target of creating at least five ORAs in every village it serves. By 2001, CD managed to create an average of three ORAs in each village in Yogyakarta and Central Java (CD-Bethesda 2001: 4). CD's capacity to lobby the government was tested in 1991 when the organisation was involved in a row with the Ministry of Health over the inclusion of alternative medicine which led to a subsequent ban on its KKD training programme. The ministry refused alternative medication on two counts: (1) its ability to cure patients was not scientifically viable; and (2) its introduction would discourage villagers to seek help from health facilities provided by the government, especially the Puskesmas (Wijayanto, interview, 31/01/1997). However, after some long negotiation and lobbying activities, CD managed to regain its license to train KKDs. More importantly, the Ministry of Health also allowed CD to train the Prokesa and Apsari cadres in alternative medication. This was done amid the government's encouragement of self-help activity in the health sector. In the post-Suharto era, the decline of the government's capacity to provide subsidised health care to the poor has forced the government to welcome CD's contribution in the health sector. Small-enterprise development remained the weak point for CD as manifested in its trivial contribution (only 1.20 per cent) to the organisation's total revenue in 2000 (Table 5.7). One main reason was the fact that this sector is not the priority of CD's organisational mission (Subiyono, interview, 06/07/2001).

Drucker (1990: 113–14) argued that attempts to measure impact of the voluntary sector must be contextually determined and interpreted by various constituencies the organisation serves. In the context of development NGOs, Fowler (1997: 173) maintained that impact should be judged on the basis of 'the effective satisfaction of the rights and interests of legitimate stakeholders[27] in keeping with its mission'. Thus, a high-performing NGO must have the capacity to satisfy or influence its stakeholders, while a low-performing NGO lacks this capacity (Hashemi 1995; Ul Karim 1995). Using this definition, it appears that both BSY and CD are low performing NGOs because their accountability is usually directed 'upward'[28] towards the executive body (directors or vice-directors) and sometimes donors. Public accountability in terms of formal notification of activities and expenditures has never been pursued. Meanwhile, the government receives a full version of project reports only occasionally.

There are several reasons for this lack of 'downward' accountability. First, the funding structures of both BSY and CD, which indicate a heavy reliance on commercial activities, have limited the scope of accountability only to directors and senior managers. Uphoff (1995) noted that there is little difference between service-oriented NGOs and the for-profit sector in their relations with beneficiaries or customers because neither NGOs nor the for-profit sector are accountable to those who receive the goods and services provided. Although beneficiaries of an NGO may receive more benign treatment than do customers of a business, they have no right to make decisions about the goods and services provided (Uphoff 1995: 178). Thus, just like the for-profit sector, in which customers are in a 'take-it-or-leave-it' relationship, neither BSY nor CD feel obliged to provide detailed reports or project evaluation to their target groups.[29] Second, as has been mentioned in Chapter 4, in order to avoid regulation under the Law of Mass Organisations No. 8/1985 many NGOs set themselves up as foundations (*yayasan*) which required only a very general statement of objectives to be granted legal status by a local notary office. The *yayasan* arrangement has generally proved successful in evading potential take-over or co-optation by the state agencies because the state, as stated in Supreme Court Decision No. 124/1973, is not allowed to intervene in the management of a *yayasan* (Prijono 1992: 446). Moreover, as a *yayasan* NGOs can be exempted from payment of taxes as stipulated in the Tax Law of 1984 (Prijono 1992: 447). However, a *yayasan* is a highly undemocratic institution because control over the organisation's strategic matters is in the hands of an executive body (*badan pelaksana*) whose members are appointed rather than elected from among top managers and founders (Soemitro 1993: 164). Operating as *yayasan*, both BSY and CD tend to be held back from gaining experience of legal democratic processes and their structure of accountability to the target groups and the general public does not exist (Eldridge 1997: 211). The two organisations, however, conduct regular project evaluations – every three months (for BSY) and two months (for CD) – in which area managers, section heads and fieldworkers are held accountable to the executive body. Reports are made of every project and distributed to top leaders and donors, but not to representatives of target groups. Third, because most villagers are accustomed to the state's top–down approach whereby development agencies (both NGOs and the state) serve as patrons in initiating people's development, demands for NGOs' accountability from villagers are low, if not non-existent (Fakih 1996: 145–6). This may support Fowler's contention that there is not much NGOs can do to enhance their external accountability if the general public are indifferent, if the media are not concerned with voluntary activities and if the government (which serves as a key actor of development) is part of the problem (Fowler 1997: 183).

# 6 Building constituencies and institutionalising a movement
The case of women's NGOs

## The rise of women's movement

The rise of women's movements in developing societies can be attributed to the changing views of the role of women in the development process that generates a new kind of awareness among women to translate their self-protection efforts into political action.[1] While women are poorly represented in political bodies and power structures, they have learned to use other avenues to turn their aspirations into political action (Arce *et al.* 1994: 167; Karl 1995: 19). This leads to the formation of new organisations dedicated entirely to women. The socialist and radical activists tend to form revolutionary women's clubs, women worker's associations and radical political organisations. Likewise, concerned women of the upper-class may also form various social reform organisations addressing welfare and equality for women. The rise of women's NGOs in developing societies can therefore be understood in this context.

### Perspectives on women and development

Up until the early 1970s, development policies and programmes were considered to be gender-neutral, that is, they did not distinguish between men and women but were assumed to benefit automatically all people, women as well as men (Karl 1995: 94). Attention was given to women primarily as mothers and carers, or as particularly 'vulnerable' groups who were at the receiving end of any development assistance (Smillie 1995: 85). Consequently, programmes directed at women were related mainly to nutrition, child care, health and population control (Kabeer 1994: 3). By the mid-1970s, however, following the declaration of the 'decade for women' (1975–1985) by the United Nations, the perspective on the role of women in development had changed. Inspired by Ester Boserup's groundbreaking publication titled *Women's Role in Economic Development* (1970), researchers and activists began to make women more visible as active participants in production, households and other sector of society. The initial implication of Boserup's work was the shift of attention for women in the development process from welfare to equality, that is, from a focus on women's role as carers to a bold women agenda which called for the achievement of equality between the sexes

(Kabeer 1994: 7). Known as the women in development (WID) approach, this new perspective attempted to meet women's 'practical gender needs' for income and their 'strategic gender needs' for equality with men through legislative interventions by government and non-government development agencies[2] (Moser 1993: 62-4).

In the 1980s, the WID approach was increasingly criticised for its failure to offer solution for women's subordination in social relations (Kabeer 1994: 41). Radical women's researchers and activists proposed a more fundamental effort to bring women from the margins into the centre of the main development programmes. Known as gender and development (GAD) approach, this new perspective adopted a revolutionary method of empowerment by focusing on: (1) the strengthening of women's units, groups and organisations to ensure gender awareness, to act as pressure groups and to monitor the policies on women; and (2) the establishment of a critical mass of women inside development-oriented organisations (Karl 1995: 103). There were some who saw the GAD approach as having the potential to bring in a breakthrough in women's vision of development. For example, the Canadian Council for International Co-operation, as quoted by Karl (1995: 102), stated:

'Gender and development' is emerging as a progressive approach to development from women's perspectives and experiences. It is part of the larger work of creating an alternative development model, for a world view which moves beyond an economic analysis to include environmental, sustainable and qualitative (personal, ethical and cultural) aspects in its definition of development.

Without doubt, GAD has contributed to the rise of a new wave of women's movement in developing societies. This movement was fuelled by the realisation that women are still far from participating equally in society although some gains in the social, economic and political spheres might have been achieved. In Latin America, for instance, women's movement of the 1980s was strongly influenced by the influx of women militants who were no longer prepared to occupy traditional servicing roles or to accept the marginalisation of women's issues which was manifested in the formation of grassroots groups such as the people's kitchens and other community groups that began to flourish in the 1970s and 1980s (Sternbach et al. 1992: 212; Karl 1995: 32). The major concern of this movement was a continuous process of marginalisation of women as they tend to work longer days and are paid less than men. As Smillie put it: 'Women's long work day remains largely unrecorded in national statistics and is therefore unrecognised by planners, development agencies and the families for whom they fetch water and wood, for whom they are producers and reproducers, and for whom they cook meals almost everyday of the year' (Smillie 1995: 82). Women are also subject to a continuous subordination as their competence is often less respected and their decision-making abilities are less trusted than those of their male counterparts (Berninghausen and Kerstan 1992: 60). The limited choice for women, according to Kabeer (1994: 228), has curtailed their ability to 'know' other ways of being and to engage in the analytical process by which their structural, rather than individual, interests as a subordinated category come more clearly into view. Structural adjustment programmes implemented in some countries to reduce financial imbalances by increasing efficiency and greater productivity have also produced adverse effects on women. By reducing government social sector expenditure, especially in the health sector, these programmes place a greater burden on women as they have to pursue their own health care for their family (Smillie 1995: 84). Meanwhile, cutbacks in public sector employment tend to produce not only the decline of demand for ancillary services generally provided by women, but also job losses for low income households that force women to search for additional income in the informal sector (Johnson 1992: 161–2; Haddad *et al.* 1995: 882–4). For these reasons, women's NGOs have begun to flourish since the mid-1980s in many developing societies.

## Women's movements in Indonesia

In Indonesia, women's movements had begun from the early twentieth century. Kartini (1879–1904) was one of the first Indonesian women who pioneered the idea of women's emancipation as she argued for the right to education and access to professional occupations for Indonesian women (Jayawardena 1986: 141). The first women's organisation in Indonesia, *Putri Mardika* (Independent Women), was formed in 1912 to carry out a nationalist campaign and rejection of child marriage. It was followed by the formation another organisation, *Isteri Sedar*, which was active in promoting women to participate in politics (Jayawardena 1986: 151–2). In the 1920s, these organisation had contributed to the rise of a new concept of personal freedom, self-determination and social uplift manifested in the famous Youth Oath (*Sumpah Pemuda*) of 1928 declaring commitment to one country, one nation and one language (Taylor 1997: 95). But women's activity at that time was not independent because men stood at the centre stage and directed women to subordinate positions in running political organisations (Blackburn 1994: 172; Taylor 1997: 94). Likewise, in the 1960s, despite the success of GERWANI (Indonesian Women's Movement), a women's organisation of the Indonesian Communist Party, in mobilising women to serve as political cadres, women participating in politics were considered only as auxiliaries and the issue of equality between men and women was never pursued (Berninghausen and Kerstan 1992: 59–60; Taylor 1997: 95).

Under the New Order government, women's activities faced a setback when the state took the initiative to organise, control and mobilise Indonesian women for political purposes (Blackburn 1994: 174). Various state-sponsored women's organisations were formed during the 1970s and 1980s. Wives of civil servants and military personnel were organised into women's groups. *Dharma Wanita*, with three million members, was for wives of civil servants. Its main function was to assist the husbands of its members in performing their duties and it was sheltered under the banner of the ruling party, Golkar (Thorbecke and van der Pluijm 1993: 274; Nadia 1996: 240). *Dharma Pertiwi*, a similar association for wives of police and military personnel, was subdivided by the military service branch. The social hierarchy within these organisations generally corresponded to the husbands' rank (Blackburn 1994: 174). The most influential state-sponsored women's organisation at the grassroots level, however, was the PKK (Family Welfare Guidance). Created in 1973 by the Ministry of Home Affairs as a non-political women's movement, PKK sought to instill in rural women the appropriate knowledge, attitudes and skills to perform their domestic role which covered 10 basic segments of family life: (1) family relations; (2) household economy; (3) child education and guidance; (4) household management; (5) food and nutrition; (6) physical and emotional security; (7) housing; (8) family planning; (9) health; and (10) clothing and handicrafts (Thorbecke and van der Pluijm 1993: 276). PKK members were mainly village adult females. Its leadership was similar to *Dharma Wanita* in which the wife of the Ministry of Home Affairs was its national leader and the wife of village head was the leader at village level. The main umbrella body for women's organisations was KOWANI (the Indonesian Women's Congress), whose duty was to ensure the full co-ordination of the women's efforts on behalf of development according to the government's guidelines.

These organisations were formed to perpetuate existing gender ideology picturing women both as mothers and housewives carrying out domestic duties. As a mother, Indonesian women were supposed to serve their children: getting them ready for school, helping them with their homework, cooking them meals, while as a housewife they were expected to concentrate on reproductive and productive tasks: breeding, caring or performing some work in order to augment their husbands' income (Postel-Coster 1993: 133). In addition to their domestic duties, Indonesian women were also charged with a 'political duty', as expressed by President Suharto in his 1984 Mother's Day speech:

> Women are the keepers of cultural morals and national values which must be passed down through the generations. It is the special duty of Indonesian women to filter out influences from other cultures which have penetrated Indonesia, to develop self-discipline and to prevent their children from developing destructive elements such as egotism and vanity.
> (Berninghausen and Kerstan 1992: 31)

Various existing programmes in Indonesia provided institutional support to help rural women, including those in the areas of family planning, health and nutrition, agricultural extension, vocational and literacy skills training, and those related to income-generation activities. In 1983, the Ministry for the Role of Women was established and charged with duties to: (1) prepare and plan the formulation of policies to enhance the role of women in all fields of development; (2) co-ordinate all activities of government institutions concerning programmes involving women; and (3) submit regular reports, information and recommendations to various government institutions concerning the enhancement of the role of women in development (Thorbecke and van der Pluijm 1993: 273). Most of the government's programmes on women were based on the WID approach since they put

172  *Building constituencies and institutionalising a movement*

emphasis more on how to make women play a greater role in development activities rather than on women's equal rights *vis-à-vis* men.

Some argued that the New Order government's programmes on women were both 'functionalist' – as they gave priority to the function women can have for development and the family – and 'patronising' – since they were based on the assumption that women have to serve the purposes of powerful organisations and, ultimately, of the state (Berninghausen and Kerstan 1992: 29; Postel-Coster 1993: 132). An example of this kind of programme was certainly the P2W-KSS (Programme for the Improvement of Women's Social Welfare) which was introduced in the early 1980s to complement the PKK programme at village level. This programme included several activities: (1) basic activities: training in literacy, home-gardening, immunisation, maternal and child care and the use of latrines; (2) following-up activities: income-generation for participants of the government's family planning programme (*Keluarga Berencana*) which was aimed at increasing skills of small-entrepreneurship and petty-trading in the informal sector; and (3) support activities: a special course for women to internalise the principles of *Pancasila*, the official ideology (Thorbecke and van der Pluijm 1993: 277; Utrecht and Sayogyo 1994: 64). The families that participated in the P2W-KSS programme were selected by village heads (*Lurah*) on PKK recommendation with referral to the LKMD (Village's Defense Council) and daily co-ordination by sub-district heads (*Camat*) and district heads (*Bupati*) (Utrecht and Sayogyo 1994: 64). Because PKK leadership was in the hands of the wife of local officials (*Lurah, Camat* and *Bupati*) and LKMD members were drawn from rural elites, the selection of participants in the programme was determined by the local elite groups (Utrecht and Sayogyo 1994: 63). While one would not deny the role and achievement of the government's programmes on women, there was a serious concern regarding the insufficient genuine participation of rural women in those programmes. Moreover, these programmes also failed to address the issue of equality between men and women as pronounced by the GAD approach.

The GAD approach was brought by a group of feminists[3] (many of whom are university students, researchers and lawyers) in the late 1980s. These activists set up a foundation for a new wave of women's movements focusing on gender equality. They argued that women's movements must be focused not only on an effort to drive women out from the domestic world to an active participation in development, but also on a deliberate attempt to liberate women from a continuous process of exploitation and discrimination (*Annisa*, December 1996). While rejecting the view that an improvement of women's economic position will automatically lead to an improvement in their social position, they demanded an end to the explication of women as the guardians of their families' well being by arguing that women should be recognised as individuals who have the same rights as men to personal development and support (Berninghausen and Kerstan 1992: 209; Nadia 1996: 241).

These feminists attempted to establish a kind of 'collective identity'[4] among Indonesian women, which included two sets of strategy. First, they directed their attack against the process of '*priyayisation*'[5] of Indonesian women, that is, the formation of a middle-class image in which women are expected to be much more home and family-oriented. Through the educational system and the media, the *priyayi*'s image of women (viewing work outside the home as lowering status for women since the man alone is expected to provide material support for his family), penetrated the society to the village level. It was viewed that women's responsibility was simply to be active in charitable or other social organisations and thereby raises the social status of their families (Berninghausen and Kerstan 1992: 77). Feminists tried to change this view by spreading the idea of gender-equality to the grassroots people. Second, in a situation where norms of seclusion and segregation curtailed women's ability to participate independently in community-based networks, Indonesian feminists stressed the need to build up or strengthen the networks or alliances among the marginalised women. They often talked about *pemberdayaan perempuan* (women's empowerment) which included the processes of making women more aware of their powerlessness and of organising women to free themselves from the state's control (Nadia 1996: 243). However, since women's assertive behaviour was not acceptable to Indonesian culture, such awareness-building could not attack directly the repressive structures between the sexes; rather, it had to use women's day-to-day lives (i.e. the unequal distribution of workload of men and women) as a starting point of the gender-equality campaign. Thus, contrary to Western emancipatory movements, the Indonesian women's movement did not wish to use method of confrontation, but rather mutual co-operation between men and women (Berninghausen and Kerstan 1992: 210).

In the post-Suharto era, women's movement has become more prominent in playing its role in expressing the concern among Indonesian women on the economic crisis and in protecting the victims of the May 1998 riots. In February 1998, Karlina Leksono, Gadis Arivia and Wilasih formed an organisation called SIP (Voice of Concerned Mothers) which raised the issue of the negative impact of increasing prices of food and milk on women's reproductive health and children's nutrition (*Suara Pembaruan*, 24 February 1998). But SIP moved beyond the issue of food as it began to support students when they carried out demonstration demanding Suharto's resignation. While food was SIP's most visible ammunition in sustaining the students' protest action, as members prepared and delivered supplies of food and drink each day, one may assume that this group had contributed to the process of democratisation in its own way (Kalibonso 1999: 336). When rapes of women of Chinese descent took place as part of the devastating May riots, it was women's NGOs which took action by helping the rape victims and by bringing the crime to public attention. *Mitra Perempuan* (Friends of Women) was the first women's NGO to put out an urgent public call to support the survivors of the sexual assaults and mass rapes that occurred during and a few weeks after the May riots (*The Jakarta Post*, 5 June 1998). Together with Fr Sandyawan from ISJ (the Jakarta Social Institute), *Mitra Perempuan* set up the *Tim Relawan Untuk Kemanusiaan* (the Volunteers for Humanity) to provide rape victims with medical assistance, counseling and legal advice. They also compiled accounts of the circumstances of the assaults and presented the report to international human rights organisations. Their statement revealing the involvement of military and paramilitary vigilante groups in these crimes were published in almost every national daily newspaper and the internet which brought the issue to national and international attention (*Kompas*, 21 June 1998).

## NGOs and the target groups

Taylor and Whittier (1995: 169) argued that women's movements are an example of how norms and interpretive frames generate mobilisation because they illustrate the use of feminist views of gender relations in organising the challenge against the structures of seclusion. Other writers put women's movements in the category of 'new social movements' that resist the alienating effect of capitalist development, search for new alternatives and place a high value on participation and popular democracy[6] (Johnson 1992: 166). In a society in which grassroots activity has not yet well developed, women's movements outside the state tend to be generated by NGOs. Kabeer (1994: 229–30) identified several advantages of NGOs in addressing women's issues: (1) they tend to be less rule-governed which makes them more flexible; (2) their face-to-face interactions with their constituencies have given them both a greater advantage in promoting innovative strategies and capacity to develop a participatory process. In Indonesia, because the traditional women's grassroots organisations[7] concentrate on welfare or spiritual activities and their function are increasingly directed towards the implementation of official programmes at village level, the appeal for gender equality tends to be carried out by women's NGOs (Smyth and Grijns 1999: 90).

### *The NGOs*

Although both SBPY and Yasanti are not the only NGOs in Yogyakarta that represent movement NGOs, the two organisations are the closest to our category of movement NGOs (discussed in Chapter 4) in that they develop an anti-bureaucratic attitude, deliberately claim to be a movement as well as an NGO, concentrate on conscientisation and mobilisation, serve as representatitives for their constituencies and adopt a direct opposition to the state. Although they may not carry the ideology of *basismo*[8] that objects the formal apparatus of liberal democracy as well as the modern state as depicted by Lehmann (1990: 192), they nevertheless try to represent the 'voice of the voiceless' that make them share the main characteristics of a social movement. Information about the two organisations was gathered from my own observation and interviews, reports, leaflets and bulletins written by NGOs themselves and other relevant published materials such as newspapers, journals and books. I benefited from studies made by Wolf[9] (1992), Soewito (1994), Laomang and Assariroh (1995) and Smyth and Grijns (1999) on female factory workers in Java; Alexander (1987), Krisnawati and Utrecht (1992) and Evers (1993) on female market traders; and Berninghaussen and Kerstan (1992) and on Javanese women more generally. However, due to the absence of a detailed study on both SBPY and Yasanti, I must rely on my observation, interviews, newspapers, NGOs' reports, leaflets and bulletins.

*The Yogyakarta women's joint secretariat*

SBPY (the Yogyakarta Women's Joint Secretariat) emerged from a student movement with 22 members spread across branches in several university campuses and research institutes in Yogyakarta (SBPY 1997: 2). It operated as a 'formal' women's NGO from December 1992, after serving as a campus-based study group since 1986. Its activity was dedicated to women, that is, organising and mobilising the oppressed women. Generating an average revenue of around Rp 300 million (US$30,000) per year and employing eight all-women staff, SBPY attempted to reach out to women in the informal sector, especially the *bakuls* (petty traders) and *pembantu rumah tangga* (house-keepers), who were not represented by any organisations or associations.

Unlike the two development NGOs discussed in Chapter 5, SBPY depended entirely on foreign funding. Contracts were made with two funding institutions – Oxfam-UK and ICF (Indonesia–Canada Foundation) – most of which lasted between one and three years. In order to cover the operational costs during the interlude between the old and new contracts, SBPY allocated the so-called *dana cadangan* (reserved fund) deducted from the institutional fees of each project. Donors seems to welcome this idea since they think that the fund can help the NGO to maintain its programmes and contacts with target groups, while the organisation is waiting for the new contracts.[10] In 2001, SBPY claimed to have around Rp 20 million reserved fund (Wibowo, interview, 05/07/2001).

Led by reform-minded women activists, this organisation was inspired by the GAD approach. SBPY believed that improvement of women's bargaining position *vis-à-vis* men can only be made through the process of conscientisation and mobilisation through which women can build their confidence in demanding structural changes (SBPY 1997: 3). This organisation challenges the seclusion of women by refusing to use the Indonesian term '*wanita*' for women. Instead of *wanita*, SBPY prefers to use another Indonesian term, '*perempuan*' as a general classifier in referring to women. It is claimed that *wanita*, derived from a Sanskrit word, *vanita*, denotes female subordination, whereas *perempuan*, also a Sanskrit word, supposedly implies more independence and assertiveness (Gayatri, interview, 04/07/2001). As has been discussed in Chapter 2, SBPY's insistence on conscientisation and mobilisation strategy seems to contradict Eldridge's claim that women's NGOs in Indonesia tend to be low-profile, behind-the-scenes problem solving and consensus-building rather than strident assertion of women's rights (Eldridge 1995: 153).

Initially, SBPY attempted to organise both house-maids and petty traders. However, it began to concentrate on the petty traders when its plan to form a household workers' union faltered. Dian Gayatri, the co-ordinator of the programme, argued that the failure had to do with the absence of personnel in her organisation with sufficient knowledge of labour movements and the lack of time and interest on the part of the house-keepers to organise among themselves (Gayatri, interview, 12/12/1996). Meanwhile, Berninghausen and Kerstan (1992: 92) associated the failure with two factors. First, the NGO's approach by lobbying the middle- and upper-class women to allow their house-maids to form their own unions was inappropriate because employees, who were worried that the emergence of such organisations would lead to a call for an improvement in working conditions and higher salaries for their maids, were reluctant to support the idea of a household labour union. Second, the house-keepers themselves, who were very isolated in their work, were not prepared to form interest groups because their long working hours would not allow them to spare time and energy for organisational activities.

*The Annisa Swasti foundation*

Yasanti (the *Annisa Swasti* Foundation) originated from a weekly student discussion group initiated by six young feminists from various university campuses in Yogyakarta. From the beginning, Yasanti devoted its commitment entirely to women. Claiming the poor women – both in urban and rural areas – as its main target groups, Yasanti focused on advocacy, research, publication, education and training (Strintzos 1991; Yasanti 1996). It was originally formed to serve as an alternative to the state-sponsored women's organisations (PKK, *Dharma Wanita, Dharma Pertiwi* and Kowani) since its founders believed that the state's monopoly could only be ended by setting up a new women's organisation operating outside the state's circles (Berninghausen and Kerstan 1992: 210). Its monthly tabloid, *Annisa*, has been used as a means to spread the 'gender equality' idea in which it contains most radical views of women's equal roles in social, economic and political activities.

With respect to financial resources, this organisation was dependent entirely on foreign donors whereby its Rp 500 million (US$50,000) revenue in 2000 came from the Ford Foundation (USA) and the Bread for the World (Germany). Some occasional contributions also came from other agencies such as Oxfam-UK and the USC-Canada (Muftiyanah, interview, 05/07/2001). Like SBPY, Yasanti allocates some amount of *dana cadangan* to provide a temporary back-up to cover the operational costs during negotiation for new contracts. In 2000, Yasanti claimed to have around Rp 35 million (Muftiyanah, interview, 05/07/2001).

Having realised that bureaucracy is not compatible with feminism, Yasanti deliberately avoids the imposition of strict procedures and rules in implementing programmes. It relies, instead, on personal communication and negotiation in distributing jobs among workers. Employing 12 all-women staff members and fieldworkers, this organisation deliberately attempts to form a constituency. It normally begin by forming *arisan* (credit-saving rotation groups) as an entry point through which the ideas of gender equality and the need of women to organise among themselves are introduced (Kusyuniati 1990).

Initially, Yasanti made a serious effort to reach out to the poor women as it tried to speak out on behalf of women working both in the formal and informal sectors such as the *bakul jamu* (herb peddlers), *buruh gendong* (load-carriers), *pelayan toko* (shop-attendants) and *buruh pabrik* (factory workers) (Sinaga 1994: 133; Yasanti 1996: 3). However, since the early 1990s it began to put more emphasis on female factory workers whose position was vulnerable to exploitation and manipulation by the factories. Herb peddlers and shop-attendants were difficult to organise due to their mobility (moving quickly from one area to another) and the intervention of the state-sponsored union, the SPSI (All-Indonesia Workers' Union) (*Annisa*, September 1994). Meanwhile, in the case of female load-carriers, Yasanti's attempt to organise also faltered due to the substantial decline of this sector. It was estimated that by 1996 the number of female load-carriers in Yogyakarta decreased to only 80 from around 1,200 in 1993, although it increased again to 500 in 2000 (Yasanti 1996: 17; Muftiyanah, 05/07/2001). Two factors might have caused the decline. First, the local government's progressive attempt to turn them into trading activities through the provision of small-credits and entrepreneurship guidance (*Annisa*, September 1996). Second, the growing public condemnation against female load-carriers as many people (including women's activists) viewed load-carrying unsuitable (*tidak patut*) for women. As Tadjuddin Noor Effendi, a politician and academic at Gadjah Mada University, put it: 'Women carrying heavy loads for living is both inappropriate and inhuman. It is inappropriate because load carrying lowers women's status as they often run around chasing their customers for just a small amount of money. It is inhuman because it reminds us of the slavery system' (*Annisa*, January 1993). During the 1997 economic crisis, however, women were forced to retain their load-carrying jobs due to the job scarcity in their villages. This leads to an increase of load-carrying female workers in Yogyakarta.

## The target groups

One of the features that makes the two NGOs different from development NGOs discussed in Chapter 5 is that they treat women as their constituencies, more than simply a target of their programmes. Unlike BSY and CD which provide their target groups with material and technical assistance as indicated in their programmes, the two organisations try to represent the interests of the oppressed women in their dealings with other actors. On many occasions, both SBPY and Yasanti speak and act on behalf of the women in negotiation with the state officials and factory managers. There are two groups of women with whom the two organisations established their links: the market petty traders in the Beringhardjo market, Yogyakarta and the factory workers in Gadingan, Central Java.

### The market petty traders

Since the early 1970s, there has been an important shift on the part of the female workforce away from the agricultural sector towards the service sector and industry. Collier (1980: 19) noted that in the 1920s the work input of the female agricultural workers in Central Java was 65 per cent of the total workforce in the 1920s. This percentage decreased to 53 per cent by the end of the 1960s and to

37 per cent by the end of the 1970s. This decline was due mainly to the introduction of new methods of planting, harvesting and processing in the course of the 'green revolution'. First, the introduction of HYVs (high-yielding rice varieties) and the *tebasan* system[11] in which the *penebas* (middlemen) tended to employ a gang of male harvesters using sickles rather than the one-sided small blade (*ani-ani*) used by women to cut stalks individually (White 1982: 311; Siahaan 1983: 44; Papanek 1985: 25). For example, in Kali Loro, Yogyakarta, Stoler (1977: 88) found that under the *tebasan* system about 60 per cent of landless women loss their jobs. Second, the HYVs required the increased amount of fertilizer (usually spread manually onto the field by men) which led to the reduction of demand for female workforce (Berninghausen and Kerstan 1992: 86). Third, the mechanisation in rice-hulling which replaced the traditional hand-pounding performed by women was also responsible for the displacement of the female workforce by the technology (Timmer 1973: 73–4; Stoler 1977: 87; White 1982: 311). Collier (1980: 21) estimated that in the early 1970s about 1.5 million women lost the possibility of earning the equivalent of about two month's wages per year because of this mechanisation process.

Many women in rural areas who lost their jobs had to turn to the non-farming sector. While their low education and lack of sufficient skill prevented them from entering the formal sector, the majority of them ended up in the informal sector. In his survey in Central Java, Evers (1993: 4) estimated that in 1990 women workers constituted 81.6 per cent of the total workforce in the informal sector which included petty trading and service sector (house-keeping). Of all sectors of the informal economy, *bakul* (petty trading) had the highest percentage of female workers. It was estimated that in the early 1990s there were only 59 men for every 100 women involved in this sector in Java (Berninghausen and Kerstan 1992: 88). Women were more inclined to engage in trading activities that needed a relatively small outlay of capital and that did not require traveling long distances because they tended to be more restricted in their physical mobility than men and their activities more confined to the immediate environment of their homes, a situation which was encouraged by the prevailing notion associating women with domestic works (Krisnawati and Utrecht 1992: 48). Women were also considered to be more suited than men to petty trading because their experience in household management, particularly in making ends meet, made them more skillful and accurate in bargaining and handling small amount of cash (Chandler 1985: 56). Moreover, the flexibility of work in this sector allowed women to combine it with housework (Prastiwi 1994: 14). But one should bear in mind that the earnings from petty trading are very small and that as soon as higher capital investments (and potentially higher profits) are involved, more male traders tend to appear on the stage (Alexander 1987: 52–3). Thus, the particular 'suitability' of women to petty trading reflects the genuine possibilities and limitations of the situation of women; but at the same time, it serves as a legitimation of a social order in which women have relatively less access to resources than men (Krisnawati and Utrecht 1992: 49). Most of female petty traders run their businesses in the traditional marketplace (*pasar*). Alexander (1987: 53) noted that *pasar* is the domain of women because they predominate among both vendors and customers, although many of the larger traders and all the market administrators are men. In the mid-1990s, the percentage of female traders in the markets around Central Java was between 69 and 76 per cent.

In Yogyakarta, petty traders, especially those in the Beringhardjo market (the largest marketplace in the city), have always been subject to the government's attempt to 'formalise' their activities. In 1992, the government launched an ambitious project to turn the traditional market into a modern shopping centre by allocating a budget of Rp 10.5 billion (US$1.2 million). When the project was completed, the local government issued *perda* (the local government's regulation) No. 5/1992 requiring traders to pay a new tax between Rp $250/m^2$ and Rp $750/m^2$ per day for their shops or stalls in the market, indicating a dramatic increase from between Rp $45/m^2$ and Rp $100/m^2$ per day as stipulated by *perda* No. 9/1982 (Table 6.1). The difference between the two regulations was that while the new *perda* obliged the informal traders to pay tax, the old *perda* classified the traders' payment as the cleaning fee (*uang sapon*). Predictably, this new tax system generated resistance from petty traders who were not prepared to pay higher overhead costs. Evers (1993: 10) estimated that given the smallness of their scale (which implied the small profits), more than one-third of the petty traders in the Beringhardjo market will collapse if the government went on with the new taxation policy because they earned less than the amount of tax they should pay.

In working with female market traders, SBPY focused on attempts to generate awareness among the female traders of their vulnerable position to the government's regulation and a possible take-over by male traders. SBPY began its activities by

*Table 6.1* The rates of cleaning fee (regulated by Perda No. 9/1982) and the new tax systems of 1992 and 2000

| Type of establishment | Cleaning fee (Perda No. 9/1982) (in Rupiah/$m^2$/day) | New tax system (Perda No. 5/1992) (in Rupiah/$m^2$/day) | New tariff in April 2000 (in Rupiah/$m^2$/day) |
|---|---|---|---|
| Shop/Kiosk | 100 | 750 | 2,500 |
| Stall inside the shopping area[a] | 75 | 600 | 1,000 |
| Stall outside the shopping area | 50 | 450 | 750 |
| Stall outside the market[b] | 45 | 250 | 500 |

Source: *Berita Nasional*, 1 April 1993; 3 April 2000.

Notes
a The Beringhardjo market is divided into two: the shopping area (where shops, kiosks and stalls are placed side by side) and the non-shopping area available for those selling groceries and cheap items (worn out articles, second hand furnitures etc.).
b Stall outside market refers to those who sell their item in an open area outside the marketplace who must provide their own protection from the sun or rainfall.

organising around 1,740 female traders in a number of traditional marketplaces in Yogyakarta, about 80 per cent of whom were running their businesses (foodstuffs, vegetables, furniture, spices, worn-out articles and so on) in the Beringhardjo market (Gayatri, interview, 12/12/1996). It helped the traders to form a number of *paguyuban* (community groups) which were classified according to different types of businesses – namely, the batik traders' community (*paguyuban pedagang batik*), the second-hand items traders' community (*paguyuban pedagang barang bekas*), the vegetables traders' community (*paguyuban pedagang sayur*) and so forth – each of which having 50–80 members (SBPY 1996: 9). Once in two weeks, members of these groups held a meeting, discussing their immediate problems accompanied by SBPY's fieldworkers.

In April 2000, as part of its attempt to raise revenue from local sources, the government increased the tax once again to between Rp 500/m$^2$ and Rp 2,500/m$^2$ (see Table 6.1). However, at that time such an increase was less dramatic, especially to the petty traders who run permanent or semi-permanent stalls inside or outside the market. The new tariff was implemented in favour of small traders as they were asked to pay only between 66 and 100 per cent more than the old tariff. Meanwhile, large-scale traders – who run permanent shops or kiosks inside the market – had to face more than 230 per cent increase. This approach seemed to be acceptable to both small and large traders; and they did not conduct any resistance. One shop-owner inside the market commented: 'Although we have to pay much more than the petty traders (*pedagang kecil*), we still think that the new tariff contains some sense of justice (*rasa keadilan*). As long as the tariff is reasonable and within our reach, we have no reason to resist' (Indras, interview, 03/07/2001).

*The female factory workers*

Thus far, the most important constituency of Yasanti has been the female factory workers (*buruh pabrik*). As has been discussed in Chapter 1, rapid industrialisation since the late 1970s has brought with it factories providing employment for both men and women. In many industrial cities in Java – such as Majalaya, Tangerang and Sumedang in West Java, Ungaran, Bawen and Salatiga in Central Java, and Pandaan, Bangil and Sidoarjo in East Java – factories have also entered into rural areas (Manning 1987: 53–5; Guinness and Husin 1993: 272). The main attraction of rural and semi-rural areas for investors was the low prices of land, utilities and labour that substantially cut the production costs (Wolf 1992: 112). In Gadingan village in Ungaran district, Central Java, where Yasanti carried out its activities, there were 12 factories owned by foreign and domestic investors employing nearly 6,000 workers (Yasanti 2001: 12).

Table 6.2 indicates female domination in the village's industrial workforce as they constituted 69.50 per cent of the total factory workers. However, their domination does not necessarily entail a better status. In terms of salary, female workers receive less than their male counterparts. While in 2001 each female worker received a salary ranged between Rp 240,000 and Rp 270,000 per month

*Table 6.2* Rural factories and workforce in Gadingan (2000)

| Factory | Number of female workers | Number of male workers | Percentage of female workers | Percentage of male workers | Total workers |
|---|---|---|---|---|---|
| Textiles | 2,413 | 416 | 85.29 | 14.71 | 2,829 |
| Noodles | 114 | 27 | 80.85 | 19.15 | 141 |
| Biscuits | 412 | 109 | 79.08 | 20.92 | 521 |
| Garments | 228 | 66 | 77.55 | 22.45 | 294 |
| Spinning | 641 | 511 | 55.64 | 44.36 | 1152 |
| Confectionery | 27 | 14 | 65.85 | 34.15 | 41 |
| Bread | 47 | 35 | 57.32 | 42.68 | 82 |
| Glassware | 28 | 116 | 19.44 | 80.56 | 144 |
| Leatherware | 61 | 273 | 18.26 | 81.74 | 334 |
| Furniture | 4 | 63 | 5.97 | 94.03 | 67 |
| Plastic Bags | 21 | 77 | 21.43 | 78.57 | 98 |
| Transport | 6 | 49 | 10.90 | 89.10 | 55 |
| Total | 4,002 | 1,756 | 69.50 | 30.50 | 5,758 |

Source: Yasanti. 2001. *Profil Daerah Binaan:Ungaran dan Dinamika Kehidupannya.* Yogyakarta: Yayasan Annisa Swasti.

for 192 to 212 hours of work, a male worker received between Rp 400,000 and Rp 450,000 for a similar amount of work hours, indicating a clear sexual discrimination (Yasanti 2001: 65). These figures support an early study by Wolf stating that male factory workers were paid at least 50 per cent more than female workers were (Wolf 1992: 117). In 2000, the government set the UMR (regional minimum wages) at Rp 245,000 per month for Central Java and Rp 237,500 per month for Yogyakarta (*Annisa*, March 2001). A survey by Yasanti (2000) indicated that female workers worked for an average of 202 hours and received an average salary of Rp 230,000 per month. From the data we can calculate that female factory workers received an average salary of Rp 1,138 per hour. Thus, a female worker working for eight hours per day, for instance, would receive only Rp 9,109.

From the factory's point of view, preference to employ female workers is based on a common assumption that females are easier to control (*mudah diatur*), quicker (*lebih gesit*), more diligent (*lebih teliti*), less paid and are less likely to disrupt the production process with complaints or labour protests (Smyth and Grijns 1999: 89; Muftiyanah, interview, 05/07/2001). Wolf (1992) argued that by relying on female workers, factories appeared to manipulate gender ideology in the community that portrays females as economic dependents of males, working mainly to supplement family income which is used to justify low female wages. As she put it:

> Factories can rationalise paying below the minimum wage, which is itself below subsistence level, with the following interrelated arguments: according

to their ideology, females are economic dependents earning supplemental income; their families provide free lodging and food for dependent daughters, thereby decreasing the need for a higher wage; and the proximity of the agricultural economy meant that factory income is not only supplemental but surplus.

(Wolf 1992: 11997)

To many factories, employing a majority of female workers is also part of their strategy to minimise the possibility of industrial action. They employ Javanese male personnel managers whose age, sex and power would encourage the patron–client (*bapak–anak buah*) ties between female workers and their superiors to reduce the potential strike or protest because in the Javanese culture daughters tend to be hesitant and fearful to express an opinion that would disagree with their fathers (Wolf 1992: 124). Some factories even go further by forming *kelompok pengajian* (Koran reading groups) and inviting Islamic teachers to preach and provide religious justification for non-defiant and less assertive behaviour for women (Smyth and Grijns 1999: 89).

In addition to wage discrimination, female workers also suffer from unfair treatment from their employers. While the law guaranteed paid benefits such as a two days menstruation leave every month, a three months maternity leave and one or two weeks' annual vacation, there was only one factory in Gadingan that actually granted its female workers paid benefits. Examples of factories ignoring health and safety regulations were also common in Ungaran. For instance, according to labour laws workers should be provided with a cap, a nose and mouth cover and glasses to prevent irritation of the lungs and eyes and to avoid on-the-job accidents; but most factories in the site did not supply their workers with any of these items. These blatant transgressions of labour laws were made possible by the rampant corruption in which state inspectors often received bribes to write a positive evaluation of the factories concerned. Meanwhile, the only labour union recognised by the state (at least during the New Order government), the SPSI, already under the control of the state officials, existed in the factories in form only since its leaders were either handpicked by management or, more typically, was part of the personnel manager (Singarimbun 1995: xiii). My observation on several branches of SPSI at the factory level indicates that while representatives of women in their leadership were small (only 6 out of 26 positions in the unions' officials were occupied by women), their activities tended to be focused on social activities such as organising volleyball, *karate* (a Japanese martial art), table tennis or badminton games instead of negotiating women's rights with the management.

These problems had prompted Yasanti to act as a pseudo-union for female workers whose gender-specific interests were hardly been represented by the existing labour unions. Like SBPY, Yasanti attempts to organise and generate awareness among female workers of their powerlessness. A branch office with five fieldworkers was established in the Gadingan village, which was also used as the venue for its gender training programme. In order to attract female workers,

Yasanti started with *arisan* (credit-and-saving rotation groups). *Arisan* is the only way for factory workers to save some of their income not only because it reduces the danger of loss or corruption, but also because it serves as a mechanism for them to escape from parents and siblings who continually ask for some amount of money from them (Wolf 1992: 188). In this way, workers felt compelled to participate in the *arisan*. In Gadingan, every payday members of the *arisan* met and contributed a certain cash to a pool. One or two members' names were drawn to receive the cash. It is a fixed lottery in that each person receives the cash before a new round is started. As for Yasanti, *arisan* appeared to be the most, if not the only, effective way to establish relations with its constituencies because a direct appeal for organising and mobilising tended to discourage women – who might have been intimidated by factory managers, husbands, parents or even the local authorities – to join (Muftiyanah, interview, 05/07/2001; Handayani, interview, 06/07/2001). Moreover, in order to avoid resistance, Yasanti deliberately concealed its feminist agenda by announcing to the public that its weekly gathering was aimed simply at improving women's skills of domestic works (tailoring, knitting and beauty care).

## The problem of representation

It is important to note that both SBPY and Yasanti do not arise spontaneously through the efforts of the poor women themselves. Rather, they come into existence through the efforts of the more powerful actors who have access to the funds, contacts and information necessary to set them up. As 'outsiders' to the people whom they serve, the two NGOs seem to face dilemmas with regard to the conflict between values and objectives, a temptation to believe that outsiders' knowledge is more valid than the poor people's knowledge for achieving a certain goal, and a trade-off between short- and long-term costs and benefits. Chambers (1983: 145) argued that the danger for grassroots empowerment initiated by outsiders is the tendency of the outsiders to think that they know best and that the poor do not know what is in their interests.

### *NGOs as 'virtual representatives'*

Working in a situation where the gap (in terms of power, knowledge, intellectual capability and so on) between outsiders and insiders is substantial, NGOs must be careful about tailoring their approach to the people. NGOs now routinely refer in their policy declarations to the concept of empowerment which, in the context of women's movements, can be defined as the process of organising, awareness building and capacity building of the oppressed women in order to transform unequal relationships between men and women, to increase the decision-making power of women in the home and community and to stimulate greater participation of women in politics (Karl 1995: 109). For Kabeer, empowerment must entail as an ultimate goal the ability of the disempowered women to act collectively in their own practical and strategic interests (Kabeer 1994: 256). NGOs try to translate the concept of empowerment into action by acting as representatives for their target groups, that is, speaking and acting on their behalf in dealing with more powerful actors.

In the general political context, 'representation' is understood as a concept of power relations involving leaders (representatives) and followers (constituencies) whether in the governments, political parties, churches or other social organisations. There are at least two categories of representation with respect to the way in which people can trust their representatives: (1) direct or elective representation; and (2) virtual or non-elective representation (Sills, ed. 1968: 461). Direct or elective representation normally follows from an electoral procedure in which the people whose interests are represented freely and periodically elect a body of representatives. While representatives carry out activities under the elector's instructions, the electors consent to the decisions of their representatives. In many instances, direct representatives often act as 'trustees', that is, those who decide according to the expressed preferences of the people they represent (Gutmann and Thompson 1985: 170). Direct representation often entails accountability in which representatives are obliged to answer to the electors (Sills 1968: 462). The failure to do so will normally cause the loss of opportunity for reelection (Grolier Incorporated 1990: 414). Meanwhile, virtual or non-elective representation does not come from an electoral procedure. In this system, representatives are often 'appointed', rather than elected, by the people simply because of their concern or familiarity with particular issues. In most cases, virtual representatives often act as 'delegates', that is, those who act and decide according to their own judgment or evaluation of a particular problem (Gutmann and Thompson 1985: 170). Although this system does not involve accountability to the degree pursued in the direct representation, representatives are obliged to protect the interests of the constituencies because they owe allegiance to those who appoint them (Grolier Incorporated 1990: 411).

Because NGOs do not emerge from an electoral procedure, they tend to establish themselves as 'virtual representatives' for their constituencies. It is therefore crucial for NGO workers to have a good knowledge or sensitivity to the situation faced by their constituencies. However, the gap between the powerful representatives and the powerless constituencies seems to complicate NGOs' position as virtual representatives. First, in their attempt to generate a collective action there is a potential difficulty in forming a common objective and strategy. This problem may arise out of a 'structural gap' between the powerful outsiders and the powerless insiders in which outsiders are conditioned to give more weight to interests which are national and urban rather than local and rural, while insiders tend to put priority on particular, immediate and personal needs (Chambers 1983: 148). Put differently, outsiders may suggest a far-fetched solution, while insiders may opt for action that can guarantee their pragmatic needs. As outsiders, NGOs may opt for what Wignaraja (1993: 19) terms a 'big bang' solution of social problems by persuading people to revolt, while their powerless constituencies, who must shoulder the economic and political risks of their action, may choose a more restrained strategy. Second, there is also a question of who should initiate and control the collective action. A strong sense of personal control or efficacy, according to Lofland (1996: 219), is the most crucial factor that stimulates individuals to engage in a movement. Thus, little internal control on a particular action would reduce individuals' motivation to participate in a movement. It is therefore important for movement-oriented NGOs to allow their constituencies to play a major part in the collective action if they are to succeed in acting as 'virtual representatives' for them.

To support these arguments, I will examine the experience of SBPY and Yasanti in acting as virtual representatives for the marginalised women. SBPY's experience in representing female petty traders in the Beringhardjo market in their attempt to resist the local government's policy that threatens their businesses may be useful in illustrating the dilemma of representation. Because published materials about SBPY was not available and because the event occured a few years before my fieldwork, I relied on information gathered mainly from the local newspapers, particularly *Berita Nasional*, which carried out extensive coverage on the case and from my interviews with staff members of SBPY and the traders who remained on the site or moved to the streetside. I was so grateful that SBPY recorded a detailed report and account on the case to which I could get access. Meanwhile, Yasanti's experience in dealing with female factory workers in the village of Gadingan in the district of Ungaran, Central Java, may illustrate NGOs' difficulty in trying to convince their constituencies of the merit of a particular action. I gathered information from my visits to the site during April–June 1997 and again in June 2001, from reports made by Yasanti, and from published materials about female factory workers in Gadingan.

## *SBPY and the Beringhardjo market petty traders*

Following its failure to form a household workers' union, SBPY began to turn its attention to female petty traders, the majority of whom run their businesses in the Beringhardjo market. The Beringhardjo market, where no less than 2,200 traders (mainly women) involved in small and medium scale businesses, is located in the centre of the city of Yogyakarta from which most lower- and middle-class families in the city buy their groceries and other basic items (SBPY 1993: 5). When the new tax system was introduced in January 1993, traders reacted desperately because the dramatic increase of the cleaning fee (between 600 and 800 per cent) was considered by many of them as unrealistic (*Berita Nasional*, 8 January 1993). For example, Mbok Pawiro, who sells cheap furniture said that she had to give up her stall because she could not survive under the new arrangement. Before the renovation, she paid only Rp 900 cleaning fee per day for her 12-m$^2$ stall, but under the new system she had to pay Rp 7,200 per day. While she could only sell an average of three sets of furniture per day, which gave her some Rp 6,000 profit, the new fee had certainly crippled her business (SBPY 1993: 8). Meanwhile, Mbok Amat Suwarno (aged 72), who sells scrap iron and worn out articles, shouted at a tax collector: '*Kulo niki nek gadhah nggih matur gadhah, nek mboten nggih mboten. Kulo niki mboten gawe-gawe!*' (If I had the money I would say

186  *Building constituencies and institutionalising a movement*

I have. I said I don't have money because I really don't have it. I am not making up stories!) (*Berita Nasional*, 6 April 1993). It was estimated that around 630 traders (28.5 per cent of a total of 2,200 traders in the market), most of whom were the poorest, refused to pay the new tax, amid the government's threat to expel them from the market (*Jawa Pos*, 3 April 1993).

For most traders, although the renovation had created a cleaner environment and a better sanitation, its modern appearance focusing on comfort and pleasure did not fit with the concept of a traditional market focusing on accessibility and affordability (Soetiyoso 1993: 3). Most traders lost their 'strategic' places as the government moved those who sell foodstuffs, vegetable, spices and second-hand furniture to the top floors which caused problem in loading and moving the merchandise. More importantly, their access to customers decreased (SBPY 1993: 22). For example, Bu Muhadi, who sells spices and vegetables, complained: 'I lost many customers after moving to the new vegetable stall on the third floor because no one would seem to go upstairs just to buy a bunch of spinach or onion leaves' (*Berita Nasional*, 4 April 1993). Since the majority of the petty traders are women, SBPY decided to act by forming and co-ordinating a task force consisting of representatives of the petty traders, academics and other NGOs whose main duty was to represent the traders and to put pressure on the local government to renounce the new tax system (SBPY 1994: 13). The agenda of this task force was to organise female traders and to form public opinion through seminars and statements published in the local newspapers about the unfairness of the new tax system. Among the traders, initially there were 528 members of different *paguyuban* (community groups) who agreed to work together with SBPY to resist the new tax system (Gayatri, interview, 12/12/1996).

However, after a long process of lobbying and negotiation involving representatives of the task force and government officials, there was no sign of compromise on the part of the government. Widagdo, the mayor of Yogyakarta, defended the new policy: 'It is a pity that some traders refuse to pay the new tax, but we need to increase our PAD (original regional income) to support our increasing development budget. Because we think that the tax rate is realistic and that we have informed them in advance, we should go on with this policy no matter what other people say' (*Berita Nasional*, 13 May 1993). Having failed to persuade the authorities to suspend the new policy, SBPY decided to engage in protest action. It started with organising a *dengar pendapat* (hearing) at the office of the DPRD Tingkat II (people's representative body at the district level) criticising the government's uncompromising approach towards the traders, which was followed by street demonstration involving hundreds of NGO activists, traders and students carrying posters and banners (*Berita Nasional*, 18 June 1993). A few days later, many more groups joined the protest action. This time, a group called *Kelompok Seniman Muda Indonesia* (the Young Indonesian Artists Group), conducted their own way of protest. About 50 artists with their bodies covered in dirt and red colour (representing the repressed traders) were whipped and dragged along the streets by well-dressed persons (representing the state bureaucrats) to visualise the traders' agony, while around 100 students joined the procession and read their statements demanding the suspension of the new tax system (*Berita Nasional*,

22 June 1993). A few more similar protests were subsequently carried out. Predictably, the government responded with coercion. Troops were sent to put down the street demonstrations. Dozens of protesters, who were labelled as perpetrators (*provokator*), were arrested. Meanwhile, around 50 traders who refused to pay the new tax were forced to report to the police station and threatened (*Kedaulatan Rakyat*, 2 September 1993).

When the local government began to expel some traders from the market, other traders withdrew their participation in the task force and refused to go on with the protest action. They, instead, carried out their own 'protest' by retreating to the streetsides around the Beringhardjo market. Others created a 'spontaneous market' (*pasar tiban*) on the Sriwedari street, a few miles to the northeast of the Beringhardjo market (*Berita Nasional*, 4 July 1993; Gayatri, interview, 12/01/1997). In such a desperate situation, the expelled traders preferred to keep their business by becoming streetside traders although they had to protect themselves from sunshine and rainfall. This withdrawal reflected the traders' rejection of protest action led by NGOs. As Bu Kawit Mawardi, one of the traders' representatives in the task force, put it: 'The protest action and demonstration are both too aggressive (*terlalu berani*) and inappropriate (*tidak patut*) for the Javanese women because they will inflict a deeper conflict with the authorities and raise an image of disobedience (*tidak loyal*) of the Javanese women' (*Kedaulatan Rakyat*, 21 August 1993). Because the traders had found their own solution, NGOs' protest action became ineffective which subsequently led to its termination. Disturbed by the lack of support from the petty traders, one of SBPY staff members commented: 'It was a pity that the traders finally withdraw their support (from the protest action). In the future we must first try to understand what our target groups have in their minds before we take further action' (Gayatri, interview, 12/12/1996). When I visited the site, around 300 female traders opened their stalls on the streetsides around the Beringhardjo market, while around 150 run their businesses in the *pasar tiban* on the Sriwedari street. Thus far, the local government had not taken any action, except that it charged a small amount of cleaning fee of around Rp 500 per day.

Explanations of this withdrawal can perhaps be found in the Javanese culture. Koentjaraningrat (1985: 251) argued that Javanese who go against their leaders, who are critical or go their own way (*susah diatur*), are considered 'rebellious' (*duraka* or *mbalelo*) because they breach the Javanese value of harmonious integration (*rukun*). In a similar vein, Mulder (1994: 67) noted that in a Javanese society, defiant behaviour will be punished by supernature; and in severe cases, where it is felt that the good name of a particular leader has been injured, the community may even disavow the dissenters because the obnoxious behaviour towards leaders is considered as distasteful and highly unacceptable. The traders' rejection of continuing the protest action appears to reflect their reluctance to expose the weakness of not being capable of living in an agreeable existence.

### Yasanti and the female factory workers

Since the early 1990s, female factory workers have received most serious attention from Yasanti. Although in theory their interests and aspirations should be represented by the SPSI, the only labour union sanctioned by the New Order government, in practice women's participation in labour movement appeared to be very low. Among the obstacles to women's involvement in trade unions, according to Karl (1995: 48), is the domination of male workers which often prevent women from reaching leadership positions and the fact that unions' activities tend to be gender-blind as they have never addressed issues that directly concern the practical and strategic gender needs such as maternity care, menstruation leave, maternity leave and equality in wage rates. In Indonesia, the SPSI's agenda is generally constructed from a male perspective, while gender-specific issues associated with women such as child care and equal opportunities for promotion are not regarded as priority (*Annisa*, December 1996). In Ungaran, during 1995–1996 there were several labour strikes demanding an increase of the UMR (regional minimum wages). But women's involvement in those strikes was too small and the newspapers' coverage of the action had never mentioned gender-specific issues (*Annisa*, December 1996). In the post-Suharto era, although a number of new labour organisations – such as FNPBI (Indonesian Worker's Union National Front), Forbis (Worker's Solidarity Forum), PRD (People's Democratic Party), and so on – have been formed, male domination still persists to the disadvantage of female workers. None of these newly formed organisations is willing to raise gender-specific issues.

In order to represent women's interest in labour movements, Yasanti focused its activities on organising female workers to persuade them to engage in protest action demanding the recognition of women's rights for equal promotion and salary, paid benefits and protection from possible sexual harassment from male superiors (Yasanti 1996: 11). Once in a week Yasanti's office in Gadingan was packed with workers drawing their lottery saving and discussing their practical and strategic gender needs under the guidance from Yasanti's fieldworkers. The most preferred topic was indeed the failure of most factories on the site to comply with the laws on labour, especially the Ministry of Manpower's regulation (*peraturan menaker*) No. 3/1989 – granting female workers the rights for a two days per month full-paid menstruation leave and a three months maternity leave – and the law on workforce (*peraturan tenaga kerja*) No. 3/1992 which obliges employers to provide social insurance (*jamsostek*) for their workers. According to a reasearch by Yasanti's staff members, out of a total 332 factories in the sub-district of Girimulyo, Ungaran, only 36 factories had SPSI branches, 25 factories granted their female workers paid benefits and 20 factories provided *jamsostek* for their workers (Laomang and Assariroh 1995: 7).

Yasanti managed to stage some industrial actions as female workers expressed their protest by hanging posters on the factories' walls, parading on the main roads, dancing (inside their factory), banging doors and equipment to make noises, slowing down production lines and strikes. In some extreme cases, female workers expressed their protest through mass hysteria in which they screamed and cried in a group while stopping the production line (Handayani 1995: 276–7). Despite Yasanti's success in generating awareness of female workers of their powerlessness, participation of female workers in industrial actions staged by the

NGO remained small. It was estimated that only 24 out of 161 labour strikes during 1998–1999 in Central Java had involved a substantial number of female workers (Yasanti 2001: 74). One reason for this lack of female participation is that it is often difficult for women to find the time for organisational activity because of their double burden of work outside and inside their home. One of Yasanti's staff members acknowledged the difficulty in persuading female workers to be bolder and more assertive in their attitude towards the factory management, despite their awareness of a continuing process of oppression and transgression of labour rules. As Handayani put it:

> It is difficult to convince them (the workers) that they have the right to protest when they are treated unfairly by their employers. Whenever we organise any protests or strikes, many of them fail to turn up because they are afraid (*takut*) of being punished by the factory managers or worried (*khawatir*) that the action will invite the security personnel to intervene.
> (Handayani, interview, 06/08/1997)

Thus, rather than engaged in direct confrontation against the management, female workers tended to pursue their own choice of indirect actions which included withdrawal, absenteeism, stealing and cheating aimed at evading the corrupt system for their individual benefits (Muftiyanah, interview, 05/07/2001). In Gadingan, workers' withdrawal was manifested in high degree of job exchanges between factories. One worker in a plastic factory, for example, had moved six times from different factories (biscuit, bottling, textile, spinning and glassware) in just a period of two years. Absenteeism was also a common practice in Gadingan as female workers often collaborated with their immediate supervisors for truancy, amid the factory's threat of an immediate dismissal of those who were absent for more than four days in one month (*Annisa*, December 1996). A personnel manager of a biscuit factory with 521 workers (79 per cent of whom are women) estimated that there was an average of 30 reported truancy per day in his factory (Pak Damiri, interview, 20/06/1997). Stealing factories' materials or products were occasionally conducted on individual or group basis as a sign of their indirect protest of unfair treatment. In a garment factory with 294 workers (77.5 per cent of whom are women), for example, a group of female workers doing a night shift deliberately stole elastic belts, buttons and other materials from the factory because they thought that the factory had unfairly forced them to work over-hours, while the promise of wage increase had never been materialised. It was estimated that there was an average of 35 reported stealing cases per day in the factory. One of Yasanti's staff members argued that the number of stealing by workers in Gadingan was higher (between 25 and 40 cases per day) in factories with poor working conditions and lower (between 0 and 15 cases per day) in factories with better working conditions (Muftiyanah, interview, 05/07/2001). This reality seems to support other studies stating that female workers tend to use acceptable forms of Javanese resistance within the factory context which include different types of indirect protest action: walkouts related to visions of ghosts and spirits, stayouts, cheating and stealing (Wolf 1992: 128–32; Saptari 1995: 216; Smyth and Grijns 1999: 98–9).

One reason behind workers' selection of indirect protest action is the presence of an inhibiting factor that have discouraged workers to participate in aggressive action organised by NGOs. Writing in the context of the psychological aspect of participants of a protest action, Dollard *et al.* (1997: 177) argued that the strength of inhibition of any act of aggression varies positively with the amount of punishment anticipated to be a consequence of that act; and the greater participants' perception of the possible punishment for their action, the more probable will be the occurrence of less direct acts of aggression. Punishment from powerful individuals or agents against protesters may include physical injury, insults, ostracism, deprivation of goods or freedom (Dollard *et al.* 1997: 176). In Gadingan, the perception of punishment for a defiant behaviour appeared to many female workers to be too hard to bear. In their mind, the case of Marsinah, a female factory worker in Sidoardjo, East Java, who was brutally tortured and murdered in May 1993 due to her active role in organising a series of labour strikes and protests, was an example of one of the worst punishments for a female worker active in industrial actions (Soewito 1994: 11). They were also stunned by the mysterious death of Titi Sugiharti, a female worker of a textile factory in Sumedang, West Java, who was allegedly tortured for her role in instigating labour strikes in May 1994 (Soewito 1994: 12). In both cases, although the authorities had conducted investigation, there was no clear sign of who committed the murders. However, the investigating committee of Komnas-HAM (the National Commission for Human Rights), a state-sponsored organisation, indicated in its report the involvement of local military officers (Widadi 1999: 103–4). Referring to the two incidents, one female worker in a garment factory in Gadingan commented:

> The death of both Marsinah and Titi (Sugiharti) have been the most precious lesson (*pelajaran berharga*) for us of how severe the punishment against women who tried to instigate protests against the factory that usually received support from the local apparatus. It is dangerous for a woman to get involved on the front line (*barisan depan*) of a demonstration because the merciless security personnel can always harm her both mentally and physically.
> (Suwarsi, interview, 10/05/1997)

Indeed, the fear of being severely punished by male security personnel or military officers has prompted female factory workers to pursue their own choice of indirect protest which is hardly effective in persuading employers to meet their demands. Rumours of the use of rape and other physical abuse against women in the police or military detention centres are widespread among female factory workers in Gadingan (Muftiyanah, interview, 05/07/2001). Unprepared to face these risks, female factory workers have opted for indirect action in resisting the system that bears injustice and exploitation.

## The challenge on PAR method

Like other types of social movements, women's movements have as their unshakeable core a commitment to breaking down the structure of gender subordination and a vision for women as full and equal participants with men at all levels of societal life (Sen and Grown 1987: 79). In the contexts of female market traders in Yogyakarta and factory workers in Ungaran, both SBPY and Yasanti used the method of PAR[12] in trying to help women pursue their own development. Activists of the two organisations believe that the PAR method is significant in generating a women's movement for at least two reasons. First, in a politically repressive situation, where the state constantly attacked women's social and economic status and where class-based organisations were severely restricted, PAR would help generate women's awareness of the need to organise among themselves and to establish coalitions and alliances cutting across different religious, ethnic and political boundaries (Gayatri, interview, 12/12/1996; Nadia 1996: 242). Second, because large segments of the Indonesian population, especially women, are still illiterate or unused to the printed words, the method learned in the 'pedagogy of the oppressed' can be useful in generating awareness about women's subordination and the need to challenge structures that bear injustice against women (Muftiyanah, interview, 05/07/2001).

### *Indonesian feminists and PAR*

One method used by women's NGOs in translating Freire's ideas of conscientisation into practice is the so-called 'gender analysis training'. Some argue that 'gender analysis training' is an important means by which feminist advocates and practitioners are seeking to de-institutionalise male privilege within development policy and planning (Rao *et al.* 1991; Kabeer 1994; Karl 1995). This method is meant to provide activists with an awareness of women's and men's interrelated and changing reproductive and productive roles in order to ensure that women can gain an equal position *vis-à-vis* men in their social, economic and political activities (Rao *et al.* 1991; Johnson 1992). Its basic analytical tool is a matrix of questions that focuses attention on gender divisions in production as well as in access and control over resources and benefits. It helps NGO activists to identify gender roles in a given place: namely, what men and women do and how their roles are interrelated, what control men and women have over resources and how men and women overcome constraints that obstruct their own advancement (Rao *et al.* 1991; Johnson 1992; Karl 1995).

In Indonesia, the idea of 'gender analysis training' was first introduced at a national women's seminar in December 1987, in which many feminist researchers and NGO activists from all over the country participated. Some of the discussions resulted in the agreement to conduct gender analysis training courses to propagate a movement to challenge discrimination against women in the productive sector (Berninghausen and Kerstan 1992: 79). From then on many women's NGOs, including SBPY and Yasanti, used 'gender analysis training' as a method of building a wider consciousness of the inequalities and inequities in the relationship between men and women with the aim of changing their attitudes and behaviour (Assariroh, interview, 20/01/1997; Muftiyanah, interview, 05/07/2001). SBPY's attempt to organise a collective action to resist the new tax system imposed on the market traders began with a process of conscientisation in which traders were invited to discuss their rights to defend themselves against the state's exploitation. Because the majority of the market traders were female, while the state officials were mostly male, SBPY put the issue in the context of the exploitation of powerful male officials over powerless female traders (SBPY 1993: 9). In order to make the traders' grievances known by the general public, SBPY organised a seminar involving representatives of the market traders, academics, NGO activists and students. The seminar produced a joint statement (*pernyataan bersama*) expressing refusal of the new taxation widely published by both the local and the national newspapers (*Suara Pembaruan*, 27 April 1993). Although this effort had failed to force the government to back off from its original plan, it had nevertheless generated public sympathy towards the traders.

Yasanti's attempt to promote gender-related issues was also carried out through gender analysis training courses in which women were brought together to discuss the problems they faced in the workplace. This training was conducted once a week in two different places: one in its head office in Yogyakarta, and another in its branch office in Ungaran. Its main purpose was to generate awareness among women that they were vulnerable to exploitation by men and sexual discrimination. In order to attract more participants, Yasanti used traditional theatres as a medium for conveying message to the constituencies. In co-operation with the *Yayasan Teater Rakyat Indonesia* (Indonesian People's Theatre Foundation), Yasanti used the *ketoprak* (a traditional Javanese theatre) and *wayang wong* (stage show dramatising Hindu epics) as a means of raising women's consciousness of their marginal positions (Eldridge 1995: 161). In the *ketoprak*, the play (*lakon*) usually symbolised powerful, greedy male employers of *priyayi* families exploiting weak, vulnerable female workers of peasant backgrounds. Meanwhile, in the *wayang wong*, the most popular play among the workers was the *Ramayana* epic picturing Shinta, the female heroine who follows her spouse Rama into exile, shares all suffering with him, and steadfastly resists the promises and threats of the demonic prince who has kidnapped her, until she is rescued by Rama (Berninghausen and Kerstan 1992: 33). Another play was the *Mahabarata* epic presenting Srikandi, an active, energetic, argumentative, generous and brave woman who played an important role in the war against the *Kurawa*. The use of both the *ketoprak* and the *wayang wong*, according to Muftiyanah, was to make the concept of gender equality become 'easily digested' (*mudah dicerna*) by the workers especially those with no adequate education (Muftiyanah, interview, 05/07/2001). Although it is difficult to measure the extent to which this method of conscientisation can effect a change in norm orientations of the Javanese women, Yasanti has nonetheless claimed that their constituencies have become more aware of their practical and strategic-gender needs in their productive and reproductive activities.

## The challenges on PAR

There are some glowing accounts of the apparent success of PAR. For example, Rahman (1993: 48, 77–8) regarded the success of Bhoomi Sena (discussed in Chapter 2) – in organising the *adivasis* in Maharastra, India, to generate people's power against the ruthless *sawkars* – and the ability of Proshika in Bangladesh – in facilitating group solidarity and collective action for the realisation of the basic economic and social rights of the underprivileged – as examples of the success of the PAR method in generating a movement. Meanwhile, in the context of women's empowerment, the experience of SEWA (Self-employed Women's Association) – in making Indian women become more financially independent and to think of themselves in terms other than those imposed by their traditional domestic, caste and community roles – was often considered as the success story of 'empowerment from below' through the use of the PAR method (Kabeer 1994: 253–5).

But it is risky to generalise that PAR can always guarantee success in empowering the vulnerable people. Thomas (1992: 138) identified three sources of challenges in the implementation of PAR. First, the community is not always supportive towards the idea of endogenous knowledge-generation or consciousness-raising as depicted by PAR theorists. Because PAR proposes new values that are not necessarily compatible with existing customs or norms, some parts of the community may resist it. Second, because PAR opposes all forms of elite domination over the masses, its implementation by any NGOs may generate opposition from the ruling elite. Third, because the implementation of PAR requires a strong ideological basis, sufficient knowledge of radical social theories, technical competence and management, many NGOs have failed to meet this requirement due to the weak ideology, lack of expertise, poor management, and so on. We can usefully refer to Thomas' categories in examining the problems faced by SBPY and Yasanti in implementing the PAR method.

### Barriers in the community

To be successful, PAR needs an extensive infrastructure supporting participation and equality between men and women as reflected in the traditional institutions or the local culture (Elden and Levin 1991: 129; Berninghausen and Kerstan 1992: 209). However, not all society has the infrastructures which are compatible with the principles of PAR. For example, in Indonesia, an improvement of the social status of women as an individual was not reconcilable with the community ideology which regarded women as a mother and a housewife whose main duty was to look after their children and serve their husband and whose work was just to provide supplementary income for the family (Berninghausen and Kerstan 1992: 198). Since this gender ideology has been embedded in the society for a long time, attempts to organise and mobilise women to act beyond their traditional role would seem to generate resistance.

Commentators argued that when an action is directed against powerful and dominant local interests, resistance against it from the community will normally

194  *Building constituencies and institutionalising a movement*

be great (Maclure and Bassey 1991: 200; Thomas 1992: 140). My observation in Gadingan indicated that men were generally cynical towards Yasanti's gender analysis training activity as they suspected that the NGO might teach women to revolt (*memberontak*) against their husbands or parents (Mas Yono, interview, 10/05/1997). In one occasion, Yasanti's fieldworkers were threatened by a man whose wife left him (*minggat*) after a rift because he thought that Yasanti had influenced her wife to revolt (*membangkang*) against him. The story about the row was reported by Widiawati (1995: 138–42). It involved Koeri (a pseudonym), a poor peasant in Gadingan, and his wife Giyah (a pseudonym) who was working in a local biscuit factory and a member of Yasanti's *arisan* and gender-training group. The couple was involved in a family row which ended up with Giyah's departure. Koeri started to blame Yasanti as he believed that his wife had become more assertive (*berani*) after joining Yasanti's gender trainings. I confirmed this story with Sih Handayani (one of Yasanti's staff members) who said that it was *Bu Lurah* (the wife of the village head) who convinced Koeri that his wife's defiant behaviour had nothing to do with Yasanti (Handayani, interview, 20/01/1997). Meanwhile, in the case of SBPY, Bu Mawardi's comment about her refusal to go on with protest action cited earlier appeared to indicate the incompatibility between NGOs' values and the traditional image of the Javanese women with regard to their appropriate behaviour towards their husbands, parents and leaders.

In his study of a Javanese rural community in Mojokuto, East Java, Jay (1969) described the relation between husband and wife in the Javanese family. As he put it:

> The husband is the cultural arbiter of the family, the one with some skill in the blend of traditional theology, philosophy and aesthetics that guides much of the Javanese intellectual activity. The wife responds to her husband's guidance with gentle attentiveness, while skillfully but unobtrusively managing his domestic needs, so that their detail may not distress him.
>
> (Jay 1969: 89)

This premise, which is derived from the *priyayi* family, reflects the subordination of women. The husband, with his 'superior' knowledge and authority, is expected to make important decision in the household, while the wife, due to her 'inferior' intellectual capacity, must accept her husband's guidance and concentrate on her domestic works. In the Javanese society, women's high social status is associated with the absence of pressure to work outside their home, with the exception of certain prestigious positions unattainable for most women (Jay 1969; Koentjaraningrat 1985). Thus, the stated goal in the Javanese family is usually to free women from the burden of income-producing activities, so that they may devote themselves solely to their families' status, that is, taking care of a presentable home, overseeing the raising of their children and nurturing social contacts. The media, along with the national family welfare programme, the PKK, spread this ideology of the *priyayi* family as far as the smallest village (Berninghausen and Kerstan 1992: 37).

Morever, in the Javanese family parents deliberately teach their daughters to feel *isin* (shame) and to be *manut* (obedient), a very significant concept in measuring attitudes in social relations. Daughters are often expected by their parents to develop the habit of obediently giving in (*mengalah*) to other people with whom they do not know how to deal (Koentjaraningrat 1985: 122). In many cases, being *manut* is considered as a key factor in keeping good relations with others, especially those with more power and control. Among the *priyayi*, a daughter is considered good and will be successful in her future life when she is *manut*, because obedience is thought to be a sign of the ideal human virtues (Koentjaraningrat 1985: 250). Javanese daughters are therefore constantly pressured by their parents to approximate these ideals. NGOs' attempt to make women bolder and more assertive was also hindered by the tendency of Javanese parents to teach their children a pessimistic view about life, where hardships and misfortune are constantly present. Early in their lives Javanese daughters are taught to feel concern (*prihatin*) over the hardship of life and to be submissive (*nrimo*) in dealing with the misfortunes (Koentjaraningrat 1985: 121). These cultural values are normally incompatible with the principles of PAR focusing on critical thinking, self-reliance, independence and assertiveness. At this point, Yasanti's use of popular theatre might not contribute much to the radicalisation of female factory workers because as a part of the Javanese culture, the basic plays (*lakon*) both in the *ketoprak* and the *wayang wong* generally depicted women as being submissive, obedient and concerned about hardships as widely understood by the Javanese community, despite the occasional presentation of the heroine such as Shinta and Srikandi (Berninghausen and Kerstan 1992: 32–5).

*Pressure from the state*

The PAR method, according to Thomas (1992: 141), is potentially revolutionary since it may lead to the articulation of particular local group interests against other powerful interests. Many participatory action researchers claimed to have been inspired by the idea of historical materialism. Rahman (1993: 82) noted that although PAR activity is independent from leftist political parties, it implicitly carries the notion of 'class struggle' as opposed to class harmony because it separates the poor and the oppressed from the powerful and because it attempts to generate class consciousness among the poor. As a process, PAR normally starts at the grassroots as a micro level activity and seeks to stimulate and assist grassroots processes to develop into a wider movement (Rahman 1993: 84; Lende 1995: 248). The close association of PAR with revolutionary movements tends to put participatory action researchers in a direct opposition with the ruling elite, particularly in places where grassroots mobilisation is severely repressed by the state (Elden and Levin 1991: 131–2; Thomas 1992: 142).

In Indonesia, where leftist ideology has always been considered as the public 'enemy' – especially by the military as well as the Islamic organisations – PAR method is thought to be potentially dangerous as it may lead to the resurgence of communist ideology. As has been discussed in Chapter 3, the phobia of the 'communist threat' has prompted the state leaders – especially during the New Order era – to suppress any organisations that can be associated with leftist ideology. Although the state officials had never openly expressed their objection against PAR (as they might not be aware of this new approach), strongly worded warnings of 'perpetrators' (*provokators*) using communist tactics to agitate the poor to revolt should be interpreted as an indication of the state's rejection of any kind of grassroots mobilisation. In the case of the protest movement against the new taxation on informal market traders in Yogyakarta, for example, state officials constantly warned the traders that their protest action may be used by the perpetrators to create disorder and that any disruption to public order is subversive. The traders responded to this warning by discontinuing their protest action. As one of the traders put it: 'If we go on with our protest action, the authorities will think that we are a group of dissidents (*mbalelo*) working together with the perpetrators (*provokators*)' (*Berita Nasional*, 24 May 1993).

In Central Java, following a series of labour strikes demanding wage increase, the Commander of the Diponegoro Regional Military Office, who was responsible for keeping security and order in Central Java and Yogyakarta provinces, warned the workers and the 'third party' (*pihak ketiga*)[13] to end their strikes immediately. As he put it:

> There are some indications of attempts by '*pihak ketiga*' (the third party), to take advantage (*menunggangi*) of the labour strikes by exposing the issue of class conflict to create public disorder and instability. These must be stopped immediately. In order to prevent industrial actions from spreading throughout Central Java, I will personally visit the industrial sites to calm down the workers. Any attempt to spread the idea of class struggle to the workers will face a severe punishment.
> 
> (*Kedaulatan Rakyat*, 4 February 1994)

In response to this threat, workers decided to discontinue their strikes. Although the factories did not meet their demands for higher UMR (regional minimum wages), the payment of the *tunjangan hari raya* (Idul-Fitr[14] bonuses) and better working conditions, many workers decided to go back to their jobs because they were afraid of being severely punished by the military apparatus (Soewito 1994: 19). They were also worried that being identified as the *pihak ketiga*, they may face difficulty in dealing with the local authorities.

Political labels such as *pihak ketiga* (third party), *anti-pembangunan* (anti-development), anti-*Pancasila, mbalelo* (dissidents) or *antek*-PKI (ex-PKI), according to Kartjono (1996: 56), were effective in discouraging people from resisting government policies, especially during the New Order government. Indeed, people with certain 'political labels' could be summoned for questioning by military officers at any time. The local authorities might also reject the politically labeled people's application for an identity card (*kartu tanda penduduk*), traveling permit (*surat jalan*), good behaviour certificate (*surat keterangan kelakuan baik*) required for traveling, school admission and job application.[15] In the post-Suharto era, despite the success of reform movement to remove some of the administrative burdens of the society, ex-PKI members are still considered 'dangerous' by the majority of military leaders, state officials and Islamic leaders. Although President Wahid had attempted to rehabilitate the ex-PKI members, the fear of a possible resurgence of a communist party has prompted the military and the Islamic organisations to continue their denunciation of leftist organisations. In Jakarta, Solo and Yogyakarta, for example, radical Islamic groups threaten and intimidate NGOs which are considered 'leftist' in their ideological leaning. Operating in this political situation, it is almost impossible for Yasanti to inject a certain degree of militant behaviour among its constituencies. The female factory workers' choice to go on with their own indirect protest action (absenteeism, stealing, withdrawal, cheating and so on) should therefore be understood as the only way of expressing their dissatisfaction without having to face political intimidation or elimination.

*Obstacles from the NGOs themselves*

Elden and Levin (1991: 129) argued that the success of PAR campaign is determined, among others, by the presence of a vision of the 'good organisation', that is, the one based on self-management, development of human potential, power equality and democratic principles. Thus, if NGOs are to succeed in their PAR activity they must develop a solid organisational form or, to use Handy's (1993) terminology, a strong 'organisational culture', because the implementation of PAR will include the process of recruiting, deploying, training and maintaining the commitment of NGO activists to work in all the local projects. Whether or not such a deliberate strategy is attempted, organisational processes that may evolve within NGOs can affect staff members' attitudes, integrity and competence (Thomas 1992: 143). In the context of women's movement, Kabeer (1994: 245) noted that the most important step in women's empowerment is to incorporate women's own needs and priorities into an organisational framework with a clear agenda for action.

However, there are at least two different sets of internal problems for NGOs in their attempt to implement the PAR method. First, NGOs' lack of ability to set up a clear, solid vision of a women's movement due to the hitherto women's fragmentary vision of their perceived roles and the lack of capacity among women to articulate the links between development, individual liberty and equality (Sen and Grown 1987: 93–4). Second, the lack of human resources with competence and commitment to maintain the original value base of the organisation and to translate participatory ideas into practice (Thomas 1992: 143–4). To a greater and a lesser extent, SBPY and Yasanti are facing these two sets of problems.

With regard to the vision of a movement, both SBPY and Yasanti suffer from a lack of clarity in their concept of emancipation. On many occasions, activists of the two organisations express their doubt whether a blatant attack on the conventional vision or policies on women is appropriate given the fact that among the Indonesian society feminine traits such as soft (*halus*), fear (*takut*) and obedient (*manut*) are still commonly used as a positive identification of women. As one women's activist put it: 'We situate the gender equality concept in the context of oriental values (*adat ketimuran*) and religious norms (*norma agama*) well preserved in our society. We must therefore avoid Western ideas of absolute freedom (*kebebasan tanpa batas*) and individualism' (*Berita Nasional*, 22 July 1997). My interviews also indicated reservation towards liberalism among women's activists in Yogyakarta. They were caught between the Western feminist value focusing on individual liberty and the traditional rules and norms focusing on modesty and harmony (Wahyuni, interview, 10/12/1996; Gayatri, interview, 12/12/1996; Muftiyanah, interview, 05/07/2001). On this point, it appeared that Indonesian feminists bear more ambiguity in terms of their appeal and their struggle against sexist exploitation compared to the more established Western feminists. As Berninghausen and Kerstan put it:

> While we (the Western feminists) attempt to struggle against pornography, rape and other forms of male violence against our bodies without giving up the individual and sexual freedoms we have fought for, Indonesian women increasingly retreat to the traditions and rules of Islam, which guarantee them a certain amount of security.
> 
> (Berninghausen and Kerstan 1992: 46)

By maintaining the traditional roles of women, Indonesian feminists, according to Berninghausen and Kerstan (1992: 244), have failed to effect a progressive change in the definition of women's sphere of activity that will result in a breakthrough in sexist power relationships. This may explain the dilemma of SBPY and Yasanti in their attempt to help their constituencies to move beyond their traditional values and roles.

Meanwhile, in terms of competence and capability to execute the PAR method, both SBPY and Yasanti face a shortage of staff members with sufficient background in skill and knowledge of adult teaching-and-learning. Although all of their staff members have completed their university education, none of them have background in adult teaching-and-learning activity (see Table 6.3). Conscientisation through adult-education classes is important to ensure that women will mobilise around their self-defined priorities and concerns (Johnson 1992; Kabeer 1994; Karl 1995). This usually takes place through a learning-teaching process in which literacy is taught through dialogue around words and themes that have a deep resonance in women's daily lives which may include 'political' themes such as wages, industrial relations, labour union, the informal economy, household economy, laws on workforce, government's acts of violence as well as gender-based ones such as sexual harassment, divorce laws and violence. Consequently, conscientisation requires staff with sufficient knowledge of these issues. The absence of staff with knowledge in these areas (see Table 6.3) appeared to have cost SBPY and Yasanti an opportunity to link women's issues with other important themes such as human rights, social movements, state corporatism and popular resistance.

In the case of SBPY, its attempt to recruit staff with appropriate background has failed because this organisation is unable to provide an attractive salary or

Table 6.3 Background of specialisation of staff members of SBPY and Yasanti

| Specialisation | Number of staff | |
|---|---|---|
| | SBPY | Yasanti |
| Literature studies | — | 1 |
| Sociology | 2 | 2 |
| Psychology | 2 | 1 |
| Journalism | — | 1 |
| Islamic studies | 3 | 3 |
| Politics | 2 | 2 |
| Anthropology | 2 | 1 |
| Economics | 1 | — |
| Total | 12 | 11 |

Source: Own data collection.

other material benefits for its employees (Gayatri, interview, 03/07/2001). There was no such fixed salary for SBPY's workers. Only six of the total 12 permanent staff members (*pegawai tetap*) received salary based on SBPY's contract with various funding agencies of Rp 500,000 per month in 2001, while the rest received the so-called *uang kunjungan* (visiting fees) paid whenever they visited the target groups. Meanwhile, Yasanti faces a shortage of human resources in its attempt to represent its constituencies. My observation indicates that the number of fieldworkers in Gadingan was too small to handle gender training activities in the village with 12 factories employing more than 5,000 female workers. In 2001, there were five fieldworkers in Gadingan, but two of them were based in the head office in Yogyakarta. Because Gadingan is relatively far from Yasanti's main office (about 80 km to the south of Yogyakarta), the frequency of their visits to the target groups is very low, ranging from once in two weeks to once in a month. This seems to support Sinaga's study stressing that Yasanti's fieldworkers tended to be overburdened and had a very limited time to focus their attention on their constituencies because they had to perform other functions such as making regular reports, doing administrative works and attending regular meetings, in addition to their main duties as co-ordinators of the courses and as facilitators for group discussions (Sinaga 1994: 14). It can therefore be argued that women's NGOs tend to face a lack of competent fieldworkers with adequate skill and time to stay and work together with their constituencies.

## The management of a movement

Developing a professional management is not the priority of movement-oriented NGOs. Their insistence on being a movement, rather than an institution, has prevented these NGOs from pursuing management in terms of budgeting, career progression, strategic planning and institutional development. Rahman (1993: 208)

200  *Building constituencies and institutionalising a movement*

argued that for those NGOs committed to grassroots movements, apart from performing basic administration, 'management' is expected to perform three major functions: (1) to manage collective affairs by initiating and co-ordinating collective action; (2) to manage mass participation, that is, to ensure that the activities are undertaken according to mass priorities and that the wider body of people have sufficient opportunity to fulfil themselves by active participation in the action; and (3) to nurture solidarity, that is, to ensure that some elements of the movement do not develop at the expense of other elements that may hinder the whole action. In the case of SBPY and Yasanti, their main challenge is how to maintain performance and sustainability without necessarily jeopardising their main objective of being a movement. This section will discuss the NGOs' ambiguity towards 'management' and the way they develop leadership to maintain performance and sustainability.

## *NGOs as movements and institutions*

As has been discussed in Chapter 2, NGOs share the characteristics of both a rigid-formal bureaucracy and a flexible-informal private or associational world (Billis 1993). While development NGOs appear to be closer to a bureaucracy, movement-oriented NGOs are closer to the associational world. For movement-oriented NGOs, an effective result can be achieved through informal communication with the constituencies in the form of spontaneous action based on specific goals and a relatively short-term perspective (Johnson 1992: 169). Declaring themselves as movement-oriented NGOs, both SBPY and Yasanti put more emphasis on flexibility in their approach towards their constituencies by deliberately avoiding bureaucracy. Some female NGO activists whom I interviewed maintained that bureaucratic and feminist principles are fundamentally incompatible because bureaucracy, which is based on a hierarchy of power, embodies a masculine value, while feminists seek egalitarian relations and collective management.[16] However, the pressure for efficiency, good performance and sustainability have made the two NGOs feel it necessary to establish a kind of organisational structure that holds the responsibility in managing their programmes. Moreover, given that 100 per cent of their budgets were funded by foreign funding agencies, both SBPY and Yasanti had to comply with their demands for administrative and financial discipline.

Caught in these two opposing directions, the two NGOs tended to develop ambiguous attitudes towards organisational issues such as professional management, career progression, staff development and managerial authority. Both SBPY and Yasanti were not sure whether they should develop a professional management because they identified themselves more as a movement rather than a professional institution. Handayani, a staff member of SBPY and a former staff of Yasanti, for example, argued: 'In order to get our proposals approved by a particular funding agency, we have to ensure that we operate as a formal organisation with a proper management that can perform basic administrative works' (Handayani, interview, 06/08/1997). But at the same time, she also maintained: 'Although a solid organisation and a professional management are important for us, we should not push too hard in this direction because after all our main objective is to perform as a movement for women's emancipation (*gerakan emansipasi perempuan*)' (Handayani, interview, 06/08/1996). Neither did the two organisations regard career progression and staff development as crucial matters because they believed that their organisations were guided by good intention and commitment rather than by technical competence or professionalism (Muftiyanah, interview, 05/07/2001). They were also not clear whether a director should concentrate on managerial duties (establishing standard operating procedures, making processes work well, ensuring people to work according to contract and so on) or on leadership (guiding people to work more, creating a long-term vision, setting up broad purpose and direction and so forth[17]). This seems to corroborate Billis's (1993: 164) argument that as part of the voluntary sector, NGOs tend to face ambiguity in management since their formal character conflicts with their informal intention.

## *Leadership, performance and sustainability*

How leadership is exercised seems to affect NGOs' success or failure to sustain their programmes or even their existence. On the basis of their type of leadership, Lofland (1996: 149–51) identified two types of what he called 'social movement organisations'.[18] First, the 'collectivist-democratic' organisations which share the characteristics of being 'collective' where authority resides in the collectivity as a whole and 'democratic' where management is based on egalitarian values and workers are granted freedom to perform their work without facing hierarchy of power. This is parallel with Handy's (1993: 188) category of 'task culture' where power and influence are widely distributed among staff members and the outcome is determined by a team work that utilises the unifying power of the group. Second, the 'professional-unitary' organisations which share the characteristics of being 'professional' where a large proportion of human resources have exclusive access to particular skill or knowledge and 'autocratic' where leadership is in the hands of a strong charismatic individual or a board of trustees who determine the policy of the organisation. Again, this description matches Handy's (1993: 190) category of 'person culture' whereby the fate of the organisation depends on a prominent figure who dominates the management of the organisation. The two models have their own strengths and weaknesses. The 'collectivist-democratic' or 'task culture' model is chosen by NGOs because it can ensure the mutual respect among employers and the flexibility as well as the sensitivity of the organisation to the environment, although it may face difficulty in imposing control mechanism since everyone seems to perform their work without restrictions on time, space or materials (Handy 1993: 188–9). Meanwhile, the 'professional-unitary' or 'person culture' is believed to be able to displace bureaucratic obstacles and to provide guidance to the unsophisticated members, but it suffers from the lack of sustainability because the survival of the organisation depends on the existence of a prominent figure and his/her ability to control members (Handy 1993: 190–1). Judging from their type of leadership, SBPY seems to fall into the category of 'collectivist-democratic' or 'task culture' organisations, while Yasanti comes closer to the 'professional-unitary' or 'person culture' organisations.

From the beginning, SBPY realises that *yayasan* (foundation) is not the appropriate form of organisation because it is highly undemocratic in which decisions are made by individual leaders or the board of founders (Gayatri, interview, 12/12/1997). However, like most NGOs in Indonesia formed during the New Order government, SBPY registered with the local notary as a *yayasan* in order to avoid the Law on Mass Organisation No. 8/1985 which obliges NGOs to receive guidance from the government. But this is just a formality because in reality SBPY operates as a joint secretariat (*sekretariat bersama*) relying on a 'collective leadership'. As noted in SBPY's constitution, collective leadership refers to a system in which: (1) authority is distributed more or less equally among members;[19] (2) information, resources and incentives are equally shared among staff members; (3) the director is only a temporary role assumed by each staff member through a rotation; (4) decision-making must involve all employees and members; and (5) the division of labour among staff members is kept to a minimum level and specific tasks are rotated based on flexible negotiation (SBPY 1995: 3–4).

With this type of leadership, SBPY has the chance to operate in a democratic atmosphere. My observation indicates that the working spirit and motivation of staff members are high as they actively contribute their views in most of their internal meetings and gatherings. They tend to use the traditional way of *musyawarah* (deliberation) or voting to settle internal problems. For example, they used voting to decide the protest action when they failed to lobby the local government in the case of the Beringhardjo renovation project. By adopting a collective leadership, SBPY was relatively successful in avoiding association with a particular figure within the organisation. Respect was initially put on Sih Handayani, one of the founders and the most experienced member (she had also worked for Yasanti for about 12 years),[20] but later on Dian Gayatri and Yos Sutiyoso. The reason for this shift of attention was the fact that Gayatri and Sutiyoso became more popular to donors and staff members, while Handayani was too busy with her side activities. Each member, regardless their experience or age, was given the opportunity to make their own decisions for the organisation. In such a situation, SBPY was able to develop a team culture, in which staff members interacted on the basis of mutual respect and a good working condition. Everyone could carry out their work without much pressure. As Handayani put it: 'By focusing on collective leadership, our organisation can maintain the working spirit among its staff members so that our programmes can be implemented without major internal obstacles' (Handayani, interview, 06/08/1997).

By 2001, however, the team culture in the organisation began to falter. The growing popularity of Dian Gayatri and Yos Sutiyoso as central figures in the executive body (*pengurus harian*) had generated the feeling of jealousy among members of the board of members (*musyawarah anggota*) which raised tension in the organisation. This personal quarrel suddenly turned into a deeper conflict between the executive body and the board of members. While the board of members accused the executive body of deviating the original purpose of SBPY as a network of women's activists rather than an NGO, the executive body opposed the intervention of the board of members in the daily activities of the organisation. This conflict had brought disharmony to the organisation especially when staff members began to take sides; many of whom were in favour of the executive body (Wibowo, interview, 06/07/2001). In May 2001, the board of members handed a motion of non-confidence which led to the resignation of both Dian Gayatri and Yos Sutiyoso. Their sudden resignation had raised anger among staff members who felt that both Gayatri and Sutiyoso had been treated unfairly by the board of members. In July 2001, three prominent staff members – Budi Wibowo, Fitri and Shinta – resigned leaving the organisation in uncertainty. When I visited SBPY's office in August 2001, there were no activities in the organisation. Okti, a member of the board, was appointed as a new executive director. Asked of what is in her mind to save her organisation, she answered: 'I will do my best to save this organisation by recruiting new staff members and by putting it back to its original function as a network rather than an NGO' (Okti, interview, 08/08/2001). But she also admitted that she had no clear agenda that can be converted to actions and programmes. As she put it: 'Frankly, I have no idea of what kind of programmes or activities we will become involved from now on. We should sit together and think what to do in the next two or three years' (Okti, interview, 08/08/2001). It is a great pity that an organisation with such a reputation as SBPY has to fall apart due simply to personal disputes which lead to institutional breakdown.

Meanwhile, Yasanti faces a slightly different situation. At the beginning of its existence, consistent with its identification as a 'professional-unitary' or 'person culture' organisation, Yasanti relied on a prominent figure, Sri Kusyuniati, also known as Mbak Kus (a Javanese term for sister Kus). She was one of Yasanti's founders and a long-serving director. This organisation's success during its 'high' period in the late 1980s and early 1990s was a result of the indefatigable effort of Mbak Kus whose hard work had attracted foreign funding agencies. Indeed, for many years Mbak Kus came into sight as the personalisation of Yasanti. As Mohtar Mas'oed, an NGO observer and academic, put it: 'To many people Yasanti is Mbak Kus, and Mbak Kus is Yasanti' (Mas'oed, interview, 03/08/1997). Even Yasanti's staff members acknowledged her important, if not dominant, contribution to the organisation. Mukarnawati, for example, commented: 'Mbak Kus was the only person with capability, competence and connections to keep our organisation going, while other staff members had to stay behind due to their mediocrity' (Mukarnawati, interview, 20/01/1997). Under Mbak Kus' leadership, Yasanti was successful not only in developing relations with its constituencies but also in obtaining national and international recognition. Through her personal acquaintance, Yasanti was involved both in national and international NGO networks during the late 1980s and early 1990s, most notably INFID (the International NGO Forum for Indonesian Development) and CAW (Committee of Asian Women). It was her ideas that attracted foreign funding agencies to provide financial support for Yasanti's gender analysis training courses and various research and publications on women's issues.

At the same time, other staff members carried out their work under Mbak Kus' guidance. Since she was the only one with the experience, information and knowledge about women's organisations and problems, staff members always relied on her suggestion and advice in carrying out their tasks (such as writing formal letters, report preparation, project evaluation, attending meetings with state officials, making contact with foreign institutions and so on). In 1993, the problem began to appear when Mbak Kus won a scholarship to pursue a further study at Swinburn University, Australia. Her sudden departure created a setback to the organisation because no one was prepared and was able to take over Mbak Kus' role. Just as organisational procedures and rules were almost non-existent, so staff members did not know how to distribute jobs among themselves. As a result, many important programmes, including gender analysis training courses in Gadingan, had to be postponed because no one was prepared to take the full responsibility of programme management. Sih Handayani recounted the decline of Yasanti following the departure of Mbak Kus:

> Yasanti seems to be inseparable from its founders, especially Mbak Kus. When she left us for a further study in Australia, our programmes had to be scaled down or even cancelled for several reasons. The first reason was that there were no other staff with some degree of competence and connection to take over Mbak Kus' role, especially in attending international conferences or in maintaining contacts with the national and international NGO networks. For example, we were no longer able to raise fund to pay for traveling costs to participate in those activities because we were relatively unknown to those whom used to be approached by Mbak Kus. The second reason was the failure of the board of trustees to allow staff members to come up with their own ideas with regard to future action and strategies. Members of the board were lacking confidence that junior staff could take a full responsibility in managing important programmes. The third reason was the fact that funding bodies began to leave us, partly due to the changing policies of international donors to Indonesian NGOs and partly due to our failure to convince them that we could proceed in the absence of Mbak Kus.
> 
> (Handayani, interview, 06/08/1997)

In 1996, the board of trustees decided to control the daily activities of the organisation. It appointed Budi Wahyuni, also one of Yasanti's founders, as an interim executive director. The tendency of the board of trustees to control the organisation's operation had generated frustration among Yasanti's staff members because they could hardly accept the inflexible and unitary approach of the board. By September 1997, Yasanti faced a serious organisational crisis. Sih Handayani – the most senior staff – resigned and moved to SBPY. Other staff members followed suit. Mukarnawati moved to another organisation in Jakarta, and Nita Kariani moved to *Rifka Annisa*, another women's NGO in Yogyakarta. Losing three of its most prominent staff, who used to serve as the 'backbone' of the organisation especially after the departure of Mbak Kus, Yasanti moved closer to a total collapse. While advocacy and training programmes had to be cancelled, Yasanti could only manage to maintain its research and publication activities albeit at a much lower scale. Its ambitious project of low-cost housing for female workers in Ungaran was also cancelled due to the withdrawal of the funding agency. New recruits were brought in, but it took a long while before they could deliver innovative programmes.

Despite this organisational crisis, in the post-Suharto era Yasanti continues to exist. After about 12 months of vacuum under Wahyuni's leadership,[21] in 1998 Yasanti began to operate on a 'normal' scale. Many programmes which were previously postponed or cancelled were reactivated. For this change, Yasanti owed much to Amin Muftiyanah, an experienced fieldworker in Ungaran who was promoted as an executive director in 1998. Realising that Yasanti was lacking working spirit and commitment especially among the new recruits, she put more emphasis on consolidation rather than on programme planning and implementation during the first year of her leadership. Muftiyanah regularly took new staff members to a 'field trip' to Ungaran in order to allow them learn about the situation faced by female factory workers during the economic crisis. They were subsequently asked to design their own programmes for the workers, while senior staff members served as facilitators. This approach seemed to be acceptable to all staff members who were enthusiastically involved in every discussion and brainstorming. Muftiyanah was also able to shift Yasanti's leadership style from 'personal-unitary' or 'person culture' to 'collectivist-democratic' or 'task culture' in which she distributed task and authority to all staff members regardless their age or seniority. Gradually, Yasanti was able to recover from the organisational crisis in the previous year. In August 2001, when I visited the organisation, Yasanti had already reactivated almost all of its programmes during its high performance in the early 1990s, which included gender equality training, research, publication, and networking. What we can learn from both SBPY and Yasanti's is that leadership seems to play an important role for organisations which claim to operate as a pseudo-movement. It appears that the survival of such organisations is determined by the quality of their leaders.

# 7 Developing democracy through a local network
## The case of the Yogyakarta NGO Forum

### The rise of popular resistance in the 1990s

For many observers, the 1990s were a 'decade of motion' in Indonesian politics when social movements across the region sprang up and became more assertive in expressing their demands for better and more tolerable social, economic and political conditions (Crouch 1994a: 121–2; Aspinall 1995: 28; Uhlin 1997: 60–1; Hadiwinata 1999: 7). Among the middle-class, criticism of the government was expressed in various kinds of critical writings, theatrical performances and informal gatherings. Frustrated members of the opposition parties held rallies, ignoring the threat of suppression from the military. Students' organisations and NGOs had also become increasingly involved in the promotion of democratic values and in facilitating collective action to resist the authoritarian government (Budiman 1994a: 233; Aspinall 1995: 30–1; Uhlin 1997: 111–15). Among the lower-class, people became bolder in expressing their grievances and demands for policy changes (Santoso 1993: 3–4). While in rural areas peasants stood up to defend their lands, in urban areas workers increased their demands for better working conditions and higher wages (Budiman 1994a: 230–2; Hadiz 1994: 192–3; Ramage 1996: 149). Commentators regarded the 1990s as the beginning of the rise of a strong Indonesian civil society (Fakih 1996: 37–8; Hikam 1996: 65; Ibrahim 1998: 55).

This chapter discusses the dynamics of an NGO network in the contexts of the growing pro-democracy movements in Indonesia during 1995–1997 and the subsequent transition to democracy in the post-Suharto era. It argues that the government's repression of campus-based student activities in the 1970s and 1980s had led to the rise of cross-sectoral pro-democracy coalitions in which NGOs played a leading role. Frustrated with the government's control of their activities, students began to turn their attention to the NGO sector. In Yogyakarta, the influence of student activism on NGOs was evident in the activities of the Yogyakarta NGO Forum. Also known as Forum, this local NGO network played an active role in the promotion of democracy before and after the fall of Suharto. Dominated by ex-student activists, Forum served as a pro-democracy coalition in Yogyakarta.

However, the fact that Forum consists of different organisations representing different values, ideologies and interests raises the question of whether it can maintain its coherence. Also, the facts that Forum is only a loose network whose governing body has no power to oblige members to follow particular rules or procedures and that its funding depends entirely on external donors also raise the question of whether or not it is sustainable. By presenting Forum's experience, this chapter attempts to illustrate the challenges faced by a network in its attempt to incorporate different organisations and to sustain collaboration. Some of the challenges have to do with the character of the network itself: (1) members are not ready to be governed by structures outside their own organisations and they are confused about who should pay the costs of the secretariat; (2) the process of institutionalisation tends to slow down due to members' fear of bureaucratisation; and (3) sustainability and performance are limited by over-ambitious goals and by heavy reliance on external funding agencies. Other challenges are external to the network. As we shall see, the change from a simple co-ordination to a pro-democracy coalition appears to bring new problems which includes a greater challenge from the state and a growing resistance from anti-democracy groups. In the post-Suharto era, Forum's effort to establish linkages with workers and the urban poor has raised suspicion from the radical Muslim groups which accused them of attempting to revive the communist ideology and of running programmes that contradict Islamic Law.

## *Structural conditions*

Popular resistance – or at least, the impulse among the people to resist – came from three quarters: those who believed themselves to be materially disadvantaged by appropriation without adequate compensation, those who believed themselves to be politically disadvantaged by restrictions on speech and public association, and those angered by government's acts of violence. The first quarter of resistance put emphasis on attempts to simply defend physical existence and other basic human rights (Schuurman 1993: 191). In the case of resistance in disputes over land ownership, for example, people organised themselves into groups, expressed their grievances and demanded fairer dealings. Land pressure, both in rural and urban areas where more and more people were forced to give up their lands for hydro-electric dams, factories and other modern business establishments, had generated frustration among those whose lives depended on a piece of land for vital income (in the case of small farmers) and for shelter (in the case of the urban poor). Lehmann (1990: 158) argued that movements against the dams and other modern construction projects quintessentially represent what a new social movement should be: their social base is heterogeneous, including smallholders, sharecroppers, squatters, artisans and the like who found themselves under threat and subsequently took 'collective action'.[1]

In Indonesia, in order to allow the domestic economy to become more exposed to the global market economy, the New Order government decided to take all possible measures to ensure rapid industrialisation. More lands were taken from the agricultural sector to be given to the industrial sector and this seizure subsequently raised the feeling of exploitation and impoverishment among the marginalised population (Soetrisno 1995: 40–1; Nasikun 1995: 60). Between 1994 and 1996, thousands of families in Yogyakarta and Central Java were evicted from their inherited land because new modern business establishments, housing estates and hydro-electric dams were to be constructed in the area, as was the case in the Solo Permai housing construction project in Sukohardjo, the Borobudur recreation centre in Magelang, the Prambanan tourism project in Sleman, the Mrica power plant in Banjarnegara, the Kedung Ombo dam project in Boyolali, the Paranggupito recreational project in Wonogiri, the Malioboro supermall in Yogyakarta and the batik factory construction in Bantul (Ismanto 1995: 120–1). People were often forced to leave without adequate material compensation or alternative employment (Juliantara 1995: 177). Their voices were not heard because the government tended to avoid prolonged negotiations, which would reduce the speed of industrialisation (*Kedaulatan Rakyat*, 2 January 1996). In a number of cases, villagers were forced to put their signature, indicating 'voluntary' displacement (Ismanto 1995: 132; YLBHI 1997: 201). Frustrated by these unfair dealings, with assistance from movement-oriented NGOs and students' organisations, people began to organise resistance in the forms of protest, demonstration or even violent action.

The second quarter of resistance grew out of an increasing level of frustration over strict government control and regulation of grassroots political activities. In countries where political parties and other political organisations had been ineffective, popular movements were most likely to emerge and press for room to manoeuvre (Fals Borda 1992: 309). In Indonesia, people were frustrated by the New Order government's systematic control over society where public gatherings and freedom of expression were strictly regulated. In 1995, the chief of the national police force, General Banurusman, emphasised that although article 28 of the 1945 constitution guarantees every Indonesian freedom of expression (*kebebasan menyatakan pendapat*), its implementation had to refer to the Law concerning public gathering No. 5/1963 and the Law on security and order No. 20/1982 stipulating that every gathering involving more than ten individuals requires a special permit issued by the local authorities. The failure to provide such a document would lead to dismissal and imprisonment of the organisers (*Berita Nasional*, 4 May 1995). Hadix, an NGO activist in Yogyakarta, described the complicated procedure that was involved in obtaining permission for a gathering as stipulated in the Law on public gatherings (*Undang-undang keramaian*) No. 5/1963. First of all, an individual or an institution must write a formal letter asking for permission. This letter, together with the proposal, must be signed by the *Ketua Rukun Warga* (chief of neighbourhood administration), the *Lurah* (village head), the *Camat* (sub-district head), the *Danramil* (sub-district military commander) and the *Kapolsek* (the sub-district police chief). At the next stage, this letter has to be presented to the *Kapolda* (the provincial police chief) and the *Kaditsospol* (the provincial head of social and political directorate), who will decide whether or not to grant the letter of permission (*surat ijin kegiatan*) (*Berita Nasional*, 20 June 1995). Annoyed by this complicated procedure, some NGOs chose to ignore it even though they realised what the consequences would be.

The third quarter of grassroots resistance sprang from public anger at the state's acts of violence. Giddens (1994: 231) noted that violence[2] was part of a long-term process of 'internal pacification' in the modern state. He argued that because premodern states were vulnerable to disorder (brigandage, banditry, piracy and the like), they depended entirely on the use of violence as the only way of enforcing obedience and of maintaining order. Indeed, through the centralisation of military power and the use of surveillance mechanisms, nation-states became 'sovereign powers': the agency of government was able to achieve much greater administrative control over its people (Giddens 1994: 232). Violence remained a part of the modern nation-states, as it was often used by regimes with an extremely narrow and largely superficial base of legitimacy – such as the communist regimes of Eastern Europe – to enforce the obedience of their citizens (Diamond 1993: 44). In many parts of developing world, authoritarian regimes persisted, not because of any belief in their moral entitlement to rule, but because they were able to impose coercive measures to repress opposition (Diamond 1993: 45).

In Indonesia, the New Order government relied on the use of violence to ensure its control over society. For example, it exercised domestic surveillance during the 1990s by imposing bans on individuals who were accused of spreading views hostile to Suharto's government. During 1995–1996, prominent individuals such as Emha Ainun Najib (a poet and critic who was popular among students), Abdurrahman Wahid (the then chair of the *Nahdlatul Ulama*), Megawati (the leader of the opposition party, the PDI), Adnan Buyung Nasution (the former director of YLBHI), Sri Bintang Pamungkas (an academic and politician), Gunawan Mohammad (a poet and former chief editor of the banned *Tempo* magazine) and many others, were banned from making public appearances for spreading anti-government feeling (*Kedaulatan Rakyat*, 3 June 1995; *Berita Nasional*, 4 June 1995; Juliantara 1996b: 114).

The state's acts of violence had gone so far as to include the use of physical force and murder. One example was the case of Fuad Muhammad Syarifuddin (Udin), a journalist for a local newspaper in Yogyakarta, *Berita Nasional*, who was brutally murdered for his reports on a corruption scandal involving a local government official. Shortly before his death on the 13 August 1996, Udin published reports on manipulation of the implementation of IDT (presidential instruction on less-developed villages) programmes and the falsification of land certificates in the Parangtritis recreational centre project committed by the head (*Bupati*) of Bantul district. The most serious report was on a corruption scandal in which the *Bupati* was reported to have bribed *Yayasan Dharmais* – one of President Suharto's 'charity' organisations – by involving the village head (*Lurah*) of Godean, who happened to be Suharto's close relative. He published a copy of a letter, signed by the *Bupati* and the *Lurah*, revealing the *Bupati*'s agreement to pay Rp 1 billion to the *yayasan* if reappointed for a second term[3] (*Berita Nasional*, 29 July 1996). This report was published in *Berita Nasional* shortly after the *Bupati* was actually reappointed. On 9 August 1996, eight members of the Bantul district security force threatened *Berita Nasional*'s chief editor, Bambang Sigap Sumantri, and forced him to apologise to the *Bupati* (YLBHI 1997: 52; Sumantri, interview, 10/08/1997). On 13 August 1996, Udin was found dead in front of his own house after receiving some mysterious guests. People in Yogyakarta were convinced that Udin's death had to do with his report on the

*Bupati*. They were devastated, not only by the murder itself, but also by the local police's attempt to manipulate the investigation of the case. On 21 October 1996, the police arrested a local man, Iwik, and linked him with the murder. It was later known that the police had fabricated the arrest by intoxicating Iwik with alcohol and by forcing him to make a false confession that he had murdered Udin for having an affair with his wife (*Berita Nasional*, 16 January 1997). Due to the lack of substantial evidence, this case was finally dropped when it reached the provincial court (*Kedaulatan Rakyat*, 29 August 1997). This case, according to Professor Loekman Soetrisno, a sociologist at Gadjah Mada University, had generated resentment among the people of Yogyakarta against the police force for their conspiracy in protecting the *Bupati* (Soetrisno, interview, 01/03/1997). While it was unclear to what extent the *Bupati* and the local police had been involved in Udin's murder, people in Yogyakarta began to develop strong anti-government feelings. Since then, students and NGO activists have become bolder in setting up a movement to challenge corruption and collusion involving state officials.

However, intensity of public reaction does not necessarily guarantee success in influencing the state, since a movement should also have the opportunity to organise and the right momentum to launch its action (Alberoni 1984: 170). Writing in a Latin American context, O'Donnell and Schmitter (1986: 16) argued that the rise of the pro-democracy movement in the 1980s was prompted partly by the growing tension within the ruling elite, particularly between the 'hard-liners', who believed that the perpetuation of authoritarian rule was necessary to ensure stability and the 'soft-liners', who became increasingly aware that the authoritarian regime would need some form of electoral legitimacy and a certain degree of freedom to make it acceptable both to the domestic opposition groups and to the international community. This tension can open up a space for grassroots groups to launch their resistance.

In Indonesia, the first signs of a crack in the New Order became evident in the late 1980s. Robison (1993: 50) noted that the military's lucrative forestry and transport monopolies had largely evaporated as better capitalised conglomerates and new family enterprises closely related to Suharto moved in. As a result, some parts within the army leadership began to feel uncomfortable with the take-over of their business enterprises by President Suharto's family and friends. Tension between Golkar and the army also increased. The rift between a group of army officers and leaders of Golkar, as manifested in the struggle for the nomination of vice-president in the 1988 and the 1993 parliamentary sessions, appeared to illustrate the beginning of conflict within the elite circle (Liddle 1993: 32; Uhlin 1997: 60). Some army officers were also disturbed by the greater political role of President Suharto's children. In 1993, two of Suharto's children – Bambang Trihatmodjo and Siti 'Tutut' Hadiyanti – were appointed as members of Golkar's Central Executive Board, which irritated some army officers (Aspinall 1995: 23). There was also dissatisfaction within the officer corps linked with the sudden or 'unfair' promotions and transfers (especially in the case of Prabowo, Suharto's son-in-law) and interference by non-military officials in the purchase of armaments (especially the role of B.J. Habibie, then Minister of Research and Technology, in determining the selection of military aircrafts and battleships) (*Far Eastern Economic Review*, 18 August 1994). These developments raised considerable concern and resentment among at least some of the military leaders. In 1996, the tension intensified as state officials began to humiliate their colleagues in public, for example, in the cases of the Minister of Transportation, Haryanto Danutirto, and the Minister of Mining and Energy, I.B. Sudjana. In both instances, insiders leaked the information to the media of an alleged case of corruption which subsequently raised controversy (Heryanto 1997: 120).

This evidence of the fragility of relations in the ruling elite allowed some clandestine relations between some parts of the military and the students to surface. Frustrated intelligence officers 'encouraged' (*mendorong*) students to continue holding protests, although at the same time they stressed their concern about national stability and warned students against infiltration by the 'extreme' left (Aspinall 1995: 35). For example, at an early stage of the campaign on the land dispute issue in the Kedung Ombo dam project, a prominent military officer (initially disguised as a journalist), visited the activists on the site and offered his help to finance the making of posters and banners, and to provide supplies for the protesters. Fr Mangunwijaya, a Catholic priest and activist who led the campaign, recalled: 'One day an army colonel came up to me and said that he was sent by a prominent military general, whom might have been General Murdani (then the Armed Forces Commander), to support activists in carrying out their resistance' (Fr Mangunwijaya, interview, 19/02/1997). This contention was supported by Aspinall's study in which one of the student activists whom he interviewed claimed that an army officer, who was known as General Murdani's right-hand man (*tangan kanan*), came to the site and encouraged students to go on with their anti-Suharto campaign (Aspinall 1995: 35). Similar incidents were reported in other cities such as Jakarta, Bandung and Surabaya where military intelligence officers visited the boarding-houses (*kos-kosan*) of activists and offered their sympathy for the students' protest against corruption committed by Suharto and his cronies.[4] The cracks in the fabric of the establishment appeared to have inspired the pro-democracy activists to increase their pressure for more political space and room to manoeuvre.

## *Actors and strategies*

The main agents of popular resistance in the 1990s were indeed students. The fact that Yogyakarta is a city of education where university students constituted nearly 40 per cent of the city's total population highlights the role of students in generating popular movements. Aspinall (1999: 229) argued that students became the central agent of these movements because other elements of civil society (political parties, Islamic organisations, labour unions, professional associations, interest groups and so on) were all too weak to challenge Suharto's power. Students tended to pursue militant politics because they live in key urban centres (where they have unlimited access to information and communications). They are not yet weighed down by the obligations of employment and family life and they have access to critical thinking through 'academic freedom' (*kebebasan akademis*) unavailable to other groups (Aspinall 1999: 229–30).

In the mid-1980s, as a result of the NKK/BKK policy (see Chapter 3), the students' movement retreated to off-campus activities. Students organised a number of study groups whose main activity was to promote radical social theories. In Yogyakarta, among these groups, Palagan was renowned for its radical orientation and ability to attract activists to discuss radical political discourses (Marxism, dependency theory, critical theory, among others).[5] In 1987, this group faced a crisis when two of its activists – Bambang Isti Nugroho and Bambang Subono – were caught red-handed while selling the banned novels of Pramoedya Ananta Toer (an ex-PKI member and a political prisoner). About a year later, Bonar Tigor, its founder, was arrested in Jakarta. The three activists were found 'guilty' of conducting subversive activity (that is, disseminating the strictly prohibited Marxist–Leninist doctrine) and were sentenced to eight years imprisonment (Uhlin 1997: 107). Other groups soon took over Palagan's activities. In the early 1990s groups such as FKMY (the Yogyakarta Student Communication Forum), DPMY (the Yogyakarta Council for Youth and Students), the SMY (the Yogyakarta Students' Solidarity) and SMID (the Indonesian Student Solidarity for Democracy, an organisation with several branches in major cities in Java) managed to follow Palagan's lead to link radical theories with the call for grassroots movements. Although these groups were severely repressed by the government, their formation indicated the birth of politically-concerned organisations outside university campuses seeking support from peasants and workers (Lane 1991: 18–19; Uhlin 1997: 110).

According to the method used in communicating ideas, resistance initiated by student activists can be classified into two categories: symbolic and practical resistance. Symbolic or indirect resistance includes various kinds of indirect actions against the state, whose main purpose is to express social grievances in a symbolic manner where criticism is expressed delicately and sometimes humorously (Hadiwinata 1999: 11). The main channel of this action was the mass media (particularly newspapers) and popular theatres. The two leading local newspapers in Yogyakarta, *Kedaulatan Rakyat* and *Berita Nasional*, regularly carried students' critical commentaries on various political events or topics such as human rights abuses, corruption, manipulation, repression, democratisation and so forth. Students (mainly from the drama schools scattered all over the city) also formed theatrical groups to address their grievances. In most performances, groups such as *Jeprik* and *Gandrik* expressed social criticism humorously by picturing greedy and lazy officials, pretentious social climbers, hypocritical and holier-than-thou moralists who manipulated and exploited '*wong cilik*' (the little people) for their personal advancement. Creative figures such as Heru Kesawamurti, Jaduk Ferianto, and Butet Kertarajasa, had staged critical theatrical performances that became increasingly popular among the middle-class audience, especially through television.

Meanwhile, practical or direct resistance refers to direct action to challenge particular policies. These activities can be associated with street demonstrations, protest action, strike and condemnation directed against particular government policies or officials (Hadiwinata 1999: 13). In Yogyakarta, students have begun to link themselves with peasants and workers since the early 1990s. Juliantara noted that one major difference between students' movement of the 1990s and their predecessors in the 1960s and 1970s was that students of the 1990s put more emphasis on local issues and established linkage with NGOs and grassroots organisations (Juliantara 1996b: 104). In a number of land dispute cases, for instance, students worked together with farmers and petty traders in conducting street demonstrations, in organising petitions and in lobbying the local representative assembly (DPRD) for a better compensation and alternative jobs (Hadiwinata 1999: 14).

From the mid-1990s, amid the growing dissatisfaction with Suharto's government, students became increasingly involved in practical and direct resistance in which street demonstration was their major choice. Crude anti-Suharto slogans such as 'Hang Suharto!' (*Gantung Suharto*), 'Drag Suharto to an extra-ordinary parliamentary session!' (*Seret Suharto ke Sidang Istimewa*), 'Suharto is the culprit of all troubles!' (*Suharto Dalang Segala Bencana*), and the like were frequently shouted and written in their posters. Although there were differences among the students with regard to the extent to which confrontation with the government should be pursued or whether Islam should be used as the basis for their resistance, they had nevertheless agreed to share common purposes which included: (1) a demand for the maximum protection of human rights; (2) an appeal to ensure the rule of law and the reduction of the state's power; (3) a call for free and fair elections; and (4) an appeal for the reduction of military role in politics (Uhlin 1997: 145). Golkar's domination in the general elections was also the main target of popular resistance in the 1990s. For example, in May 1997 groups of students and youngsters removed the symbols of all parties – Golkar, PPP and PDI – from the streets around the city and replaced them with white flags and banners symbolising the identity of *golput* (the non-voters).[6] It was followed by a procession involving thousands of youngsters on their motorcycles carrying an empty bier symbolising the death of democracy. In most corners of the streets, people put empty biers and banners chanting, among other things: 'Long live the Non-voters!' (*Hidup Golput*), 'Our democracy has died!' (*Demokasi Kita Sudah Mati*), and the like (*Kompas*, 16 May 1997). Meanwhile, groups of youngsters were roaming around the city on their motorcycles almost everyday, causing major traffic problems in the city (*Berita Nasional*, 28 May 1997). Towards the end of the New Order government, students' demonstrations began to take place on a greater scale. In various places they sporadically organised demonstrations demanding Suharto's resignation. In 1998, endless demonstrations carried out by students in major cities such as Jakarta, Medan, Bandung, Yogyakarta, Surabaya and Ujung Pandang had contributed to the fall of Suharto. The students' occupation of the parliamentary building in Senayan, Jakarta, in May 1998 was considered as the final blow which resulted in Suharto's resignation.

## Multi-group networks in Yogyakarta

Lende (1995: 248–52) argued that a multi-group network is generally formed to perform two major functions. First, groups need to identify channels for strengthening their networking capabilities from the community level to global contexts by organising dialogues among local grassroots initiatives. Second, a cross-fertilisation (i.e. cross-sectoral sharing of knowledge and information) must be developed in order to bridge the gap between community leaders, NGO activists and other advocates of the network. It is expected that different participants can become further sensitised to what has been tried in one region and apply it to another.

In the Philippines, a cross-sectoral effort was launched in the late 1980s to unite peasants long divided by ideological, territorial and regional disputes. NGOs such as PHILDHRRA (Philippine Partnership for the Development of Human Resources in Rural Areas), the PPI (Philippine Peasant Institute), PRRM (Philippine Rural Reconstruction Movement) and FRC (Forum for Rural Concerns) played important roles in forming a network between NGOs and popular organisations in order to link local level struggles to national level debates (Clarke 1998: 124–6). In Indonesia, students initiated a broad network through their off-campus activities. Radical organisations formed by students or ex-student activists such as PIJAR, GENI, LAPERA, LBH Nusantara, RUMPUN, PRD (People's Democratic Party), PIPHAM (Centre for Human Rights Information and Education), LEKHAT, ALDERA, SBPY (Yogyakarta women's joint secretariat) and Yasanti established informal coalitions to pursue joint human rights campaigns (Uhlin 1997: 111). Some (GENI, LAPERA and ALDERA) considered themselves more as student groups rather than NGOs because their major aim was to establish coalitions among different student groups to address issues concerning the marginalisation of the powerless (workers, peasants, children and women) rather than act as intermediary organisations with paid staff and a permanent office.[7]

## Different types of networking

The development of networks has been described by NGO writers as a part of NGOs' scaling-up process, that is, an attempt to achieve wider social and political impact and to articulate local needs on a broader regional, national or even international stage (Korten 1990: 113–18; Clark 1991: 83–4; Edwards and Hulme 1992: 14). By establishing a network, NGOs are expected to form a link not only among NGOs themselves but also between the NGO community and other social movements such as student organisations, professional associations, labour unions, peasant associations, religious groups and grassroots organisations (White 1994: 377; Tandon 1996: 119; Bunnell 1996: 196–8). Clark (1991: 106) argued that collaborative action among different actors is important to generate resistance because bigger battles can only be fought by large numbers of similar groups coming together in coalitions or networks to support each other's struggle.

NGO networks can be divided into two categories: vertical and horizontal networks. While in a vertical network members are tied into regional federations and are required to follow the rules of that federation, in a horizontal network they operate at the same level and retain their autonomy (Clark 1991: 99). A vertical network is the most coherent type of collaboration because it is based on a system of governance whereby members have more obligation to synchronise their efforts and resources in order to achieve a collective goal (Fowler 1997: 112). Meanwhile, a horizontal network is 'loose' because initiators are not mandated by the membership which is essentially self-selected and can come and go at any time (Fowler 1997: 113). A survey of 150 NGOs in South Asia conducted in 1981 showed that NGOs that were linked vertically performed better than isolated organisations, but those that were linked horizontally performed even better (Uphoff 1987). Fisher (1993) divided NGO networks into formal and informal ones. A formal network normally functions as an umbrella or consortium of NGOs with paid staff and boards of directors. In most cases, formal networks are promoted and funded by foreign donors to provide members with services: information, skill, funding sources, and so forth (Fisher 1993: 140). An informal network, on the other hand, does not generally create formal organisational structures and is less likely to have paid staff or boards. They may grow spontaneously out of the contacts made at a conference or other events, or because one group or individual takes the initiative to convene others to get together on a more or less regular basis (Fisher 1993: 143; Eade 1997: 155). Although these distinctions represent more of a continuum than rigid categories, it is important to understand them before discussing how well or badly NGO networks perform.

## Students and the informal networks

From the late 1980s, students, intellectuals and NGO activists in Yogyakarta realised the importance of a cross-sectoral network. Professor Loekman Soetrisno of Gadjah Mada University initiated a regular discussion which was intended to set up a dialogue between academics, researchers, students and NGO activists. Once a month he invited speakers from inside or outside Yogyakarta to discuss various topics in the area of rural development, grassroots organisations, human rights, democracy, labour affairs, and the informal sector, among others in his well-known research institute, the P3PK (Research Centre for Regional and Rural Development). Similar efforts were initiated by NGOs such as *Dian Desa*, LBHY (Yogyakarta Legal Aid Institute), LKPSM-NU (a community development unit of the *Nahdlatul Ulama*) and *Yayasan Satunama* to establish informal links between students, academics and NGO activists. However, these efforts were criticised for having failed to include grassroots groups in their activities. As Fajar Sudarwo, a staff of *Yayasan Satunama*, put it: 'Although interactions between activists increased as a result of the regular discussions organised by various institutions, it was far from creating a grassroots network because popular organisations were not involved in those activities' (Kusumohadi *et al.* 1997: 168).

The initial cross-sectoral networks involving grassroots people emerged in the early 1990s when students and a fraction of NGOs established linkage with informal traders, workers and peasants. The experience of SBPY in working with petty market traders and of Yasanti with factory workers discussed in Chapter 6 were examples of these grassroots-oriented networks. But the biggest collaborative effort was the campaign against the construction of Kedung Ombo hydro-electric dam in Central Java. The thirty megawatt hydropower project required some

6,125 hectares of land, 1,500 of which were cultivated land from which more than 30,000 people had been forcibly displaced (Mayer 1996: 196). On the whole, 37 villages from seven *kecamatan* (sub-districts) and three *kabupaten* (districts): Boyolali, Grobogan and Sragen had to be cleared. Co-funded by the World Bank (45 per cent), the government of Indonesia (28 per cent) and the Japanese Export-Import Bank (27 per cent), the US$283 million worth project was meant to provide supplies of drinking water (a critical necessity for people in the area), to create electricity power supply, to serve as flood control, fish breeding and as a tourist attraction (Sinaga 1994: 151). Problems arose when around 8,000 villagers, who were dissatisfied with the inadequate compensation[8] and the absence of alternative jobs, refused to leave the area. When the water began to rise behind the dam in early 1989, villagers moved to higher ground that became islands in the middle of the rising lake and ignored the eviction order by the security apparatus (*Suara Merdeka*, 28 April 1989).

The local authorities responded by calling those who refused to leave the site 'anti-development', 'extremists', even 'communists' (*Suara Merdeka*, 8 May 1989). President Suharto himself addressed them as *mbalelo* (dissidents) (*Kompas*, 2 June 1989). Those who were regarded as masterminds of the resistance had their identity card stamped with the letters E.T., meaning *ex-tapol* (ex-political prisoner), indicating that they had been involved in the PKI's 30 September 1965 movement. This was followed by the use of coercion including physical force, arrests and intimidation (Sinaga 1994: 172). The extensive publication of this case generated sympathy from students, NGO activists, intellectuals, and religious leaders. Around 150 students from various universities in Semarang, Solo, Salatiga and Yogyakarta formed a task force called KSKPKO (the Solidarity Group for the Victims of Kedung Ombo Construction Project) whose main task was to accompany (*mendampingi*) the villagers by setting up a solidarity camp site in the village and to bring the case to public attention by organising street demonstrations in Solo, Semarang, Yogyakarta and Jakarta (Sinaga 1994: 158; Uhlin 1997: 105). They were joined by Fr Mangunwijaya (a Catholic priest) and Kyai Hammam Ja'far (an Islamic teacher of the Pabelan *Pesantren*), who held marches and vigils in solidarity with the inundated villagers (Stanley 1990: 34; Mayer 1996: 196). Meanwhile, NGOs – especially LBHS (Semarang Legal Aid Institute) and LBHY (Yogyakarta Legal Aid Institute) – joined the campaign, focusing on the court settlement by filing a case against the government for using political intimidation and manipulation in displacing villagers. Judging from the status of its membership and the absence of organisational structures, KSKPKO seems to match Clark's horizontal and Fisher's informal network.

Predictably, after operating for about one year, KSKPKO soon collapsed. Apart from being too informal, KSKPKO was also weakened by internal conflicts, especially between NGO activists and the students (Eldridge 1995: 124). This conflict was illustrated in a sharp exchange between George Aditjondro and Arief Budiman, both of whom were lecturers and activists at Satyawacana Christian University, Salatiga, Central Java. For Aditjondro, the Kedung Ombo campaign was seriously undermined by the gap between radical-oriented student activists and a few legal-minded NGOs. In his view, while the student movement claimed victory prematurely, as they were satisfied with their success in bringing the case to the national or even international attention, NGOs were more concerned with a court settlement and were not interested in the political struggles (Aditjondro 1990: 46–8). Budiman, on the other hand, argued that students had played complementary roles in supporting NGOs' attempt to provide a legal solution. In his view, although the problems faced by villagers remained unsolved, students had helped to fan the flames that provided moral support for NGOs in their attempt to file the case against the local government (Budiman 1990: 54–7). While it is important to note the differences between NGOs and student activists as argued by Aditjondro, one should also consider Budiman's account of the compatibility of political struggles and legal actions. Combining the two views, Eldridge (1995: 42) commented that despite the partial success of the Kedung Ombo collaborative effort to bring the case to public attention, the coherence of KSKPKO had been undermined by a continuing 'cold war' between NGOs and student activists which led to its collapse.

## The Yogyakarta NGO Forum

In Yogyakarta, the first formal NGO network was formed in 1986. It was charged with the duty to establish co-ordination among different NGOs. Known as the Yogyakarta NGO Forum, or simply Forum, this co-ordinating body was considered by some commentators as the first Indonesian regional NGO network formed through local initiatives (Eldridge 1995: 203; Bunnell 1996: 199; Kusumohadi, interview, 25/07/1997). Forum was co-founded by *Yayasan Purba Danata*, an NGO specialised in borrowing-and-lending activities, and the Bappeda (the Development Planning Board) of the Central Java region to achieve two major aims: (1) to co-ordinate relationships between the NGO community and the local government; and (2) to remind one another (*saling mengingatkan*) of the appropriate conduct of community development activities (Kartjono 1986: 4–6; Setiawan 1986: 3–4). Although Forum has a governing body with organisational structures, permanent office and paid staff, the fact that its members retain absolute freedom and full autonomy makes it fall into Clark's category of a horizontal network.

Its daily activities were controlled and managed by an executive board (*badan pelaksana*) consisting of an executive director, a secretary general, a treasurer and four ordinary members (Forum 1996: 83). The executive director was responsible for devising standard operating procedures and co-ordinating activities of different *ad hoc* committees (Ujianto, interview, 06/07/2001). To ensure the balance of power within the governing body, a steering committee (*badan pengurus*) – consisting of seven individuals taken from member organisations – was formed. The main duty of the steering committee was to check and monitor the works of the executive director, the secretary general and the treasurer (Forum 1996: 76). In addition to these structures, 10 *ad hoc* committees (labour affairs, networking, publication, community development, public health, informal sector, legal aid, land disputes, art and culture and education and training) were formed to plan, implement and monitor programmes (Forum 1996: 1–42). Members of these committees were selected from various participating organisations; and each committee elected a co-ordinator to provide guidance and leadership. In 1998, however, Forum rationalised its *ad hoc* committees by limiting their number to only four: research and discussion, publication, advocacy and training. This rationalisation was carried out for two reasons: (1) as an attempt to develop a more simple management; and (2) as a response to donor's demand to scale down its organisational size (Forum 2000: 15).

From 1986 to 1992, under the leadership of Imam Yudotomo (1986–1989) and Din Yati (1989–1992), Forum served as an agent of information exchange and a co-ordinating body of joint community development projects between the Bappeda and NGOs in Yogyakarta and Central Java. It concentrated on training programmes for small NGOs. Each of the participating NGOs was asked to bring a leading village activist and a representative of the state-sponsored grassroots organisation, the LKMD (village people's defense council), to participate in 10 days of training in community development skills (namely, new methods of farming, cattle breeding, micro-credit, handicrafts and the like). This was followed by a one month internship in respective villages to identify local problems and needs. The programme ended with a final gathering to discuss project designs and proposal writings (Din Yati, interview, 12/12/1996). Occasionally, Forum also carried out joint projects with the Bappeda as manifested in the *mbangun deso* (rural development) project in several villages in Kulon Progo in which rural cadres were trained and helped to form pre-co-operative groups mainly in the area of saving-and-borrowing (Hariadi, interview, 04/08/1997). In 1992, these programmes were terminated due to the poor communication between Forum and its funding agencies (the *Sekretariat Bina Desa*, the Group of Thirteen and WALHI) (Eldridge 1995: 203). By 2000, although there were 81 NGOs registered with Forum, the actual members of this regional network were fewer. For example, in its regular meeting in Kaliurang in August 2000, there were only 42 individuals representing 32 organisations that can be considered as Forum's actual members (Forum 2000: 32). According to Forum's membership list, there were 17 (21 per cent) out of the total 81 members who were either inactive or had disappeared. This indicates a relatively high percentage of what Constantino-David called COME'NGOs in Yogyakarta where fly-by-night activists formed organisations, registered with Forum and then disappeared for various reasons ranging from shortage of funding to boredom.

## Forum's pro-democracy campaigns

Aspinall (1995: 33) and Uhlin (1997: 112) argued that since the early 1990s students who were frustrated with the government's tough regulation of campus-based activities had begun to turn their attention to the NGO sector in their search for more effective solutions for social and political problems. In the 1993 election for Forum's governing body, both students and ex-student activists outnumbered the non-student members. Consequently, students were able to control three top positions in Forum's organisational structure. Dadang Juliantara, a prominent figure in the student movements of the late 1980s, was elected as the executive director, Untoro Hariadi, another ex-student activist, was elected as the secretary general, and Budi Astuti Azhar, a final year student, served as the treasurer (Forum 1996: 21).

Juliantara brought with him a number of young activists – many of whom were still pursuing their studies – into Forum's governing body at the expense of the non-student members. If we look at the age distribution of members of Forum's governing body, during 1996–1998, 29 out of the total 42 members were under 29; and only 13 were over 30 which indicated the domination of young student activists[9] (Table 7.1). With regard to members of *ad hoc* committees, 21 out of the total 28 members were under 29; and only seven were over 30 (Table 7.1). It also appears in the table that 14 out of 42 members of Forum's governing body were under 25; and 15 were aged between 26 and 29. Considering that 24–26 years of age is the normal age of Indonesian university graduates, the data seems to indicate that at least one-third of members of Forum's governing body were still pursuing their studies; and about 35 per cent were just finishing their courses. In describing the impact of students' domination on Forum's policy direction, Farid, a non-student member of Forum, argued that by controlling the strategic positions of Forum's governing body, students could achieve their political agenda, that is, to use Forum as a supporting body to intensify their pro-democracy campaigns (Farid, interview, 28/01/1997).

*Table 7.1* Age distribution of members of Forum's governing body during 1996–1998 and 1998–2000

| Position | Age distribution | | | | | | | | Total | |
|---|---|---|---|---|---|---|---|---|---|---|
| | 19 or under | | 20–25 years | | 26–29 years | | 30 or over | | | |
| | 1996 to 1998 | 1998 to 2000 | 1996 to 1998 | 1998 to 2000 | 1996 to 1998 | 1998 to 2000 | 1996 to 1998 | 1998 to 2000 | 1996 to 1998 | 1998 to 2000 |
| Executive board | — | — | 2 | — | 3 | — | 2 | 4 | 7 | 4 |
| Steering committee | — | — | 1 | — | 2 | 2 | 4 | 7 | 7 | 9 |
| Ad hoc committees | 2 | — | 9 | 1 | 10 | 11 | 7 | 16 | 28 | 28 |
| Total | 2 | — | 12 | 1 | 15 | 13 | 13 | 27 | 42 | 41 |

Source: Own data collection.

220  *Developing democracy through a local network*

In the post-Suharto era, although ex-student activists continue their control over Forum's governing body, most of them have gained relatively long experience in the NGO sector. The election of Anggerjati Wijaya, an ex-student activist and a staff member of the KTRI (the Indonesian Association of People's Theatre), as Forum's new executive director in February 1998 had signified the involvement of experienced NGO activists in Forum's governing body. Wijaya brought with him some ex-student activists with long experience in NGO operations such as Ari Suseta from the LBHY (the Yogyakarta Legal Aid Foundation), Mohammad Najib from the YKF (the women's organisation of the *Nahdlatul Ulama*), and Odi Shalahuddin from the SAMIN (the Indonesian Free Children's Association). Wijaya's attempt to mobilise ex-student activists with sufficient experience in NGO operations was followed by his successor, Martinus Ujianto, another ex-student activist and a staff member of the YLKI (the Indonesian Consumers' Association). After his election as Forum's new executive director in August 2000, Ujianto filled top positions in Forum's governing body with experienced NGO activists: Taufiqurrahman (a staff member of the LKPSM-NU or the Community Development Arm of the *Nahdlatul Ulama*) as the secretary general, Amin Muftiyanah (the director of Yasanti) as the treasurer, and Agus Hartana (a staff member of IDEA or the Institute for Democracy and Electoral Assistance) as the project officer. He also appointed some activists from various movement-oriented NGOs as co-ordinators of the *ad hoc* committees. With regard to the age distribution of Forum's governing body (see Table 7.1), during 1998–2000 there was a substantial change: most members were between 26 and 29 (13 out of 41 members) or over 30 years old (27 out of 41 members). This indicates an increase of maturity among the members of Forum's governing body.

*Propagating the idea of people's sovereignty*

With ex-student activists and members of movement-oriented NGOs controlling its governing body, Forum's role was increasingly transformed from a co-ordination of rural development projects to a network for the pro-democracy campaign. No longer serving as a liaison agency between the NGO community and the local government, Forum began to adopt a confrontational strategy in which critical comments against the state were expressed more directly and openly. In the New Order era, using the local media – especially the newspapers – Forum tried to bring people's grievances and dissatisfaction with Suharto's government to public attention. Although the strategy appeared to be too risky, especially when the government was so determined to thwart any political opposition, the commitment to democracy among the radical activists had encouraged Forum to go on with its confrontation strategy. In March 1994, for instance, Forum organised a workshop on the issue of labour movement. At the end of the workshop, activists signed a petition criticising the government's repression of labour activism by referring to a number of cases – especially the death of Marsinah and Titi Sugiharti (two women labour activists who were allegedly killed by security officers for their involvement in labour strikes) – and the banning of independent labour unions (*Berita Nasional*, 20 March 1994). A few weeks later, Forum expressed concern about the government's use of coercion in a number of land dispute cases such as the Prambanan recreational project and the Batik factory construction in Bantul (*Berita Nasional*, 3 April 1995). Many other statements followed focusing on a wide range of issues such as democracy, political freedom, labour rights, land disputes, the state's acts of violence, press freedom, the protection on women workers and so on.

The boldness of Forum's strategy was also manifested in a number of protests. On 23 December 1994, it organised a rally in the front yard of the DPR (People's Representative Body) building in Jakarta expressing concern about the government's continuous violation of human rights as manifested in the banning of the three weekly magazines (*Tempo*, *Editor* and *DeTik*), the forced resettlement in Kedung Ombo dam project, the banning of seminars organised by NGOs and the prohibition of critical individuals to make public appearances (*Republika*, 26 December 1994). This action was repeated on 16 January 1995 when dozens of Forum's representatives handed in a petition to the DPR demanding the representative body to warn Suharto and his ministers for denying the rights of workers to organise. Forum attacked the enactment of the *Peraturan Menteri Tenaga Kerja* (Minister of Manpower regulation) No. 1/1994 stipulating that the government only recognises SPSI (a state-sponsored labour union) as the only organisation for workers (*Merdeka*, 17 January 1995).

The TNI (the Indonesian armed forces) was also a target of Forum's campaign. On 30 December 1995, in a written statement distributed to the local newspapers, Forum demanded an end of the 'security approach' which allowed the government to use military force to repress any kind of political opposition. More specifically, Forum called on the abolition of the military's dual function (*Dwifungsi*)[10] and the reduction of the number of TNI representatives in the MPR (People's Consultative Assembly)[11] (*Kedaulatan Rakyat*, 31 December 1995). When the 1997 general election was approaching, Forum began to question the use of manipulation by the government to force Golkar's absolute majority. In January 1996, Forum demanded the formation of an independent committee to monitor and to ensure free and fair elections (*Berita Nasional*, 13 January 1996; *Yogya Post*, 13 January 1996). Altogether, from December 1993 to January 1996, Forum had produced 33 political statements covering various issues (see Table 7.2).

Predictably, the government responded by imposing a more severe approach, especially in dealing with radical NGOs. On 12 April 1995, the Commander of the Regional Military Office in Central Java, warned: 'Any NGO which exaggerates the issue of social-economic inequality to provoke peasants and workers to engage in revolutionary action will face serious punishment (*hukuman berat*) from the security apparatus', as he feared that Forum's comments on socio-economic inequality would provoke class struggles (*Berita Nasional*, 13 April 1995; *Jawa Pos*, 13 April 1995). Meanwhile, the Minister of Justice, Oetojo Oesman, threatened that the government might 'crystallise' (*mengkristalisasi*) NGOs in order to 'put them back into their original function' (*mengembalikan ke fungsi sebenarnya*) by introducing a law especially designed to regulate NGO

*Table 7.2* Forum's political statements 1993–1996

| | Date | Issues concerned |
|---|---|---|
| 1 | 30/12/93 | Criticism of the governments' non-participatory development approach |
| 2 | 12/01/94 | Protest against the use of coercion in government's handling of students' demonstrations |
| 3 | 24/01/94 | Protest against the government's Nuclear Power Plant project in Jepara, Central Java |
| 4 | 07/02/94 | Concern about the need to protect women migrant workers (TKW) against any abuse |
| 5 | 19/03/94 | Calling on the recognition of labours' rights to organise |
| 6 | 02/04/94 | Protest against political engineering (*rekayasa politik*) against community organisations |
| 7 | 08/06/94 | Demand a greater role of NGOs in public policy making |
| 8 | 11/06/94 | Concern about the use of coercion in handling industrial disputes |
| 9 | 26/06/94 | Protest against the banning of the three weekly magazines (*Tempo, Editor* and *DeTik*) |
| 10 | 08/07/94 | Call for the press freedom and the lifting of the restrictions on the press |
| 11 | 03/08/94 | Protest against the ban on Emha Ainun Nadjib, a poet and writer. |
| 12 | 23/09/94 | Protest against restrictions on public meetings |
| 13 | 26/09/94 | Demand a greater freedom for NGOs |
| 14 | 22/12/94 | Concern about government's negligence of women migrant workers (TKW) |
| 15 | 23/12/94 | Concern about the government's continuous violation of human rights |
| 16 | 04/01/95 | Concern about the growing social and economic inequality |
| 17 | 16/01/95 | Demand a higher regional minimum wages (UMR) for workers |
| 18 | 25/01/95 | Protest against the use of coercion in land dispute cases |
| 19 | 01/02/95 | Call for the abolition of the law on subversion used against student activists |
| 20 | 14/03/95 | Protest against police brutality in handling criminals |
| 21 | 07/04/95 | Protest against the use of coercion against students' peaceful protest action |
| 22 | 12/04/95 | Protest against the threat from military leaders to thwart movement NGOs |
| 23 | 20/06/95 | Concern about the deterioration of individual freedom |
| 24 | 05/07/95 | Protest against the government's lack of political will to investigate the mysterious death of a woman migrant worker in Singapore |
| 25 | 11/07/95 | Protest against rampant corruption and brutality within the police force |
| 26 | 15/08/95 | Concern about the New Order's authoritarian rule |
| 27 | 01/09/95 | Call on the implementation of rule of law that guarantees freedom and equality |
| 28 | 25/09/95 | Concern about the banning of Abdurrahman Wahid (the leader of the *Nahdlatul Ulama*) and of Megawati (the leader of the PDI) |
| 29 | 25/09/95 | Concern about government intervention in NGOs' internal affairs |
| 30 | 30/10/95 | Reject the government's association of radical NGOs with OTB (formless organisations) |
| 31 | 30/12/95 | Call on the abolition of the military doctrine of *Dwifungsi* and the reduction of military representatives in the MPR |
| 32 | 02/01/96 | Demand a fair general election and the neutrality of the military |
| 33 | 12/01/96 | Call on the formation of an independent committee to monitor the general election process |

Source: Compiled from Forum, 1996. *Laporan Pertanggungjawaban Kepengurusan Periode 1993–1996.* Yogyakarta: Forum LSM/LPSM DIY.

activities (*Kompas*, 9 April 1995). These threats were followed by a surveillance on NGO activities by the security forces. Juliantara recalled: 'In most of our seminars or discussions during 1994–1995, we felt intimidated by the presence of *intel* (intelligence officers) who noted or recorded every political remark made by the speakers as well as the participants' (Juliantara, interview, 23/08/1997). On 26 August 1995, Forum's seminar on the politics of regulation on grassroots organisations was dissolved by the local police on the grounds that the organiser had not followed the proper procedure for gaining permission from the local authorities (*Kedaulatan Rakyat*, 27 August 1995). About a month later, around 60 participants in Forum's seminar on freedom of expression were sent home for the same reason (*Kedaulatan Rakyat*, 28 September 1995). In November 1995, a group of police officers raided Forum's office, accusing the NGO network of conducting an 'illegal' gathering. Hariadi, Forum's secretary general, recalled that during the raid the policemen counted the number of tea cups used in the meeting. Because there were more than 20 cups on the table, they insisted that the meeting required permission from the local authorities before it could be allowed to proceed (Hariadi, interview, 04/08/1997).

Indeed, during 1995–1997 Forum was forced to bow to the government's tough regulation. The continuing government's surveillance had depressed some of its members who subsequently suggested a low profile approach. Budi Wahyuni recalled that some non-student members, including herself, demanded Forum return to training programmes and adopt a 'wait-and-see' strategy until an opportunity to go on with the pro-democracy campaign arose (Wahyuni, interview, 10/12/1996). In January 1996, when Juliantara's term as the executive director was due to end, Forum returned to its original conflict-avoidance approach. Din Yati, a non-student member and Forum's former executive director (1989–1993), was re-elected as the new executive director. Under his leadership, Forum deliberately avoided controversial issues that might invite the security forces to intervene and decided to concentrate on consolidation among members by holding a regular gathering twice a month. This move had generated frustration among the radical members. Dadang Juliantara and a number of ex-student activists resigned from membership of Forum's committees. By 1997, Forum seemed to be happy with its 'wait-and-see' approach, although it had to lose many of its radical activists (Wijaya, interview, 12/08/1997).

A dramatic change in Indonesian politics in May 1998 which led to the resignation of president Suharto had brought Forum back to political activities. This coincided with the election of Anggerjati Wijaya as Forum's executive director in February 1998. Being an ex-student activist, Wijaya was really determined to make Forum play a greater role in developing democracy, at least at local level. He argued that in the post-Suharto era, Forum should safeguard the reform agenda (*agenda reformasi*) at local level by making political statements with regard to the protection of human rights, the promotion of anti-corruption campaigns, the protection of minority rights, the encouragement of non-violent actions, and the introduction of a free election both for national and local public officials. On top of that, Wijaya was also keen on organising public hearings to allow local people to communicate their grievances to local officials. On these occasions, Forum also expressed its critical evaluation of various local issues such as extra charges on electricity bills, forced resettlement cases, corruption by village officials and fraud in the election of local officials. During Wijaya's leadership (1998–2000) there were no fewer than 27 political statements and public hearings held by Forum (see Table 7.3).

*Table 7.3* Forum's political statements and public hearings, 1998–2000

| | Date | Issues concerned |
|---|---|---|
| 1 | 08/05/98 | Protest against police brutality in the government's handling of protests and demonstrations |
| 2 | 21/05/98 | Protest against the use of coercion in handling students' demonstrations of May 1998 |
| 3 | 21/05/98 | Call on democratisation after President Suharto's resignation in May 1998 |
| 4 | 30/06/98 | Demand for an agrarian reform to allow local people's direct control on local assets |
| 5 | 10/07/98 | Demand for a disclosure of the main actors behind the May 1998 riots in Jakarta, Solo and Medan |
| 6 | 23/07/98 | Call on the protection of children against abuse and violence |
| 7 | 08/06/98 | Appeal for a fair election of the Governor of Yogyakarta Province |
| 8 | 11/06/98 | Call on the removal of *Pancasila* as the sole ideology for every organisation |
| 9 | 25/11/98 | Public hearing to protest extra charges on electricity bills in Magelang District |
| 10 | 22/01/99 | Call on an immediate end to violence committed both by the security apparatus and the people |
| 11 | 05/02/99 | Public hearing to protest corruption by village officials in Bantul District |
| 12 | 24/03/99 | Appeal for an immediate end to violent actions committed by members of political parties |
| 13 | 02/04/99 | Public hearing to protest against forced resettlement of local people in Muntilan Sub-district |
| 14 | 12/04/99 | Call on a free and fair general election in order to support the democratic agenda |
| 15 | 14/04/99 | Public hearing with members of the local parliament to demand for a fair and free election in Yogyakarta Province |
| 16 | 15/04/99 | Demand for the dismissal of the District Head of Bantul who was allegedly involved in the murder of a local journalist in 1996 |
| 17 | 19/04/99 | Protest against corruption by local officials in the disbursement of funds in the Social Safety-nets programme |
| 18 | 09/06/99 | Call for an investigation in the corruption scandal involving the state's Attorney General, Andi M. Ghalib |
| 19 | 31/07/99 | Demand for the cancellation of the Malioboro construction project due to the lack of adequate compensation for the street vendors |
| 20 | 29/09/99 | Public hearing with the local parliament to protest against the new public transportation tariff |
| 21 | 07/10/99 | Public hearing with members of local parliament in Bantul District to demand for an investigation of corruption in the local election fund |

*Table 7.3* (Continued)

|    | Date     | Issues concerned |
|----|----------|------------------|
| 22 | 11/10/99 | Demand for an immediate removal of banners and posters associating NGOs with communism |
| 23 | 29/03/00 | Demand for the delay of the price increase of petrol, kerosene and gas |
| 24 | 09/05/00 | Concern about a possible come-back of the military in Indonesian politics |
| 25 | 15/07/00 | Demand for NGOs' support of the newly formed Yogyakarta Corruption Watch (YCW) |
| 26 | 25/07/00 | Demand for a fairer deal for people who had to lose their land for the Giwangan bus station construction project |
| 27 | 18/08/00 | Concern about the growing religious and ethnic conflicts in Aceh and Ambon |

Source: Compiled from Forum, 2000. *Laporan Pertanggungjawaban Dewan Pengurus Periode 1998–2000.* Yogyakarta: Forum LSM/LPSM DIY.

However, making political statements and conducting public hearings were not the only activities carried out by Forum in the post-Suharto era. To many of its activists, the democratic transition in the post-Suharto era appeared to be too volatile in which mass mobilisation carried out by different political forces to win popular support went out of control. Many of them used thugs and the growing number of unemployed groups to threaten their potential rivals (Forum 2000: 6). As a result, riots and violent clashes between different political groups – including political parties – became more frequent, while the security apparatus was unable to take necessary actions due to an increasing deterioration of morale and lack of competence. In Yogyakarta, for example, recurring violent conflicts involving the fanatical members of political parties – especially the PPP (the United Development Party) and the PDIP (the Indonesian Democratic Party of Struggle) – had generated pessimism among grassroots people about the prospect of Indonesian democracy.

## *Facing the Islamic challenge*

Another new development which posed a serious threat to democracy was the formation of radical Islamic groups. Serving as the so-called 'defenders of the Islamic faith', these groups attacked those who were considered to be the enemies of Islam. In major cities in Java – especially Jakarta and Solo – these groups routinely carried out campaigns wrecking night clubs, cafes and even restaurants which were suspected of selling alcohol especially during the *Ramadhan* (the Muslims' fasting period). They also attacked the media who ran unpleasant stories about their activities. In April 2000, for example, a number of journalists – Usman Asyari from BBC-Indonesia, Victor Cahyadi from the AFP, and Hinarius, a freelance journalist – were violently attacked by members of the *Lasjkar Jihad* (the so-called ready-to-die Islamic Troops) for running unfavourable news about the organisation's involvement in a violent religious conflict in Maluku (*Alert,*

August–September 2000). In March 2000, the Sasitania Radio Station in Solo, Central Java, bore the brunt of displeased listeners when a group called the FPIS (the Islamic Defense Front of Surakarta) protested the station's programme on 'Efforts to Deal with Inter-religious Conflicts' broadcasted on 24 February 2000. The demonstration involved the participation of approximately 300 individuals who considered the programme an assault on the Islamic faith. Protesters demanded that the radio station issue an apology letter and broadcast it five times daily for seven days in a row. In addition, FPIS demanded that the police seize the radio station's equipment as material evidence. The Solo police fulfilled this second request and since then the Sasitania Radio Station has been unable to broadcast (*Alert*, August–September 2000). Similar actions also took place in other cities. These incidents had encouraged people to think that democracy has actually created anarchy.

In order to reduce pessimism and frustration with democracy among grassroots people, Forum began to make a more serious attempt to disseminate the idea of tolerance, pluralism and anti-violence to the local people. There were four main programmes in this area. First, workshops on 'the role of NGOs in civil society empowerment'. These workshops were designed to enable NGOs in Yogyakarta and Central Java to identify local problems and to design an action plan in order to facilitate the formation of a strong civil society in the area (Forum 2000: 29–30). During 1998–2000, Forum organised four workshops involving more than 100 NGO representatives in Yogyakarta and Central Java. Second, cultural orations featuring local prominent figures including both the Sultan of Yogyakarta, Hamengku Buwono X, and a well-known essayist, Bondan Winarno. These events were aimed at bringing local people – religious leaders, students, local officials, security apparatus and representatives of civil society organisations – together to call for an immediate end to the use of violence by different social and political groups. Third, anti-violence campaigns through the distribution of posters, flyers and leaflets stressing the importance of peace-making and peace-keeping. Forum also formed a prayer group consisting of different religious groups which prayed routinely for a peaceful life in Yogyakarta. Fourth, Forum organised regular theatrical performances in which NGO activists and local artists performed together in an auditorium that belongs to the Indonesian Institute of Arts. The plays were meant to present a satirical image of the local social and political situation such as labour disputes, violent clashes involving members of political parties, forced resettlement cases, violent acts by particular religious groups, discrimination against women, and so on. This theatrical performance was aimed at generating public condemnation of particular misconduct committed by different groups in society.

However, despite the success of these programmes to attract NGOs and a number of civil society organisations in Yogyakarta, the radical Islamic groups[12] were suspicious towards Forum's attempt to establish linkage with grassroots people and to introduce the idea of tolerance, pluralism and gender equality. For these groups, NGOs' attempt to link themselves with grassroots people – especially workers, peasants and women – was similar to the Indonesian Communist Party's strategy of mass mobilisation during the early 1960s. Most of their leaders warned NGO activists in Yogyakarta not to revive the banned communist ideology (Taufiqurrahman, interview, 06/07/2001). They were particularly hostile towards women's NGOs since they thought that NGOs' gender equality campaign tended to contradict the Islamic Law (Muftiyanah, interview, 06/07/2001). Although these radical groups had never committed any harmful action against Forum, some of their fanatical members had threatened its staff members for their involvement in mobilising workers, peasants and women. In July 2001, these radical Islamic groups placed banners and posters on most street corners around the city. Crude anti-NGO slogans were written on their banners and posters, such as 'NGOs must stay away from workers and peasants!', 'We declare *jihad* (holy war) against those who persuade women to revolt!', 'We will punish those NGOs which introduce an anti-Islamic way of life!' and the like. Asked of what he thought of the impact of these growing radical Islamic groups on NGO activities in Yogyakarta, Taufiqurrahman (Forum's secretary general) commented:

> NGOs in Yogyakarta have always been in a difficult position. If in the past the main enemy of NGOs was the New Order government, which tended to use coercion to thwart those NGOs failing to conceal their radical agenda. Today, although we live in a democratic political system, NGOs seem to have a new enemy, namely the radical Islamic groups which felt threatened by NGOs' attempt to introduce the idea of tolerance, equality, justice and non-violence to society. Even though their threat was not as serious as that of the New Order government, NGOs have to be very careful about implementing their programmes. It is therefore highly recommended for NGOs to avoid any direct confrontation with any of those radical Islamic groups.
> (Taufiqurrahman, interview, 06/07/2001)

## Surviving internal conflicts

Despite the fact that some networks may have been successful in facilitating collective actions, there are some limitations that seem to have influenced their effectiveness in achieving co-ordination and collaboration. First, different expectations among participants over the possible outcome of a particular action can disturb the coherence of a network. Referring to popular resistance in land dispute cases in Central Java, Eldridge (1995: 205–8) noted that NGO activists, students and peasants applied different standards in measuring the outcome of a particular campaign. While NGOs tended to consider an action successful if the peasants were willing to file a case against the authorities in defending their land, students tended to judge success on the basis of their ability to expose the state's arbitrariness to the national or even international audience. Meanwhile, peasants measured success on the basis of the reversal of the government's policy or better material compensation. These differences often led to misunderstandings between participants in determining the values that should be addressed in the joint effort and in judging the success or failure of their action. Thus, in order to succeed in its co-ordinating effort, a network should be able to manage internal differences and reach agreement on goals, strategies and values of the collaborative action.

Second, a network may also suffer from poor performance and a lack of sustainability because members tend to lack the willingness to develop a coherent institutional framework. Because NGOs consider themselves to be the proponents of democracy, their activists are often sceptical about the hierarchy of power embedded in a bureaucracy as they prefer to be governed by collective agreement and absolute administrative transparency (Cardoso 1992: 296; Fals Borda 1992: 305). A network formed to serve as a pro-democracy coalition tends to face internal challenges because members are ambivalent about the development of rules and power structures. Members of a network are also uncertain whether or not they should cover the whole cost of networking. Fowler (1997: 116) argued that because the benefits of a network can sometimes be distant and diffuse (since meetings or consultations do not guarantee immediate changes), members tend to be reluctant to provide sufficient financial or technical support. As a result, an NGO network is often dependent upon external funding agencies. This section will illustrate these problems by looking into Forum's experience.

Melucci (1995: 45) argued that when different groups – whose identity, ideology and strategy are different from one another – begin to form a collective identity which guides their action, they must interact, communicate, negotiate and influence each other. In practice, however, actors often face difficulties in reaching agreement over what values and strategies the collective action should be based on. In the context of NGOs, Bennett (1994: 15) argued that it is often difficult to manage a network because members tend to spend too much time debating internal organisational matters regarding what strategies should be adopted to achieve goals, who should receive the credit for particular changes, and what ideology should lead the collective action.

In the case of Forum, there were several areas in which members could not agree with one another. The first disagreement was on the way Forum should develop its interaction with the government. Eldridge (1995: 204) noted that one of the major problems that disturbed Forum's unity was the ongoing conflict between the pro- and anti-government members. This conflict started in the early 1990s following Forum's changing approach from 'co-operation' to 'confrontation' with the government. It is important to note that Forum was co-founded by NGO activists and some reform-minded local government officials at the Bappeda and was originally meant to bridge relations between NGO community and the local government. Thus, when younger activists who controlled the governing body began to organise street demonstrations and issue various statements criticising the government, senior members who opted for a 'co-operative' strategy were worried that Forum would lose support and blessing of the local government. It was this fear that had encouraged a number of senior members such as Din Yati, Idham Ibty, Budi Wahyuni and Yos Soetiyoso to resign from Forum's steering committee in 1994 (Din Yati, interview, 12/12/1996). In the post-Suharto era, however, this conflict is no longer relevant since the government's consent is not the most important factor that can guarantee Forum's survival. Operating in a democratic political setting, today Forum can avoid control from local government. Yet, the tension between senior and junior members is not over. This time around, the conflict has been shifted to a disagreement between the anti-grassroots mobilisation and the pro-grassroots mobilisation groups. Some senior members are worried that Forum's attempt to establish linkage with grassroots people may turn the local NGO network into a political organisation mobilising local people to achieve a certain political ambition (Soetiyoso, interview, 07/07/2001). Younger members, however, refute this claim as they believe that in order to be more effective and to make a greater impact on society, Forum has to link itself with various grassroots organisations and groups (Ujianto, interview, 06/07/2001; Taufiqurrahman 06/07/2001).

The second area of disunity was an element of tension between the more and the less established members (Siregar 1988: 25; Mas'oed, interview, 03/08/1997). While on the one hand the more established members (often associated with large NGOs) tended to view small NGOs as lacking seriousness and professionalism in project design and implementation, the less well-established NGOs, on the other hand, suspected large NGOs of trying to use Forum as a means to impose their influence on small NGOs (Wahyuni, interview, 10/12/1996). Siregar (1988: 25) noted that Forum's unity had been undermined by competition and mutual accusation between large and small NGOs, which prevented members from developing communication and co-ordination, let alone co-operation. The tension was manifested in an exchange between Gilman D. Santos, an activist of a small NGO, and Petrus Swarnam, the staff member of *Dian Desa* (one of the largest NGOs in Yogyakarta). While Santos argued that large NGOs tried to use the network to dictate their agenda and values to smaller NGOs, Swarnam blamed small NGOs for lacking the discipline and commitment needed to ensure better performance and sustainability (Kusumohadi *et al.* 1997: 136–7).

The third area of conflict arose out of different orientations towards values on which the network should be based. Juliantara argued that from the early 1990s NGO activists were 'contaminated' by religious cleavages as some NGOs were used by Islamic organisations, especially the ICMI (the Indonesian Association of Muslim Intellectuals), to mobilise grassroots support to achieve their political ambitions (Juliantara, interview, 23/08/1997). As has been discussed in Chapter 3, the formation of ICMI marked the resurgence of Islamic thinking in Indonesian politics. By the mid-1990s, a significant number of intellectuals, government officials, military leaders, party cadres and NGO activists joined the ICMI. The appointment of Adi Sasono, a prominent NGO activist, as ICMI's secretary general had raised the feeling of fear among activists that ICMI's political views might affect NGO activities (Mas'oed, interview, 03/08/1997). At the same time, Muslim intellectuals began to demand NGOs to take Islamic values (*nilai-nilai keislaman*) more seriously and condemned NGOs which failed to address human rights violation cases against Muslims in Aceh, Flores and East Timor (Juliantara, interview, 23/08/1997). As a result, some NGOs hesitated over pursuing their campaign due to the fear of a possible accusation of being anti-Islam. In the case of Forum, members were divided between those who supported the 'Islamisation' of NGOs and those who stood for the 'neutrality' of NGOs (Hariadi, interview, 04/08/1997). Ertanto, a staff member of a street children NGO, recalled that many of Forum's discussions and meetings in the mid-1990s were used by activists to debate religious issues. The fact that these centered particularly on the question of whether Islam should be considered as the ultimate values of NGOs made Christian NGOs feel uneasy about joining such meetings (Ertanto, interview, 13/01/1997). Surprisingly, in the post-Suharto era, this religious tension tends to fade away. Members of Forum finally agree that NGOs should remain neutral and avoid direct involvement in religious debates. One reason for this change is the fact that in the past few years, Islamic groups – especially those with radical orientations – have begun to create a gap with the NGO sector in Yogyakarta. Their continuous accusation that NGOs have attempted to revive communist ideology and to introduce an anti-Islamic way of life has separated Islamic groups from the NGO sector. Forum members – who initially believed that Islamic faith can support NGO activities – are beginning to realise that NGOs are under the constant threat of the radical Islamic groups. This realisation has engendered a spirit of unity among Forum members as they begin to brush religious issues aside.

The first serious internal conflict within Forum's organisational structure, however, took place in July 1994 when 24 members held a secret meeting to protest Juliantara's leadership and Forum's failure to address the interests of Muslims. This meeting produced a letter demanding two things: (1) a more democratic leadership; and (2) a more active campaign to protect the rights of Muslims in Flores and East Timor[13] (Forum 1996: 54; Juliantara, interview, 23/08/1997). The problem was settled when Juliantara personally apologised to the concerned members and promised to take the issue of human rights violation in Flores and East Timor more seriously. The biggest conflict, however, took place in July 1996 when senior members protested against Forum's involvement in street demonstrations and demanded a less direct attack on the government (Forum 1996: 66–7). This protest overshadowed Forum's meeting in January 1996 to re-evaluate programmes and to elect new members of its governing body. Predictably, the meeting faced a deadlock as members disagreed over Forum's future direction. While senior members wanted Forum to return to its original function as a liaison agent between NGO community and the local government, younger members insisted on the pro-democracy campaigns (Wijaya, interview, 12/12/1996). A compromise was reached when Din Yati, the former executive director, who was acceptable to both sides, was re-elected as Juliantara's successor. Under his leadership Forum adopted a low profile approach by avoiding controversial issues such as the promotion of political freedom, the anti-military campaigns, the protection of human rights, the demand for free and fair elections, and the like.

Realising that he had lost the battle against senior members, Juliantara, the man behind Forum's radical activities, resigned from membership of the executive board. In reflecting upon his experience as Forum's executive director, Juliantara commented:

> Most of our time and energy had been wasted on solving internal tensions. Time and again we organised dialogues. But instead of developing co-operation

*Developing democracy through a local network* 231

or getting a concrete agenda for action, we always ended up with arguments and mutual accusations. In the end, we were all bored and exhausted.
(Juliantara, interview, 23/08/1997)

Outsiders like Sumartana, an NGO activist and a Christian leader, for example, saw Forum's experience as a recurrence of the old conflicts between the 'co-operative' and the 'non-co-operative' nationalist leaders who differed sharply in their attitudes towards the colonial government and between Muslim and Christian leaders who failed to reach agreement on the role of Islam. Despite the conflicts, he argued, the resistance against the colonial government could be maintained (Sumartana, interview, 24/03/1997).

In general, activists had learned from Forum's experience that NGOs need to get together to discuss their differences and seek a way to bridge the gaps that have separated them. In April 1994 a workshop on NGO collaboration in Kaliurang was organised by nine NGOs from Solo, Jakarta, Bandung and Yogyakarta to seek out the possibility of policy co-ordination between NGOs (Mahmudi *et al.* 1994: 1–2). In December 1996, another workshop was organised in Yogyakarta by *Yayasan Satunama* to allow NGO activists to resolve their differences (Kusumohadi *et al.* 1997: iv). How far these workshops have succeeded or failed to bridge the gap between different NGOs is difficult to measure. However, there were signs of confidence among activists that in the future NGOs can achieve a mutual understanding. Mahmudi, an activist who initiated the 1994 workshop, for example, argued that through a regular dialogue activists began to learn from one another to combine efforts in building the political consciousness of grassroots people (workers, peasants, petty traders, small artisans and so on) and in resisting policies that threaten the rights of the poor (Mahmudi *et al.* 1994: 6–7). Meanwhile, Kusumohadi, the director of *Yayasan Satunama* and the initiator of the 1996 workshop, argued that dialogues between NGO activists had allowed personal contacts to take place so that any differences that might undermine co-ordination and consensus building can be settled through personal negotiations (Kusumohadi *et al.* 1997: 143).

## The question of performance and sustainability

Another crucial problem for an NGO network is how to maintain performance. Eade (1997: 157) defined 'performance' as the capacity of a co-ordinating body to implement programmes according to what has been planned. Performance is closely related to the concept of sustainability, that is, the capacity of a network to ensure a long-term collaborative effort and to maintain confidence among its participants (Eade 1997: 158). Whether or not a network can maintain its performance and sustainability depends on how it develops its institutional framework, how it turns ideas into practical programmes, and how it arranges its own budgeting. A network may not be well-performing or sustainable if there are no rules that govern relationship among members, if its goals are too difficult to achieve, and if the programmes are determined by external agencies who pay the operational costs. Ideally, a network should have at least three crucial aspects.

First, it should have formal organisational structures, rules and procedures to regulate relations among members and to ensure an effective co-ordination (Bennett 1994: 21–2; Eade 1997: 155–6). Second, it should be based on realistic goals because too high an expectation can generate disappointment, which subsequently lowers the morale of the participating members (Bennett 1994: 32–3; Fowler 1997: 112–13). Third, it should be funded by its own members to ensure the sense of belonging and the commitment of the participants (Bennett 1994: 26–7).

## *The problem of institutionalisation*

Sztompka (1993: 289) argued that in order to guarantee success, a collective action needs a minimum degree of institutionalisation[14] of norms and values, which will regulate internal relations between actors and ensure a common purpose. In the context of an NGO network, Covey (1995: 178) argued that institutional mechanisms for information-sharing and decision-making are fundamental in developing negotiations between groups on specific strategies and goals, and in maintaining the balance of power between different participants. If a network were to succeed in its co-ordination it should have a statute that sets the limits of what the co-ordination body can and cannot do and it must make sure that all participants comply with the wishes of its membership (Bennett 1994: 15).

But there are some obstacles that seem to have prevented participants form developing a sustainable institutional framework. First, the fact that NGOs operate on the basis of flexibility, non-hierarchical structures, participatory decision and informality appears to create internal resistance towards the process of institutionalisation (Lende 1995: 246; Eade 1997: 158). Rejection of institutionalisation often arises out of fear that a coherent institutional framework will serve as a 'control mechanism' that may jeopardise the autonomy of participants (Bennett 1994: 15; Fowler 1997: 117). Referring to his experience in the *Sekretariat Bina Desa*, one of the first NGO networks in Indonesia, Kartjono (1986: 3) argued that obligation among NGO activists to preserve flexibility, democracy and participatory decision-making had turned his organisation into a loose network which had no power to impose rules on members. Second, NGOs are often expected to compromise their freedom and autonomy as they are obliged to subscribe to a common agenda of action by joining a network. Fowler (1997: 111) argued that collaboration between NGOs often put participants in a trade-off between the 'costs' of sacrificing their complete sovereignty of decision-making and action and the 'benefits' of information-sharing, greater leverage, mutual support and co-operation. The greater the perceived benefit, the more likely an NGO would be to compromise its autonomy in joining a network. But most NGOs are not prepared to reduce their autonomy or agree to be governed by a governing body above their own institutional structures (Fowler 1997: 112). As a result, a network is often lacking sufficient power to oblige members to follow certain rules or procedures.

In the case of Forum, members had been divided between the pro- and the anti-bureaucracy ones since the beginning of its operation. The tension between the two sides was manifested in a conflict over the design of Forum's organisational statute (Juliantara 1996a: 144). While on the one hand the pro-bureaucracy members wanted to draft a statute that would enable the governing body to exercise its power to ensure effective co-ordination, the anti-bureaucracy members, on the other hand, wanted a statute that would guarantee the absolute sovereignty and full autonomy of all members (Farid, interview, 28/01/1997; Juliantara, interview, 30/08/1997). In July 1994, in response to the pressure from the funding agency, Juliantara assigned a team to draft a statute. The team consisted of ten representatives from different NGOs (Fritz Panggabean, Hadi Wahono, Nur Ismanto, Din Yati, Yos Soetiyoso, M. Farid, Kumara Dewi, Raziku Amin, Amir Panzuri and Dadang Juliantara), with Panggabean serving as its co-ordinator (Forum 1997: 69). From August to October 1994 they worked to draft a statute which was finally agreed on by the majority of members after several long debates. However, the agreed statute did not seem to contain rules that obliged members to endorse the statute. Farid, one of the ten members of the team, commented that Forum's statute appeared to be weak because it failed to provide the power to the governing body to withdraw any member which was found to have deliberately ignored their obligations as stated in the statute (Farid, interview, 28/01/1997). As a result, Forum remained unable to demand a full commitment from its members. In most of Forum's annual meetings to elect leaders or to devise programmes, for example, the number of participants was normally low. Ujianto argued that from 1996 to 2000, the number of participants in Forum's annual meetings was usually less than 40 per cent of the total members (Ujianto, interview, 06/07/2001).

One way to observe Forum's performance is by looking at the activities of its *ad hoc* committees. Some argued that Forum did not perform well because its members were lacking the seriousness and commitment to follow up on programmes planned by the *ad hoc* committees (Din Yati, interview, 12/12/1996; Wahyuni, interview, 12/12/1996; Hariadi, interview, 04/08/1997). From 1993 to 1996, for instance, only two committees (public health and education and training) out of the ten *ad hoc* committees managed to implement and complete their planned programmes, four committees (labour affairs, networking, publication, and legal aid) were able to implement but unable to complete their programmes, and four others (art and culture, land disputes, the informal sector and community development) were unable to implement a single programme (see Table 7.4).

Imam Yudotomo, Forum's former executive director, argued that the members of Forum's *ad hoc* committees seemed to suffer from 'high levels of amnesia' to follow up plans, which subsequently made co-ordination almost impossible to achieve (Eldridge 1995: 204). Forum's secretary general under Din Yati's leadership, Mohammad Nadjib, pointed to the domination of immature student activists as the major cause of the problem. He argued that because most students worked as part-timers for NGOs and the fact that not all of them expected to continue working in the NGO sector after their graduation, they could not be expected to commit fully to support Forum's programmes; and Forum could not do anything when many of them 'disappeared' to continue their studies or take new jobs elsewhere (Nadjib, interview, 12/12/1996). Meanwhile, Budi Santoso, the co-ordinator of the labour affairs committee, pointed to the poor discipline among members

Table 7.4 Performance of Forum's *ad hoc* committees, 1993–1996

| Name of committee | Programmes planned | Completion |
| --- | --- | --- |
| 1 Labour affairs | Discussion and workshop on labour issues | + |
| | Labour advocacy: training, protest action etc. | 0 |
| 2 Networking | Workshop on grassroots networking | + |
| | Establish internal and external networks | 0 |
| 3 Publication | Writing political statements | + |
| | Book publishing | + |
| 4 Community development | Workshop on models of rural development | 0 |
| | Policy co-ordination of development-oriented NGOs | 0 |
| 5 Public health | Training sessions on alternative medicine | ++ |
| | Discussion about low-cost community health care | ++ |
| 6 Informal sector | Seminar and workshop on the role of the informal sector | 0 |
| 7 Legal aid | Discussion about repression and democracy | + |
| | Training on Human Rights | 0 |
| 8 Land disputes | Peasants' advocacy: training, protest, demonstration, etc. | 0 |
| 9 Art and culture | Organising an alternative art festival | 0 |
| 10 Education and training | Training sessions on self-help organisations | ++ |
| | Training sessions on strategic management | ++ |

Source: Adapted from Forum, 1997. *Tahap Konsolidasi dan Dinamika Forum.* Yogyakarta: Forum LSM/LPSM DIY.

Notes
++ = programmes are both implemented and fully completed.
+ = programmes are implemented, but not completed.
0 = programmes are not implemented.

(as manifested in the low attendance and the high degree of withdrawal) as the main reason behind his committee's poor performance. He argued that from October 1994 to January 1996 the committee of labour affairs could only hold two discussions and one workshop on labour movements, while other programmes such as attempts to provide training for workers to embolden them to express their demand for higher wages and to facilitate the formation of independent workers' associations had to be cancelled due to the shortage of personnel (Santoso, interview, 20/01/1997).

During Wijaya's leadership (1998–2000), however, pressure from donors to increase their performance had encouraged Forum's *ad hoc* committees to improve their activities. In order to avoid duplication and overlapping, Wijaya decided to rationalise the *ad hoc* committees by reducing their number from ten to four: (1) discussion and workshop; (2) publication; (3) advocacy; and (4) training. The 'discussion and workshop' committee was charged with the duty of organising discussions, workshops and seminars on various issues such as democracy, elections, political parties, policy reform, labour affairs, conflict resolution, and so on. During 1998–2000, this committee was successful in accomplishing its main target by organising six discussions and seven workshops. The publication committee was responsible for publishing the seminars or workshops' proceedings. It was also responsible for the publication and the distribution of Forum's bulletin called *Media Forum*. During 1998–2000, this committee was able to publish three books (*Political Order in the New Indonesia, Village Government Reform* and *Grassroots Participation in the Post-Suharto Era*) and ten editions of the bulletin. The advocacy committee carried two main duties: (1) drafting and circulating political statements to the local media; and (2) conducting public hearings to express local problems to the local officials and members of the local parliament. During 1998–2000, there were 27 political statements and public hearings carried out by this committee. The training committee was responsible for organising trainings targeting small enterprises, paralegal activists and NGOs in Yogyakarta and Central Java. During 1998–2000, it carried out five trainings on small enterprises, paralegal activities, project management, gender equality and fund raising management involving around 125 participants. The performance of these committees during 1998–2000 can be seen in Table 7.5. Judging from the completion rate of the planned programmes, it appears that Forum's *ad hoc* committees under Wijaya's leadership performed better than those under Juliantara's leadership. There are at least two explanations for this improvement. First, Wijaya's decision to downsize the number of Forum's *ad hoc* committees seems to have increased the capacity of the governing body to control the activities of the committees. By controlling the *ad hoc* committees, the governing body was able to oblige them to implement programmes. Second, the 'maturity' of Forum's membership – as indicated by the growing number of experienced NGO activists who controlled strategic positions in the network – had significantly increased the capacity of the *ad hoc* committees to design and implement realistic programmes. Being full-time NGO workers, these activists were ready to dedicate their time and energy to support Forum's activities.

*Too high expectations*

Another challenge for an NGO network is that members often put too much pressure on the co-ordinating body to provide resources to fulfil the individual requirements of each participating organisation. But when they realise that the network cannot meet their expectations, attendance begins to decline because members are either frustrated or bored (Bennett 1994: 32–3). In the case of Forum, especially during Juliantara's leadership, members of the governing body often came up with the ambition to do big things, but their spirit diminished as soon as they realised that their target was too difficult to achieve (Kusumohadi, interview, 25/07/1997). For a network with a high degree of internal conflict, too ambitious goals can further damage coherence among members because disappointment can exploit differences, which in turn can cause mutual accusation.

Table 7.5 Performance of Forum's *ad hoc* committees, 1998–2000

| Name of committee | Programmes planned | Completion |
|---|---|---|
| 1 Discussion and workshop | Discussions on grassroots alliance, the military in the post-Suharto era, village government, the protection of female workers, the role of the media and Islamic revivalism | ++ |
| | Workshops on political order in the post-Suharto, civil society empowerment, political parties, village government reform, repositioning NGOs, political freedom and conflict resolution | ++ |
| 2 Publication | Publishing and distributing workshop/seminar proceedings | + |
| | Publishing and distributing Forum's bulletin, *Media Forum* | ++ |
| 3 Advocacy | Making political statements on various local and national social, political and cultural issues | ++ |
| | Organising public hearings to express local concerns to the local officials or members of the local parliaments | ++ |
| 4 Training | Trainings sessions on small enterprises, paralegal activities, gender equality, fund raising management and project management | ++ |

Source: Adapted from Forum, 2000. *Laporan Pertanggungjawaban Dewan Pengurus Periode 1998–2000*. Yogyakarta: Forum LSM/LPSM DIY.

Notes
++ = programmes are both implemented and fully completed.
+ = programmes are implemented, but not completed.

The experience of the art and culture committee – which was dominated by student activists – may illustrate this problem. During its first meeting on 30 April 1994, the younger members – Eko Winardi, Syamsul Bachri, Mohammad Jihad and Tommy – came up with the idea of organising an annual cultural exhibition as an alternative to the state-sponsored *Festival Kesenian Yogyakarta* (the Yogyakarta Art Festival) which was held annually by the Yogyakarta provincial government in co-operation with the Ministry of Tourism, Postal and Telecommunications. These young activists accused the government of using the festival to impose its control on the local popular art; and by organising an alternative programme they thought they would be able to 'return art to the people's hands' (*mengembalikan seni ke tangan rakyat*).[15] This plan was discussed in depth between members of the committee; but they were unable to draft a concrete proposal as they faced two major problems. First, because they were lacking any experience in organising such a big event, it was difficult to generate adequate funding for such an alternative cultural exhibition. The committee failed to convince the ICF (the Indonesia-Canada Foundation), Forum's funding agency during 1994–1996, that such an event was effective to prevent the state from dominating the local culture and was therefore worth funding (Forum 1996: 39). Second, the plan did not receive adequate support from Forum's members because most of them thought that cultural exhibition was irrelevant to NGO network and co-ordination (Wijaya, interview, 12/12/1996).

These obstacles appeared to generate friction among radical members of the committee. As Winardi put it: 'When we realised that our plan to organise an alternative cultural exhibition did not attract donors and other members (of Forum), many of us began to lose enthusiasm and blame each other for being over-ambitious or for being incompetent' (Winardi, interview, 12/08/1997). By January 1996, when Forum's two-year contract with the ICF was due to end, the committee had not been able to deliver a single programme and most members disappeared without any clear reason (Nadjib, interview, 12/12/1996). One possible explanation for their withdrawal was the feeling of disappointment and boredom because too many meetings were used to debate the state's domination over the local culture and the relevance of an alternative cultural festival to networking instead of searching for more realistic programmes (Forum 1997: 38–9). Kusumohadi, a former member of ICF's executive board, argued that it was the romanticism and immaturity of student activists within Forum's *ad hoc* committees that seemed to have produced unrealistic goals and a lack of responsibility, which subsequently brought Forum close to a stalemate (Kusumohadi, interview, 25/07/1997).

## *The problem of budgeting*

Forum's budget is mainly derived from external funding agencies. For example, Forum was funded by three different national NGO networks from 1986 to 1993: the *Sekretariat Bina Desa*, the Group of Thirteen and WALHI (Eldridge 1995: 202). Between 1993 and 1996, it was funded by the ICF, a group consisting of several Indonesian and Canadian NGOs (Forum 1996: 81). Such a heavy reliance on external funding agencies had made Forum unable to evolve independently as a co-ordinating body for local NGOs. Most programmes had to be formulated through consultation with the external funding agencies. By 1992, following criticism from members that Forum had served as the regional arm for the *Sekretariat Bina Desa*, the Group of Thirteen and WALHI, contracts with external agencies were terminated, which led to the decline of its activities. Since then Forum has tried to focus on consolidation among members by organising regular bi-monthly gatherings (Eldridge 1995: 203–5). Attempts to raise funding from its own members were not successful because they were not convinced that regular gatherings would bring immediate changes or advantages to their organisations (Kusumohadi *et al*. 1997: 140–1).

After about one year of recess, Forum was able to attract a new funding agency. On 15 December 1993, it signed a memorandum of understanding (MoU) with the ICF. The MoU contained two important agreements: (1) the arrangement of a three-year project-based[16] co-operation; and (2) the setting up of collaborative effort in which ICF served as the provider of technical and financial assistance for all of Forum's programmes which put emphasis on the development of NGO co-ordination in the region (ICF 1994: 18). However, it took more than a year before ICF finally agreed to allocate its funding. The delay was partly caused by ICF's dissatisfaction with Forum's organisational structure and the absence of a statute that would ensure stability and continuity (Din Yati, interview, 12/12/1997). On 22 July 1994, negotiation was reopened after Dadang Juliantara agreed to assign a special team to draft the statute. Abdi Suryaningati, the Indonesian director of the ICF, promised to allocate a maximum amount of Rp 22 million per year to cover Forum's programmes as soon as the team began to work (Forum 1996: 66).

During 1995–1996, Forum managed to raise more than Rp 23 million in revenue, about 95 per cent of which (Rp 21 million) came from the ICF, while members' contribution constituted only less than one per cent (Rp 223 thousand) of the total revenue (see Table 7.6). Around 54 per cent (Rp 12 million) of the total expenditure went to administrative expenses (salaries, secretariat, telephone, electricity and rent); and only 46 per cent went to programmes. A network spending too much on administrative expenses would not seem to impress funding agencies because they believe that project-based activities, rather than organisational development, tend to produce more direct and viable results (Bennett 1995: 10). Forum's allocation of more than half of donor's contribution on administrative expenses was considered by the ICF as a failure because it breached the initial agreement that ICF would only pay for Forum's programmes as stipulated in the MoU (Suryaningati, interview, 25/07/1997). In evaluating Forum's 1995/1996 budget, a member of ICF's executive board, commented:

> Initially we thought that by pouring our money into Forum, we could get a strong NGO coalition and co-ordination in Yogyakarta that can be used as a model for regional NGO networks throughout Indonesia. But after about two years of co-operation (with Forum), we found that too much money was spent on salaries and other administrative expenses which should have been paid by members. What we had expected from Forum was programmes that could increase communication, information exchange and co-operation between NGOs.
> 
> (Kusumohadi, interview, 25/07/1997)

In January 1996, the ICF decided to postpone the negotiation for a possible renewal of its two-year contract with Forum. Since then Forum has not done anything notable. From October 1996 to August 1997, members of Forum's governing body continued to meet twice a month, but mostly to discuss the current political issues and personal matters instead of programmes or collective actions. When I visited the secretariat in August 1997, Din Yati, who in 1996 was re-elected as the executive director, had resigned. No longer able to afford its own office, Forum shared an office with the *Yayasan Purba Danata* during 1996–1998 and failed to design or implement any programmes. Forum's experience under Din Yati's leadership appears to corroborate Bennett's (1994: 26–8; 1995: 10–11) contention that networks funded by external funding agencies, instead of by its own members, tend to face a sustainability problem because their activity is determined more by short-term project-based contracts than by the long-term commitment of membership.

However, the election of Anggerjati Wijaya as Forum's executive director in 1998 brought the local NGO network back to business. Supported by experienced NGO activists who controlled Forum's governing body, he managed to draft an impressive project proposal which attracted the ICF to negotiate a new contract. In 1998, the ICF changed its name and used an Indonesian acronym, YAPPIKA (*Yayasan Penguatan Partisipasi, Inisiatif dan Kemitraan Masyarakat Indonesia* or the Foundation for Indonesian People's Participation, Initiative and Partnership), to be more familiar to its Indonesian partners. Impressed by Forum's new management, the YAPPIKA decided to offer a three-year contract and promised to allocate a maximum amount of Rp 120 million per year to support Forum's activities. Learning from the past experience, Forum worked harder to spend the money more efficiently. In its 1999/2000 budget, Forum made a big improvement in the financial management. It appears that Forum was able to cut down the administrative costs from 54 per cent (in the 1995/1996 budget) to 23 per cent of its total expenditure (see Table 7.6). Moreover, Forum was also able to increase the amount of members' contribution from Rp 223 thousand (in 1995/1996) to Rp 6 million (in 1999/2000), which indicated a substantial increase of members' commitment to support Forum's programmes.

In September 2000, following Martinus Ujianto's election as Wijaya's successor, the YAPPIKA renewed its commitment by offering another three-year contract worth more than 600 million *rupiah*. This seems to indicate the donor's growing confidence in Forum's capability to deliver effective and cost-efficient programmes. There are at least two reasons behind the donor's growing confidence in Forum. First, Forum's ability to improve the performance of its *ad hoc* committees as a result of the slimming down of their numbers carried out during

*Table 7.6* Forum's annual budgets in 1995/1996 and in 1999/2000 (in rupiah)

| Revenue | 1995/1996 (in Rupiah) | 1999/2000 (in Rupiah) | Expenditure | 1995/1996 (in Rupiah) | 1999/2000 (in Rupiah) |
|---|---|---|---|---|---|
| *External* Donors' contribution Interest rates | 21,735,600 304,389 | 112,800,000 13,536,000 | *Administrative costs* (salaries, secretariat, telephone, facsimile, electricity, rent etc.) | 12,280,799 | 30,314,000 |
| *Internal* Programme remuneration Members' contribution | 738,800 223,125 | — 6,250,000 | *Programme costs* (discussions, seminars, workshops, training sessions, advocacy, publication etc.) | 10,599,955 | 101,486,000 |
| Total | 23,001,914 | 132,586,000 | Total | 22,880,754 | 131,800,000 |

Source: Forum, 1996. *Laporan Pertangungjawaban Kepengurusan Periode 1993–1996.* Yogyakarta: Forum LSM/LPSM DIY, Appendix 3; and Forum, 2000. *Laporan Pertangungjawaban Kepengurusan Periode 1998–2000.* Yogyakarta: Forum LSM/LPSM DIY.

Wijaya's leadership. Second, Forum's ability to increase its efficiency by substantially reducing the proportion of its administrative costs to the total expenditure. What we can learn from Forum's experience is that an organisation whose budget depends on the donor's contribution must always work hard to make sure that the donor is confident about the organisation's ability to improve its performance and to deliver cost-efficient programmes.

# 8 Conclusion

### 'Context' in NGO operation

This book describes and analyses NGOs operating under different social and political circumstances in a country undertaking a rapid political transformation from authoritarianism to democracy. It argues that NGOs have to struggle to serve as both promoters of grassroots-oriented development and advocates for people's coalitions and movements. In a situation where authoritarian government imposed pervasive control on the political activities of society such as the New Order Indonesia, NGOs had cautiously confined their activities to community development. However, when opportunity to become involved in grassroots mobilisation activities arose, NGOs had helped society to form grassroots resistance to challenge the state's domination. When the political setting had been dramatically transformed from authoritarianism to democracy, NGOs played their role in strengthening of civil society by forming grassroots coalitions and networks.

'Context', according to Swidler (1995: 35), can be defined as the immediate situation or setting under which actors or agencies evolve. To explain how context influence agencies, I can usefully refer to the work of Goertz (1994) who examines some specific environments (history, structure and norms) that influence state behaviour. In his *Contexts of International Politics* (1994), Goertz argued that context can influence agencies in two different ways. First, context may serve as some sort of 'cause' that makes things happen. It is often the case that some higher-level factors such as socio-political structures, the state's power, or cultural values can serve as the major cause of the behaviour of particular agencies (Goertz 1994: 16). In the case of NGO activities, factors such as legislation, political situation, procedures of operation, management, the behaviour of target groups and so on can force NGOs to select particular strategies and programmes. Second, context may be seen as a 'barrier' in a situation where actors or agencies cannot achieve their goals or ambitions due to the strong influence of both external and internal factors (Goertz 1994: 20–1). As a barrier, context prevents things from happening. For example, NGOs operating in an authoritarian political context may not be able to promote grassroots initiatives due to the political constraints imposed by the authorities, whereas NGOs operating in a democratic political context may have more opportunity to carry out grassroots empowerment and mobilisation activities.

This book observes Indonesian NGOs operating in the last years of the New Order regime and the subsequent transition to democracy in the post-Suharto era. In the New Order era, the fear among the political leaders of a possible national disintegration due to the division in society alongside the territorial, ethnic, religious and *aliran* (streams) boundaries had led to the rise of a centralised state that would use coercion to ensure order and political stability. In this situation, the chance for grassroots political activities was slim. When resistance against Suharto from different quarters of society became stronger in the mid-1990s, the chance for grassroots mobilisation activities was greater. In the post-Suharto era, grassroots political activities begin to flourish which indicate the beginning of the formation of a vibrant civil society. However, not all of the newly formed grassroots organisations are sympathetic towards NGOs. Many of them – particularly those radical Islamic organisations – are suspicious of NGOs' grassroots mobilisation activities and gender equality campaign. These factors serve both as a 'cause' and a 'barrier' for NGO activities. They serve as a 'cause' insofar as they shape the activities of NGOs in facilitating the transition to democracy by disseminating the idea of people's sovereignty and by helping grassroots people to organise among themselves. They act as a 'barrier' insofar as they prevent NGOs from making a greater impact to the people they serve.

## NGOs and grassroots-oriented development

This book examines NGOs in two different capacities: as development institutions whose main purpose is to alleviate poverty, and as social movements whose main agenda is to challenge social and political structures that have created poverty and injustice. As development institutions, NGOs are expected to play their part in facilitating self-managed income generating activities to ensure the stability and regularity of income of the underprivileged. In addition to economic benefits, NGOs are also expected to produce a range of social benefits such as reduced dependence on money lenders, greater independence in decision-making, lower seasonal out-migration, reduced social and sex discrimination (Robinson 1992: 31). This role had gained currency in the so-called 'grassroots-oriented' development in the 1980s and 1990s. Disappointed with the failure of the conventional development strategy (focusing on economic growth and productivity), which expected the benefits of economic development to 'trickle down', scholars began to search for a new alternative with more emphasis on grassroots participation, empowerment, bottom-up (as opposed to top–down) planning, and indigenous (instead of expert) knowledge (Stirrat and Henkel 1997: 67). Under this mandate, development planners were required to listen more to the voices of grassroots people. It was felt that as 'outsiders' to the underprivileged who received their assistance, development planners should take the time to open dialogue with the poor rather than imposing their own policy preferences. The key text of this new orthodoxy was Chambers's *Rural Development: Putting the Last*

*First* (1983) in which he argued that:

> Outsiders' views of the poor are distorted in many ways. Lack of contact or communication permits them to form those views without the inconvenience of knowledge, let alone personal exposure. Poor people are rarely met; when they are met, they often do not speak; when they do speak, they are often cautious and deferential; and what they say is often either not listened to, or brushed aside, or interpreted in a bad light. Any attempt to understand the poor, and to learn from them, has to begin with introspection by the outsiders themselves.
>
> (Chambers 1983: 104)

Reversal in the management of rural development is therefore necessary. The strategy of rural development, according to Chambers (1983: 147), should include an attempt to help the poorest (small farmers, tenants and the landless) to impose more control on the benefits of development; and outsiders must alter the way they communicate with the poor by talking less and listening more.

Nowadays, scholars celebrate this new belief as part of their agenda to overturn the forms of neo-colonialism and to challenge the state's domination in rural development (Arce *et al.* 1994: 159). This raises the expectation that there would be a move in NGO activities from 'development' to 'empowerment'. Scholars begin to talk about the role of NGOs in the context of 'popular participation', a term Smillie (1995: 221) defined as a process by which people, especially the disadvantaged, are informed of and involved in the implementation or benefits of development activities. The term also suggests that people can and should exercise influence over, and ultimately take responsibility for things which affect their lives (Long and van der Ploeg 1994: 64). The appeal for popular participation has provided both ideological and theoretical grounds to support the role of NGOs in encouraging grassroots initiatives to manage their own development (Stirrat and Henkel 1997: 67). Some believe that NGOs have demonstrated the capacity to design and to implement effective development programmes, using innovative approaches without governmental hassles and bureaucratic red tape, which actually reach the people at grassroots level (Long and van der Ploeg 1994: 66; Aubrey 1997: 25). But NGOs tend to face barriers in their attempt to revitalise popular participation. We should not allow ourselves to oversimplify NGOs' activities by ignoring their contradictions and barriers, although we should equally balance our analysis by acknowledging their achievement and contribution to rural development.

Our cases in Chapter 5 have illustrated both NGOs' problems as well as their contributions to rural development. The first problem for NGOs has to do with the way in which they develop their vision and ideology. Turner and Hulme (1997: 216–17) described the dilemma of NGOs operating in authoritarian states in which adherence to the state's ideology will render criticism of being subservient or of being the state's development arm, while the adoption of radical ideology may invite repression. Indonesian NGOs find themselves under constant pressure to purge both their vision and their ideology of anything that might be construed as 'radicalism' by the New Order government. Juliantara, for example, argued that it was impossible for Indonesian NGOs during Suharto's government to embrace an ideology that used radical terms such as *perjuangan kelas* (class struggle), *kekuatan rakyat* (people's power) or *revolusi sosial* (social revolution) because it might lead to a ban or even a closure (Juliantara, interview, 23/08/1997). In the case of BSY and CD-Bethesda, for instance, although they claimed that empowerment was part of their agenda, they were forced to concentrate on areas that complemented the official development programmes such as small credit, primary health care and other income generation activities because the failure to do so would have put themselves at risk of being shut down.

Some argued that Indonesian NGOs' modest, welfare-oriented approach had to do with the conservative political stance of the Indonesian middle-class who formed NGOs in the early 1970s (Oepen 1988: 126–7; Fakih 1996: 101–2). The problem with this view is that the middle-class people are not necessarily conservative and that welfare-oriented NGOs are not necessarily lacking an empowerment agenda. As has been described in Chapter 5, NGOs' modest style and conflict avoidance approach appear to result from a deliberate strategic choice rather than a lack of political resolve. Their focus on income generation was derived from considerations of political calculation to guarantee survival. The experience of BSY and CD-Bethesda has illustrated that Indonesian NGOs have developed considerable skill in exploiting areas of rhetorical convergence with official ideology in order to secure space for participation in rural development and access to establish direct contact with villagers. In the case of BSY, the trauma of the 1965 killings and the conviction of the ex-PKI members among the villagers in Wedi led the NGO to deliberately avoid grassroots mobilisation because such activity would not only invite military intervention, but also put the potential beneficiaries at risk. Meanwhile, syncretism was the only solution for CD-Bethesda to enfold its Christian values in secular idioms and to incorporate *Pancasila* into its own ideology. There is a reason to agree with Juliantara (1997: 27–30) that the tendency of Indonesian NGOs in the New Order era to adopt a moderate ideology was not caused by their ignorance or lack of political will, but it was rather caused by the fact that the political pressure imposed by the government was too strong to confront. In the post-Suharto era, however, when opportunity to embrace a radical ideology arises, Indonesian NGOs begin to implement radical programmes. CD-Bethesda, for example, deliberately turns its KKDs (village health cadres) into ORAs (people's organisations) sustaining a new duty of controlling the decision-making process at village level. Likewise, BSY changes its approach by adopting the PRA method in order to encourage villagers to determine their own development. Although BSY is not interested in political mobilisation, it nevertheless attempts to build villagers' awareness of their social and political situation.

The second challenge relates to the effect of primordialism on NGO activities. Geertz (1973: 259) defined 'primordialism' as sentiments that stem from something 'given' (assumed blood ties, language, region, religion and custom). He argued that in developing societies, where the tradition of civil politics is weak and where the technical requirements for an effective welfare government are poorly understood, primordial attachments tend to be repeatedly proposed and widely acclaimed as preferred bases for the demarcation of autonomous political units (Geertz 1973: 261). Community leaders often use these sentiments to court the masses by appealing to traditional loyalties. In promoting new ideas to their target groups NGOs may sometimes face difficulties in dealing with primordialism, especially when it involves religious issues. In Bangladesh, for example, the idea of gender equality and small credits (which oblige customers to pay interests) has placed NGOs in a direct confrontation with Islamic organisations, especially the *Jamiat-I-Islami*, which later issued *fatwa* (decrees) against women's independent status and rural credit schemes (Feldman 1997: 47). In Indonesia, religious issues have their effect on NGO activities. Christians in Indonesia have historically experienced great difficulties in conducting political activities since they are forced to remain low profile to avoid a possible attack from extreme Islamic groups. The fact that many income-generating NGOs are run by groups or individuals of Protestant or Catholic origins seems to put NGOs in a sensitive relationship with their Muslim beneficiaries. The case of CD-Bethesda in Donorojo (discussed in Chapter 5) has illustrated how important it is for an NGO (run by a Christian organisation) to maintain a good relationship with local authorities who will 'protect' them from hard-line Muslim groups. It turned out that CD-Bethesda had to convince the state, the potential beneficiaries and the general public that its operation had no connection with any Christian missionary activity. It is therefore understandable if NGOs of this kind need to adopt a low-profile approach to ensure their acceptability.

The third challenge has to do with NGOs' capacity to develop an effective management system that will ensure professionalism, competence, flexibility and stability. Smillie (1995) posited a somewhat pessimistic view of NGOs' attitude towards professionalism. As he put it: 'Like small boys playing football, too many NGOs swarm down the field after the ball, without strategy and without positions. Dismissed by bemused spectators, they are easily relieved of the ball by bigger players' (Smillie 1995: 240). In a similar vein, Bebbington (1997: 126–7) argued that NGOs are currently facing a 'crisis of legitimacy' in which practices of transparency and accountability with regard to the use of the resources they receive from donors as well as beneficiaries are not being pursued; and their structure of governance appears to be overlapping, which generates conflicts of interest between different organisations. This is certainly the challenge for Indonesian NGOs in the post-Suharto era. A number of corruption scandals involving NGO activists have generated concern of NGOs' accountability system. In general, NGOs rarely pay serious attention to the management sector because activists often share the view that management, if it has any legitimate place at all, should stay in the statutory sector where it belongs and that NGOs should be run on the basis of goodwill, flexibility, commitment and natural ability (Billis 1993: 129). As a result, NGOs tend to suffer from a lack of planned growth in which organisational expansion, greater scope of activities and increase of budgets are not followed by sufficient staff development, strategic management or institutional development. The case of BSY (discussed in Chapter 5) may indicate the extent of this problem. However, in the case of CD-Bethesda, management received a more serious attention. Operating at a larger scale, this organisation realised that greater attention to financial management, staff development, planning and leadership was necessary to guarantee survival.

However, this is not to say that Indonesian NGOs are entering a logical dead-end by which they are doomed to failure. Although they are facing ideological, political and management challenges, this does not mean that they have been ineffectual. It is fair to say that Indonesian NGOs have made significant contributions to participatory rural development. Due to their capacity to innovate, their ability to make breakthroughs and their close touch with the ideas of popular participation, Indonesian NGOs can deliver alternative programmes that come close to the new orthodoxy in development thinking focusing on grassroots initiatives. Turner and Hulme (1997: 96) argued that rural development tends to suffer from a 'bureaucratic bias' where the reality of rural lives is often misconstrued through misreporting, especially in the exaggeration of government performance, through the selected use of unrepresentative sources of information and through the tendency to treat villagers as passive recipients of assistance. One major contribution of NGOs to rural development is that they have been able to remove the 'bureaucratic bias' from rural development by revealing the reality of what is actually happening in rural areas. Moreover, NGOs' income generating programmes have provided safety-nets for vulnerable groups (especially women) in dealing with the strains of daily rural economic activities. Because NGOs usually have dedicated staff members who live and work with the people they seek to assist, they have the capacity to understand the needs of micro-entrepreneurs and to invoke trust and co-operation. They also tend to be more flexible, willing to take risks and are less subject to political controls and intervention than public development institutions (Carr 1989: 167). In the case of BSY, for example, its ability to reduce the transaction costs of the rural micro-credits and to increase the repayment rates of the rural borrowers has made the rural micro-enterprises more 'bankable' and more capable of carrying out productive activities. Likewise, CD-Bethesda's health care programmes have generated self-help initiatives among the poor in the health sector. No one can deny Indonesian NGOs' positive contributions to any of these sectors. Also, one should not ignore NGOs' ability to mobilise their own financial resources to support their programmes. BSY and CD-Bethesda should be praised for their ability to reduce dependence on foreign funding. Their cost-recovery projects had enabled them to ensure financial stability and to run long-term programmes. However, the only disadvantage of the market-driven activities was perhaps the tendency of the NGOs to be accountable to the top managers, rather than to the target groups or more precisely, the customers.

## NGOs as part of the 'pro-democracy' movements

Since the late 1980s the NGO sector in developing societies has moved much more decisively to the range of activities focusing on attempts to help the underprivileged increase their capacity to organise among themselves, to raise people's awareness of their own problems, and to help them find their own solutions.[1] A new generation of graduates has entered the NGO sector and brought with it new ideas and new perspectives. No longer satisfied with NGOs' role in service delivery and income generation, these activists have begun to see development in terms of empowerment, or to use another term, of 'training for transformation' (Elliott 1987: 58). They see poverty as the result of political processes (exploitation, marginalisation and alienation) and are therefore committed to enabling people to search for their own empowerment. They believe that NGOs share the responsibility to initiate grassroots collective action. At this point, NGOs enter to the arena of social movements. Fowler (1996: 25) argued that as a movement, NGOs can regain their 'legitimacy' in two ways. First, they can make the political process more inclusive, that is, to increase the number and level of engagement of citizens interested in and able to participate in the political arena. Second, they can make governments more accountable for their behaviour and performance, which often entails increasing people's capacity to assert themselves in both the institutional and the non-institutional political processes.

In this context, NGOs are seen as agencies with responsibility to strengthen civil society. A civil society, that is to say, flourishing associations that promote and defend various interests, is broadly considered to serve both to pressure governments and to protect their members from adverse interference from governments. Blair (1997: 28) argued that NGOs can contribute to the strengthening of civil society by: (1) providing political education and mobilising citizens to exercise their right to participate; (2) encouraging previously marginalised groups (women, minorities and the poor) to participate in the political arena; and (3) building a complex network of groups whose members have multiple affiliations, thereby moderating the potentially destabilising effects of single membership in exclusive groups – especially those based along ethnic, religious, territorial or economic cleavages. Meanwhile, Alvarez and Escobar (1992) saw NGOs as crucial forces in the democratisation of authoritarian social relations. Referring to the case of the women's movement, they argued that feminists have articulated their calls for change by establishing their own constituencies and by expanding their action to include training on empowerment and self-organisation (Alvarez and Escobar 1992: 325–6). The activities of two women's NGOs in Yogyakarta, as depicted in Chapter 6, have illustrated attempts to encourage, educate and mobilise poor women to press for the recognition of their rights to organise among themselves and the need to change structures that have caused their marginalisation.

However, as I have discussed in Chapters 6 and 7, Indonesian NGOs have to face some barriers in their attempt to strengthen civil society. The first barrier has to do with the social and political factors that forced NGOs to adopt a 'damage-limitation' strategy in expressing their demands for change. NGOs speaking out about human rights abuse are often faced with a cruel choice. When they speak out against the authorities, they run the risk of expulsion, which will put their beneficiaries and partners at risk (Smillie 1995: 228). This is especially true in a situation where democracy is ineffective because NGOs can be considered as 'public enemy' or more seriously, become a target of terrorist attacks from the extreme groups, on the whim of a single politician. Likewise, when they raise issues that require radical changes to values or norms, they may face resistance from those who feel obliged to preserve the status quo. For example, women's NGOs carrying out gender equality campaign tend to face challenges from conservative leaders (both men and women) who are not ready to accept radical changes in the relationship between the sexes. For NGOs working under such circumstances, both circumspection and self-censorship are a necessity (Smillie 1995: 234). In the case of SBPY and Yasanti, for example, their decision not to confront the Javanese and Islamic interpretations of the relationship between men and women should be understood as an act of self-censorship. In the post-Suharto era, the rise of radical Islamic groups with commitment to purge those who insult or challenge Islamic law has warned women's NGOs to be more careful about carrying out their gender equality campaign. One can therefore agree with Billis (1993: 129) who suggested that donors and observers should not blame NGOs for not pursuing radical changes because the social and political 'barriers' under which they operate are often too difficult to surmount.

The second obstacle can be associated with the problem in implementing the PAR method. When NGOs speak about conscientisation and awareness-creation – advocated by the Brazilian educationalist, Paulo Freire – it is understandable if they use PAR as a way to encourage grassroots participation and self-reliance. However, the implementation of PAR in the field is often more difficult than it appears in theory. Elliott (1987: 59) argued that it is far from easy to combine the processes of the development of a critical consciousness with the processes of creating and managing a productive capacity that delivers a surplus to the underprivileged. For Brown (1996: i–ii), problems in the application of Freire's ideas derive from, among other things, their 'domestication' in the interests of the established social-political order, and not from any weaknesses in the approach itself. When applied in concrete social and political contexts of developing societies, Freire's model seems to face two crucial challenges: a possible lack of support from the target groups because the poor cannot be easily persuaded to embrace new values; and that any action which is taken will tend to reflect the interests of those in the dominant position rather than those from the marginalised group. This is because the dominant class will, of course, do whatever it can to maintain the status quo. Thus, in order to solve these problems the method of PAR is often 'domesticated', in which Freirean doctrine becomes subsumed beneath a 'revised' terminology, one which, rather than promoting the liberation of the oppressed, strives to incorporate (or conceal) them within the current political status quo (Brown 1996: 18). For example, 'oppression' is substituted with 'poverty', 'praxis' with 'problem-solving' and so on. As a result, the notion of indigenous knowledge and grassroots initiative is often manipulated and distorted, for which Freire should take no responsibility (Brown 1996: 19).

At this point, I disagree with Brown for I believe that the domestication of the PAR method has been done by NGOs in their attempt to avoid resistance from external agencies or their own target groups; and that it should not be seen as the manipulation of Freire's ideas or a deliberate attempt to incorporate the PAR method into the current political status quo. Any reform, and any revolution too, however truly revolutionary it might be, always takes place in circumstances in which the initiators have to compromise. In the case of SBPY and Yasanti, feminists had to adjust to the local situation by avoiding action that would place poor women in direct confrontation with the authorities, factory owners/managers or conservative community leaders, because protest action and strike are considered too radical and unsuitable (*tidak pantas*) for women pictured in the Javanese culture as individuals with the characteristics of being *manut* (obedient), *setia* (adherent) and *lemah-lembut* (kind-hearted). SBPY's attempt to hold street demonstration to protest the local government's new tax policy, for instance, was denied by the female market traders who preferred their own way of protest, that is, giving up their stalls inside the market and moving to the street-sides. Similarly, Yasanti had to bow to the female factory workers' choice of indirect protest action (absenteeism, stealing, cheating and so on) instead of direct action of strikes or demonstrations. In the post-Suharto era, although the changing political situation has allowed grassroots groups to express their grievances more openly, the general attitude of the people towards women remains unchanged. It is therefore the challenge of women's NGOs in Indonesia to form a 'critical mass' who will pave the way to a new understanding of equality between men and women.

The third obstacle has to do with the tendency of Indonesian NGOs to suffer from a 'paternalistic bias' in which activists impose their subjective preferences on target groups. NGOs often try to break the 'culture of silence' (fatalism, apathy, naivety and the like) of the underprivileged by suggesting that particular actions should be taken in order to produce changes (Brown 1996: 23–4). When Indonesian NGOs start their activities in a particular area, they normally come in with their own agenda. Elliott (1987: 66) argued that any intervention from 'outside' is already preventing the community from acting on its own terms and in accordance with its own inner dynamics. The fact that many NGOs in developing societies are formed and run by charismatic leaders – who control the policy direction of their organisations and who are determined to share their experience with the people – has made intervention more difficult to avoid. This often leads to what Smillie (1995: 151) termed a '*guru* syndrome' where experienced NGO leaders and activists with charisma, energy, political savvy and a strong, value-based commitment to community development dictate their preferences to NGO staff members and target groups. Our cases in Chapter 6 have illustrated how under different circumstances NGOs have encountered this 'syndrome'. Although both SBPY and Yasanti shared the same view that bureaucratic and feminist principles are fundamentally incompatible because bureaucracy embodies a masculine value that conflicts with feminists' emphasis on egalitarianism and informality, they differed sharply in managing their organisations. SBPY's attempt to develop a 'collective leadership' and a 'task culture', where power and influence were widely distributed among staff members, appeared to allow some degree of internal democracy and flexibility to emerge, although the organisation had to face a lack of discipline, as manifested in the long delays of programme implementation and completion. Meanwhile, Yasanti's focus on 'strong leadership' and a 'person culture', where power was concentrated in the hands of a prominent figure and the board of trustees, had led to Smillie's *guru* syndrome', whereby staff at the middle level had no power to make decisions. This subsequently created a gap between top leaders and staff members, especially during Kus Yuniati and Wahyuni's leadership.

The final obstacle relates to the problem of how to develop an effective network. The formation of pro-democracy coalitions and networks appears to be the major purpose of movement-oriented NGOs, because collective action to challenge the state's domination can only be pursued if different actors (NGO activists, religious leaders, academia, peasants, workers, students and so on) can be incorporated into a set of cross-cutting relationships. Without doubt, co-ordination is important for NGOs to provide political back-up for their actions. However, this seems to be difficult to achieve because NGOs are often slow to co-operate with each other or with other elements of social movements due to their different philosophies, structures, histories and approaches. Moreover, harsh competition for money and limelight among NGOs has also discouraged inter-NGO networking (Smillie 1995: 233). Forum's experience (discussed in Chapter 7) has illustrated the problem a network must face in its attempt to ensure performance and sustainability. Despite its serious efforts to disseminate the idea of people's sovereignty, to facilitate the formation of a broad pro-democracy coalition and to lift the morale of local NGOs to become more actively involved in NGO movement, Forum has not done much in developing a coherent co-ordination as indicated by the low level of members' participation in its annual meetings. Its co-ordinating activity appears to suffer from three kinds of difficulties. First, too much time and energy have been spent on attempts to resolve internal conflicts. This has limited Forum's capacity to deliver programmes. Second, Forum has never been able to develop a strong institutional framework for co-ordination because members are not prepared to sacrifice their autonomy and are unwilling to be governed by an institution outside their own organisational structures. Third, Forum's dependence on grants from external funding agencies has created a situation in which the networking body has to accommodate donors' preferences and is unable to act on the basis of the choice of its own members. Given that members have no capability or willingness to cover Forum's operational costs, this problem will seem to persist. In the post-Suharto era, the capability of the new executive director to increase members' contribution seems to indicate the growing commitment to support Forum's activities. Yet, the small proportion of members' contribution to the total budget shows that in the near future Forum will remain dependent on donors' financial support.

However, we should not understate the capacity of movement-oriented NGOs in generating collective action. Despite the four barriers discussed above, Forum and other movement-oriented NGOs in Indonesia have played crucial roles in mobilising grassroots population and in disseminating the discourse of democracy to the people. First, because movement-oriented NGOs always operate beyond ethnic, religious, class and other exclusive social-cultural boundaries, they contribute to what Turner and Hulme (1997: 209) have called the process of 'social energisation', a process in which individuals and groups mobilise mental and physical resources to act in terms of both self-interest and in the interests of others. In Indonesia, movement-oriented NGOs and students' groups can be credited for their ability to forge new patterns of alliance with workers, farmers, informal traders and squatters. Their activities since the early 1990s have shown that it is possible to defy government restrictions on strikes and demonstrations to a greater extent than had previously been thought possible in New Order Indonesia. They took up issues of immediate needs, instead of opinions, of various target groups, such as higher wages, improvement of working conditions in the industrial sector, fairer deals in the land dispute cases, human rights protection, a more democratic governance, and so forth. Second, NGOs have kept the idea of people's sovereignty (*kedaulatan rakyat*) alive amid the systematic attempts by the New Order government to repress grassroots initiatives. Historically, the slogan of *kedaulatan rakyat* has been mainly associated with leftist ideology. It was brought to the national political arena by Mohammad Hatta and Tan Malaka during the period immediately following the proclamation of Indonesian independence in 1945 (Feith 1970). While Hatta saw *kedaulatan rakyat* in terms of government accountability through elected legislatures, Malaka and his radical youth supporters stressed direct mass action (Anderson 1972). Some elements of this tradition have inspired today's grassroots resistance, as manifested in many local struggles organised by radical students and NGOs. Third, through their conscious attempt to establish constituencies, movement-oriented NGOs have made contribution to self-organisation by providing marginalised groups with room to manoeuvre (Arce *et al*. 1994: 167). Consistent with being part of social movements, Indonesian NGOs have contributed to the process of liberating the underprivileged from the structures of exploitation and injustice. Despite the failure to implement their radical agenda, the two women's NGOs discussed in Chapter 6 appeared to have made important contribution to the process of consciousness-raising and self-organisation among the marginalised women. Both SBPY and Yasanti have generated awareness of the structures of male domination and gender exclusion and a sense of solidarity among their constituencies. Meanwhile, through its democratic campaigns Forum has laid a strong foundation for the pro-democracy movements. Its widely published political statements have also inspired societal groups to put more pressure on the New Order government and to boost the transition to democracy in the post-Suharto era.

## Alleviating poverty and developing democracy in the post-Suharto era

What role can be played by Indonesian NGOs after the fall of the New Order government? There are at least two areas in which NGOs seem to play a greater role in the post-Suharto era. The first area has to do with attempts to mitigate the adverse effects of the 1997 economic crisis on the poor. The financial crisis had forced the state to reduce its expenditure and to terminate many of its community development projects. This substantially reduced the state's capacity to provide health care, subsidies on basic items and other material benefits to the poor. Meanwhile, under the pressure of financial bankruptcy, both state-owned and private enterprises had been forced to make lay-offs. Due to their dependence on the faltering industrial sector, the urban poor seemed to suffer the most. Lane (1999) described the appalling quality of life among the urban poor in Jakarta during the financial crisis:

> [T]he urban poor – factory workers, shop assistants, supermarket employees (mostly women), coolies, public transport drivers, street stall owners, etc. – live in squalid *kampung*. Rubbish is piled up everywhere, there is no water, the drains are blocked, mosquitoes abound, the rooms are tiny so that people pile up against each other like sardines to sleep, and they wash and defecate in public toilets where they have to pay. Electricity is around 100 watts total per household (if you are a bit better off you can get up to 450 watts). It is rare for anyone to get a senior high school or university education. Incomes are around 100–300 thousand *rupiah* (US$10–30) a month. Most families have two to five members. Children regularly suffer from cholera, typhus, meningitis, dysentery, skin disorders, influenza, sinus and eye infections and malnutrition.
>
> (Lane 1999: 247)

The economic crisis and widespread impoverishment after the collapse of the *rupiah* in 1997 brought new demands from society to which NGOs cannot turn a blind eye. In the area of community development, for instance, development NGOs devised programmes to remedy the impact of the economic crisis on the poorest section of society. BSY's attempt to carry out 'Project Support to Home Workers' Response to the Economic Crisis' (discussed in Chapter 5) is an example of this type of activity. At the national level, a collective effort to mitigate the impact of the economic crisis on the poorest was also carried out. In 1999, for example, twenty-seven NGOs from all over Indonesia formed a consortium to introduce a community recovery programme (*Program Pemulihan Keberdayaan Masyarakat* or PKM). To administer the implementation of PKM, the consortium established the DPN (the National Advisory Council) whose membership was taken from representatives of NGOs, academia, and government agencies. This consortium managed to secure some US$20 million funding from donor countries (Canada, USA, United Kingdom, Norway, Denmark and Italy), from an international agency, the UNDP (United Nations Development Programme) and from the Indonesian government, where Bappenas (the National Development Planning Board) agreed to contribute Rp 1 billion to support the PKM programme (*Suara Pembaruan*, 7 August 1998).

Another area in which Indonesian NGOs appear to have played a significant role is to keep the political reform going. In a situation where NGOs appear to be freer, those organisations committed to 'democratisation' have much to do to create a condition that will allow the democratisation to proceed. What role can be expected from Indonesian NGOs in order to sustain a democratic governance? To start a steady transition to democracy, Indonesia needs more time and favourable conditions that will allow experts and representatives of many voices to work through the crucial philosophical, legal, institutional and procedural issues, which will frame a durable democracy. According to Diamond (1992: 7), democratisation 'from below', requires a steady growth of civil society: a process where manifold social movements (neighbourhood associations, women's groups, religious organisations, intellectuals and students) and civic organisations from all classes (lawyers, journalists, trade unions and entrepreneurs) attempt to constitute themselves in an ensemble of arrangements so that they can express their interests. This process is significant since a strong civil society can uphold a fledgling democracy in several ways. First, it can provide a reservoir of resources (political, economic, cultural and moral) to check and balance the power of the state. Second, when a wide range of interests are organised, it will provide an important basis for democratic competition where groups in society are able to press their interests. Third, associational life supplements the role of political parties in stimulating political participation and in promoting an appreciation of the obligations and rights of democratic citizenship. Fourth, a strong civil society can train or educate citizens of how to organise their neighbours or co-workers effectively, how to mediate their conflicts and produce consensus, and how to manage their associations more responsibly (Diamond 1992: 8–10). In the Philippines, for instance, during the late 1980s and early 1990s, the political prominence of NGOs increased as they consolidated and strengthened through a plethora of coalitions (especially the national and regional networks) and established relations with grassroots organisations that led Clarke (1998: 126) to remark that the Philippines has 'the most organised and well-developed NGO community in the world'.

In Indonesia, NGOs have struggled to enable grassroots people learn about and exercise democratic principles. The legacy of centralised colonial rule, authoritarian government and state-led development has taken its toll on the capacity of citizens to organise independently. As a result, the associational cultures are often fragile, crudely reflective of the structures of power within society. Existing grassroots organisations appear to have been vulnerable to external control and manipulation. If they managed to survive under Suharto's authoritarian rule, their ability to influence the state was weakened by complicated class, ethnic, religious and gender relations. What Indonesian NGOs can do in this situation is to educate people of how to exercise democratic political activities: interest articulation, representation, negotiation, lobbying, bargaining, consensus building and so on. The activities of CD-Bethesda, BSY, SBPY, Yasanti and Forum (discussed in Chapters 5–7) in establishing self-reliant groups, in disseminating the idea of people's sovereignty, and in forming grassroots coalitions clearly indicate NGOs' significant contribution to the strengthening of Indonesian civil society.

What has been initiated by these NGOs before and after the fall of the New Order government has now been replicated by other organisations. One of them is a Jakarta-based organisation called INPI-Pact (Indonesian NGOs Partnership Initiatives) which put emphasis on discussion, publication and training of social organisations. Funded by USAID (United States Agency for International Development), this organisation established co-operations with various institutions (universities, research centres, private firms and so forth) and grassroots groups (co-operatives, neighbourhood associations and the like) to provide education and training on how democracy should operate at grassroots level (INPI-Pact 1998: iv–v). This action was carried out simultaneously in several places all over Indonesia such as Aceh, Padang, Jakarta, Yogyakarta, Denpasar and Ambon. Another group worth mentioning is the Indonesian Women's Coalition for Justice and Democracy. Representing over ninety NGOs and individuals nationwide, the coalition has been active in political networking and in advocating the principles they represent: popular democracy, justice and equality. Its first national congress on 15–17 December 1998 in Yogyakarta was attended by over 500 women representing different organisations (*Berita Nasional*, 19 December 1998). In its statement, the coalition expressed its intention to push for a 50 per cent quota for women in the legislative, executive and judicial arms of government (Kalibonso 1999: 340). Similar actions on a smaller scale have also been initiated by local NGOs all over the country. However, it is too early to say whether these organisations have succeeded or failed in their attempts to promote the idea and practice of democracy. But the enthusiasm of their activists to press for *reformasi total* (total reform) has generated hope that grassroots people will somehow have more choice and freedom to express their voices.

However, there is a reason to believe that during the transition to democracy Indonesian NGOs may still face obstacles. The situation in the post-Suharto era has undoubtedly enabled Indonesian NGOs to play a greater role than ever before. But it will take a long while before NGOs can produce a major transformation. For example, organisations such as BSY and CD-Bethesda have to be patient in their attempt to free both KSMs (self-reliant groups) and ORAs (people's organisations) from domination by village officials because it will take sometime to remove the '*priyayi* culture'[2] from the rural social relations. Although the new favourable climate will allow NGOs to implement the PAR method without obstruction from the government, they may still have to be patient in persuading their target groups to accept radical strategies. In the case of SBPY and Yasanti, for example, activists must first resolve their role as 'virtual representatives' by listening more to their constituencies and by allowing them to initiate and to impose control on their collective action. One may agree with Townsend (1995: 101) who argued that outsiders can do no more than facilitating the poor to seek out their own solutions to their own problems.

In a democratic political context, there could also be a cost for NGOs in which political parties and other groupings could exploit their connections with the grassroots and possibly pervert NGOs' purposes. NGOs' attempt to establish pro-democracy coalitions at both regional and national levels may attract groups competing for political power and who could thus use NGOs as a means to achieve their political ambitions. Because NGOs have the access and the capacity to organise and to mobilise people at grassroots level, political groups may be interested in using NGOs' reach to secure popular support. It is therefore advisable for

Indonesian NGOs to stay away from the political terrain that belongs to political parties and the state because involvement in this area may encourage more internal conflict. If Indonesian NGOs are to remain true to their role as promoters of grassroots-oriented development and as parts of social movements, their activists must not allow their organisations to become involved in current political struggles between the secular-nationalists and the Islamic fundamentalists, and between the conservatives and the reformists. As the third sector organisations representing the interests of the underprivileged, NGOs are not designed to compete for political power. They must instead concentrate on their symbolic role of initiating indirect popular resistance because this is clearly what NGOs can do best.

Another crucial challenge for Indonesian NGOs is how to maintain the trust put in them by their donors, beneficiaries, the government and the public. Although professionalism and efficient management system may not be the landmark of the NGO sector, there is a growing need for NGOs to develop their staff members, to ensure financial stability, to improve their management system and to develop accountability system. Our cases indicate that NGOs capable of providing better 'motivators' and 'hygiene factors' (salary, fringe benefits, career path and so on) have greater chance to achieve organisational stability. In terms of professionalism, it appears that small NGOs tend to face less pressure of professionalisation, which affects their seriousness in developing the technical and managerial skills of their employees. Our cases also indicate that different style of leadership has produced different effects on NGOs' performance and capacity to sustain their programmes. Each style has its own strengths and weaknesses.

In the case of development NGOs, it appears that small organisations tend to develop a 'power culture' in which the fate of the organisation depends on a strong leader, while large organisations develop a 'role culture' in which activities are guided by rules and procedures. Reliance on 'power culture' can ensure strong leadership and flexibility, but at the same time it denies organisational stability as indicated in the case of BSY. Meanwhile, dependence on 'role culture' appears to guarantee predictability and sustainability, but at the same time it entails bureaucratic rigidities as manifested in the case of CD-Bethesda. For movement-oriented NGOs, the adoption of 'collective leadership' (in the case of SBPY) can ensure internal democracy, but it entails a lack of discipline. Meanwhile, dependence on a prominent individual leader (as indicated in the case of Yasanti) seems to guarantee strong leadership, but it denies the exercise of internal democracy.

In judging NGOs' accountability, one should look at both the external and internal dynamics of their operation. Factors such as NGOs' legal status of being *yayasan* (which implies a non-democratic environment), the lack of serious concern on management, and the low level of demand for accountability both from target groups and public in general appear to have prevented Indonesian NGOs from developing a downward accountability. These problems may not seriously threaten NGOs' contribution to the democratisation in Indonesia. However, in order to respond to the growing demand for more professionalism and accountability from donors, beneficiaries and community, Indonesian NGOs should put more serious attention to efficient management, staff development and accountability system.

# Glossary

| | |
|---|---|
| *Abangan* | nominal Muslims |
| *Aksi Sepihak* | one-sided action (PKI's land-reform campaign) |
| *Aliran* | political and religious streams |
| *Arisan* | traditional credit-and-saving rotation group |
| *Azas Tunggal Pancasila* | the concept of *Pancasila* as the sole ideology of the state |
| *Bakul* | a Javanese term for petty-traders |
| *Bhinneka Tunggal Ika* | unity in diversity (Indonesia's slogan of national unity) |
| *Bupati* | district head |
| *Buruh Pabrik* | factory workers |
| *Camat* | sub-district head |
| *Demokrasi Terpimpin* | guided democracy |
| *Dharma Pertiwi* | the association for the wives of Indonesial military personnels |
| *Dharma Wanita* | the association for the wives of Indonesian civil servants |
| *Dusun* | hamlet |
| *Dwifungsi* | Indonesian military doctrine of dual function |
| *Gotong Royong* | mutual self-help activity |
| *Gubernur* | provincial governor |
| *Haji* | Muslims who made pilgrimage to Mecca |
| *Jimpitan* | Javanese traditional food security groups |
| *Kamituwo* | a Javanese term for hamlet head |
| *Kampung* | a residential area situated behind street side houses in the city |
| *Karang Taruna* | the state-formed village youth groups |
| *Kecamatan* | sub-district administration |
| *Kedokan* or *Ceblokan* | the traditional sharecropping in which non-labour input costs and harvests are shared on the basis of two-thirds to the landowner and one-third to the tenant |
| *Keluarga Berencana* | family planning programme |
| *Kemitraan* | partnership |
| *Ketoprak* | a traditional Javanese theatre |
| *Kontak Tani* | the state-formed farmers' group |

## Glossary

| | |
|---|---|
| *Kristenisasi* | an Indonesian term for conversion to Christianity |
| *Kromo inggil* | refined Javanese language |
| *Kyai* | traditional Islamic teachers |
| *Lasykar Jihad* | the ready-to-die Islamic troop |
| *Lurah* | village head |
| *Makelar* | a middleman who purchases commodities directly from farmers |
| *Manut* | a Javanese term for obedient behaviour |
| *Modin* | a religious official in the village |
| *Muhammadiyah* | literally means 'the followers of Muhammad' is the second biggest Islamic organisation in Indonesia |
| *Musyawarah* | a traditional process of deliberation in decision making |
| *Nahdlatul Ulama (NU)* | literally means 'the awakening of leaders' is the biggest Islamic organisation in Indonesia representing the traditional stream |
| *Negara Kesatuan* | an Indonesian conception of 'unitary state' |
| *Organisasi Nir-Laba* | non-profit organisations |
| *Pancasila* | Indonesia's official ideology of 'Five Principles' |
| *Pasar* | traditional marketplace |
| *Pembinaan* | guidance |
| *Pengajian* | Koran reading group |
| *Penyuluhan* | extension |
| *Pesantren* | traditional Islamic boarding school |
| *Pribumi* | indigenous people |
| *Priyayi* | traditional Javanese bureaucrats |
| *Reformasi* | political reform in the post-Suharto era |
| *Rupiah* | the Indonesian currency |
| *Sambatan* | collective activities for construction or repair of houses, dykes and so forth |
| *Santri* | devout Muslims |
| *Sawah* | rice fields |
| *Sekretaris Desa* | the village secretary |
| *Selapanan* | traditional Javanese weekly meeting groups |
| *Sidang Istimewa* | a special session of the people's consultative assembly (MPR) |
| *Staatsblad* | state's law |
| *Sumpah Pemuda* | youth oath of 28 October 1928 |
| *Swadaya Masyarakat* | people's self-reliance |
| *Swasembada Pangan* | food self-sufficiency |
| *Syariah* | Islamic law |
| *Tanah Bengkok* | a block of cultivated land allocated to village officials as a source of income while serving their positions |
| *Tebasan* | a pre-harvest purchase of crops by middlemen directly from farmers |
| *Wayang Kulit* | traditional Javanese shadow puppet show |
| *Wayang Wong* | stage show dramatising themes from Hindu epics |
| *Yayasan* | an Indonesian term for 'foundation' |

# Notes

## 1 Introduction

1 For a useful discussion about the relations between the 'first', 'second' and 'third' sectors, see Billis (1993:159–65), Hudson (1995: 26–9) and Fowler (1997: 21–7).
2 In the Indonesian context, 'empowerment' (*pemberdayaan*) is understood as an attempt to strengthen the bargaining position of *wong cilik* (the little people) – e.g. poor peasants, workers, petty traders and squatters – *vis-à-vis* the state and the market (Kartjono 1996: 51). *Pemberdayaan*, according to Prijono, includes three processes: (1) developing (*mengembangkan*) people's knowledge and skills; (2) defending (*membela*) and protecting (*melindungi*) them against unfair dealing and exploitation; and (3) making them more independent (*memandirikan*) and self-reliant (*menswadayakan*) in carrying out their own development (Prijono 1996: 97).
3 A clear definition of 'civil society' is provided by Gellner (1995: 32) who defined the term as 'a set of diverse non-governmental institutions, which is strong enough to counterbalance the state and, whilst not preventing the state from fulfilling its role of keeper of the peace and arbitrator between major interests, can nevertheless prevent the state from dominating and atomising the rest of society'.
4 Guinness (1986) and Sullivan (1992) argued that in Yogyakarta, Javanese people strongly maintained their traditional social relations as manifested in their routine *slametan* (ritual feasts), *gotong-royong* (mutual help), *arisan* (credit-and-saving rotation groups), *sambatan* (collective works: construction and repair of houses, dykes and so forth), *jimpitan* (food security groups) and so on.
5 In most urban areas in Java, *kampung* – literally means hamlet – is commonly understood as a residential area situated behind streetside houses and characterised by a large proportion of substandard housing among a maze of narrow winding pedestrian pathways, occupied by a densely settled population with poor sanitation. Important studies on the Javanese *kampung* were made by, among others, Geertz (1965) and Guinness (1986).
6 Resource mobilisation theory argues that a movement is likely to evolve at the presence of organised core groups who are capable of designing strategies, common goals, symbols and beliefs. More information regarding the theory will be provided in Chapter 2. In Yogyakarta, the presence of a large number of students with organisational and intellectual capacity to design a movement has generated a necessary condition for the emergence of social resistance.
7 Susenas (the national social-economic survey) is a household sample survey conducted once in a year by the BPS (Centre of the Statistical Bureau) in each province. The 1999 survey, for example, used 204,416 households taken from all over Indonesia to collect information about the current social-economic indicators (BPS 1999: viii).

8 There are two distinct aspects in a quantitative study: (1) statistical assessment of relationships 'between variables'; and (2) generalisability of findings which requires careful sampling, most usually randomised.
9 The word 'constituency', when applied to NGO advocacy, can be defined as any citizen or community group who: (1) may be organised to provide a base of support for advocacy because they will either directly benefit from the solution or because they care about the cause; or (2) need information or discussion so that policy and legal reform can transform attitudes, values and behaviour (Vene-Klasen 1996: 233).

## 2 NGOs, community development and social movements

1 Korten (1990: 115–27) also added another category which he called 'fourth-generation NGOs', i.e. those NGOs still evolving and relatively undefined but essentially promoting institutional and structural reform through increasing NGOs and coalition of popular organisations. While a more detailed analysis of this type of NGOs is not available, this study will concentrate on the three types of NGOs described by Korten and Elliott.
2 Participatory rural appraisal (PRA) is a method of grassroots empowerment in which the collection of data and information for rural development is provided by 'insiders' (i.e. local people) and the technology and methods used in the project are derived from local knowledge. In PRA, 'insiders' appraise, analyse, plan, experiment, implement and monitor their own programmes, while 'outsiders' (i.e. NGO activists or government officials) listen, encourage and facilitate them (Chambers 1992).
3 'Acceptability' is a concept referring to the degree of 'acceptance' or welcome received by NGOs *vis-à-vis* their beneficiaries. Writing in the context of development NGOs in Yogyakarta, Widaningrum (1988) argued that an NGO receives a high degree of acceptability if its method is not 'alien' to the local culture, if its technology is applicable, if its programme brings direct benefits to the participants and if its existence is sanctioned by the local authorities.
4 The word *mag-uugmad* is a Cebuano term meaning 'tiller'.
5 This definition seems to match Gellner's definition of civil society discussed in Chapter 1.
6 For more discussion on the effect of the 'Third Wave of Democratisation' on political activism in Indonesia, see Uhlin (1997).
7 INGI (International NGO Forum on Indonesia) is a national NGO network in Indonesia. This network was formed by a number of Indonesian and Dutch NGOs in June 1985.

## 3 The social and political settings

1 Schmitter (1974: 103–4) defined 'corporatism' as a system of interest representation in which the constituency units are organised into a limited number of singular, compulsory, non-competitive, hierarchically ordered and functionally differentiated categories which are recognised, created, or otherwise controlled in leadership selection or interest articulation by the state and which exercise a monopoly of representational activity within the respective categories.
2 *Cendana* is the name of a street in Central Jakarta where Suharto's private home is located.
3 Also known as the Huk, this organisation was formed by radical peasants in Central Luzon and was influential throughout the country especially during 1942–1962. Peasant leaders took advantage of the Second World War to bring together groups of tenant farmers who, since the 1920s, had been angered by poverty and degradation they had suffered at the hands of landowners. For a more detailed account about this organisation, see Davis (1989), among others.
4 See Chapter 2 for a brief discussion about this ideology.
5 Baramuli, one of Habibie's close associates, organised a support group called *Kelompok Iramasuka* (the Irian Jaya, Maluku, Sulawesi and Kalimantan group) within Golkar

whose purpose was to make sure that Habibie is elected as Indonesia's fourth president (*Tempo*, 5 September 1999). The political manoeuvre of this group, had generated a split within Golkar, especially between the Habibie–Baramuli group and the Akbar Tanjung–Marzuki Darusman group over Habibie's candidacy. The Indonesian media called the first group 'Golkar Hitam' (black Golkar) and the second 'Golkar Putih' (white Golkar). The split increased as the presidential election approaching.
6 The Bank Bali corruption scandal involved a number of businessmen, top government officials, Golkar functionaries of the Habibie–Baramuli circle and Habibie's relatives. In its attempt to collect an inter-bank loan from the BPPN (the National Body for the Reconstruction of the Banking Sector), Bank Bali (one of the troubled Indonesian private banks), was asked to pay a great deal of 'debt collection fee' of Rp 546 billion (about 60 per cent of the total amount of the debt collected) to a private company, Era Giat Prima Limited. It was believed that most of the money went to the Habibie–Baramuli circle to fund the pro-Habibie presidential campaign (*Tempo*, 29 August 1999).
7 *Bruneigate* is a term used by the Indonesian media in reference to a 'grant' from the Sultan of Brunei given to President Wahid. Critics argued that the president should not have used the US$1 million grant for his personal purposes.
8 *Buloggate* refers to the illegal use of approximately 40 billion *rupiah* (US$400,000) money from BULOG (the Indonesian food logistics agency) by those who are suspected to be President Wahid's close associates.
9 Mohammad 'Bob' Hassan is one of Suharto's close allies who was sent to jail on corruption charges.
10 He was arrested in Bintaro, South Jakarta, on 28 November 2001.

### 4 NGOs in Indonesia: strategies and approaches

1 *Pesantren* is a traditional Islamic boarding school led by traditional leaders (*kyai*) widely available in Java in which the students (*santri*), both male and female, learn about Islamic teaching.
2 In the Indonesian context, *yayasan* is defined as non-profit organisations carrying out social and humanitarian activities (Soemitro 1993: 162). In a *yayasan*, the founders (who often claim to be the owners) dominate the decision-making and control the policy direction; and staff members are accountable only to the founders who employ them. In most cases, however, top leaders are usually selected from a group of founders whose position has no particular time limit (Soemitro 1993: 164).
3 My interviews with Anton Soedjarwo (29 January 1997), Aleks Wiyarto (20 January 1997) and Sigit Wijayanto (14 June 1997).
4 Interviews with Aleks Wiyarto (19 May 1997) and Aryanto Soedjarwo (2 August 1997).
5 This term was used by Juni Thamrin, a staff of the *Yayasan Akatiga*, an NGO in Bandung, West Java, in his speech titled *LSM dan Paradigma Perubahan* (NGOs and the Changing Paradigm), at the opening session of the Cisarua NGO meeting, West Java, 18–19 June 1993.
6 Structural adjustment policies (SAPs) which include budget cuts, the liquidation of inefficient public or private corporations, tax increase and higher interest rates are policies implemented by countries undertaking economic recovery programmes under IMF's supervision. Prior to the commencing of IMF's rescue plan, a particular state must indicate SAPs in its letter of intent (LoI).

### 5 Development, empowerment and professionalism: the case of development NGOs

1 Chambers (1983: 147) defines 'rural development' as a strategy to enable a specific group of villagers (small-scale farmers, tenants, the landless and women) to gain for themselves and their children more of what they want and need. It involves

helping the poorest who seek a livelihood to demand and control more of the benefits of development.
2 The interest rate of commercial borrowing in Indonesia at that time was between 20 per cent and 30 per cent per year.
3 NGO writers could not agree on a standard of criteria that defines large NGOs. While in South Asia some define BINGOs (big NGOs) as those having at least 500 staff members, an annual budget of at least US$1 million and working directly in 100,000 or more rural households, in Latin America, where such large NGOs are rare, the criteria for BINGOs are: a minimum of 125 staff members, an annual budget of US$ 1.2 million and an outreach covering 25,000 families (Wils 1995: 54). In Indonesia, there were only a few NGOs with more than 200 workers, one of which was *Dian Desa*, an NGO specialised in appropriate technology, with more than 300 workers. In Yogyakarta, most NGOs employ an average of 50 workers, run an annual budget between US$200,000 and US$900,000 and serve between 2,000 and 80,000 households.
4 As has been discussed in Chapter 3, the 'floating mass' was introduced by the New Order government in the mid-1970s to prevent villagers from conducting any political activity by prohibiting political organisations from opening branches or establishing direct contacts with villagers.
5 Data are collected from *Monografi Desa Wedi* (Wedi village statistics) of 2000.
6 In the *tebasan* system, the standing crop is sold by the owners to a middleman (*penebas*) just before the harvest, who then organises the harvest and pays the workers in cash. Many argue that *tebasan* reflects the growing commercialisation of crop-growing as a result of the agricultural revolution of the 1960s and 1970s, in which a substantial increase in non-labour input costs has made traditional sharecropping unbearable to landless tenants (Schweizer 1987: 41).
7 Vermicelli (*soun*) is a kind of noodle made of a high quality of *aren* tree and is an important ingredient of the famous *soto ayam* (chicken soup) and *bakso* (meat-ball soup) dishes popular among Indonesians.
8 Unfortunately, reliable information on the number of ex-PKI members and followers in the village was not available. Pak *Sekdes* (the village secretary), whom I interviewed, said that records on former political prisoners are strictly confidential and accessible only to military officers. Meanwhile, villagers were reluctant to talk about political prisoners in their village. One villager, however, mentioned that there had been several hundreds of ex-PKI followers in Wedi.
9 Islam has been important in both the cultural and spiritual life of the local society in Jepara for a long time. Jepara was one of the port cities through which Islam entered Java more than five centuries ago. In the early sixteenth century, Jepara was involved in an extensive trade with Malacca (the Islamic Kingdom in Southeast Asia) in which Muslim traders also introduced Islam to the local communities (Schiller 1996: 48). Nowadays, about 95 per cent of the population is at least nominally Muslim. The Central Java's Regional Office of Religious Affairs estimated there were 3,800 mosques in Jepara in 1997, compared to 80 Protestant churches, one Catholic church, eight Hindu temples and 30 Buddhist *viharas* (Kanwil Departemen Agama Propinsi Jawa Tengah 1997: 30).
10 *Kedokan* or *Ceblokan* is the dominant sharecropping in Central Java which requires the tenant to cultivate modern rice varieties and apply appropriate levels of fertilizers and pesticides. Non-labour input costs and harvests are shared on the basis of two-thirds to the landowner and one-third to the tenant. Each worker who performs all tasks except ploughing and harrowing receives one-ninth to one-twelfth of the harvest (Hart 1986: 179).
11 In Indonesia, different institutions have their own definitions of SSCIs. The Ministry of Industry, for example, defines SSCIs as enterprises owned by an Indonesian citizen with a total asset value not exceeding Rp 600 million, excluding the value of housing and land occupied by the plant (Sandee *et al.* 1994: 118). The BPS (Centre of the

262  *Notes*

Statistical Bureau) defines SSCIs in terms of the number of personnel involved in the activities, that is, small-scale industry comprises firms of 5–19 workers, while cottage industries employ less than five workers (Husaini *et al*. 1996: 8). However, the definition provided by the Directorate General of Small Industries, which refers to firms with assets of less than Rp 5 million, appears to be more commonly used in identifying rural small enterprises (Sandee *et al*. 1994: 121).

12 This point was made by the *Ketua Bappeda* in his speech titled *Arah Pembangunan Daerah di Yogyakarta dan Peran LSM* (The Direction of Regional Development in Yogyakarta and the Role of NGOs), at a government-sponsored NGO meeting in Kaliurang, Yogyakarta, 24 November 1986.

13 The 'accompanying fee' is determined by a 12 per cent margin in borrowing rates imposed by BSY on KSMs. The banks allocated the credit to BSY with 21 per cent annual loan rates, while BSY distributed the money to the KSMs with 33 per cent annual loan rates. Meanwhile, the KSMs charged their members with 44 per cent annual loan rates (Wiyarto, interview, 20/01/1997). It appeared that BSY gained 12 per cent of the total money distributed per year, and the KSMs gained 11 per cent of the total money distributed to their members. Although the loan rate paid by individual borrowers was high (44 per cent per year), it was relatively lower than the rates imposed by private money-lenders in the village. A petty trader in Wedi, whom I interviewed, said that the *bank plecit* (a Javanese term for private money lenders) charged borrowers between 25 per cent per week and 50 per cent per month of each credit they received (Bu Sastro, interview, 22/02/1997).

14 In the context of NGO, Fowler defined 'legitimacy' as a valid public perception that an NGO is a genuine agent of development that will do what it promises to do and will conform to generally accepted standards of development behaviour and performance (Fowler 1997: 183).

15 During my interviews with a number of villagers, I could sense the reservation against outsiders, especially among the older generation who might have witnessed the 1965 killings in the village.

16 I must thank CD's staff members in the Jepara office, especially Andreas Subiyono, for sharing the details of this incident.

17 These remarks were made by an Islamic preacher who led the protest action against CD-Bethesda, as quoted in the CD's Central Java office's *notulen* (meeting minutes) on 2 October 1995.

18 The dialogue between the local authority, CD's staff members and the people of Donorojo in that meeting was recorded in CD's *notulen* (meeting minutes) of 24 August 1995.

19 Based on my interviews with Andreas Subiyono (CD's executive director) on 6 July 2001, Julius Tongaretang (CD's fieldworker) on 6 July 2001, Antoro (member of ORA from Panggang) on 2 August 2001 and Sahid (also member of ORA from Panggang) on 2 August 2001.

20 In the context of NGOs, institutional development refers to the process of increasing NGOs' capacity which includes improvement in roles and power distribution between actors inside the organisations and building interactions with other sectors of society (Fowler 1997: 190).

21 Pusphar Sandar says of the Indian situation that the reason for a lack of funds available to organised charity is not because individuals are less charitable, but only that individual charity is informal and flows spontaneously to individuals needing help on a one-to-one basis and does not go to organised bodies (Fowler 1997: 148). This argument, in my view, is also applicable to the Indonesian context.

22 The data are gathered from BSY's annual reports of 1993–2000.

23 This approach was initiated by the Grameen Bank, a leading small-credit institution in Bangladesh, which used peer group to choose, monitor and evaluate members in obtaining credit and in using their money for productive activities. By using peer

support and pressure the bank can minimise the administrative costs of loan and increase the repayment rates because groups tend to put pressure on members who try to violate Grameen rules and provide support at times when members face difficulty in pursuing their economic aims (Yunus 1989: 144).
24 Its small size has prevented BSY from developing a sufficient system of career promotion for its workers. In 1997, there was only one position of director who supervises five heads of section (general affairs, guidance, small enterprises, consultancy and production and marketing). While Aleks Wiyarto has served as the director since the formation of the organisation, 'section head' is the only top position available for other staff.
25 Strategic management is an attempt to create a clear view throughout the organisation of its mission and objectives and the development of strategies and plans that lead to their achievement. It normally deals with some critical questions: what specifically does the organisation want to achieve in the next few years? How should it allocate resources between different objectives? What quality standards should it aim to achieve? What has it learned from past experiences? What improvements are required to enable it to make better use of resources? (Hudson 1995: 89–90).
26 Information on CD's strategic planning activity was gathered from *notulen* (meeting minutes) made by staff members in the process of discussion and brainstorming during July–November 1995.
27 Stakeholders are all those parties who either affect or are affected by an organisation's behaviour, actions and policies. In the context of development NGOs, stakeholders include: (1) those to whom the organisation has a formal obligation: board members, staff and target groups; (2) other parties whom the NGO is obliged to satisfy: donors and governments; and (3) groups or individuals who have an 'imperative interest' to influence the NGO for whatever personal or ideological reason: elite groups who may be threatened by empowerment, the military, religious leaders, and the like (Fowler 1997: 174).
28 Edwards and Hulme (1995a) made a useful distinction between NGOs' 'upwards' accountability – directed towards their executive body, trustees, donors and host governments – and 'downwards' accountability – directed toward target groups, partners, fieldworkers and supporters.
29 My interviews with the directors of the two NGOs indicate that neither BSY nor CD regard those who receive their goods or services as members or constituencies with any associated rights or duties to get involved in the decision-making process or project evaluation.

## 6 Building constituencies and institutionalising a movement: the case of women's NGOs

1 In the context of movement NGOs, political action does not only concern the exercise of power relations in the state institutions or economic organisations; it also includes attempts to re-organise the daily life of men and women, to repudiate existing structures and to call for changes (Johnson 1992: 165).
2 The term 'practical gender needs' refers to what women require to fulfil their role in existing sexual division of labour (sanitation, children's nurseries, higher wages and health care), while 'strategic gender needs' are those arising from a desire to challenge women's subordination and existing gender relations benefiting men (e.g. changes in divorce laws to give women equality with men, an end of sexual discrimination, and so on) (Molyneaux 1985: 225–54; Moser 1993: 65).
3 The Indonesian feminists of the 1980s can be associated with individuals such as Julia Suryakusumah, Ita F. Nadia, Nursyahbani Katjasungkana, Wardah Hafidz, Ani Soemantri, Kartini Syahrir, Arianne Katoppo, Myra Diarsi, Sri Kusyuniati and Murniati whose articles and papers depicted the idea of gender equality.

264  Notes

4 Kabeer (1994: 253) noted that women's movement tends to develop a kind of 'collective identity' which includes: (1) the recognition of the shared aspects of gender subordination which would form the basis of strategies for change; and (2) the shared feeling of powerlessness (i.e. inability to participate independently in community-based networks) which would generate the need to organise among themselves.
5 '*Priyayi*' is a Javanese term for people in the higher position. Their status is determined not only by power and prosperity, but also by their refined (*halus*) behaviour and the 'cleanliness' of their occupation.
6 The term 'popular democracy' refers to a system whereby the broad masses of the people have an effective voice in shaping macro policy and in conducting public affairs. Neither the democracy of the 'liberal' nor the 'socialist' worlds has ensured this natural right of the people since leadership is determined by the 'powerful' (Rahman 1993: 210).
7 In the Javanese community, the traditional grassroots organisations such as *arisan* (credit-and-saving rotation groups) and *kelompok pengajian* (Koran reading groups), which involves women in rural areas, tend to focus on the welfare and the spiritual aspects of women and they have become increasingly co-opted by the state-sponsored women's organisations, especially the PKK (Tjondronegoro 1984: 183–6).
8 See Chapter 1.
9 Coincidently, Wolf's study was carried out in Gadingan, a village in Central Java where Yasanti carried out its female factory workers' advocacy.
10 My interviews with Mansour Fakih, the Indonesian director of Oxfam-UK (22/12/1996) and Meth Kusumohadi, the Indonesian director of USC-Canada (25/07/1997).
11 See Chapter 5.
12 This method and its implementation in the Indonesian context have been briefly discussed in Chapter 2.
13 The term is often used by the state officials and military leaders as an indirect reference to the leftist activists both during and after Suharto's government.
14 Idul-Fitr is the Muslims' New Year during which employers pay bonuses to their workers. The amount of this reward varies, between one and two months of the workers' salary.
15 Antlov (1994: 81–2) provided a somewhat detailed illustration of the importance of these letters for most Indonesians in their attempt to get advanced education or jobs both in the private and public sectors. For civil service and the military, for example, applicants must be able to produce letters of 'good behaviour' (*surat keterangan kelakuan baik*), 'self cleanliness' (*surat bersih diri*) and 'clean environment' (*surat bersih lingkungan*) issued by the sub-district administration, the police station and the military office. The 'good behaviour' certificate normally states that the holder has not been involved in any criminal offence or any anti-state activities; the letter of 'self cleanliness' states that the holder has not been member of any forbidden organisations, does not oppose *Pancasila* and the 1945 constitution; and the letter of 'clean environment' states that the holder and his/her relatives have not been involved in any anti-*Pancasila* activities or have been member of forbidden organisations. Without these letters it was almost impossible for villagers to get education, job or run businesses outside the village.
16 This view was expressed by some female staff members of NGOs in Yogyakarta: Assariroh (Yasanti), Sih Handayani (Yasanti and SBPY), Dian Gayatri (SBPY), Suswati (LKPSM-NU) and Budi Wahyuni (PKBI).
17 Although the difference between 'managers' and 'leaders' is not crystal clear, the distinction between the two is important because organisations need an appropriate type of management or leadership in order to ensure performance and sustainability. In the context of voluntary organisations, Hudson (1995: 242) tried to make a distinction between managers and leaders as he argued that while, on the one hand, managers try to link people together in an organised way, leaders, on the other hand, try to motivate people to engage in collective action and spread particular values or norms.

18 Lofland (1996: 2–3) defined 'social movement organisations' as associations of persons making idealistic and moralistic claims about how human personal or group life ought to be organised in order to construct realistic, reasonable and morally justifiable social relations. In North America, where his study is based, the term covers a wide range of social movements: the Anti-Saloon Leagues of the prohibitionist movement, the Industrial Workers of the World of the labour movement, the Student Non-violent Co-ordinating Committee of the civil rights movement, the Berkeley Free Speech Movement of the student movement and the National Organisation for Women of the women's liberation movement.

19 SBPY's definition of members seems to be too broad as it states in one of its leaflet: 'Membership is open to everybody concerned with women's issues. Individuals as well as organisations are welcome' (SBPY 1997). However, SBPY did make a distinction between 'members' and 'target groups'. While the former refers to people who contribute their ideas, time, energy and money to the organisation, the latter refers to those who are oppressed and receive assistance from SBPY (Gayatri, interview, 12/12/1996 and 06/08/1997). In 2001, SBPY had 22 female 'members' coming from various backgrounds: students, researchers, lawyers and academics.

20 I interviewed Sih Handayani in several occasions in two different capacities: as a staff member of Yasanti and the founder of SBPY. In June 1997, she decided to leave Yasanti to be fully active in the management of SBPY.

21 One reason for the lack of activity during 1997–1998 was the fact that Budi Wahyuni, Yasanti's interim director, could not be fully involved in the organisation's daily activities given that she was also an executive director of the Yogyakarta chapter of the PKBI (Indonesian Family Planning Association), another NGO operating at national scale.

## 7 Developing democracy through a local network: the case of the Yogyakarta NGO forum

1 Melucci defined 'collective action' as the events in which a number of individuals act collectively, combine different orientations, involve multiple actors and implicate a system of opportunities and constraints that shape their relationships (Melucci 1995: 43). A collective action, according to Gamson (1995: 90), is shaped by a cognitive process in which people develop a sense of individual harm, destitution and suffering. This cognitive process may be shaped by intolerable structural conditions such as poverty, exploitation, oppression, and so on. Seen in this context, collective action appears to express a feeling of dissatisfaction with existing structural conditions which encourages people to act together to resist them.

2 Violence has sometimes been defined in a very broad way. Galtung (1990: 11) defined violence as any barrier which impeded the realisation of potential, where such a barrier is social rather than natural. As he put it: 'if people are starving when this is objectively affordable, then violence is committed ... '. However, I prefer to use the term in a more straightforward and conventional sense as interpreted by Giddens who defined it as 'the use of force to cause physical harm to another' (Giddens 1994: 231).

3 According to the Law on Local Government (*Undang-undang pemerintahan daerah*) No. 5/1970, the *Bupati* is appointed by the provincial governor with approval from the Minister of Home Affairs. But this system was always vulnerable to corruption and manipulation due to a non-transparent procedure of selecting candidates.

4 My interviews with Pius Lustrilanang, a prominent student activist in Jakarta and Bandung (20/06/1997) and Bambang, a student activist at Airlangga University, Surabaya (04/01/1997).

5 During 1986–1987, I attended several discussions organised by Palagan in Yogyakarta, in which students enthusiastically discussed radical social theories and theories of social movements with references to cases of popular resistance in Latin America, South Korea and the Philippines.

6 In Indonesia, groups or individuals who refuse to be associated with any political parties and who deny their right to vote in the general elections address themselves as the *golongan putih* (the white group), also known as *golput*.
7 My interviews with Budiawan, an ex-member of GENI (13/04/1997); Juliantara, the founder of LAPERA (23/08/1997); and Pius Lustrilanang, one of the founders of ALDERA (20/06/1997), indicated that most radical students' organisations refused to be put into the category of NGOs because they wanted to remain informal and because they did not want to be isolated from campus-based activities.
8 The Kedung Ombo dam project was marked by a high level of manipulation in the payment of compensation to the farmers. Some village heads and middlemen tried to reap material benefits from the project by manipulating the price of the land. For example, the Ministry of Home Affairs announced that the compensation was set at Rp 3,000/m$^2$, while in practice villagers received only between Rp 300–700 per m$^2$ (Stanley 1990: 26).
9 Under the current educational system, the 'normal' age of university graduates in Indonesia with *Sarjana Strata Satu* (S-1) degree, a five-year degree course equivalent to master degrees, is between 24 and 26. But, in most cases, students (especially the activists) can go on to pursue their studies beyond that range.
10 *Dwifungsi* is a doctrine used by the Indonesian military forces to justify their role in politics which allows military officers to become state officials at all levels, from *Bupati* (district heads), to *Gubernur* (provincial governors), members of people's representative bodies, and cabinet ministers.
11 By 1997 there were 100 non-elected members of the MPR representing the armed forces. President Suharto had absolute control of their appointment together with other non-elected MPR members such as *Utusan Daerah* (the regional representatives) and *Utusan Golongan* (group representatives).
12 In the post-Suharto era, there were a number newly formed paramilitary groups in Yogyakarta representing different radical Islamic organisations such as the *Hamka Radikal* (from Mrisi, Bantul), the *Hajar Azwad* (from Padokan, Bantul), the Joxin Brigade (from Kauman, Yogyakarta) and the *Buto Ijo* (from Mangiran, Bantul). Some of them even named their groups after some radical organisations in Sri Lanka and the Philippines such as the Tamil Tiger Muslim Youth Group (from Jejeran, Bantul) and the Abu Sayyaf Muslim Youth Group (from Ngabehan, Yogyakarta).
13 During 1993–1994, there were a number of incidents of rioting in Maumere (Flores) and Dili (East Timor) where Muslims of Javanese and Buginese origins were attacked by local people. Those incidents were sparked by arguments between local people and migrants from Java and Sulawesi (many of whom run shops and kiosks). Because in those areas the majority of the population are Catholics and Protestants, while the migrants are mainly Muslims, Islamic leaders saw the incidents as an action against Islam.
14 The term 'institutionalisation' refers to a process whereby ideas, actions or structures become taken for granted, or taken as a rule (Bordt 1997: 134). This process involves institutional work that is carried out by actors with political interests as well as self-interest. Once the outcome of an institution is achieved, organisational practices or structures take on a rule-like status, or a life of their own and are beyond the reach of political and individual interests (Di Maggio 1988; Di Maggio and Powell 1991).
15 Members of the committee for art and culture (many of whom were students from various drama and art schools) were disappointed at the state's control over popular culture, especially the local theatre. Eko Winardi, the co-ordinator of the committee, for example, argued that the state had used the traditional popular theatres such as *wayang kulit* (a shadow puppet-show) and *ketoprak* (traditional Javanese theatre) to serve as the speakers for the ruling party, Golkar. It is therefore the duty of concerned artists, he argued, to hand back art to the people (Forum 1997: 37).
16 The initial arrangement as stipulated in the MoU was a three-year contract, but it was cut short into a two-year contract with a possible extension for another year due to the

long delay in its implementation. One reason for the delay was that it took almost a year for Forum to meet the conditions set by ICF that Forum must first have a stable organisational structure and a clear organisational statute.

## 8 Conclusion

1 See my references on those who argue that NGOs are part of social movements in Chapter 2.
2 Young (1999: 84) argued that one possible obstacle to democratisation in Indonesia is the '*priyayi* culture': a kind of relationship that puts the aristocratic *priyayi* and bureaucrats as patrons for the *wong cilik* (little people), which is taken for granted and institutionalised in the society, especially in rural areas.

# Bibliography

## Books, journals, papers and reports

Aditjondro, George. 1990. 'Dampak Sistematik dan Kritik Yang Terlupakan: Suatu Refleksi Terhadap Kampanye Kedung Ombo Yang Lalu'. *Kritis* 4(3) 44–51.
—— 1993. *Memahami Gerakan LSM*. Unpublished Paper. Jakarta: CPSM.
Alberoni, Francesco. 1984. *Movement and Institution*. New York: Columbia University Press.
Alexander, Jennifer. 1987. *Trade, Traders and Trading in Rural Java*. Singapore: Oxford University Press.
Alvarez, S. E. and Escobar, A. 1992. 'Conclusion: Theoretical and Political Horizons of Change in Contemporary Latin American Social Movements'. In S. E. Alvarez and A. Escobar (eds). *The Making of Social Movements in Latin America: Identity, Strategy and Democracy*. Boulder: Westview Press.
Anderson, Benedict R. O'G. 1972. *Java in a Time of Revolution: Occupation and Resistance, 1944–1946*. Ithaca: Cornell University Press.
—— 1990. 'Old State, New Society: Indonesia's New Order in Comparative Historical Perspective'. In B. R. O'G. Anderson. *Language and Power: Exploring Political Cultures in Indonesia*. Ithaca: Cornell University Press.
Anderson, B. R. O'G. and McVey, R. T. 1971. *A Preliminary Analysis of the October 1, 1965, Coup in Indonesia*. Ithaca: Cornell University.
Anderson, Perry. 1974. *The Lineage of Absolutist State*. London: New Left Books.
ANGOC (Asian Non-Governmental Organisation Coalition). 1991. 'GO–NGO Relations in Six Asian Countries'. *Lok Niti: Journal of the Asian NGO Coalition* 7(2) 12–18.
Annis, Sheldon. 1987. 'Can Small-Scale Development be Large-Scale Policy? The Case of Latin America'. *World Development* 15(Suppl.) 129–34.
Antlov, Hans. 1994. 'Village Leaders and the New Order'. In H. Antlov and S. Cederroth (eds). *Leadership on Java: Gentle Hints, Authoritarian Rule*. Surrey: Curzon Press.
—— 2001a. 'Village Governance: Past, Present and Future'. *Renai* I(2) 26–41.
—— 2001b. 'Village Governance and Local Politics in Indonesia'. Unpublished paper.
Arce, A., Villareal, M. and de Vries, P. 1994. 'The Social Construction of Rural Development: Discourses, Practices and Power'. In D. Booth (ed.). *Rethinking Social Development: Theory, Research and Practice*. London: Longman.
Arief, S. and Sasono, A. 1981. *Indonesia: Dependency and Underdevelopment*. Kuala Lumpur: Meta.
Aspinall, E. 1995. 'Students and Military: Regime Friction and Civilian Dissent in the Late Suharto Period'. *Indonesia* No. 59 21–44.

Aspinall, E. 1999. 'The Student Uprising of 1998'. In A. Budiman *et al.* (eds). *Reformasi: Crisis and Change in Indonesia*. Monash Papers on Southeast Asia No. 50. Monash Asia Institute. Monash University, Clayton.
Aubrey, Lisa. 1997. *The Politics of Development Cooperation: NGOs, Gender and Partnership in Kenya*. London: Routledge.
Bank Indonesia. 1990. *Indonesian Financial Statistics*. Jakarta: Bank Indonesia.
Bappenas (National Development Planning Board). 1997a. *Public Finance Statistics*. Jakarta: Badan Penerbit Bappenas.
—— 1997b. *Laporan Kondisi Keuangan Daerah*. Jakarta: Badan Penerbit Bappenas.
—— 2001. *Menatap ke Depan Perekonomian Nasional Indonesia*. Jakarta: Badan Penerbit Bappenas.
Baroto, A. 1992. 'Indonesia's 1992 General Election: Changes and Continuity'. *The Indonesian Quarterly* 20(3) 244–56.
Barton, Greg. 1997. 'Indonesia's Nurcholis Madjid and Abdurrahman Wahid as Intelectual Ulama: The Meeting of Islamic Traditionalism and Modernism in Neo-Modernist Thought'. *Islam and Christian-Muslim Relations* 8(3) 323–50.
Bebbington, Anthony J. 1997. 'Reinventing NGOs and Rethinking Alternatives in the Andes'. In J. L. Fernando and A. W. Heston (eds). *The Role of NGOs: Charity and Empowerment*. Philadelphia: The Annals of the American Academy of Political and Social Science.
Bebbington, A. *et al.* 1993. *NGOs and the State in Latin America: Rethinking Roles in Sustainable Agricultural Development*. London: Routledge.
Bebbington, A. and Riddell, R. 1997. 'Havy Hands, Hidden Hands, Holding Hands? Donors, Intermediary NGOs and Civil Society Organisations'. In D. Hulme and M. Edwards (eds). *NGOs, States and Donors: Too Close for Comfort?* London: MacMillan.
Bennett, J. 1994. *NGO Coordination at Field Level: A Handbook*. Oxford: ICVA NGO Coordination.
—— 1995. *Meeting Needs: NGO Coordination in Practice*. London: Earthscan.
Berman, Evan M. 1998. *Productivity in Public and Non-profit Organizations: Strategies and Techniques*. London: Sage.
Berninghausen, J. and Kerstan, B. 1992. *Forging New Paths: Feminist Social Methodology and Rural Women in Java*. London: Zed Books.
Biggs, S. and Neame, A. 1995. 'Negotiating Room for Manoeuvre: Reflections Concerning NGO Autonomy and Accountability within the New Policy Agenda'. In M. Edwards and D. Hulme (eds). *NGOs Performance and Accountability: Beyond the Magic Bullet*. London: Earthscan.
Billah, M. M. 1993. *Visi, Masalah, Posisi dan Paradigma ORNOP di Indonesia Serta Upaya untuk Mengatasinya*. Unpublished paper. Jakarta: CPSM.
—— 1994. 'Pengendalian Negara Atas Hak-Hak Buruh Indonesia'. *Kawah* 3(3) 3–10.
—— 1996. 'The Role of NGOs in Democratization Based on People's Sovereignty'. In R. Ibrahim (ed.). *The Indonesian NGO Agenda: Towards the Year 2000*. Jakarta: LP3ES.
Billah, M. M. and Nusantara, A. H. G. 1988. 'LSM di Indonesia: Perkembangan dan Prospeknya'. *Prisma* 17(4) 16–28.
Billis, David. 1993. *Organising Public and Voluntary Agencies*. London: Routledge.
Bimo. 1985. 'Penanganan Kesehatan di Pedesaan'. In P. Hagul (ed.). *Pembangunan Desa dan Lembaga Swadaya Masyarakat*. Jakarta: Rajawali.
Blackburn, Susan. 1994. 'Gender Interests and Indonesian Democracy'. In D. Bourchier and J. D. Legge (eds). *Democracy in Indonesia, 1950s and 1990s*. Monash Paper on Southeast Asia No. 31. Centre of Southeast Asian Studies. Monash University, Clayton.

Blair, Harry. 1997. 'Donors, Democratisation and Civil Society: Relating Theory to Practice'. In M. Edwards and D. Hulme (eds). *NGOs, States and Donors: Too Close for Comfort?* London: MacMillan.
Block, Fred. 1977. 'The Ruling Class Does Not Rule: Notes on Marxist Theory of the State'. *Socialist Revolution* No. 7 6–28.
Blumer, Herbert. 1995. 'Social Movements'. In S. M. Lyman (ed.). *Social Movements: Critiques, Concepts, Case Studies*. London: MacMillan.
Booth, Anne. 1992. 'Income Distribution and Poverty'. In Anne Booth (ed.). *The Oil Boom and After: Indonesian Economic Policy and Performance in the Suharto Era*. Singapore: Oxford University Press.
Bordt, Rebecca L. 1997. 'How Alternative Ideas Become Institutions: the Case of Feminist Collectives'. *Nonprofit and Voluntary Sector Quarterly* 26(2) 132–55.
Boserup, Esther. 1970. *Women's Role in Economic Development*. New York: St Martin's Press.
Bourchier, David. 1996. *The Lineage of Organicist Political Thought in Indonesia*. Ph.D. dissertation. Department of Politics. Monash University, Clayton, Australia.
BPS (Biro Pusat Statistik) Daerah Istimewa Yogyakarta. 1994. *Indikator Kesejahteraan Rakyat*. Yogyakarta: Kantor Statistik Propinsi DIY.
—— 1995. *Hasil Survei Sosial-Ekonomi Nasional*. Yogyakarta: Kantor Statistik Propinsi DIY.
—— 1996. *Yogyakarta Dalam Angka*. Yogyakarta: Kantor Statistik Propinsi DIY.
—— 1997. *Profil Kependudukan*. Yogyakarta: Kantor Statistik Propinsi DIY.
—— 1999. *Daerah Istimewa Yogyakarta Dalam Angka*. Yogyakarta: Badan Pusat Statistik.
—— 2000. *Statistik Indonesia*. Jakarta: Badan Pusat Statistik.
Bradlow, D. and Grossman, C. 1996. 'Adjusting the Bretton Woods Institutions to Contemporary Realities'. In J. M. Griesgraber and B. G. Gunter (eds). *Development: New Paradigms and Principles for the Twety-First Century*. London: Pluto Press.
Bratton, Michael. 1986. 'Beyond the State: Civil Society and Associational Life in Africa'. *World Politics* 41(3) 407–30.
—— 1989. 'The Politics of Government-NGO Relations in Africa'. *World Development* 17(4) 569–97.
Bresnan, John. 1993. *Managing Indonesia: The Modern Political Economy*. New York: Columbia University Press.
BRI (Bank Rakyat Indonesia). 1987. *Model Hubungan Keuangan antara Lembaga Swadaya Masyarakat dengan Bank*. A paper for the Seminar on the Development of NGO-Bank Relations. Jakarta, 22–24 July.
Brown, David. 1996. *Strategies of Social Development: Non-government Organizations and the Limitations of the Freirean Approach*. The New Belshume Papers. Department of Agricultural Extension and Rural Development. University of Reading, United Kingdom.
BSY (Bina Swadaya Yogyakarta). 1992. *Evaluasi Program Kerja 1992*. Yogyakarta: Satwil Bina Swadaya Yogyakarta.
—— 1994. *Evaluasi Program Kerja 1994 dan Perencanaan Program Kerja 1995*. Yogyakarta: Satwil Bina Swadaya Yogyakarta.
—— 1995. *Evaluasi Program Kerja 1995 dan Perencanaan Program Kerja 1996*. Yogyakarta: Satwil Bina Swadaya Yogyakarta.
—— 1996. *Realisasi Kerja Tahun 1995*. Yogyakarta: Satwil Bina Swadaya Yogyakarta.
—— 1997. *Realisasi Kerja Tahun 1996*. Yogyakarta: Satwil Bina Swadaya Yogyakarta.

BSY (Bina Swadaya Yogyakarta). 1999. *Laporan Kerja Tahun 1999*. Yogyakarta: Guswil Bina Swadaya Yogyakarta.
—— 2001. *Laporan Kinerja Tahun 2000*. Yogyakarta: Guswil Bina Swadaya Yogyakarta.
Budiman, Arief. 1990. 'Gerakan Mahasiswa dan LSM: Ke Arah Sebuah Unifikasi'. *Kritis* 4(3) 53–9.
—— 1994a. 'From Lower to Middle-Class: Political Activities Before and After 1988'. In D. Bourchier and J. D. Legge (eds). *Democracy in Indonesia, 1950s and 1990s*. Monash Paper on Southeast Asia No. 31. Centre of Southeast Asian Studies. Monash University, Clayton.
—— 1994b. 'Dimensi Sosial-Ekonomi Dalam Konflik Antar Agama di Indonesia'. In INTERFIDEI. *Dialog: Kritik dan Identitas Agama*. Yogyakarta: INTERFIDEI.
—— 1999. 'The 1998 Crisis: Change and Continuity in Indonesia'. In A. Budiman *et al.* (eds). *Reformasi: Crisis and Change in Indonesia*. Monash Papers on Southeast Asia No. 50. Monash Asia Institute. Monash University, Clayton.
Bunnell, Frederick. 1996. 'Community Participation, Indigenous Ideology, Activist Politics: Indonesian NGOs in the 1990s'. In Daniel S. Lev and Ruth T. McVey (eds). *Making Indonesia*. Southeast Asia Program, Cornell University, Ithaca.
Byres, Terry. 1989. 'Agrarian Structure, the New Technology and Class Actions in India'. In H. Alavi and J. Harris (eds). *Sociology of Developing Societies: South Asia*. London: MacMillan.
Canel, Eduardo. 1992. 'Democratisation and the Decline of Urban Social Movements in Uruguay: A Political-Institutional Account'. In S. Alvarez and A. Escobar (eds). *The Making of Social Movements in Latin America: Identity, Strategy and Democracy*. Boulder: Westview Press.
Cardoso, Ruth L. 1992. 'Popular Movements in the Context of the Consolidation of Democracy in Brazil'. In S. Alvarez and A. Escobar (eds). *The Making of Social Movements in Latin America: Identity, Strategy and Democracy*. Boulder: Westview Press.
Caroll, Thomas. 1992. *Intermediary NGOs: The Supporting Link in Grassroots Development*. West Hartford, Connecticut: Kumarian Press.
Carr, Marylin. 1989. 'Institutional Aspects of Microenterprise Promotion'. In J. Levitsky (ed.). *Microenterprises in Developing Countries*. London: Intermediate Technology Publications.
CD-Bethesda. 1995. *Laporan Pelaksanaan Program dan Rencana Program 1994–1995*. Yogyakarta: CD-Bethesda.
—— 1996a. *Laporan Pelaksanaan Program dan Rencana Program 1995–1996*. Yogyakarta: CD-Bethesda.
—— 1996b. *Strategic-Plan 1996–2002*. Yogyakarta: The Community-Development Unit of Bethesda Hospital.
—— 1997. *Laporan Pelaksanaan Program dan Rencana Program 1996–1997*. Yogyakarta: CD-Bethesda.
—— 2000. *Laporan Pelaksanaan Program Tahun 2000*. Yogyakarta: CD-Bethesda.
—— 2001. *Laporan Hasil Pertemuan Organisasi Rakyat dan Organisasi Professional Mitra CD-Bethesda*. Yogyakarta: CD-Bethesda.
Cerna, L. and Miclat-Teves, A. G. 1993. 'MFI Experience of Upland Technology Development in the Philippines'. In J. Farrington *et al. NGOs and the State in Asia: Rethinking Roles in Sustainable Agricultural Development*. London: Routledge.
Chambers, Robert. 1983. *Rural Development: Putting the Last First*. London: Longman.
—— 1992. *Rural Appraisal: Rapid, Relaxed and Participatory*. Discussion paper No. 311, Institute of Development Studies, University of Sussex, Brighton.

Chambers, Robert. 1995. 'Paradigm Shifts and the Practice of Participatory Research and Development'. In N. Nelson and S. Wright (eds). *Power and Participatory Development: Theory and Practice*. London: Intermediate Technology Publications.

—— 1997. *Whose Reality Counts? Putting the First Last*. London: Intermediate Technology Publications.

Chandler, G. 1985. 'Wanita Pedagang Pasar Desa di Jawa'. *Prisma* 10(2) 50–8.

Chazan, Naomi, et al. 1988. *Politics and Society in Contemporary Africa*. London: MacMillan.

—— 1994. 'Engaging the State: Associational Life in Sub-Saharan Africa'. In J. S. Migdal et al. (eds). *State, Power and Social Forces: Domination and Transformation in the Third World*. Cambridge: Cambridge University Press.

Clark, John. 1991. *Democratising Development: The Role of Voluntary Organisations*. London: Earthscan.

Clarke, Gerrard. 1996. *Non-Governmental Organisations and Politics in the Developing World*. Papers in International Development No. 20. Centre of Development Studies, University of Swansea, United Kingdom.

—— 1998. *The Politics of NGOs in Southeast Asia: Participation and Protest in the Philippines*. London: Routledge.

Clayton, Andrew. 1996. 'Introduction'. In A. Clayton (ed.). *NGOs, Civil Society and the State: Building Democracy in Transitional Societies*. Oxford: INTRAC.

Commins, Stephen. 1997. 'World Vision International and Donors: Too Close for Comfort?'. In M. Edwards and D. Hulme (eds). *NGOs, States and Donors: Too Close for Comfort?* London: MacMillan.

Constantino-David, Karina. 1992. 'The Phillipine Experience in Scaling-up'. In M. Edwards and D. Hulme (eds). *Making a Difference: NGOs and Development in a Changing World*. London: Earthscan.

Collier, David (ed). 1979. *The New Authoritarianism in Latin America*. Princeton: Princeton University Press.

Collier, William. 1980. *Declining Labour Absorption in Javanese Rice Production, 1978 to 1980*. Occasional Paper No. 2. Bogor: Institut Pertanian Bogor.

Covey, Jane. 1995. 'Accountability and Effectiveness in NGO Policy Alliances'. In M. Edwards and D. Hulme (eds). *NGOs Performance and Accountability: Beyond the Magic Bullet*. London: Earthscan.

CPSM (Centre for Participatory Social Management). 1993. *Laporan Pertemuan LSM/LPSM di Cisarua, Bogor, 18–19 Juni 1993*. Jakarta: CPSM Working Committee.

Creswell, John W. 1994. *Research Design: Qualitative and Quantitative Approaches*. London: Sage.

Crone, Donald. 1988. 'State, Social Elites and Government Capacity in Southeast Asia'. *World Politics* 40(2) 252–68.

Crouch, Harold. 1978. *The Army and Politics in Indonesia*. Ithaca: Cornell University Press.

—— 1979. 'Patrimonialism and Military Rule in Indonesia'. *World Politics* 31(4) 571–87.

—— 1994a. 'Democratic Prospects in Indonesia'. In D. Bourchier and J. D. Legge (eds). *Democracy in Indonesia: 1950s and 1990s*. Monash Paper on Southeast Asia No. 31. Centre for Southeast Asian Studies, Monash University, Clayton.

—— 1994b. 'Indonesia: The Period of Uncertainty'. In Daljit Singh (ed.). *Southeast Asian Affairs 1994*. Singapore: Institute of Southeast Asian Studies.

Dahl, Robert. 1967. *Pluralist Democracy in the United States*. Chicago: Rand MacNeely.

Dahm, Bernard. 1971. *History of Indonesia in the Twentieth Century*. London: Pall Mall Press.
Darmaputera, Eka. 1988. *Pancasila and the Search for Identity and Modernity in Indonesian Society*. Leiden: E. J. Brill.
Dasgupta, Biplap. 1977. *Agrarian Change and New Technology in India*. Geneva: UNSRID.
Davies, Rick. 1997. 'Donor Information Demands and NGO Institutional Development'. *Journal of International Development* 9(4) 613–20.
Davis, Leonard. 1989. *The Revolutionary Struggle in the Philippines*. London: MacMillan.
De Fonseka, Chandra. 1991. 'Alliance of Convenience'. *Lok Niti: the Journal of the Asian NGO Coalition* 7(2) 4–9.
De Janvry *et al*. 1995. 'State, Market and Civil Organisations: New Theories, New Practices and Their Implications for Rural Development'. In De Janvry *et al*. (eds). *State, Market and Civil Organisations*. London: MacMillan.
De Jouvenal, Bertrand. 1962. *On Power: Its Nature and the History of Its Growth*. Boston: Beacon Press.
Department of Social Affairs of the Republic of Indonesia. 1997. *Rekapitulasi Data Organisasi Kemasyarakatan Di Bawah Pembinaan Departemen Sosial di Seluruh Indonesia*. Jakarta: Sub-Direktorat Pendataan dan Pendaftaran.
Desai, Vandana and Howes, Mick. 1995. 'Accountability and Participation: A Case Study from Bombay'. In M. Edwards and D. Hulme (eds). *NGOs Performance and Accountability: Beyond the Magic Bullet*. London: Earthscan.
Dhakidae, Daniel. 1993. *Posisi dan Peran ORNOP di Indonesia*. Unpublished Paper. Jakarta: CPSM.
Diamond, Larry. 1992. 'Introduction: Civil Society and the Struggle for Democracy'. In Larry Diamond (ed.). *The Democratic Revolution: Struggles for Freedom and Pluralism in Developing World*. New York: Freedom House.
—— 1993. 'The Globalisation of Democracy'. In R. O. Slater *et al*. (eds). *Global Transformation and the Third World*. Boulder: Lynne Rienner.
Di Maggio, P. J. 1988. 'Interest and Agency in Institutional Theory'. In L. G. Zucker (ed.). *Institutional Patterns and Organizations: Culture and Environment*. Cambridge, M.A.: Ballinger.
Di Maggio, P. J. and Anheier, H. K. 1994. 'The Sociology of Non-Profit Organisations and Sectors'. In Sharon M. Oster (ed.). *Management of Non-Profit Organisations*. Brookfield, USA: Dartmouth.
Di Maggio, P. J. and Powell, W. W. 1991. 'Introduction'. In P. J. Di Maggio and W. W. Powell (eds). *The New Institutionalism in Organizational Analysis*. Chicago: Chicago University Press.
Di Palma, Gabriel. 1978. 'Dependency: A Formal Formal Theory of Underdevelopment or a Methodology for the Analysis of Concrete Situations of Underdevelopment?'. *World Development* 6(1) 881–924.
Djiwandono, J. S. 1997. 'Elections in the Political System of the New Order'. *The Indonesian Quarterly* 25(2) 94–7.
Dollard, J., *et al*. 1997. 'Aggression Follows Frustration'. In J. C. Davies (ed.). *When Men Revolt and Why*. New Brunswick, USA: Transaction Publishers.
Drabek, Anne G. 1987. 'Development Alternatives: The Challenge for NGOs – An Overview of the Issues'. *World Development* 15(Suppl.) ix–xv.
Drucker, P. 1986. *The Frontiers of Management*. London: Hienemann.
—— 1990. *Managing the Non-Profit Organisation*. London: Butterworth-Hienemann.

Eade, Deborah. 1997. *Capacity-Building: an Approach to People-Centered Development.* Oxford: Oxfam Publication.

Easton, David. 1967. *The Political System: An Inquiry into the State of Political Science.* New York: Alfred A. Knopf.

Echeverri-Gent, John. 1993. *The Sate and the Poor: Public Policy and Political Development in India and the United States.* Berkeley: University of California Press.

Eckstein, H. 1963. 'Group Theory and the Comparative Study of Pressure Group'. In H. Eckstein and D. Apter (eds). *Comparative Politics.* New York: Free Press.

Edwards, Michael. 1994. 'International Non-Governmental Organisations, Good Government and the New Policy Agenda: Lessons of Experience at the Programme Level'. *Democratization* 1(3) 504–15.

Edwards, M. and Hulme, D. 1992. 'Scaling-Up the Development Impact of NGOs: Concepts and Experiences'. In M. Edwards and D. Hulme (eds). *Making a Difference: NGOs and Development in a Changing World.* London: Earthscan.

—— 1995a. 'NGOs Performance and Accountability: Introduction and Overview'. In M. Edwards and D. Hulme (eds). *NGOs Performance and Accountability: Beyond the Magic Bullet.* London: Earthscan.

—— 1995b. 'Beyond the Magic Bullet? Lessons and Conclusions'. In M. Edwards and D. Hulme (eds). *NGOs Performance and Accountability: Beyond the Magic Bullet.* London: Earthscan.

—— 1997. 'NGOs, State and Donors: an Overview'. In M. Edwards and D. Hulme (eds). *NGOs, State and Donors: Too Close for Comfort?* London: MacMillan.

Elden, M. and Levin, M. 1991. 'Cogenerative Learning: Bringing Participation into Action Research'. In W. F. Whyte (ed.). *Participatory Action Research.* London: Sage.

Eldridge, Philip. 1985. 'The Political Role of Community Action Groups in India and Indonesia: In Search of a General Theory'. *Alternatives* 10(3) 401–34.

—— 1989. *NGOs in Indonesia: Popular Movement or Arm of Government?* Working Paper No. 55. Centre for Southeast Asian Studies, Monash University, Clayton, Australia.

—— 1990. 'NGOs and the State in Indonesia'. In A. Budiman (ed.). *The State and Civil Society in Indonesia.* Monash Papers on Southeast Asia No. 22. Centre for Southeast Asian Studies. Monash University, Clayton.

—— 1995. *Non-Government Organisations and Democratic Participation in Indonesia.* Kuala Lumpur: Oxford University Press.

—— 1997. 'NGOs, the State and Democratisation in Indonesia'. In J. Schiller and B. Schiller (eds). *Imagining Indonesia: Cultural Politics and Political Culture.* Athens: Ohio University Press.

Elliott, Charles. 1987. 'Some Aspects of Relations Between North and South in the NGO Sector'. *World Development* 15(Suppl.) 57–68.

Emmerson, Donald K. 1976. *Indonesia's Elite: Political Culture and Cultural Politics.* Ithaca: Cornell University Press.

Erlandson, D. A., et al. 1993. *Doing Naturalistic Inquiry: a Guide to Methods.* Newbury Park, CA: Sage.

Evans, P., Rueschemeyer, D. and Skocpol, T. (eds). 1985. *Bringing the State Back In.* Cambridge: Cambridge University Press.

Evers, Hans-Dieter. 1993. *Arah dan Strategi Pembinaan Pedagang Pasar: Sebuah Analisa Kebijaksanaan Kenaikan Retribusi Pasar.* Unpublished Paper. Yogyakarta: Pusat Penelitian Kependudukan. Gadjah Mada University.

Evers, Hans-Dieter. 1994. 'Transformation of the Informal Sector: Social and Political Consequences'. In D. Bourchier and J. D. Legge (eds). *Democracy in Indonesia, 1950s and 1990s*. Monash Paper on Southeast Asia No. 31. Centre for Southeast Asian Studies. Monash University, Clayton.
—— 1995. 'The Growth of an Industrial Labour Force and the Decline of Poverty in Indonesia'. In Daljit Singh and Liak Teng Kiat (eds). *Southeast Asian Affairs 1995*. Singapore: Institute of Southeast Asian Studies.
Fakih, Mansour. 1996. *Masyarakat Sipil Untuk Transformasi Sosial: Pergolakan Ideologi LSM di Indonesia*. Yogyakarta: Pustaka Pelajar.
Falaakh, M. F. 1999. 'Islam and the Current Transition to Democracy in Indonesia'. In A. Budiman et al. (eds). *Reformasi: Crisis and Change in Indonesia*. Monash Papers on Southeast Asia No. 50. Monash Asia Institute. Monash University, Clayton.
Fals Borda, Orlando. 1981. 'The Challenge of Action Research'. In A. Rahman. *Some Dimension in the Bhoomi Sena Movement*. Participation Occasional Paper, UNSRID, Geneva.
—— 1992. 'Social Movements and Political Power in Latin America'. In S. Alvarez and A. Escobar (eds). *The Making of Social Movements in Latin America: Identity, Strategy and Democracy*. Boulder: Westview Press.
Farrington, John, et al. 1993a. *Reluctant Partners?: NGOs, the State and Sustainable Agricultural Development*. London: Routledge.
—— 1993b. *NGOs and the State in Asia: Rethinking Roles in Sustainable Agricultural Development*. London: Routledge.
Fauzi, Noer. 1996. 'Penghancuran Populisme'. *Kawah* 5(5) 10–17.
Feith, Herbert. 1962. *The Decline of Constitutional Democracy in Indonesia*. Ithaca: Cornell University Press.
—— 1970. 'Introduction'. In H. Feith and L. Castles (eds). *Indonesian Political Thinking, 1945–1965*. Ithaca: Cornell University Press.
Feldman, Shelley. 1997. 'NGOs and Civil Society: (Un)stated Contradictions'. In J. L. Fernando and A. W. Heston (eds). *The Role of NGOs: Charity and Empowerment*. Philadephia: The Annals of the American Academy of Political and Social Science.
Fields, G. S. 1994. 'Poverty Changes in Developing Countries'. In R. van der Hoeven and R. Anker (eds). *Poverty Monitoring: An International Concern*. London: MacMillan.
Fincham, R. and Rhodes, P. 1996. *The Individual, Work and Organization*. Second Edition. Oxford: Oxford University Press.
Fisher, Julie. 1993. *The Road from Rio: Sustainable Development and the Non-governmental Movement in the Third World*. Westport, Connecticut: Praeger.
—— 1994. 'Is the Iron Law of Oligarchy Rusting Away in the Third World?'. *World Development* 22(2) 129–43.
Fisher, William F. 1997. 'Doing Good? The Politics and Antipolitics of NGO Practices'. *Annual Review of Anthropology* 26, 439–64.
Forum LSM/LPSM Yogyakarta. 1996. *Laporan Pertanggungjawaban Kepengurusan Periode 1993–1996*. Yogyakarta: Forum LSM/LPSM DIY.
—— 1997. *Tahap Konsolidasi dan Dinamika Forum*. Yogyakarta: Forum LSM/LPSM DIY.
—— 2000. *Laporan Pertanggungjawaban Dewan Pengurus Periode 1998–2000*. Yogyakarta: Forum LSM/LPSM DIY.
Foweraker, Joe. 1994. 'Popular Political Organisation and Democratisation'. In Ian Budge and David McKay (eds). *Developing Democracy*. London: Sage.

Fowler, Alan. 1993. 'Non-Governmental Organisations as Agents of Democratisation: An African Perspective'. *Journal of International Development* 5(3) 325–339.

—— 1996. 'Strengthening Civil Society in Transition Economies – From Concept to Strategy: Mapping an Exit in a Maze of Mirrors'. In A. Clayton (ed.). *NGOs, Civil Society and the State: Building Democracy in Transitional Societies*. Oxford: INTRAC.

—— 1997. *Striking a Balance: A Guide to Enhancing the Effectiveness of NGOs in International Development*. London: Earthscan.

Frantz, Telmo R. 1987. 'The Role of NGOs in the Strengthening of Civil Society'. *World Development* 15(Suppl.) 121–7.

Freire, Paulo. 1972. *Pedagogy of the Oppressed*. London: Penguin.

Friedmann, John. 1992. *Empowerment: The Politics of Alternative Development*. Oxford: Blackwell.

Galtung, Johan. 1990. 'Violence and Peace'. In P. Smoker *et al*. *A Reader in Peace Studies*. Oxford: Pergamon.

Gamble, A. 1990. 'Theories of British Politics'. *Political Studies* 38(3) 404–20.

Gamson, A. 1995. 'Constructing Social Protest'. In H. Johnston and B. Klandermans (eds). *Social Movements and Culture*. London: University College London Press.

Garreton, M. A. 1997. 'Social Movements and Democratisation'. In S. Linberg and A. Sverrison (eds). *Social Movements in Development: the Challenge of Globalisation and Democratisation*. London: MacMillan.

Gellner, Ernest. 1995. 'The Importance of Being Modular'. In John A. Hall (ed.). *Civil Society: Theory, History and Comparison*. Cambridge: Polity Press.

Gersham, J. and Bello, W. 1993. 'Struggles for Democracy and Democratic Struggle'. In J. Gersham and W. Bello (eds). *Re-examining and Renewing the Phillipine Progressive Vision*. Quezon City: FOPA (Forum for Phillipine Alternatives).

Gerth, H. H. and Mills, C. W. 1965 [1948]. *From Max W1eber: Essays in Sociology*. London: Routledge and Kegan Paul.

Geertz, Clifford. 1960. *The Religion of Java*. Chicago: The University of Chicago Press.

—— 1963. *Agricultural Involution: The Process of Ecological Change in Indonesia*. Berkeley: University of California Press.

—— 1965. *The Social History of an Indonesian Town*. Westport, Connecticut: Greenwood Press.

—— 1973. *The Interpretation of Cultures*. New York: Fontana Press.

Giddens, Anthony. 1991. *Modernity and Self-Identity: Self and Society in the Late Modern Age*. Stanford: Stanford University Press.

—— 1994. *Beyond Left and Right: The Future of Radical Politics*. Cambridge: Polity Press.

Goertz, Gary. 1994. *Contexts of International Politics*. Cambridge: Cambridge University Press.

Grolier Incorporated. 1990. *The Encyclopaedia Americana*. Danbury, Connecticut: Grolier.

Guinness, Patrick. 1986. *Harmony and Hierarchy in a Javanese Kampung*. Singapore: Oxford University Press.

Guinness, P. and Husin, I. 1993. 'Industrial Expansion into a Rural Sub-district: Pandaan, East Java'. In H. Dick *et al*. (eds). *Balanced Development: East Java in the New Order*. Singapore: Oxford University Press.

Gupta, Anil K. 1992. 'Voluntarism in Rural Development in India: Intiative, Innovation and Institutions'. In V. A. Hodgkinson, *et al*. (eds). *The Nonprofit Sector in the Global Community: Voices from Many Nations*. San Francisco: Jossey-Bass Publishers.

Gurr, Ted Robert. 1970. *Why Men Rebel.* Princeton: Princeton University Press.
Gutmann, A. and Thomson, D. 1985. 'The Theory of Legislative Ethics'. In B. Jennings and D. Callahan (eds). *Representation and Responsibility: Exploring Legislative Ethics.* New York: Plenum Press.
Hadad, Ismid. 1983. 'Development and Community Self-Help in Indonesia'. *Prisma* 12(2) 3–20.
Hadiwinata, Bob S. 1999. 'Masyarakat Sipil Indonesia: Sejarah, Kebangkitan dan Transformasinya'. *Wacana* 1(1) 7–21.
Haddad, Lawrence. et al. 1995. 'Gender Dimensions of Economic Adjustment Policies: Potential Interactions and Evidence to Date'. *World Development* 23(6) 881–96.
Hadiz, Vedi. 1994. 'Challenging State Corporatism on the Labour Front: Working Class Politics in the 1990s'. In D. Bourchier and J. D. Legge (eds). *Democracy in Indonesia, 1950s and 1990s.* Monash Paper on Southeast Asia No. 31. Centre of Southeast Asian Studies. Monash University, Clayton.
—— 1999. 'Contesting Political Change After Suharto'. In A. Budiman et al. (eds). *Reformasi: Crisis and Change in Indonesia.* Monash Papers on Southeast Asia No. 50. Monash Asia Institute. Monash University, Clayton.
Haliman, Arif. 1997. 'Suatu Kasus Kerjasama Pemda-Swasta di Tingkat Operasional'. In M. Kusumohadi et al. *Globalisasi dan NGO.* Yogyakarta: USC/Yayasan Satunama.
Hainsworth, Geoffrey B. 1983. 'Private Voluntary Organisations and Socio-economic Security and Equality in Indonesia'. *Prisma* 12(2) 46–63.
Handayani, Sih. 1994. 'Hidupku Untuk Memperbesar Pabrik'. *Kawah* 3(1) 12–17.
—— 1995. 'Sri Rejeki: Buruh Pabrik Utama Tex'. In M. Singarimbun and S. Sairin (eds). *Lika-Liku Kehidupan Buruh Perempuan.* Yogyakarta: Pustaka Pelajar and Yasanti.
Handy, Charles. 1988. *Understanding Voluntary Organisations.* London: Penguin.
—— 1993. *Understanding Organisations.* Fourth Edition. London: Penguin.
Hannam, Peter. 1988. 'Pengembangan Bentuk Pembangunan Alternatif: Pengalaman LSM Indonesia'. *Prisma* 17(4) 3–15.
Hanseman, John B. 1997. 'Indonesia and ABRI: Challenges for the Future'. In Daljit Singh (ed.). *Southeast Asian Affairs 1997.* Singapore: Insitute of Southeast Asian Studies.
Hansmann, Henry B. 1994. 'The Role of Non-profit Enterprise'. In Sharon M. Oster (ed.). *Management of Non-profit Organisations.* Brookfield, USA: Dartmouth.
Hardjosoemantri, Koesnadi. 1985. 'Peran Serta Masyarakat Dalam Pengelolaan Lingkungan Hidup'. In P. Hagul (ed.). *Pembangunan Desa dan Lembaga Swadaya Masyarakat.* Jakarta: Rajawali.
Harper, Caroline. 1996. 'Strengthening Civil Society in Transitional East Asia'. In A. Clayton (ed.). *NGOs, Civil Society and the State: Building Democracy in Transitional Societies.* Oxford: INTRAC.
Harper, Malcolm. 1989. 'Training and Technical Assistance for Microenterprises'. In J. Levtisky (ed.). *Microenterprises in Developing Countries.* London: Intermediate Technology Publications.
Hart, Gillian. 1986. *Power, Labour and Livelihood: Processes of Change in Rural Java.* Berkeley: University of California Press.
—— 1989. 'Agrarian Change in the Context of State Patronage'. In G. Hart, A. Turton and B. White (eds). *Agrarian Transformations: Local Processes and the State in Southeast Asia.* Berkeley: University of California Press.
Hashemi, Syed. 1995. 'NGO Accountability in Bangladesh: Beneficiaries, Donors and the State'. In M. Edwards and D. Hulme (eds). *NGOs Performance and Accoutability: Beyond the Magic Bullet.* London: Earthscan.

Hellman, J. A. 1992. 'The Study of New Social Movements in Latin America and the Question of Autonomy'. In S. Alvarez and A. Escobar (eds). *The Making of Social Movements in Latin America: Identity, Strategy and Democracy*. Boulder: Westview Press.

Hendrata, Lukas. 1983. 'Bureaucracy, Participation and Distribution in Indonesian Development'. *Prisma* 12(2) 21–32.

Heryanto, Ariel. 1997. 'Indonesia: Towards the Final Countdown?'. In Daljit Singh (ed.). *Southeast Asian Affairs 1997*. Singapore: Institute of Southeast Asian Studies.

Hiemann, Wolfram. 1997. 'Pengembalian Tepat Waktu Atau Produktivitas?' *Bulletin Bina Swadaya* April Edition, 16–17.

Hikam, Mohammad. 1996. 'Perijinan dan Pemberdayaan Rakyat'. In H. S. Salim and A. J. Wijaya (eds). *Demokrasi Dalam Pasungan: Politik Perijinan di Indonesia*. Yogyakarta: Forum LSM/LPSM.

Hill, David T. 1994. *The Press in New Order Indonesia*. Nedlands: University of Western Australia Press.

Hill, Hal. 1994. 'The Economy'. In H. Hill (ed.). *Indonesia's New Order: the Dynamics of Socio-economic Transformation*. Honolulu: University of Hawaii Press.

Hirschman, Albert O. 1987. *Getting Ahead Collectively: Grassroots Experience in Latin America*. New York: Pergamon.

Hodgkinson, V. A. and McCarthy, K. D. 1992. 'The Voluntary Sector in International Perspective: an Overview'. In V. A. Hodgkinson *et al.* (eds). *The Non-profit Sector in the Global Community: Voices From Many Nations*. San Francisco: Jossey-Bass Publishers.

Hodgkinson, V. A. and Sumariwalla, R. D. 1992. 'The Non-profit Sector and the New Global Community: Issues and Challenges'. In V. A. Hodgkinson *et al.* (eds). *The Non-profit Sector in the Global Community: Voices From Many Nations*. San Francisco: Jossey-Bass Publishers.

Hodson, Roland, 1992. 'Small, Medium or Large? The Rocky Road to NGO Growth'. In D. Hulme and M. Edwards (eds). *Making a Difference: NGOs and Development in a Changing World*. London: Earthscan.

Holden, Barry. 1974. *The Nature of Democracy*. London: Thomas Nelson and Sons Ltd.

Hudson, Mike. 1995. *Managing Without Profit: The Art of Managing Third-Sector Organisations*. London: Penguin.

Hulme, David. 1994. 'Social Development Research and the Third Sector: NGOs as Users and Subjects of Social Inquiry'. In D. Booth (ed.). *Rethinking Social Development: Theory, Research and Practice*. London: Longman.

Huntington, Samuel P. 1968. *Political Order in Changing Societies*. New Haven: Yale University Press.

—— 1991. *The Third Wave: Democratization in the Late Twentieth Century*. Norman: University of Oklahoma Press.

Husaini, M., *et al.* 1996. 'Small-Scale Enterprises Development in Indonesia'. In Mari Pangestu (ed.). *Small-Scale Business Development and Competition Policy*. Jakarta: CSIS (Centre for Strategic and International Studies).

Hyden, Goran, 1983. *No Short Cuts to Progress: African Development Management in Perspective*. Berkeley: University of California Press.

Ibrahim, Rustam. 1997. 'Beberapa Aspek Manajemen Sumberdaya LSM'. In M. Kusumohadi *et al. Globalisasi dan NGO*. Yogyakarta: USC/Yayasan Satunama.

—— 1998. 'Civil Society dan LSM'. In K. Sinaga *et al.* (eds). *Menuju Masyarakat Madani*. Jakarta: INPI-Pact and Lemhannas.

ICF (Indonesia-Canada Foundation). 1994. *Profil Program Yapika (Yayasan Perhimpunan Indonesia-Kanada)*. Yogyakarta: Yappika.
ICG (International Crisis Group). 1999. *Indonesia's Shaky Transition*. ICG Indonesia Report No. 1. Jakarta: ICG Indonesia.
—— 2001a. *Indonesia's Presidential Crisis*. Jakarta and Brussels: ICG.
—— 2001b. *Indonesia's Presidential Crisis: the Second Round*. Jakarta and Brussels: ICG.
INFID (International NGO Forum on Indonesian Development). 1994. *Review of Advocacy 1994*. Jakarta and The Hagues: INFID Secretariat.
—— 1995. *Review of Advocacy 1995*. Jakarta and The Hague: INFID Secretariat.
—— 1996. *Advocacy Review 1996*. Jakarta and The Hague: INFID Secretariat.
—— 1997. *Advocacy Review 1997*. Jakarta and The Hague: INFID Secretariat.
—— 2000. *Perjuangan Demokrasi dan Masyarakat Sipil: Reposisi dan Peran ORNOP/LSM di Indonesia*. Jakarta: INFID.
INGI (International NGO Forum on Indonesia). 1989. *INGI References*. Jakarta and The Hague: INGI Secretariat.
—— 1990. *Report on the 6th INGI Conference in Bonn*. Jakarta and The Hague: INGI Secretariat.
—— 1991. *Laporan Kegiatan 1990–1991*. Jakarta: INGI Secretariat.
Ingleson, John. 1986. *In Search of Justice: Workers and Unions in Colonial Java, 1886–1926*. Singapore: Oxford University Press.
INPI-Pact (Indonesian NGOs Partnership Initiatives). 1998. *Menuju Masyarakat Madani*. Jakarta: INPI-Pact and Lemhannas.
Ismanto, Nur. 1994. 'Penanganan Kejahatan di Indonesia Dalam Perspektif HAM'. *Kawah* No. 3 36–9.
—— 1995. 'Pembebasan Tanah dan Perlindungan Hukum'. In U. Hariadi and Masruchah (eds). *Tanah, Rakyat dan Demokrasi*. Yogyakarta: Forum LSM/LPSM DIY.
Ismawan, Bambang. 1985. 'Pendidikan yang Diperlukan untuk Pengembangan Pedesaan'. In P. Hagul (ed.). *Pembangunan Desa dan Lembaga Swadaya Masyakat*. Jakarta: Rajawali Press.
Jackelen, Henry L. 1989. 'Banking on the Informal Sector'. In J. Levitsky (ed.). *Microenterprises in Developing Countries*. London: Intermediate Technology Publications.
Jackson, Karl D. 1978. 'Bureaucratic Polity: A Theoretical Framework for the Analysis of Power and Communications in Indonesia'. In K. D. Jackson and L. W. Pye (eds). *Political Power and Communications in Indonesia*. Berkeley: University of California Press.
Jain, Laxmi C. 1991. 'NGOs and Government: Forever Different, Forever at Odds'. *Lok Niti: the Journal of the Asian NGO Coalition* 7(2) 19–22.
James, Estelle. 1983. 'How Non-Profits Grow: A Model'. *Journal of Policy Analysis and Management* 2(3) 350–66.
Jamhari. 1999. 'Islamic Political Parties: Threats or Prospects?' In Geoff Forrester (ed.). *Post-Suharto Indonesia: Renewal or Chaos?* Singapore: Institute of Southeast Asian Studies.
Jay, Robert. 1963. *Religion and Politics in Rural Central Java*. New Haven: Yale University Press.
—— 1969. *Javanese Villagers*. Cambridge: MIT Press.
Jayawardena, K. 1986. *Feminism and Nationalism in the Third World*. London: Zed Books.
Jemadu, Aleksius. 1992. *Peranan LSM Dalam Pembangunan: Studi Kasus Bina Swadaya Jakarta*. M. A. thesis. Department of Social and Political Sciences. University of Indonesia. Jakarta.

Johnson, Chalmers. 1966. *Revolutionary Change*. Boston: Little Brown.
Johnson, Hazel. 1992. 'Women's Empowerment and Public Action: Experiences From Latin America'. In M. Wuyts, M. Mackintosh and T. Hewitt (eds). *Development Policy and Public Action*. Oxford: Oxford University Press.
Johnson, Mary. 1990. 'Non-Government Organisations at the Crossroads in Indonesia'. In Robert C. Rice (ed.). *Indonesian Economic Development: Approaches, Technology, Small-scale Textiles, Urban Infrastructure and NGOs*. Melbourne: Centre for Southeast Asian Studies, Monash University.
Jorgensen, Lars. 1996. 'What Are NGOs Doing in Civil Society?'. In A. Clayton (ed.). *NGOs, Civil Society and the State: Building Democracy in Transitional Societies*. Oxford: INTRAC.
Judd, Mary. 1987. *Village Kader Study*. Unpublished Report. Washington DC: USAID.
Juliantara, Dadang. 1994. 'Kekerasan Dalam Pemogokan Buruh'. *Kawah* 3(1) 3–7.
—— 1995. 'Sengketa Agraria, Modal dan Transformasi'. In U. Hariadi and Masruchah (eds). *Tanah, Rakyat dan Demokrasi*. Yogyakarta: Forum LSM/LPSM DIY.
—— 1996a. 'Developing Size Without Force: Notes on Forum's Experience'. In Rustam Ibrahim (ed.). *The Indonesian NGO Agenda: Toward the Year 2000*. Jakarta: LP3ES.
—— 1996b. 'Politik Perijinan, Gerakan Massa dan Demokrasi'. In H. Salim and A. J. Wijaya (eds). *Demokrasi Dalam Pasungan: Politik Perijinan di Indonesia*. Yogyakarta: Forum LSM/LPSM.
—— 1997. *LSM, Masyarakat Sipil dan Transformasi Sosial*. Unpublished Paper. Yogyakarta: Yayasan Lapera Indonesia.
Kabeer, Naila. 1994. *Reversed Realities: Gender Hierarchies in Development Thought*. London: Verso.
Kadir, Siti A. 1995. 'Amah: Buruh Pabrik Citra Plastik'. In M. Singarimbun and S. Sairin (eds). *Lika-Liku Kehidupan Buruh Perempuan*. Yogyakarta: Pustaka Pelajar and Yasanti.
Kahn, Joel S. 1982. 'Ideology and Social Structure in Indonesia'. In B. Anderson and A. Kahin (eds). *Interpreting Indonesian Politics: Thirteen Contributions to the Debate*. Interim Report Series No. 62. Cornell Modern Indonesia Project. Cornell University, Ithaca.
Kalibonso, Rita S. 1999. 'The Gender Perspective: a Key to Democracy in Indonesia'. In A. Budiman *et al.* (eds). *Reformasi: Crisis and Change in Indonesia*. Monash Papers on Southeast Asia No.50. Monash Asia Institute. Monash University, Clayton.
Kammen, Douglas. 2001. '*Pilkades*: Democracy, Village Elections and Protest in Indonesia'. *Renai* I(2) 42–64.
Kana, Nico. 2001. 'Strategi Pengelolaan Persaingan Politik Elit Desa di Wilayah Kecamatan Suruh: Kasus Pemilihan Kepala Desa'. *Renai* I(2) 5–25.
Kandil, Amani. 1993. *Defining the Non-Profit Sector: Egypt*. Working Paper No. 10. The Johns Hopkins Comparative Non-Profit Sector Project. The Johns Hopkins University, Baltimore.
Kantor Kelurahan Desa Donorojo. 1997. *Monografi Desa Tahun 1996/1997*. Donorojo: Balai Desa.
—— 2000. *Monografi Desa Tahun 1999/2000*. Donorojo: Balai Desa.
Kantor Kelurahan Desa Wedi. 1997. *Monografi Desa Tahun 1997*. Wedi: Balai Desa.
—— 2000. *Monografi Desa Tahun 1999*. Wedi: Balai Desa.
Kantor Wilayah Departemen Agama Propinsi Jawa Tengah. 1997. *Rekapitulasi Data Rumah Ibadah di Wilayah Propinsi Jawa Tengah*. Semarang: Kanwil Depag Propinsi Jateng.
Karebet, Bani M. 1986. 'Beberapa Catatan dari Seminar Pembentukan LSM'. *Bulletin Bina Desa* 12(54) 30–2.

Karl, Marilee. 1995. *Women and Development: Participation and Decision Making*. London: Zed Books.
Karlsen, Jan I. 1991. 'Action Research as Method: Reflections from a Programme for Developing Methods and Competence'. In W. F. Whyte (ed.). *Participatory Action Research*. London: Sage.
Kartjono. 1986. *Jaringan Kerjasama Antar LSM*. Unpublished paper. Jakarta: Sekretariat Bina Desa.
—— 1988. 'Demokrasi di Tingkat Grassroots: Peranan LSM'. *Prisma* 17(6) 28–39.
—— 1996. 'Bina Desa's Experience in People's Empowerment'. In Rustam Ibrahim (ed.). *The Indonesan NGO Agenda: Toward the Year 2000*. Jakarta: LP3ES.
Kartodirdjo, Sartono. 1973. *Protest Movement in Rural Java: a Study of Agrarian Unrest in the Nineteenth and Early Twentieth Centuries*. Kuala Lumpur: Oxford University Press.
—— 1981. *The Pedicab In Yogyakarta*. Yogyakarta: Gadjah Mada University Press.
—— 1988. 'Lembaga Swadaya Masyarakat: Tinjauan Singkat'. *Prisma* 17(1) 97–101.
Kessler, Richard J. 1989. *Rebellion and Repression in the Philippines*. New Haven: Yale University Press.
Kimmel, Michael S. 1990. *Revolution: A Sociological Interpretation*. Cambridge: Polity Press.
King, Dwight Y. 1982. 'Indonesia's New Order as a Bureaucratic Polity, a Neopatrimonial Regime or Bureaucratic-Authoritarian Regime: What Difference Does It Make?' In B. Anderson and A. Kahin (eds). *Interpreting Indonesian Politics: Thirteen Contributions to the Debate*. Interim Report Series No. 62. Cornell Modern Indonesia Project, Cornell University, Ithaca.
Koentjaraningrat. 1961. *Some Social-Anthropological Observations on Gotong Royong Practices in Two Villages of Central Java*. Southeast Asia Programme. Cornell University, Ithaca.
—— 1985. *Javanese Culture*. Singapore: Oxford University Press.
Koning, Juliette. 1997. *Generations of Change: A Javanese in the 1990s*. Ph.D. thesis. University of Amsterdam.
Korten, David C. 1984. 'Strategic Organisation for People-Centered Development'. *Public Administration Review* 44(4) 341–52.
—— 1987. 'Third Generation NGO Strategies: A Key to People-Centered Development'. *World Development* 15(Suppl.) 145–59.
—— 1990. *Getting to the 21st Century: Voluntary Action and the Global Agenda*. West Hartford: Kumarian Press.
Korten, D. C. and Quizon, A. B. 1991. 'In Search of Common Ground'. *Lok Niti: the Journal of the Asian NGO Coalition* 7(2) 23–8.
Kothari, Rajni. 1993. 'Masses, Classes and the State'. In P. Wignaraja (ed.). *New Social Movements in the South: Empowering the People*. London: Zed Books.
Koyano, Shogo. 1996. 'Struktur dan Perubahan Kota Menengah Yogyakarta'. In S. Koyano (ed.). *Pengkajian Tentang Urbanisasi di Asia Tenggara*. Yogyakarta: Gadjah Mada University Press.
Krisnawati, T. and Utrech, A. 1992. 'Women's Economic Mediation: The Case of Female Petty-Traders in Northwest Lombok'. In S. van Bemmelen *et al.* (eds). *Women and Mediation in Indonesia*. Leiden: KITLV Press.
Kuroyanagi, Haruo. 1990. 'Research Note on the Social and Economic Life of Village People in Central Java: A Case Study of Two Villages in Yogyakarta Special Region'. *The Indonesian Journal of Geography* 20(60) 41–56.

Kushadiwijaya, Hari P. 1985. 'Masalah Kesehatan di Pedesaan dan Strategi Penanganannya'. In P. Hagul (ed.). *Pembangunan Desa dan Lembaga Swadaya Masyarakat*. Jakarta: Rajawali.
Kusumah, Mulyana. 1996. 'Masalah Perijinan Kegiatan Sosial Politik'. In H. S. Salim and A. J. Wijaya (eds). *Demokrasi Dalam Pasungan: Politik Perijinan di Indonesia*. Yogyakarta: Forum LSM/LPSM DIY.
Kusumohadi, Meth. *et al.* 1997. *Globalisasi dan NGO*. Yogyakarta: USC/Yayasan Satunama.
Kusyuniati. 1990. *Membangun Kesadaran Melalui Arisan*. Unpublished paper. Yogyakarta: Yasanti.
Landim, Leilah. 1993. 'Brazilian Crossroads: People's Groups, Walls and Bridges'. In P. Wignaraja (ed.). *New Social Movement in the South: Empowering the People*. London: Zed Books.
Lane, Max. 1991. *Openness: Political Discontent and Succession in Indonesia, 1989–1991*. Australia-Asia Papers No. 56, Centre of the Study of Australia-Asia Relations, Griffith University, Brisbane.
—— 1999. 'Mass Politics and Political Change in Indonesia'. In A. Budiman *et al.* (eds). *Reformasi: Crisis and Change in Indonesia*. Monash Papers on Southeast Asia No. 50. Monash Asia Institute. Monash University, Clayton.
Laomang, R. and Assariroh, N. 1995. 'Girimulyo: Daerah Penelitian'. In M. Singarimbun and S. Sairin (eds). *Lika-Liku Kehidupan Buruh Perempuan*. Yogyakarta: Pustaka Pelajar and Yasanti.
Lay, Cornelis. 1996. 'Birokrasi, Korupsi dan Pengawasan'. *Kawah* 5(5) 21–9.
Leach, E. 1976. *Culture and Communication*. Cambridge: Cambridge University Press.
Leftwich, A. (ed.). 1984. *What is Politics?* Oxford: Basil Blackwell.
—— 1993. 'State of Underdevelopment: the Third World State in Theoretical Perspective'. *Journal of Theoretical Politics* 6(1) 55–74.
—— 1995. 'Bringing Politics Back In: Towards a Model of the Developmental State'. *The Journal of Development Studies* 31(3) 400–27.
Legowo, T. A. 1997. 'Riots and the 1997/98 Draft of State Budget'. *The Indonesian Quarterly* 25(2) 102–9.
Lehmann, David. 1990. *Democracy and Development in Latin America: Economics, Politics and Religion in the Postwar Period*. Cambridge: Polity Press.
Lehmann, D. and Bebbington, A. 1996. *NGOs, the State and the Development Process: Dilemma of Institutionalisation*. Working Paper. Centre of Latin American Studies, Cambridge University.
Lende, Kari Anderson. 1995. 'Coalition-Building in Diversity'. In R. Morse, A. Rahman and K. L. Johnson (eds). *Grassroots Horizons: Connecting Participatory Development Initiatives East and West*. London: Intermediate Technology Publications.
Lev, Daniel. 1966. *Transition to Guided Democracy: Indonesian Politics, 1957–1959*. Cornell Modern Indonesia Project. Cornell University, Ithaca.
—— 1987. *Legal Aid in Indonesia*. Working Paper No. 44, Centre of Southeast Asian Studies, Monash University, Melbourne, Australia.
—— 1990. 'Intermediate Classes and Change in Indonesia: Some Initial Reflections'. In R. Tanter and K. Young (eds). *The Politics of Middle-class Indonesia*. Monash Paper on Southeast Asia No. 19. Centre for Southeast Asian Studies, Monash University, Clayton.
—— 1993. 'Social Movements, Constitutionalism and Human Rights: Comments from the Malaysian and Indonesian Experience'. In S. Greenberg *et al.* (eds). *Constitutionalism and Democracy: Transitions in the Contemporary World*. Oxford: Oxford University Press.

Lev, Daniel. 1994. 'On the Fall of the Parliamentary System'. In D. Bourchier and J. D. Legge (eds). *Democracy in Indonesia, 1950s and 1990s*. Monash Paper on Southeast Asia No. 31. Centre for Southeast Asian Studies. Monash University, Clayton.
Lewis, David J. 1993. 'NGO-Government Interaction in Bangladesh: Overview'. In J. Farrington *et al*. *NGOs and the State in Asia: Rethinking Roles in Sustainable Agricultural Development*. London: Routledge.
—— 1997. 'NGOs, Donors and the State in Bangladesh'. In J. L. Fernando and A. W. Heston (eds). *The Role of NGOs: Charity and Empowerment*. Philadephia: The Annals of the American Academy of Political and Social Science.
Liddle, R. William. 1978. 'Participation and Political Parties'. In K. D. Jackson and L. W. Pye (eds). *Political Power and Communications in Indonesia*. Berkeley: University of California Press.
—— 1985. 'Suharto's Indonesia: Personal Rule and Political Institutions'. *Pacific Affairs* 58(1) 68–90.
—— 1987. 'The Politics of Shared Growth: Some Indonesian Cases'. *Comparative Politics* 19(2) 127–46.
—— 1993. 'Politics 1992–1993: Six Term Adjustments in the Ruling Formula'. In C. Manning and J. Hardjono (eds). *Indonesia Assessment 1993: Labour Sharing in the Benefits of Growth?* Political and Social Change Monograph No. 20. Research School of Pacific and Asian Studies. Australian National University, Canberra.
—— 1997. 'Improving Political Cultural Change: Three Indonesian Cases'. In J. Schiller and B. Schiller (eds). *Imagining Indonesia: Cultural Politics and Political Culture*. Athens: Centre for International Studies, Ohio University.
—— 1999. 'Indonesia's Democratic Opening'. *Government and Opposition* 34(1) 94–116.
Lincoln, Y. S. and Guba, E. G. 1985. *Naturalistic Inquiry*. Beverly Hills, CA: Sage.
Linz, Juan. 1975. 'Totalitarian and Authoritarian Regimes' In F. Greenstein and N. W. Polsby (eds). *Handbook of Political Science Vol. 3*. Reading, MA: Addison-Wesley.
Lofland, J. 1996. *Social Movement Organisations: Guide to Research on Insurgent Realities*. New York: Aldine de Gay Gruyter.
Long, N. and van der Ploeg, J. D. 1994. 'Heterogeneity, Actor and Structure: Towards A Reconstitution of the Concept of Structure'. In D. Booth (ed.). *Rethinking Social Development: Theory, Research and Practice*. London: Longman.
Lont, H. B. 1997. *Social Security and Outside Involvement in Financial Self-Help Organisations in Yogyakarta*. A paper for the workshop on Social Security and Social Policy in Indonesia. Yogyakarta, 6–8 August.
Lowa, Anton. 1985. 'Kesan dan Pengalaman dalam Melaksanakan Proyek-Proyek Air Minum: Catatan Seorang Petugas Lapangan'. In P. Hagul (ed.). *Pembangunan Desa dan Lembaga Swadaya Masyarakat*. Jakarta: Rajawali.
Lucas, Anton and Bachriadi, Dianto. 2001. 'Who Owns the Forests? Forestry Land Reform Agenda in Wonosobo District Central Java'. Unpublished paper.
Lubis, T. M. 1993. *In Search of Human Rights: Legal-Political Dilemmas of Indonesia's New Order, 1966–1990*. Jakarta: Gramedia.
MacClelland, D. C. 1961. *The Achieving Society*. New York: D. van Nostrad.
Mackie, Jamie. 1990. 'Property and Power in Indonesia'. In R. Tanter and K. Young (eds). *The Politics of Middle-Class Indonesia*. Monash Paper on Southeast Asia No. 19. Centre for Southeast Asian Studies. Monash University, Clayton.
—— 1994. 'Inevitable or Unavoidable? Interpretations of the Collapse of Parliamentary Democracy'. In D. Bourchier and J. D. Legge (eds). *Democracy in Indonesia, 1950s and*

*1990s*. Monash Paper on Southeast Asia No. 31. Centre for Southeast Asian Studies. Monash University, Clayton.

Mackie, J. and MacIntyre, A. 1994. 'Politics'. In H. Hill (ed.). *Indonesia's New Order: the Dynamics of Socio-economic Transformation*. Honolulu: University of Hawaii Press.

MacIntyre, Andrew. 1990. *Business and Politics in Indonesia*. Sydney: Allen and Unwin.

Maclure, R. and Bassey, M. 1991. 'Participatory Action Research in Togo: An Inquiry into Maize Storage Systems'. In W. F. Whyte (ed.). *Participatory Action Research*. London: Sage.

MacPherson, C. B. 1989. 'Do We Need a Theory of the State?'. In G. Duncan (ed.). *Democracy and the Capitalist State*. Cambridge: Cambridge University Press.

Madsen, S. T. 1997. 'Between People and the State: NGOs as Troubleshooters and Innovators'. In S. Linberg and A. Sverrison (eds). *Social Movements in Development: The Challenge of Globalisation and Democratisation*. London: MacMillan.

Mahasin, Aswab. 1996. 'Empowering Civil Society: The NGO Agenda'. In Rustam Ibrahim (ed.). *The Indonesian NGO Agenda: Toward the Year 2000*. Jakarta: LP3ES.

Mahmudi, Ahmad et al. 1994. *Laporan Workshop Pendidikan Politik Untuk Aktivis Organisasi Non-Pemerintah, Kaliurang (Yogyakarta) 30 Maret–1 April 1994*. Solo: Gita Pertiwi.

Mainwaring, Scott. 1989. 'Grassroots Popular Movements and the Struggle for Democracy: Nova Iguacu'. In Alfred Stepan (ed.). *Democratizing Brazil: Problems of Transition and Consolidation*. Oxford: Oxford University Press.

Mangunwijaya, J. B. 1997. *Sejarah Perkembangan Yayasan Dinamika Edukasi Dasar*. Yogyakarta: Yayasan Dinamika Edukasi Dasar.

Manning, C. 1987. 'Rural Economic Change and Labour Mobility: A Case Study from West Java'. *Bulletin of Indonesian Economic Studies* 23(3) 52–79.

Martokoesoemo, S. B. 1994. 'Small-scale Finance: Lessons from Indonesia'. In H. McLeod (ed.). *Indonesia Assessment 1994: Finance as a Key Sector in Indonesia's Development*. Research School of Pacific and Asian Studies. Australian National University, Canberra.

Maryono, Erfan. 1996. 'Developing Small-scale Enterprise: Reflections on the NGOs Experience'. In Rustam Ibrahim (ed.). *The Indonesian NGO Agenda: Toward the Year 2000*. Jakarta: LP3ES.

Marzouk, Mohsen. 1997. 'The Associative Phenomenon in the Arab World: Engine for Democratization or Witness to the Crisis?'. In M. Edwards and D. Hulme (eds). *NGOs, States and Donors: Too Close for Comfort?* London: MacMillan.

Maurer, Jean-Luc. 1991. 'Beyond Sawah: Economic Diversification in Four Bantul Villages, 1972–1987'. In P. Alexander, P. Boomgard and B. White (eds). *In the Shadow of Agriculture: Non-farm Activities in the Javanese Economy, Past and Present*. Amsterdam: Royal Tropical Institute.

May, Brian. 1978. *The Indonesian Tragedy*. London: Routledge and Kegan Paul.

Mayer, Judith. 1996. 'Environmental Organising in Indonesia: The Search for a New Order'. In R. D. Lipschutz and J. Mayer (eds). *Global Civil Society and Global Environmental Governance*. Albany: State University of New York Press.

McCarthy, John D. and Zald, Mayer. 1977. 'Resource Mobilization and Social Movements'. *American Journal of Sociology* 82, 1212–41.

McClelland, David. 1961. *The Achieving Society*. Princeton: Van Nostrand.

McVey, Ruth T. 1996. 'Building Behemoth: Indonesian Constructions of the Nation-State'. In D. Lev and R. T. McVey (eds). *Making Indonesia*. South East Asia Programme. Cornell University, Ithaca.

Melucci, Alberto. 1980. 'The New Social Movements: a Theoretical Approach'. *Social Science Information* 19(2) 199–226.

Melucci, Alberto. 1989. *Nomads of The Present: Social Movements and Individual Needs in Contemporary Society*. London: Hutchinson Radius.
—— 1995. 'The Process of Collective Identity'. In H. Johnston and B. Klandermans (eds). *Social Movements and Culture*. London: University College London Press.
Miclat-Teves, A. G. and Lewis, D. J. 1993. 'NGO-Government Interaction in the Philippines: Overview'. In J. Farrington *et al. NGOs and the State in Asia: Rethinking Roles in Sustainable Agricultural Development*. London: Routledge.
Migdal, Joel S. 1988. *Strong Societies and Weak States: State-Society Relations in the Third World*. Princeton: Princeton University Press.
—— 1994. 'The State in Society: An Approach to Struggles for Domination'. In J. S. Migdal *et al.* (eds). *State Power and Social Forces: Domination and Transformation in the Third World*. Cambridge: Cambridge University Press.
Milliband, Ralph. 1969. *The State in Capitalist Society*. New York: Basic Books.
Moaddel, Mansoor. 1995. 'Ideology as Episodic Discourse: the Case of Iranian Revolution'. In S. Lyman (ed.). *Social Movements: Critiques, Concepts, Case Studies*. London: MacMillan.
Moll, H. A. J. and Palallo, K. 1994. 'The Cooperative Rural Finance Programme in Indonesia'. In R. H. McLeod (ed.). *Indonesia Assessment 1994: Finance as a Key Sector in Indonesia Development*. Research School of Pacific and Asian Studies. Australian National University, Canberra.
Molyneaux, M. 1985. 'Mobilisation Without Emancipation? Women's Interests, State and Revolution in Nicaragua'. *Feminist Studies* 11(2) 227–54.
Moore, M. 1993. 'Good Government?: Introduction'. *IDS Bulletin* 24(1) 1–6.
Mortimer, Rex. 1974. *Indonesian Communism Under Sukarno: Ideology and Politics, 1959–1965*. Ithaca: Cornell University Press.
—— 1982. 'Class, Social Cleavage and Indonesian Communism'. In B. Anderson and A. Kahin (eds). *Interpreting Indonesian Politics: Thirteen Contributions to the Debate*. Interim Report Series No. 62. Cornell Modern Indonesia Project, Cornell University, Ithaca.
Moser, Caroline. 1993. *Gender Planning and Development: Theory, Practice and Training*. London: Routledge.
Mouzelis, Nicos. 1994. 'The State in Late Development: Historical and Comparative Perspectives'. In D. Booth (ed.). *Rethinking Social Development: Theory, Research and Practice*. London: Longman.
Mulder, Niels. 1994. 'The Ideology of Javanese-Indonesian Leadership'. In H. Antlov and S. Cederoth (eds). *Leadership in Java: Gentle Hints, Authoritarian Rule*. Surrey: Curzon Press.
Munawar-Rahman, Budhy. 1994. 'Kesatuan Transendental Dalam Teologi: Perspektif Islam Tentang Kesatuan Agama-agama'. In INTERFIDEI. *Dialog: Kritik dan Identitas Agama*. Yogyakarta: INTERFIDEI.
Mundayat, Aris A. 1994. 'Hirarki Sosial dan Wacana Ancaman'. *Kawah* 3(1) 39–48.
Munir. 1996. 'Buruh, Negara dan Kebebasan Berserikat'. In H. S. Salim and A. J. Wijaya (eds). *Demokrasi Dalam Pasungan: Politik Perijinan di Indonesia*. Yogyakarta: Forum LSM/LPSM DIY.
Nadia, Ita F. 1996. 'The Political Role of Women's NGOs'. In Rustam Ibrahim (ed.). *The Indonesian NGO Agenda: Toward the Year 2000*. Jakarta: LP3ES.
Nandika, Mutia. 2001. *Implementasi Kebijakan Bank Dunia dalam Menanggulangi Kemiskinan di Indonesia Melalui Program Jaringan Pengaman Sosial*. B.A. thesis. Parahyangan Catholic University, Bandung, Indonesia.
Nakamura, Mitsuo. 1983. *The Crescent Arises Over the Banyan Tree*. Yogyakarta: Gadjah Mada University Press.

Nasikun, J. 1995. 'Perkembangan Konflik Pertanahan di Indonesia dalam Era Pembangunan'. In U. Hariadi and Masruchah (eds). *Tanah, Rakyat dan Demokrasi*. Yogyakarta: Forum LSM/LPSM DIY.

Nasution, Adnan Buyung. 1981. *Bantuan Hukum di Indonesia*. Jakarta: LP3ES.

Nelson, N. and Wright, S. 1995. 'Participation and Power'. In N. Nelson and S. Wright (eds). *Power and Participatory Development: Theory and Practice*. London: Intermediate Technology Publication.

Nugent, Jeffrey. 1995. 'Between State, markets and Households: A Neo-institutional Analysis of Local Organisations and Institutions'. In de Janvry et al. (eds). *State, Market and Civil Organisations: New Theories, New Practices and Their Implications for Rural Development*. London: MacMillan.

Nusantara, A. H. G. 1986. *Peranan Organisasi Swadaya Masyarakat Dalam Kerjasama Pembangunan Internasional*. A paper for the Yogyakarta NGO Seminar, Kaliurang, 25 November.

—— 1996. 'The Experience of Human Rights Advocacy'. In Rustam Ibrahim (ed.). *The Indonesian NGO Agenda: Toward the Year 2000*. Jakarta: LP3ES.

O'Donnell, Guillermo. 1978. *Modernization and Bureaucratic-Authoritarianism: Studies in South American Politics*. Berkeley: Institute of International Studies, University of California.

O'Donnell, G. and Schmitter, P. C. 1986. *Transitions from Authoritarian Rule: Tentative Conclusions About Uncertain Democracies*. Baltimore: The Johns Hopkins University Press.

Oepen, Manfred. 1988. 'Pesantren and NGOs in Rural Development: Cooperation and Controversies'. In M. Oepen and W. Karcher (eds). *The Impact of Pesantren in Education and Community Development in Indonesia*. Jakarta: Fredrich-Neumann Stifftung and P3M.

Offe, Claus. 1987. 'Challenging the Boudaries of Institutional Policies: Social Movements Since the 1960s'. In C. Maier (ed.). *Changing Boundaries of the Political*. Cambridge: Cambridge University Press.

Onghokham. 1994. 'Pluralisme Agama Dalam Perspektif Sejarah'. In INTERFIDEI. *Dialog: Kritik dan Identitas Agama*. Yogyakarta: INTERFIDEI.

Oster, Sharon M. 1994. *Management of Non-Profit Organisations*. Brookfield, USA: Dartmouth.

Pangaribuan, Luhut. 1996. 'Hukum dan Politik Perijinan di Indonesia'. In H. S. Salim and A. J. Wijaya (eds). *Demokrasi Dalam Pasungan: Politik Perijinan di Indonesia*. Yogyakarta: Forum LSM/LPSM DIY.

Papanek, G. 1985. 'Agricultural Income Distribution and Employment in the 1970s'. *Bulletin of Indonesian Economic Studies* 21(2) 24–50.

Pascual, Dette. 1992. 'Building Democratic Culture in the Philippines'. In L. Diamond (ed.). *The Democratic Revolution: Struggles for Freedom and Pluralism in the Developing World*. New York: Freedom House.

Pearce, Jenny. 1993. 'NGOs and Social Change: Agents or Facilitators?' *Development in Practice* 3(3) 222–27.

—— 1997. 'Between Co-option and Irrelevance? Latin American NGOs in the 1990s'. In D. Hulme and M. Edwards (eds). *NGOs, States and Donors: Too Close for Comfort?* London: MacMillan.

Perera, Jehan. 1997. 'In Unequal Dialogue with Donors: The Experience of the Sarvodaya Shramadana Movement'. In M. Edwards and D. Hulme (eds). *NGOs, States and Donors: Too Close for Comfort?* London: MacMillan.

Pinney, Andrew. 1983. 'Partners in Development?: Government and NGOs in Indonesia'. *Prisma* 12(2) 33–45.
Piven, F. F. and Cloward, R. A. 1977. *Poor People's Movements: Why They Succeed, How They Fail*. New York: Pantheon Books.
Plotke, David. 1995. 'What's So New About New Social Movements?'. In S. M. Lyman (ed.). *Social Movements: Critiques, Concepts, Case Studies*. London: MacMillan.
Poerwokoesoemo, S. 1984. *Daerah Istimewa Yogyakarta*. Yogyakarta: Gadjah Mada University Press.
Postel-Coster, Els. 1993. 'The Instrumentality of Indonesia's Policy Towards Women'. In J. P. Dirkse, F. Husken and M. Rutten (eds). *Indonesia's Experiences Under the New Order*. Leiden: KITLV Press.
Prajitno, Tegoeh. 1986. 'Mempertahankan Idealisme LSM-LPSM'. *Bulletin Bina Desa* 11(53) 1–3.
Prastiwi, Etty. 1994. 'Gender dan Tenaga Kerja Wanita di Sektor Informal'. *Bergetar* No. 114 10–15.
Prijono, O. S. 1992. 'Voluntarism and Voluntary Organisations in Indonesia'. In V. A. Hodgkinson *et al.* (eds). *The Non-profit Sector in the Global Community: Voices from Many Nations*. San Francisco: Jossey-Bass Publisher.
—— 1996. 'Organisasi Non-Pemerintah: Peran dan Pemberdayaannya'. In O. S. Prijono and A. M. W. Pranarka (eds). *Pemberdayaan: Konsep, Kebijaksanaan dan Implementasi*. Jakarta: Centre for Strategic and International Studies.
Rahardi, F. 1997. 'Mengapa Wong Cilik Perlu Diberdayakan?'. *Bulletin Bina Swadaya* 5(10) 25–27.
Rahardjo, Dawam. 1985. 'Masalah Komunikasi di Pedesaan'. In P. Hagul (ed.). *Pembangunan Desa dan Lembaga Swadaya Masyarakat*. Jakarta: Rajawali Press.
—— 1988. 'Dokter Soetomo: Pelopor LSM?'. *Prisma* 17(7) 11–13.
Rahman, Anizur. 1993. *People's Self-Development: Perspectives on Participatory Action Research*. London: Zed Books.
—— 1995. 'Towards an Alternative Development Paradigm'. In R. Morse, A. Rahman and K. L. Johnson (eds). *Grassroots Horizons: Connecting Participatory Development Initiatives East and West*. London: Intermediate Technology Publications.
Rais, Amien. 1999. 'Islam and Politics in Contemporary Indonesia'. In Geoff Forrester (ed.). *Post-Suharto Indonesia: Renewal or Chaos?* Singapore: Institute of Southeast Asian Studies.
Ramage, Douglas. 1995. *Politics in Indonesia: Democracy, Islam and the Ideology of Tolerance*. London: Routledge.
—— 1996. 'Indonesia at 50: Islam, Nationalism and Democracy?'. In Daljit Singh and Liak Teng Kiat (eds). *Southeast Asian Affairs 1996*. Singapore: Institute of Southeast Asian Studies.
Rao, A. *et al.* (eds). 1991. *Gender Training and Development Planning: Learning from Experience*. New York: The Population Council.
Rasyid, M. R. 1995. 'Indonesia: Preparing for Post-Suharto Rule and Its Impact on the Democratisation Process'. In Daljit Singh (ed.). *Southeast Asian Affairs 1995*. Singapore: Institute of Southeast Asian Studies.
Ravallion, M. 1988. 'Inpres and Inequality: A Distributional Perspective on the Centre's Regional Disbursement'. *Bulletin of Indonesian Economic Studies* 24(3) 53–73.
Reeve, David. 1985. *Golkar of Indonesia: an Alternative to the Party System*. Singapore: Oxford University Press.
Ricklefs, Merle C. 1981. *A History of Modern Indonesia*. London: MacMillan.

Riddell, Roger. 1990. *Judging Success: Evaluating Approaches to Alleviating Poverty in Developing Countries*. Working Paper No. 37. London: Overseas Development Institute.

Riddell, R. and Robinson, M. 1996. *NGOs and Rural Poverty Alleviation*. Oxford: Oxford University Press.

Riggs, Frederick W. 1966. *Thailand: The Modernisation of a Bureaucratic Polity*. Honolulu: University of Hawaii Press.

Rini, Kartika. 1995. 'Sudarsi: Buruh Pabrik Garmen Busana Tama'. In M. Singarimbun and S. Sairin (eds). *Lika-Liku Kehidupan Buruh Perempuan*. Yogyakarta: Pustaka Pelajar and Yasanti.

Robinson, Mark. 1992. 'NGOs and Rural Poverty-alleviation: Implications for Scaling-Up'. In M. Edwards and D. Hulme (eds). *Making a Difference: NGOs and Development in a Changing World*. London: Earthscan.

—— 1993. 'Governance, Democracy and Conditionality: NGOs and the New Policy Agenda'. In A. Clayton (ed.). *Governance, Democracy and Conditionality: What Role for NGOs?* Oxford: INTRAC.

Robinson, Mark, Farrington, J. and Satish, S. 1993. 'NGO-Government Interaction in India'. In J. Farrington et al. *NGOs and the State in Asia: Rethinking Roles in Sustainable Agricultural Development*. London: Routledge.

Robison, Richard. 1982. 'Culture, Politics and Economy in the Political History of the New Order'. In B. Anderson and A. Kahin (eds). *Interpreting Indonesian Politics: Thirteen Contributions to the Debate*. Interim Report Series No. 62. Cornell Modern Indonesia Project, Cornell University, Ithaca.

—— 1985. 'Class, Capital and the State in New Order Indonesia'. In R. Higgott and R. Robison (eds). *Southeast Asia: Essays in the Political Economy of Structural Change*. London: Routledge and Kegan Paul.

—— 1988. 'Authoritarian States, Capital-Owning Classes and the Politics of Newly Industrialising Countries: the Case of Indonesia'. *World Politics* 41(1) 52–74.

—— 1993. 'Indonesia: Tensions in State and Regime'. In R. Robison, K. Hewison and G. Rodan (eds). *Southeast Asia in the 1990s: Authoritarianism, Democracy and Capitalism*. Sydney: Allen and Unwin.

Rocamora, Joel. 1995. 'Social Movements and Democratisation in the Philippines'. In J. Hippler (ed.). *The Democratisation and Disempowerment: Problems of Democracy in the Third World*. London: Pluto Press.

Roeloffs, Jan. 1989. *Small-Enterprise Development in Indonesia*. Eschborn, Germany: GTZ (German Technische Suzammen Arbeit).

Rose-Ackerman, Susan. 1994. 'Competition Between Non-profits and For-profits: Entry and Growth'. In Sharon M. Oster (ed.). *Management of Non-Profit Organisations*. Brookfield, USA: Dartmouth.

Rositaningrum. 1994. 'Atik: Potret Perempuan Kalah'. *Kawah* 3(2) 21–9.

Sahley, Caroline. 1995. *Strengthening the Capacity of NGOs: Cases of Small-Enterprise Development Agencies in Africa*. Oxford: INTRAC.

Salamon, L. M. and Anheier, H. K. 1996. *The Emerging Non-profit Sector: an Overview*. Manchester: Manchester University Press.

Salim, Emil. 1983. 'Common Aims, Different Approaches'. *Prisma* 12(2) 70–2.

Salim, Hairus and Wijaya, A. J. (eds). 1996. *Demokrasi Dalam Pasungan: Politik Perizinan di Indonesia*. Yogyakarta: Forum LSM/LPSM DIY.

Salim, Ziad. 1983. 'Non-Government Organisations and Politics'. *Prisma* 12(2) 64–9.

Samson, A. A. 1978. 'Conceptions of Politics, Power and Ideology in Contemporary Indonesia Islam'. In Karl D. Jackson and L. W. Pye (eds). *Political Power and Communications in Indonesia*. Berkeley: University of California Press.

Samudavanija, Chai-Anan. 1992. 'Promoting Democracy and Building Institutions in Thailand'. In L. Diamond (ed.). *The Democratic Revolution: Struggles for Freedom and Pluralism in the Developing World*. New York: Freedom House.

Sandee, H., *et al*. 1994. 'Promoting Small-Scale and Cottage Industries in Indonesia: An Impact Analysis for Central Java'. *Bulletin of Indonesian Economic Studies* 30(3) 115–42.

Sandee, H and Weijland, H. 1989. 'Rural Cottage Industry in Transition: The Roof Tile Industry in Boyolali, Central Java'. *Bulletin of Indonesian Economic Studies* 25(2) 79–98.

Sangkoyo, Hendro. 1999. 'Limits to Order: the Internal Logic of Instability in the Post-Suharto Era'. In Geoff Forrester (ed.). *Post-Suharto Indonesia: Renewal or Chaos?* Singapore: Institute of Southeast Asian Studies.

Santosa, Amir. 1993. 'Hope for Democratisation in 1993'. *The Indonesian Quarterly* 21(1) 3–6.

Santosa, Paulus H. 1986. *Rumah Sakit Tanpa Dinding: Kumpulan Tulisan*. Yogyakarta: UPKM/CD-Bethesda.

Sanyal, B. 1991. 'Antagonistic Cooperation: a Case Study of NGOs, Government and Donors' Relationships in Income-Generating Projects in Bangladesh'. *World Development* 19(10) 1367–79.

—— 1994. *Cooperative Autonomy: The Dialectic of State-NGO Relationships in Developing Countries*. Research Series No.100. Geneva: International Labour Organisation.

—— 1997. 'NGOs' Self-Defeating Quest for Autonomy'. In J. L. Fernando and A. W. Heston (eds). *The Role of NGOs: Charity and Empowerment*. Philadelphia: The Annals of the American Academy of Political and Social Science.

Saptari, Ratna. 1995. *Rural to the Factories: Continuity and Change in East Java's Kretek Cigarette Industry*. Ph.D. thesis. University of Amsterdam.

Saragih, Sebastian. 1995. *Membedah Perut LSM*. Jakarta: P. T. Penabar Swadaya.

SBPY (Sekretariat Bersama Perempuan Yogyakarta). 1993. *Laporan Diskusi Panel Aspek Keadilan Sosial Dalam Pemungutan Retribusi Pasar: Kasus di Yogyakarta*. Yogyakarta: SBPY.

—— 1994. *Laporan Akhir Program Kerja 1993*. Yogyakarta: SBPY.

—— 1995. *Laporan Kegiatan Pendampingan Perempuan di Sektor Informal*. Yogyakarta: SBPY.

—— 1996. *Laporan Kegiatan Pendampingan Pedagang Pasar*. Yogyakarta: SBPY.

—— 1997. *SBPY: Informasi Kegiatan dan Struktur Organisasi*. Yogyakarta: SBPY.

Schiller, Jim. 1990. 'State Formation in Jepara'. In A. Budiman (ed.). *The State and Society in Indonesia*. Monash Papers on Southeast Asia No. 22. Centre of Southeast Asian Studies. Monash University, Clayton.

—— 1996. *Developing Jepara in New Order Indonesia*. Clayton: Monash Asia Institute.

Schmitt, Hans. 1963. 'Post-Coloinal Politics: A Suggested Interpretation of the Indonesian Experience'. *The Australian Journal of Politics and History* 9(2) 41–59.

Schmitter, Phillipe. 1974. 'Still the Century of Corporatism?'. In F. Pike and T. Strich (eds). *The New Corporatism: Social Political Structures in the Iberian World*. Notre Dame: University of Notre Dame Press.

Schneider, Cathy. 1992. 'Radical Opposition Parties and Squatters Movements in Pinochet's Chile'. In S. Alvarez and A. Escobar (eds). *The Making of Social Movements in Latin America: Identity, Strategy and Democracy*. Boulder: Westview Press.

Schuurman, Frans J. 1993. 'Modernity, Post-Modernity and the New Social Movements'. In F. J. Schuurman (ed.). *Beyond the Impasse: New Directions in Development Theory*. London: Zed Books.

Schwartz, David C. 1970. *A Theory of Revolutionary Behaviour*. New York: The Free Press.

Schwarz, Adam. 1994. *A Nation in Waiting: Indonesian in the 1990s*. Sydney: Allen and Unwin.

Schweizer, Thomas. 1987. 'Agrarian Transformation? Rice Production in a Javanese Village'. *Bulletin of Indonesian Economic Studies* 23(2) 38–70.

Sen, Gita and Grown, Caren. 1987. *Development, Crisis and Alternative Visions: Third World's Women's Perspectives*. New York: Monthly Review Press.

Sethi, Harsh. 1993. 'Action Groups in the New Politics'. In P. Wignaraja (ed.). *New Social Movements in the South: Empowering the People*. London: Zed Books.

Sethna, A. and Shah, A. 1993. 'The Aga Khan Rural Support Project (AKRSP): Influencing Wasteland Development Policy'. In Farrington et al. (eds). *NGOs and the State in Asia: Rethinking Roles in Sustainable Agricultural Development*. London: Routledge.

Setiawan, Bambang. 1986. *Jaringan Kerjasama Antar LSM di Yogyakarta*. Unpublished paper. Yogyakarta: LP3Y (Lembaga Penelitian, Pendidikan dan Penerbitan Yogyakarta).

Setiawan, Bonie. 1996. 'Organisasi Non-Pemerintah dan Masyarakat Sipil'. *Prisma* 25(7) 35–48.

—— 2000. 'Analisis Terhadap Reposisi Peran ORNOP Pasca Rejim Suharto'. In INFID. *Perjuangan Demokrasi dan Masyarakat Sipil: Reposisi Peran ORNOP/LSM di Indonesia*. Jakarta: INFID.

Shiraisi, Takashi. 1990. *An Age in Motion: Popular Radicalism in Java, 1912–1926*. Ithaca: Cornell University Press.

Siahaan, Hotman. 1983. 'Structural Pressures and Peasant Mobilisation'. *Prisma* 12(3) 41–55.

Siebert, V. S. 1986. 'Banyak Batu, Sedikit Beras: Swasembada di Daerah Termiskin di Indonesia'. In P. Santosa (ed.). *Rumah Sakit Tanpa Dinding*. Yogyakarta: UPKM/CD-Bethesda.

Sills, D. L. (ed.). 1968. *International Encyclopaedia of the Social Sciences*. New York: MacMillan and the Free Press.

Simanjuntak, Marsilam. 1994. *Pandangan Negara Integralistik: Sumber, Unsur dan Riwayat Persiapan UUD 1945*. Jakarta: Graffiti Press.

Sinaga, Kastorius. 1992. *Beyond the Edge: An Assessment of Internal Limitations of Indonesian NGOs*. Working Paper No. 182, Sociology of Development Research Centre, University of Bielefeld, Germany.

—— 1994. *NGOs in Indonesia: A Study of the Role of Non-Governmental Organisations in the Development Process*. Bielefeld Studies on the Sociology of Development No. 159, University of Bielefeld, Germany.

Singarimbun, Masri. 1995. 'Kata Pengantar'. In M. Singarimbun and S. Sairin (eds). *Lika-Liku Kehidupan Buruh Perempuan*. Yogyakarta: Pustaka Pelajar and Yasanti.

Siregar, Amir Effendi. 1987. *The Communication Patterns Among Indonesian NGOs in Yogyakarta: a Pilot Study*. M.A. Thesis. University of Iowa, USA.

—— 1988. 'Pertumbuhan dan Pola Komunikasi LSM/LPSM'. *Prisma* 17(4) 24–51.

Skocpol, Theda. 1979. *States and Social Revolutions: A Comparative Analysis of France, Russia and China*. Cambridge: Cambridge University Press.
—— 1985. 'Bringing the State Back In: Strategies of Analysis in Current Research'. In P. B. Evans, D. Rueschemeyer and T. Skocpol (eds). *Bringing the State Back in*. Cambridge: Cambridge University Press.
Smillie, Ian. 1995. *The Alms Bazaar: Altruism Under Fire – Non-profit Organisations and International Development*. London: Intermediate Technology Publications.
Smith, Brian H. 1990. *More Than Altruism: The Politics of Private Foreign Aid*. Princeton: Princeton University Press.
Smyth, Ines. 1992. 'Indonesian Women as Economic Mediators: Some Comments on Concepts'. In S. van Bemmelen *et al*. (eds). *Women and Mediation in Indonesia*. Leiden: KITLV Press.
Smyth, I. and Grijns, M. 1999. 'Unjuk Rasa Atau Protes Sadar? Strategi Perlawanan Buruh Perempuan di Indonesia'. *Wacana* 1(1) 86–105.
Soemitro, Rachmat. 1993. *Hukum, Perseroan Terbatas, Yayasan dan Wakaf*. Bandung: Eresco.
Soetiyoso, Yos. 1993. *Kebijaksanaan yang Mengacu pada Kesejahteraan Masyarakat Bawah*. Unpublished Paper. Yogyakarta: SBPY.
Soetrisno, Loekman. 1995. 'Tanah dan Masa Depan Rakyat Indonesia di Pedesaan'. In U. Hariadi and Masruchah (eds). *Tanah, Rakyat dan Demokrasi*. Yogyakarta: Forum LSM/LPSM DIY.
—— 1999. 'Current Social and Political Conditions of Rural Indonesia'. In Geoff Forrester (ed.). *Post-Suharto Indonesia: Renewal or Chaos?* Singapore: Institute of Southeast Asian Studies.
Soewito. 1994. 'Upah, Kondisi Buruh dan Pemogokan'. *Kawah* 3(1) 17–20.
Stanley. 1990. *Seputar Kedung Ombo*. Jakarta: ELSAM.
Steinberg, David J. 1986. *The Philippines: a Singular and Plural Place*. Boulder, Colorado: Westview Press.
Steinberg, Richard. 1990. 'Profits and Incentive Compensation in Non-profit Firms'. *Non-profit Management and Leadership* 1(2) 137–51.
Stepan, Alfred. 1978. *The State and Society: Peru in Comparative Perspective*. Princetoon: Princeton University Press.
Sternbach *et al*. 1992. 'Feminism in Latin America: From Bogota to San Bernardo'. S. Alvarez and A. Escobar (eds). *The Making of Social Movements in Latin America: Identity, Strategy and Democracy*. Boulder: Westview Press.
Stirrat, R. L. and Henkel, H. 1997. 'The Development Gift: the Problem of Reciprocity in the NGO World'. In J. L. Fernando and A. W. Heston (eds). *The Role of NGOs: Charity and Empowerment*. Philadelphia: The Annals of the American Academy of Political and Social Science.
Stoker, Gerry. 1995. 'Introduction'. In G. Stoker and D. Marsh (eds). *Theory and Methods in Political Science*. London: MacMillan.
Stoler, Ann L. 1977. 'Class Structure and Female Autonomy in Rural Java'. *SIGNS* 3(1) 74–89.
—— 1985. *Capitalism and Confrontation in Sumatra's Plantation Belt, 1870–1979*. Ann Arbor: The University of Michigan Press.
Streeten, Paul. 1994. 'Poverty Concepts and Measurement'. In R. van der Hoeven and R. Anker (eds). *Poverty Monitoring: An International Concern*. London: MacMillan.
—— 1997. 'NGOs and Development'. In J. L. Fernando and A. W. Heston (eds). *The Role of NGOs: Charity and Empowerment*. Philadelphia: The Annals of the American Academy of Political and Social Science.

Strintzos, Maria. 1991. 'Australian Volunteer Work in Indonesia: a Personal Account'. In H. da Costa (ed.). *Australian Aid to Indonesia*. Melbourne: Centre for Southeast Asian Studies, Monash University.

Sugiyanto, E. and Wahyuni, S. 1994. 'Program Pengembangan Usaha Kecil: Pengalaman Bina Swadaya'. *Bulletin Bina Swadaya* 2(3) 30–3.

Sukma, Rizal. 1998. 'Indonesia: A Year of Politics and Sadness'. In D. da Cunha and J. Funton (eds). *Southeast Asian Affairs 1998*. Singapore: Institute of Southeast Asian Studies.

Sukur, I. M. 1987. 'Pelayanan LSM Ibarat Warna Kulit Bunglon'. *Bergetar* No. 71 22–3.

Sullivan, John. 1992. *Local Government and Community in Java: An Urban Case Study*. Singapore: Oxford University Press.

Sundhaussen, Ulf. 1994. 'The Inner Contraction of the Suharto Regime: a Starting Point for a Withdrawal to the Barracks'. In D. Bourchier and J. D. Legge (eds). *Democracy in Indonesia, 1950s and 1990s*. Monash Paper on Southeast Asia No. 31, Centre of Southeast Asian Studies, Monash University, Clayton.

Susanto S. J., Budi. 1993. *Peristiwa Yogya 1992: Siasat Politik Massa Rakyat Kota*. Yogyakarta: Kanisius.

Suzuki, Naoki. 1998. *Inside NGOs: Learning to Manage Conflict Between Headquarters and Field Offices*. London: Intermediate Technology Publications.

Swidler, Ann. 1995. 'Cultural Power and Social Movements'. In H. Johnston and B. Klandermans (eds). *Social Movements and Culture*. London: University College London Press.

Sztompka, Piotr. 1993. *The Sociology of Social Change*. Oxford: Blackwell.

Tambunan, Tulus. 1992. 'Economic Development and Small-Scale Enterprises in Indonesia'. *Entrepreneurship and Regional Development* 4(1) 85–98.

Tandon, Rajesh. 1996. 'Local Governance, Democratic Transition and Voluntary Development Organisations: Some Lessons from South Asia'. In A. Clayton (ed.). *NGOs, Civil Society and the State: Building Democracy in Transitional Societies*. Oxford: INTRAC.

Taylor, Jean G. 1997. 'Official Photography, Costume and the Indonesian Revolution'. In J. G. Taylor (ed.). *Women Creating Indonesia: The First Fifty Years*. Clayton: Monash Asia Institute.

Taylor, V. and Whittier, N. 1995. 'Analytical Approaches to Social Movement Culture: The Culture of the Women's Movement'. In H. Johnston and B. Klandermans (eds). *Social Movements and Culture*. London: University College London Press.

Tendler, Judith. 1989. 'Whatever Happened to Poverty Alleviation?'. In J. Levitsky (ed.). *Microenterprises in Developing Countries*. London: Intermediate Technology Publications.

Thamrin, Juni. 1993. *LSM dan Paradigma-Paradigma Perubahan*. Unpublished Paper. Jakarta: CPSM.

—— 1995. 'Membangkitkan Kemampuan Permodalan Usaha Rakyat'. *Bulletin Bina Swadaya*, March Edition, pp. 11–13.

Thomas, Alan. 1992. 'Non-Governmental Organizations and the Limits to Empowerment'. In M. Wuyts, M. Mackintosh and T. Hewitt (eds). *Development Policy and Public Action*. Oxford: Oxford University Press.

Thorbecke, Eric. 1995. 'Impact of State and Civil Institutions on the Operation of Rural Market and Non-Market Configurations'. In A. de Janvry *et al.* (eds). *State, Market and Civil Organizations: New Theories, New Practices and Their Implications for Rural Development*. London: MacMillan.

Thorbecke, E. and van der Pluijm, T. 1993. *Rural Indonesia: Socio-economic Development in a Changing Environment*. New York: New York University Press.
Tilly, Charles. *From Mobilization to Revolution*. Reading, MA: Addison-Wesley.
Timberg, Thomas A. 1989. 'Comparative Experience with Microenterprise Projects'. In J. Levitsky (ed.). *Microenterprises in Developing Countries*. London: Intermediate Technology Publications.
Timmer, C. P. 1973. 'Choice of Technique in Rice Milling in Java'. *Bulletin of Indonesian Economic Studies* 9(3) 57–76.
Tjajo, Rambun. 1994. 'Upaya Membangun Kekuatan Rakyat'. *Kawah* 3(1) 20–6.
Tjondronegoro, Sediono M. P. 1984. *Social Organisation and Planned Development in Rural Java*. Singapore: Oxford University Press.
Touraine, Alain. 1981. *The Voice and the Eye: An Analysis of Social Movements*. Cambridge: Cambridge University Press.
Townsend, J. 1995. 'Who Speaks for Whom?: Outsiders Re-present Women Pioneers of the Forests of Mexico'. In N. Nelson and S. Wright (eds). *Power and Participatory Development: Theory and Practice*. London: Intermediate Technology Publications.
Trivedy, R. and Acharya, J. 1996. 'Constructing the Case for an Alternative Framework for Understanding Civil Society, the State and the Role of NGOs'. In A. Clayton (ed.). *NGOs, Civil Society and the State: Building Democracy in Transitional Societies*. Oxford: INTRAC.
Tsuchiya, Kenji. 1987. *Democracy and Leadership: the Rise of the Taman Siswa Movement in Indonesia*. Honolulu: University of Hawaii Press.
Turner, M and Hulme, D. 1997. *Governance, Administration and Development: Making the State Work*. London: MacMillan.
Uhlin, Anders. 1997. *Indonesia and the Third Wave of Democratisation: the Indonesian Pro-democracy Movement in a Changing World*. Surrey: Curzon.
Ul Karim, Mahbub. 1995. 'NGOs in Bangladesh: Issues of Legitimacy and Accountability'. In M. Edwards and D. Hulme (eds). *NGOs Performance and Accountability: Beyond the Magic Bullet*. London: Earthscan.
Uphoff, Norman. 1987. *Relations Between Governmental and Non-governmental Organisations and the Promotion of Autonomous Development*. Unpublished paper. Ithaca: Cornell Institute for Food, Agriculture and Development.
—— 1995. 'Why NGOs are not a Third Sector'. In M. Edwards and D. Hulme (eds). *NGOs Performance and Accountability: Beyond the Magic Bullet*. London: Earthscan.
Utami, Andri Y. 1995. 'Kadariyah: Buruh Pabrik Utama Tex'. In M. Singarimbun and S. Sairin (eds). *Lika-Liku Kehidupan Buruh Perempuan*. Yogyakarta: Pustaka Pelajar and Yasanti.
Utrecht, A. and Sayogyo, P. 1994. 'Policies and Interventions'. In Grijns, Mies *et al.* (eds). *Different Women, Different Work: Gender and Industrialisation in Indonesia*. Aldershot, UK: Avebury.
Van Klinken, Gerry. 1999. 'How a Democratic Deal Might be Struck'. In A. Budiman *et al.* (eds). *Reformasi: Crisis and Change in Indonesia*. Monash Papers on Southeast Asia No. 50. Monash Asia Institute. Monash University, Clayton.
Van Langenberg, Michael. 1990. 'The New Order State: Language, Ideology, Hegemony'. In A. Budiman (ed.). *State and Civil Society in Indonesia*. Monash Papers on Southeast Asia No. 22. Centre of Southeast Asian Studies. Monash University, Clayton.
Van Tuijl, Peter. 1994. 'Conditionality for Whom? Indonesia and the Experience of the IGGI: the NGO Experience'. In A. Clayton (ed.). *Governance, Democracy and Conditionality: What Role for NGOs?* Oxford: INTRAC.

Van Tuijl, P. and Witjes, B. 1993. 'Popular Participation in Indonesia's Development Process'. In J. P. Dirkse, F. Husken and M. Rutten (eds). *Indonesia's Experiences Under the New Order*. Leiden: KITLV Press.

Vatikiotis, Michael. 1993. *Indonesian Politics Under Suharto: Order, Development and Pressure for Change*. London: Routledge.

Veltmeyer, H., Petras, J. and Vieux, S. 1997. *Neoliberalism and Class Conflict in Latin America*. London: MacMillan.

Vene-Klasen, Lisa. 1996. 'The Challenge of Democracy-Building: Practical Lessons on NGO Advocacy and Political Change'. In A. Clayton (ed.). *NGOs, Civil Society and the State: Building Democracy in Transitional Societies*. Oxford: INTRAC.

Wahid, Abdurrahman. 1994. 'Hubungan Antar-Agama di Indonesia: Dimensi Internal dan Eksternal'. In INTERFIDEI. *Dialog: Kritik dan Identitas Agama*. Yogyakarta: INTERFIDEI.

Wahjono, Padmo. 1982. *Negara Republik Indonesia*. Jakarta: Rajawali Press.

Watters, Patrick. 1999. 'The Indonesian Armed Forces in the Post-Suharto Era'. In Geoff Forrester (ed.). *Post-Suharto Indonesia: Renewal or Chaos?* Singapore: Institute of South-East Asian Studies.

Wanigaratne, Ranjith. 1997. 'The State-NGO Relationship in Sri Lanka: Rights, Interests and Accountability'. In M. Edwards and D. Hulme (eds). *NGOs, States and Donors: Too Close for Comfort?* London: MacMillan.

Wardani, Nila. 1995. 'Pengembangan Sistem Pemasaran: Sebuah Peluang yang Bisa Dimanfaatkan LSM'. *Bergetar* No. 121 17–24.

Weber, Max. 1930. *The Protestant Ethic and the Spirit of Capitalism*. Translated by Talcott Parsons. London: Unwin.

White, Benjamin. 1982. 'Population, Involution and Employment in Rural Java'. In John Harris (ed.). *Rural Development: Theories of Peasant Economy and Agrarian Change*. London: Routledge.

—— 1983. 'Agricultural Involution and Its Critics: Twenty Years After'. *Bulletin of Concerned Asian Scholars* No. 15 18–31.

White, Gordon. 1994. 'Civil Society, Democratisation and Development (I): Clearing the Analytical Ground'. *Democratization* 1(3) 375–90.

Whyte, W. F. 1982. 'Social Inventions for Solving Human Problems'. *American Sociological Review* 47(1) 1–13.

Widadi. 1999. 'Pelajaran Kasus Marsinah'. In D. Supriyanto (ed.). *Lima Tahun Komnas-HAM: Catatan Wartawan*. Jakarta: INPI-Pact and Forum Akal Sehat.

Widaningrum, Ambar. 1988. *Kemampuan Beradaptasi, Legitimasi dan Akseptabilitas LSM: Studi Kasus Bina Swadaya dan Mekar Bhakti di Yogyakarta*. B.A. thesis, Faculty of Social and Political Sciences, University of Gadjah Mada, Yogyakarta.

Widiawati, Helmy. 1995. 'Giyah: Buruh Pabrik Cita Rasa'. In M. Singarimbun and S. Sairin (eds). *Lika-Liku Kehidupan Buruh Perempuan*. Yogyakarta: Pustaka Pelajar and Yasanti.

Wignaraja, Ponna. 1993. 'Rethinking Development and Democracy'. In P. Wignaraja (ed.). *New Social Movements in the South: Empowering the People*. London: Zed Books.

Wils, F. 1995. 'Scaling-up, Mainstreaming and Accountability: the Challenge for NGOs'. In M. Edwards and D. Hulme (eds). *NGOs Performance and Accountability: Beyond the Magic Bullet*. London: Earthscan.

Wiratama, I. M. L. and Hasibuan, N. 1997. 'Post-Election Political Development'. *The Indonesian Quarterly* 25(3) 224–32.

Wolf, Diane L. 1992. *Factory Daughters: Gender, Household Dynamics and Rural Industrialisation in Java*. Berkeley: University of California Press.
World Bank. 1982. *Indonesia: Health Sector Review*. Washington, DC: The World Bank.
—— 1993. *The East Asian Miracle: Economic Growth and Public Policy*. New York and Oxford: Oxford University Press.
Wright, S. and Nelson, N. 1995. 'Participatory Research and Participant Observation: Two Incompatible Approaches'. In N. Nelson and S. Wright (eds). *Power and Participatory Development: Theory and Practice*. London. Intermediate Technology Publication.
Yamaguchi, Tomiko. 1998. 'A Dynamic Approach to Community Development in a Rural Area of Yogyakarta Special Region'. *Regional Development Studies* 4, 151–63.
Yasanti (Yayasan Annisa Swasti). 1995. *Laporan Kegiatan Pendampingan Buruh Pabrik di Ungaran*. Yogyakarta: Yasanti.
—— 1996. *Latar Belakang dan Struktur Organisasi*. Yogyakarta: Yasanti.
—— 2001. *Profil Daerah Binaan:Ungaran dan Dinamika Kehidupannya*. Yogyakarta: Yasanti.
YLBHI (Yayasan Lembaga Bantuan Hukum Indonesia). 1997. *Tahun Kekerasan: Potret Pelanggaran Hak Azasi Manusia di Indonesia*. Jakarta: YLBHI.
Young, Kenneth R. 1999. 'Post-Suharto: a Change of Regime?'. In A. Budiman *et al.* (eds). *Reformasi: Crisis and Change in Indonesia*. Monash Papers on Southeast Asia No. 50. Monash Asia Institute. Monash University, Clayton.
Yunus, Muhammad. 1989. 'Grameen Bank: Organisation and Operation'. In J. Levitsky (ed.). *Microenterprises in Developing Countries*. London: Intermediate Technology Publications.

## Newspapers, bulletins, magazines and the internet

*Alert: the Southeast Asian Press Alliance*
*Ajinews (http://www.indo-news.com)*
*Annisa*
*Bergetar*
*Berita Nasional*
*Bulletin Bina Desa*
*Bulletin Bina Swadaya*
*Bulletin Setia Kawan*
*Detikcom (http://www.detik.com)*
*Far Eastern Economic Review*
*Forum Keadilan*
*Gatra*
*Info Bisnis*
*Jawa Pos*
*Kawah*
*Kedaulatan Rakyat*
*Kompas*
*Media Indonesia*
*Merdeka*
*Pikiran Rakyat*
*Republika*
*Sinar*
*Suara Independen*
*Suara Merdeka*
*Suara Pembaruan*
*Tempo*
*Tempointeraktif*
*(http://www.tempointeraktif.com)*
*The Jakarta Post*
*The Guardian*
*The Times*
*Time Magazine*
*Tiras*
*Yogya Post*

# Index

*abangan* 48–9, 129, 142
accountability 43, 245, 255
Aceh 81–2, 225, 229, 254
Achmadi, Heri 63
ADB 80, 99, 125
Aditjondro, George 62, 111, 216–17
administrators 50
Admiral Widodo Sucipto 88
Africa 151
*aide memoire* 45, 99
AIPI 61
AKRSP 24
*aksi sepihak* 51
Aldera 72, 214
*aliran* 49, 68, 71, 91, 242
Alvarez, Sonia 247
Ambon 225, 254
Amnesty International 74
Anderson, Benedict 51
ANGOC 60
*Ansor* 51
Antlov, Hans 132
Apnalaya 28
*Apsari* 123, 129, 141, 143, 166
Aquino, Corry 39
Arabic 48
Arabs 48
Arce, A. 59
Arief, Sritua 111
*arisan* 90, 129, 176, 182, 194
*asal bapak senang* 98
Asia 151
Aspinall, Edward 63, 211, 218
Australia 99, 161
awareness building 103, 183
*azas tunggal Pancasila* 53, 94, 96, 105

Bachriadi, Dianto 116
Badega 63, 66
BAKIN 52, 94
BAKOR 64
Bali 63, 76, 80, 91, 117
Balinese 48

*Bandes* 124
Bandung 64–5, 73, 77, 94, 113, 116, 119, 211, 213, 231
Bandung Institute of Technology 63
Bangdes 60
Bangladesh 24, 38, 60, 69, 158, 245
Banjarmasin 76
Bank Bali 80
*Bank Muamalat* 62
Bapindo 75
Bappenas 118, 120
*basismo* 36, 68, 174
Batak 48
Baturaden declaration 42, 109–10
BBI 64
Belgium 99
Bennett, Jon 228
*beras perelek* 90
Berninghausen, Jutta 46, 174, 176, 198
*Bhinneka Tunggal Ika* 49, 113
Bhoomi Sena 38, 69, 193
Billah, M.M. 109
*Bimas* 59, 121–4, 129
Bimo 136
Bina Swadaya 91, 105, 126, 140–1, 152, 159, 161
*Biro Kerjasama Teknik Luar Negeri* 94
BKMJ 64
Bogor 63, 74, 117, 161
Bonowiratmo, S.J. 111
Boserup, Ester 46, 168
bourgeoisie 58
Boyolali 137
BPD 132–3, 146–9
BRAC 24, 159
Brazil 114
Brown, David 248
*Bruneigate* 81, 83, 86
Brussels incident 98–9
BSY 16–17, 44, 126–8, 130, 138–43, 145, 147, 150–62, 164–7, 244, 246, 252–5
BTI 90, 130
Buchori, Binny 119

Buddhism 12
Budi Utomo 4
Budiman, Arief 62, 81–2, 111, 216–17
Buginese 48
Bulatao, Gerry 66
Bulkin, Farkhan 111
Bulog 58, 83, 86, 122, 142
*Buloggate* 81, 83, 86
Bunnell, Frederick 45, 143
*Bupati* 55, 128, 131–2, 172, 209–10
Bureaucratic Authoritarianism 55
Bureaucratic Polity 54
Buru island 67
BUUD 122–3

*Camat* 55, 128, 144, 172, 208
campus autonomy 63
Canada 99, 162
Canel, Eduardo 114–15
capacity building 183
Carr, Marylin 137
Casanova, Gonzalez 111
Catholicism 12
CD-Bethesda (CD) 16–17, 44, 105, 126–8, 131, 139, 143–7, 158–9, 161–7, 244, 246, 253–5
CEBEMO 98
*ceblokan* 71, 131
Cebu 29
Cendana 59
central axis *see* poros tengah
Central Java 42, 63, 84, 99, 105–6, 109, 110, 114, 116, 120–1, 126–7, 129–30, 134, 137, 145, 147–9, 158, 164–5, 177–8, 181, 189, 196, 215–16, 218, 221, 226–7, 235
Central Sulawesi 12
Cepogo Plan 110
CGI 100
Chambers, Robert 112, 183, 242–3
Chazan, Naomi 35
Chile 39
Chinese 11–12, 48, 58–9, 75, 81, 173
Christianisation 13, 125
CIDES 62
Ciptawijaya, Eka 58
Ciputra 58
Cisarua 45, 110
civil society: characteristics 35; definitions 35; ideology 36; and the state 55
Clark, John 27, 60, 214, 217
Clarke, Gerrard 37, 253
class struggle 69–71, 141, 221, 244
clean government 83
Clinton, William 74
CODE-NGO 40
collective action 90, 153–4, 185, 192–3, 206–7, 228, 232, 238, 247, 250, 254

Collier, William 177–8
collusion 59, 77, 83, 210
Colonel Untung 51
COME'NGOs 16, 218
community development 25, 59, 91–2, 100, 135
*compradores* 111
conflict avoidance 41, 108
conscientisation 24, 112, 174–5, 191–2, 198, 248
Constantino-David, Karina 218
constituency (ies) 69, 80, 110, 114, 166, 174, 177, 183–4, 192, 198, 200, 203, 247, 251
Constitution of 1945 78
Cornell paper 51–2
corporatism 55
corruption 59, 72, 77, 80, 82–5, 88, 99, 112, 119, 183, 210, 211–12, 224, 245
counter-hegemonic movements 45
Covey, Jane 232
CPP 66
CPSM 110
Creswell, John W. 16
Criminal Law 56
Critical Theory 111
Crouch, Harold 54
*cukupan* 70
culture of silence 44, 249

*Danramil* 144, 208
Danutirto, Haryanto 72, 211
*Darul Islam* 68
Darusman, Marzuki 87
*Dasawisma* 61
Dayak 87
De Jouvenal, Bertrand 120
de-ideologisation 68, 94, 96, 101
democratisation 32, 36, 43, 114–15, 119, 132–3, 146–7, 149, 212, 224, 247, 252–3, 255
*Demokrasi Terpimpin* 51
Denpasar 63, 78, 254
de-politicisation 94, 101
developmental state 25
development-oriented NGOs 103–4, 107–9, 113–14, 150, 155, 200
*Dharma Pertiwi* 170, 176
*Dharma Wanita* 170–1, 176
Diamond, Larry 253
*Dian Desa* Foundation 16, 91, 97, 105, 160, 215, 229
Dillon, H.S. 118
direct representation 184
Djiwandono, Soedjati 76
Dollard, J. 190
Donorojo 126, 130–2, 134, 143–5, 245
dos Santos, Theotonio 111
DPR 76, 78, 82–4, 88, 101, 221
Drucker, Peter 166

## 298   Index

*Dwifungsi* 52, 73, 78–9, 221–2

Eade, Deborah 231
East Java 66, 75, 83–4, 114, 131, 180, 194
East Timor 80, 127, 158, 162, 164, 229, 230
EBJF 37
economic growth 57
Edwards, Michael 27–8, 36
Effendi, Tadjuddin Noor 177
Elden, M. 197
Eldridge, Philip 41, 43–4, 46–7, 102, 104, 108, 130, 175, 217, 227–8
elite 82, 85, 89, 112, 143, 172, 193, 210, 211
Elliott, Charles 23, 42, 102, 248–9
ELSAM 85
emancipation 170, 197, 201
empowerment 23, 41–2, 60, 100, 108, 110, 146–7, 149, 169, 183–4, 193, 242–4, 247
Ertanto 230
Escobar, Arturo 247
ethnicity in Yogyakarta 11–12
Eurasians 48
Europeans 48
Evans, Peter 54
Evers, Hans-Dieter 174, 178

Fakih, Mansour 102, 104, 109, 113
Fals Borda, Orlando 112
FAMI 64
Farrington, John 39
FBSI 65
Feith, Herbert 48, 50
Ferianto, Jaduk 212
financial crisis 113
Fincham, R. 160
Fisher, Julie 215
FKMS 64
FKMY 64, 212
floating mass 56, 128
FNPBI 188
Ford Foundation 176
FORKOT 64
Forum 206, 217–21, 223–4, 226–9, 232, 235–6, 250–1, 253
*Forum Demokrasi* 81
Fowler, Alan 40, 156, 166–7, 228, 232, 247
FPIS 226
France 99
Frank, Andre Gunder 111
Frankfurt school 63, 111
Freire, Paulo 111–13, 191, 248
*fusi* 55

G-30-S/PKI 52
GABSI 64
*Gandrik* 212

Garut 114
Gayatri, Dian 175, 202–3
GBHN 92
Geertz, Clifford 49, 70, 244
gender and development 46, 169, 172, 175
General Banurusman 208
General Bimantoro 84, 86–7
General Murdani 211
General Soesilo Soedarman 74
General Try Sutrisno 99
General Wiranto 80–1
General Yogie S. Memet 97
GENI 72, 214
Germany 99
GERWANI 90, 170
Giddens, Anthony 209
*glasnost* 111
GMKI 63
GMNI 63
Goertz, Gary 241
*gogolan* 71
Golkar 53, 55, 66, 76, 79, 80, 82–4, 88, 96, 126, 128, 131, 142–3, 170, 210, 213, 221
*Golkarisasi* 55
Golput 213
*Gono Shahajjo Shangsta* 38, 69
Gorbachev, Mikhail 111
*gotong royong* 90
Grameen Bank 158
grassroots participation 41, 242, 248
green revolution 178
GRINGOs 16
GSOs 4
*gubernur* 55
Gumelar, Agum 88
*guru* syndrome 249, 250
Gus Dur 79–89, 114, 117 *see also* Abdurrahman Wahid

Habibie, B.J. 61, 78–80, 133, 210
*hacienda* 69
Hadad, Ismid 111
Hadix, L. 208
Hadiyanti, Siti 210
*haji* 130–1
Hamburg 78
Handayani, Sih 200, 202, 204
Handy, Charles 30, 163–4, 197, 201
hard-liners 210
Hariadi, Untoro 223
Harmoko 78
Harper, Caroline 117
Hart, Gillian 60, 71, 128
Hasan, Bob 58
Hatta, Mohammad 48–9, 251
Haz, Hamzah 80, 82
HBK 138, 142, 165
health care 92, 106, 127, 135–6, 158, 164, 166, 244, 246, 252

Hegel, Frederic W. 49
Heryanto, Ariel 73, 111
high performing economies 57
Hinduism 12, 48
Hipalapa 114, 119
HIVOS 98
HKTI 55, 66, 91, 96, 126
HMI 63, 84
HNSI 91
Hong Kong 58
household economies 46
Hudson, Mike 30
*Hukbalahap* 67
Hulme, David 27–8, 36, 251
human rights 72, 77, 98, 100, 110, 198, 212–13, 215, 221, 230, 234, 247, 251
Human Rights Watch 74
Humana 100
Huntington, Samuel 32
HYVs 121, 122, 129, 178

IBRA 84
Ibrahim, Rustam 109
ICCO 98
ICF 175, 236–8
ICMI 61–2, 78, 229
IDT 124, 209
IGGI 98–100
IKADIN 61
IMF 25, 80, 84, 99, 113
IMM 84
impeachment 83
India 24, 38, 60, 69–70, 135, 158, 193
Indian Communist Party 38
Indonesian government 43
*infaq* 130
INFID 100, 117, 203
INFIGHT 72
informal sector 170, 215
INGI 98–100
*Inmas* 59, 122, 129
*Inmendagri* 95
*Inpres* 92, 94, 124
institutionalisation 232
*Insus* 122, 129
integralism 49
integralistic state 49
interventionist state 57
IPTN 100
Irian Jaya 81, 100
ISAI 61
ISEI 61
ISJ 106, 173
ISKA 61
Islamic groups 48, 68, 85, 91, 106, 197, 225–7, 229, 248
Islamic Law 48, 227, 248
Islamic parties 116–17
Islamic revivalism 65
Ismawan, Bambang 126, 140–1

Italy 99
Iwik 210

Jackelen, Henry L. 137
Jackson, Karl D. 54
Jakarta 48, 50, 62, 73–7, 80, 85, 88, 94, 98–9, 101, 144, 154, 197, 211–13, 221, 224–5, 231, 254
Jakarta Charter 48, 51
Japan 58, 99
Japanese Export-Import Bank 216
*Jaringan Merah Putih* 85
*Jaringan Pengaman Sosial see* social safety-nets
Java 50, 77, 79, 84, 91, 100, 112, 116–17, 128, 134, 174, 178, 225
Javanese 8, 11, 41, 48, 70, 103, 174, 182, 187–8, 192, 194–5
Jay, Robert 194
JBIC 125
Jember 63, 78
Jepara 130–1, 144
*Jeprik* 212
Jesuit order 67
*Jihad* 227
*jimpitan* 129
Jombang 63, 78, 131
Jopson, Edgar 66
Juliantara, Dadang 45, 63, 213, 219, 223, 229–30, 233, 238, 244
Junglepatti Thana 38

KABATID 37
Kabeer, Naila 169, 183, 197
*Kabupaten* 142
KADIN 55
*Kaditsospol* 208
Kalimantan 50, 79, 82, 91, 100, 117
Kalla, Jusuf 82, 86
*Kalpataru* Prize 127
Kalyanamitra 100
KAMMI 64, 84
*kampung* 13
Kana, Nico L. 134
*Kapolda* 208
*Kapolsek* 208
*Karang Taruna* 56, 61, 91, 123
Karl, Marilee 169, 188
Karlsen, Jan I. 112
Kartini, Raden Ajeng 170
Kartodirdjo, Sartono 65
KDP 119
Kebumen 131
*Kecamatan* 57, 101, 122, 129, 142
*kedokan* 71, 131
Kedu 116
Kedung Ombo 25, 40, 63, 66, 99, 101, 211, 215–17, 221
*kekurangan* 70
*Kelompencapir* 123, 129, 141

## 300  Index

*kelompok kematian* 90
*kelompok studi* 63
*Kelurahan* 101
*Keppres* 100, 145–6
*Keraton* 13
Kerstan, Brigit 46, 174, 176, 198
Kertarajasa, Butet 212
Kesawamurti, Heru 212
Kessler, Richard J. 70
*ketoprak* 192
Ki Hadjar Dewantara 14
KIK 123, 137
Kimmel, Michael S. 77
King, Dwight 55
*Kitab Undang Undang Hukum Dagang* 96
KKDs 127–8, 131, 139, 140, 143–4, 146–8, 158, 165–6, 244
KKN 77–8
Klaten 129–30
Kleden, Ignas 111
KMKP 123
KNPI 91, 96
*Kodim* 57
Koentjaraningrat 187
Komnas-HAM (National Commission for Human Rights) 190
*Kontak Tani* 123, 129, 141
KOPKAMTIB 52
*Koramil* 57, 101, 130
Korten, David 23, 42, 102, 118
KOWANI 171
*Kristenisasi see also* Christianisation
KSMs 127, 130, 138–9, 141–2, 147, 151–2, 158, 165, 254
KUBs 127, 138–9, 141
KUD 122–3
Kudus 78
*kumpulan* 129
*Kupedes* 124, 129
Kusumohadi, M. 237
Kusyuniati, Sri 250 *see also* Mbak Kus
KUT 124
*kyai* 75, 130–1, 134
Kyai Hammam Ja'far 216

labour movements 101
labour strikes 65, 69
Lampung 66
landowners 69
Lane, Max 252
LAPERA 214
*Lasjkar Jihad* 225
Latin America 151, 169
LBHY 215–16
Lehmann, David 174, 207
LEKHAT 214
Lende, Kari Anderson 213
Lev, Daniel 50, 85
Levin, M. 197
liberal democracy 52–3

liberation theology 63, 106, 111
Liddle, R. William 57
Liem Sioe Liong 58
Lieutenant General Suyono 73
Lieutenant General Syarwan Hamid 73–4, 97
LKMD 56, 61, 91, 123–4, 128–9, 133, 141, 146, 172
LMD 56, 91, 123, 128–9, 132–3, 141, 146
Lofland, John 185, 201
Lombok 63, 91, 117, 148–9
lower-class 61, 64, 66, 112, 185, 206
LP3ES 91
LPHAM 72
LPSM 7
LSM 6
LSP 91
Lucas, Anton 116
*lumbung paceklik* 90
*Lurah* 128, 139–41, 172, 208–9
Luzon 67

MacClelland, David 108
MacIntyre, Andrew 58
Mackie, Jamie 50, 58, 70
MacPherson, C.B. 53
Madurese 48, 87
*Mahabarata* 192
Mahasin, Aswab 109, 111
Mainwaring, Scott 114–15
Major General Hamami Nata 74
Major General Suryadi Sudirdja 74
Major General Sutiyoso 74
Makassar 116
Malaka, Tan 251
Malang 63, 77, 101
Malay 48
Malaysia 60, 161
Maluku 67, 82, 225
Manado 77
Manan, Bagir 88
Mangunwijaya, Y.B. 13, 62, 106, 113, 211, 216
Marcos, Ferdinand 26, 37, 39, 66, 67
marginalisation 169, 247
Marsinah 190, 220
Maryanto 119
Mas'oed, Mohtar 106
mass guidance *see* Bimas
mass organisations 95–6
mass violence 77
*massa mengambang see* floating mass
Masyumi 48–50
Mataram 63
May 1998 Revolution 77
Mbak Kus 203–4
MBB 78
McVey, Ruth T. 51, 109
Medan 63, 65, 74–5, 116, 213, 224

Megawati 73–4, 76, 79–82, 85–6, 88–9, 119, 209, 221
Melcher, S.J., Chris 126
Melucci, Alberto 228
Merdeka Palace 78
MFI 29
micro-enterprise 135–7, 164
middle-class 61–2, 66, 82, 85, 91, 114, 119, 173, 185, 206, 212, 244
Migdal, Joel S. 32
militancy 43, 69
military repression 69
Minangkabau 48
Ministry of Home Affairs 60, 74, 91, 94–5, 121, 170
*Mitra Perempuan* 173
mobilisation 41, 60, 100, 103, 147, 150, 174–5, 195, 225–6, 229, 241–2, 244
Mohammad, Gunawan 62, 209
money-lenders 69
Mount Apo 25, 40
Mouzelis, Nicos 57
movement-oriented NGOs 103–4, 113–14, 185, 199, 200, 208, 220, 250–1, 255
MPR 78–80, 83, 87–8, 221
Mpu Tantular 49
MSOs 4, 6
Mueller, Adam 49
*mufakat* 53
Muftiyanah, Amin 46, 192, 205, 220
*Muhammadiyah* 15, 48, 79, 84, 90, 134
MUI 55
*Muspida* 57
*musyawarah* 53, 202

Nadjib, Emha Ainun 62, 209, 222
NAMFREL 37
*Nasakom* 68
Nasikun, J. 112
Nasution, Abdul Haris 51–2
Nasution, Adnan Buyung 209
national car 72
nationalists 85
NDF 66
*negara kesatuan* 49
nepotism 59, 77, 83
NES 122, 129
Netherlands 98
New Order 43–4, 52–3, 55, 57, 59–60, 65, 67–8, 73, 91, 96, 100, 102, 105, 131, 170, 172, 196, 207, 213, 244, 251
New Order state 54–5, 57, 120
New York 74
NGOs: accountability 28, 165–7; budgeting 156–60; characteristics 2–3, 23; and civil society empowerment 35–6; and corruption 118–19; definitions 5; and democratisation 36–8, 114–15; leadership 44, 96, 163–5;
201–5; management 30–1, 44, 155, 161–3; networking and coalition 40–1, 227–8; performance 165–7, 200, 231, 233; scaling-up process 27–30, 118, 146; staff development 160–1, 201; and the state 38–9
Nilphamari 38
Nipah 66
NKK/BKK 63, 111, 212
North Sumatra 51, 114
NOVIB 98, 100
NPA 66
NU 12, 48, 50–1, 76, 79, 83, 90, 130, 134, 215, 220, 222
Nugroho, Bambang Isti 212
Nusantara, A.H.G. 109
Nusa Tenggara Timur 91

O'Donnell, Guillermo 210
ORAs 127, 131, 146–50, 165, 244, 254
OTB 73
OXFAM 4, 162, 175–6

P3M 91
PAD 120–1, 186
Padang 78, 254
Pakistan 60
Pakpahan, Muchtar 72
Palagan 212
Pamungkas, Sri Bintang 71, 73, 209
PAN 79, 116–17
*Pancasila* 52, 68, 79, 94–5, 104–5, 113, 172, 224, 244
*Pancasila* Industrial Relations 65
Pangestu, Prayogo 58
Pansus 83, 86
PAR 112–13, 191–2, 195, 197–8, 248, 254
participatory development 103
*pasar* 178
*pasukan berani mati* 84
Pasuruan 84–5
patrimonial state 54
patrimonialism 54
patron-client 182
Paul Hoffman Award 127
PBB 116–17
PDI 56, 73–4, 76, 213
PDIP 79, 82–3, 86, 117, 225
peasant movements 65–6
*Pemda* 57
*Pemuda Rakyat* 90
people-centered development 26
people's power 67, 244
people's sovereignty 115, 251
*perda* 179
*pergerakan kaum muda* 62
Pertamina 58
*pesantren* 90, 130, 216
*petinggi* 131
petty traders 179–80, 185–6

PGOs 5
Philippines 24–6, 29, 37, 39–40, 60, 66–7, 69–70, 111, 135, 161, 214, 253
Piagam Jakarta *see also* Jakarta Charter
PIJAR 72, 214
PIKI 61
Pinochet, Augusto 39
PIPHAM 72, 214
PKB 79, 83, 116–17
PKBI 97, 160
PKI 49–52, 67–8, 71, 74–5, 90, 130, 140–1, 216
PKK 56, 61, 91, 123–4, 128, 141, 171–2, 176, 194
PMII 63
PMKRI 63
PNI 49, 50–1, 79
political agitation 97
political education 115
political engineering 101
political openness 77
political opportunists 116
political parties 43, 49–50, 56, 79, 83, 96, 114–16, 184, 195, 208, 211, 226, 235, 255
*Polres* 57
*Polsek* 57, 101
popular resistance 103, 198, 206
*poros tengah* 80, 82
post-modernism 111
poverty-alleviation 60
poverty line 57
poverty reduction 9
power culture 163–4, 255
PPLs 121–2, 129
PPP 56, 73, 76, 80, 82, 116–17, 213, 225
PRA 24, 147, 151–2, 155, 244
Prabowo 210
PRD 72–5, 115, 214
Premadasa 29
pribumi 11, 48
Prijono, Onny S. 109
primordialism 244
Prisma 41
*priyayi* 48–9, 173, 194, 254
pro-democracy campaigns 43, 45, 115, 219
professional protesters 116
professionalism 155, 229, 245, 255
Prokesa 135–6, 139, 143, 166
Proshika 29, 193
Protestantism 12
PUDI 73
Purwokerto 63, 78
Puskesmas 135–6, 139
Putra, Hutomo Mandala 72

radical Muslims 85
Rahman, Anizur 112, 193, 195, 199
Rais, Amien 80–2, 88
*Ramayana* 192

Rancamaya 63, 66
*Ratu Adil* 65
Realino Foundation 14, 16
reforestation fund 100
*reformasi* 78, 114, 131, 223, 254
regional autonomy 132, 149
religious tolerance 81
Rendra, W.S. 62
Rengasdengklok 76
Repelita 120
representative government 50
Rhodes, P. 160
Riantiarno, N. 62
Ricklefs, Merle 50
Riggs, Frederick W. 54
Robison, Richard 58
role culture 163–5, 255
Roxas, Manuel 67
*rupiah* 77, 81–2, 84, 89, 114, 116, 119, 124, 127, 131, 134, 157
rural development 121, 127, 135, 215, 243–4, 246
Rustam, Supardjo 95
*ruwahan* 13

Sabirin, Syahril 86
Salatiga 63, 72, 113, 216
Salim, Emil 6, 97, 99
Samekto, Guno 165
*Sampul-D* 68
Sandee, H. 137
Sandyawan, S.J. 106, 173
Santosa, Paulus 105, 165
Santoso, Budi 77, 147, 233
*santri* 48, 49
SARA 75
Sarekat Islam 90
*Sarvodaya Shramadana* 29
Sasono, Adi 111
SBPY 16, 17, 44, 100, 174–5, 179, 183, 185–7, 191–3, 197–203, 214–15, 248–9, 251, 253–5
SBSI 65, 72
Schiller, Jim 61, 120
Schmitter, Phillipe 210
*Sekretariat Bina Desa* 91, 98, 218, 232, 237
*selapanan* 90, 129
self-censorship 248
self-management 91
self-reliance 41, 105, 149, 248
Semarang 63, 77, 154, 216
Senayan 88
Sendangsari 153–4
Setiawan, Bonie 109, 111, 115
SEWA 158, 193
share-cropping 71
shared poverty 70
Shobirin, Enceng 117
*sidang istimewa* 79
Simanjuntak, Marsilam 63, 81

Singapore 58
SIP 173
Siregar, Amir Effendi 229
Siregar, Hariman 63
Situbondo 75–6
Sjahrir 63
Skocpol, Theda 54
*slametan* 13
small credit 105, 107–8, 127, 156–7, 165, 244
small-scale industries 92
SMID 64, 74–5, 212
Smillie, Ian 169, 243, 245, 249
Sobary, Mohammad 62
SOBSI 65
social artisan 109
social indicator in Yogyakarta 9–11
social movements: categories 34; definitions 32; motives 32–3; and NGOs 102; theories 32–5
social safety-nets 116–19, 125, 224
Soedjarwo, Anton 18, 105
Soepomo 49
Soetrisno, Loekman 210, 215
soft-liners 210
solidarity makers 50
Solo 63, 73–7, 80, 94, 116, 129–30, 197, 216, 224–6, 231
South Kalimantan 76
South Korea 58, 111
Southeast Asia 58
Spinoza 49
SPSI 55, 91, 177, 182, 188, 221
SPSI 65
Sri Lanka 29, 60
Sri Paku Alam VIII 8
Sri Sultan Hamengku Buwono X 8, 226
SSCIs 136–7, 159
*Staatsspoorbond* (SS Bond) 64
stakeholders 162–3, 166
state enterprises 58, 137
state's intervention 59, 60
Stepan, Alfred 54
Stoler, Ann L. 178
strategic planning 162
structural adjustment 114, 170
student activism 62
Subiyono, Andreas 119, 127, 145, 147, 165
Subono, Bambang 212
Sudarman 151
Sudarsono, Juwono 89
Sudarwo, Fajar 215
Sudjana, Ida Bagus 72, 211
Sugiharti, Titi 190, 220
Suharto 18, 41, 46, 52, 54, 59, 62, 65, 73, 77–8, 80, 93, 100, 115, 171, 206, 210, 211, 213, 216, 221, 223
Suharto, Tommy 82 *see also* Hutomo Mandala Putra

Sukardi, Laksamana 82, 86
Sukarno 48–9, 51, 62, 65, 71
Sukarnoists 71
Sukarnoputri, Megawati *see* Megawati
Sukma, Rizal 76
Sulawesi 50, 63, 117
Sultan of Brunei 86
Sumantri, Bambang Sigap 209
Sumartana, T.H. 231
Sumatra 50, 63, 79, 91, 100, 116–17
Sumbawa 148
Sundanese 48
Sunkel, Osvaldo 111
*Supersemar* 52
Surabaya 63, 65, 73, 75, 77, 83, 101, 116, 154, 211, 213
*Surat Keputusan Bersama* 95
Suryadi 74, 76
Suryajaya, William 58
*Susenas* 57
Sutiyoso, Yos 202–3, 228
Sutrisno, S.J., Mudji 111
Swidler, Ann 241
*syariah* 48 *see also* Islamic Law
syncretism 105–6
Sztompka, Piotr 232

Taiwan 58
Taman Siswa 14–15, 90
Tanaka, Kakuei 62
Tandjung, Akbar 80
Tangerang 65
Tanzil, Eddy 71, 75
Tapos 66
Tasikmalaya 75–6
Taufiqurrahman 220
Taylor, V. 174
*tebasan* 129, 178
Thailand 54, 111, 135
The Hague 98
Thomas, Alan 193, 195
Thorbecke, Eric 121
Tigor, Bonar 212
Tjahjono, Indro 63
TNI 221
Toer, Pamoedya Ananta 212
Torre, Ed de la 66
Touraine, Alain 32
Townsend, J. 254
TPN 72
trade union 188
traditional Muslims 85
transparency 245
Trihatmodjo, Bambang 210
Turner, M. 251

Udin 209
Uhlin, Anders 111, 218
Ujianto, Martinus 220, 233, 239
Ujung Pandang 63, 76–7, 213

UMR 69, 181, 188, 196, 222
*Undang Undang Keramaian* 56
underdevelopment 111
UNDP 252
United Kingdom 99
United States 99
unity in diversity *see also* Bhinneka Tunggal Ika
University of Gadjah Mada 78, 106, 177, 210, 215
University of Indonesia 63
UPC 85
Uphoff, Norman 166
Uruguay 114
US Congress 74, 99
USAID 113, 254
USC 162, 176
*UU Ormas* 94–6, 101, 104

Vene-Klasen, Lisa 117
virtual representation 184
vote-buying 134

Wahid, Abdurrahman 12, 62, 76, 79, 81, 83, 197, 209, 222 *see also* Gus Dur
Wahyuni, Budi 204, 223, 228, 250
WALHI 98, 100, 218, 237
Wanandi, Sofyan 58
Washington, D.C. 74, 99
*wayang wong* 192
Weber, Max 53, 108
Wedi 126, 129, 130, 132, 134, 141–3, 145, 244
Weijland, H. 137
*werkwilligen* 109

West Java 45, 51, 63–4, 75, 84, 110, 114, 117, 180
West Sumatra 12
West Timor 127, 148
Whittier, N. 174
Whyte, William 112
Widaningrum, Ambar 140–1
Wijaya, Anggerjati 220, 223, 234, 239
Wijayanto, Sigit 105, 162, 165
Wiyarto, Aleks 105, 107, 141, 150, 154, 158, 162, 164
Wolf, Diane L. 174, 181
women in development 46, 169, 171
World Bank 25, 99, 100, 113, 119, 135, 216
WTO 72

YAPPIKA 239
Yasanti 16, 17, 46, 100, 174–6, 182–3, 185, 187–9, 191–4, 197–205, 214–15, 248–51, 253–5
Yati, Din 218, 223, 228, 230, 238
*yayasan* 96, 166–7, 202, 209, 255
YCW 225
YDED 106
YIS 91
YLBHI 85, 98, 100
YLKI 91, 220
Yudhoyono, Susilo Bambang 87
Yudotomo, Imam 218, 233

*zakat* 130
Zarima 71